MIND SKILLS

MIND SKILLS

A Philosopher's Notebook

JOSEPH VAN DE MORTEL

MCP - MAITLAND, FL

Mill City Press, Inc.

2301 Lucien Way #415

Maitland, FL 32751

407·339·4217

www.millcitypress.net

ISBN-13: 978-1-63505-362-3

Printed in the United States of America

CONTENTS

PART ONE

MIND SKILLS

I

MIND

The mind is not the brain, but the brain somehow holds the mind. In philosophy this puzzle is referred to as the mind-body problem: the investigation into how two very different aspects of our being coexist. We are not going to solve that puzzle right here in a theoretical way. If there is an immediate solution, it is a practical one. We want to argue for a definition of mind as ideas. Think of ideas as the mind. Then think of ideas applied to actions as judgment. Think of the body as a conduit for mind.

There is an appealing argument about mind in the Gestalt school of psychoanalysis. But, what is *Gestalt*? *Gestalt* is a German word that can only be roughly translated into English. It refers to a configuration or whole that emerges from individual events. Gestalt psychology argues that from our earliest moments in life, we experience the world as sense data. We try to develop our understanding of this sense data, perhaps translating it into a feeling of purpose or wholeness. We do not process events as isolated phenomena. We instead add them to our perception of the whole. Each day is a new layer of content to be stored in our memory, at the conscious and the subconscious levels. Each day brings experiences that affect the balance or equilibrium we seem to seek. Gestalt psychoanalysts argue that all the negative and positive events in our life become elements of our personality and our general frame of reference. Our reactions to present events (including persons as events) often connect to the memory of past events (formations) that intersect with present events. Gestalt takes a dynamic view of life rather than a static one. The dynamic synthesis of past and present is believed to explain many of our mental states, including happiness, sorrow, joy, presuppositions, prejudices, unresolved anger, and episodes of depression.

The philosopher David Hume argued that the self is a bundle of experiences. This bundle of experiences can be thematically unified by being focused, or it may be poorly organized by the inability to focus. If we cannot focus, it is often because we are overextended in too many directions. Our bundle of experiences, in this case, is threatened with becoming untied. The Gestalt school would label this as "neurosis," meaning a cognitive inefficiency resulting in a feeling of chaos. Philosophy's emphasis on reason has the potential to help us organize our decisions and interests into a meaningful hierarchy. This is one of the goals of philosophy, as it tries to define and implement virtues like wisdom, temperance, and courage.

Developing our mind philosophically is an ongoing project that relies on our natural love of learning. Our mind seems to search for content that delivers a sense of active purpose. The child's love of life is connected to this natural love of learning as experiential curiosity. We should ask ourselves, "Is this the essence of what it means to be happy, rational, and at peace? Does curiosity involve the objectivity that characterizes formation of a sense of calm and clear, unbiased thinking?" Plato calls this the sense of wonder. That sense of wonder as curiosity represents a potential to mold our life around interests that will continue to support our love of life. Sometimes, just as we think life is about to trap us into a state of boredom, the practice of thinking about things in a deeper way may create new meaning in familiar ground through fresh perspectives and awareness. We may find that there are still more sources of exuberance, enlightenment, and joy.

It is an unfortunate fact that most people view life in a more negative way than a positive one. When there is nothing to do, the human mind often settles on problems, worries, and complaints. Conversations often gravitate toward a reinforcement of pessimism and unhappiness. Sometimes our conversations are evidence of mental entropy and intellectual stagnation. And other times, through active reasoning, some of these negative mental states can be revised into useful philosophy and a more positive outlook. As a philosopher, I believe good philosophy delivers solutions to the problems of daily life. I believe we feel best when our skills match challenges, and as the degree of difficulty increases, our skills need to keep pace. That personal evolution of mind and body is part of the self-actualization process.

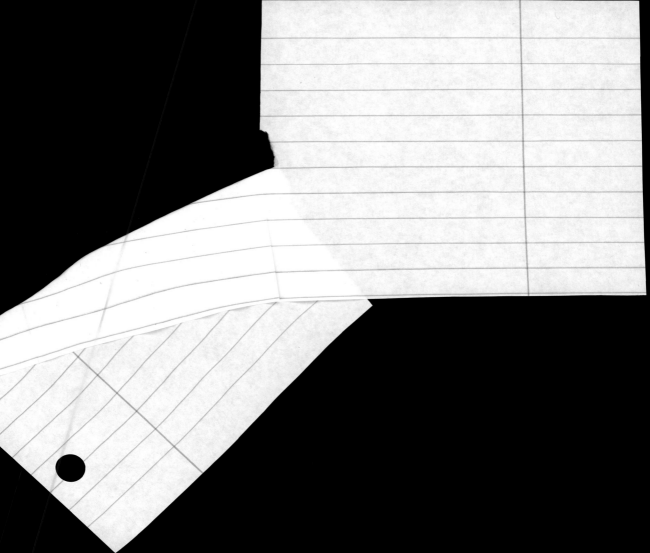

II

THE ROLE OF EPIPHANY

The word "epiphany" is a noun stemming from the Greek term *epihaneia*, which refers to a manifestation of the divine or the supernatural. In philosophical applications, and particularly in existential reference to the personality, epiphany refers to an event or experience that transforms the consciousness of the subject. An epiphany may involve a scientific, philosophic, or religious realization that leads to a deeper understanding of a problem, an interest, or a puzzle. It may follow from a long investigation or deep reflection on a problem. It is usually an inspirational experience and may be compared to the Buddhist notion of *satori*.

Epiphanies are philosophical moments of self-realization that may begin in childhood and occur throughout life. They may be accompanied by feelings of redemption. They can become sources of inspiration, transcendence, and authenticity. They can relieve suffering, frustration, and confusion. They are often the fruit of our labor, the existential moments of deep joy at having mastered a difficult challenge. And, they can provide positive direction in one's life.

Surprisingly, epiphanies sometimes arise from solitude and alienation. My parents fostered an independence that immigrants often rely on when entering a new culture. Without native skill in English, I couldn't seem to get into my education in the right way and didn't like some of my teachers, but I had a strong curiosity about nature and loved learning on my own terms. My parents supported this disposition as best they could. I was allowed to read whatever I wanted, partly because I was teaching them English, and partly because they didn't realize what I was reading. (My first philosophy book, *The Communist*

Manifesto, wouldn't have made their reading list in light of their experience with fascism.)

Since we lived in a semirural area, my parents also allowed me to catch whatever pets I wanted, from lizards to pheasants, as long as I accepted responsibility for their care. They argued that one had to catch an animal to earn ownership (epiphany). Sometimes I'd spend much of a day in the prescientific study of animals through simple observation, trying to emulate Jane Goodall. On one of these days, I experienced "the ant epiphany." Like Newton's falling apple, the ant epiphany was an accidental encounter.

There I was, sitting on a slab of concrete with my legs folded, observing pheasants, enjoying the sun, and wondering about some interesting mythical shapes in passing clouds. A single ant was also moving across the slab, a lone scout mapping and foraging the landscape for nutrients.

I had learned some fascinating facts about social roles within ant societies from library visits, so I watched and wondered about this tiny particle of intelligence. My mother was watering her vegetable garden some sixty feet away, and a field of water was expanding across the concrete slab. It quickly formed a trap around the ant, and the ant appeared to panic, moving frantically along the perimeter of a shrinking island of dry concrete, unable to escape. Absorbed in my quiet observation of this tiny creature, I wondered if it would live or die and waited for the microdrama to run its course. In a moment, my mind was absorbed in speculation about the ant's life. Was this tiny creature thinking? Did it possess a type of knowledge about what was now taking place? By its behavior, I concluded it seemed to think at some level about what was happening. Did the ant have emotions that were now displayed as fear? Could it recognize and fear its own death?

The ant's tiny island continued to shrink as the water flooded the concrete plane, and it became more agitated and reactive. It would surely perish if the water finally erased the last square centimeters of high ground. All hope of survival was about to vanish. The surrounding flood now occupied vast sections of the concrete slab, and the ant wouldn't be able to swim against the currents and escape the newly formed lakes at the delta of this temporary micro-riparian event (a "delta" refers to the three-inch waterfall at the edge of the slab).

THE ROLE OF EPIPHANY

Although I was too young to consider Berkeley's *esse est percipi* (epiphany), I still speculated about whether this event could have meaning in my absence. Did this ant's life count on some level that we didn't see? I began to wonder if I had a responsibility to save the ant, since I was observing its demise. Did my ability to save the ant translate into a duty to save the ant? I also wondered if God would intervene in my absence, should I decide to leave. I wondered if God had put me there to act on his behalf. I wondered if it even mattered that the ant might die. I wondered if its death was predestined to occur right there, and I reflected on whether my accidental presence had anything to do with this ant's life or not. How could a creature so small, and often hated by humans, have any importance anyway?

Then it occurred to me that perhaps I was also being watched by a distant observer, while living amid dangerous and unknown forces surrounding my own life. Was this drama a lesson in life's meaning and the nature of fate? An ordinary event in nature had become a catalyst for philosophical reflection, and it later explained my adolescent interest in an expanding list of favorite writers: Loren Eiseley, Charles Darwin, Aldo Leopold, Nicolaus Copernicus, Blaise Pascal, Teilhard de Chardin, Buddha, Confucius, Jesus, and Karl Marx. I wanted answers to some big questions that had emerged from a microdrama in nature, and the questions wouldn't go away.

We should notice how this kind of childlike curiosity is at the center of good critical thinking and investigative learning. It can create the basis for developing our reasoning into an interesting stream of ideas. Often the most ordinary events possess the contents for deeper scientific and philosophical understanding. Each person should examine his or her deepest natural interests to discover a field of study that may lead to a satisfying professional life. Borrowing from the Gestalt school, call it "philosophy of the obvious." If I had followed my childhood interest in nature into higher education, it might have lead to zoology or ornithology. The lateral path I followed was a general interest in philosophy, science, and religion.

With regard to learning, the young need to implement the right learning skills to master the literature in a specific field. The young may not always like school, but they should see the value of learning and its relationship to a fulfilling life. A good school can accelerate the development of students by inspiring them to learn things beyond the classroom.

It is often the curiosity of childhood that determines lifelong interests. And, studies show that what people do in their twenties, they often do for the rest of their lives. That, of course, isn't an absolute, but procrastination can do a lot of damage to possibilities. So, from a personal development standpoint, ask yourself this simple question: "What is my epiphany?"

What kind of intellectual flow can you generate when thinking about the subject that really calls to you for exploration? You may discover that this subject may represent your opportunity to find fulfillment and happiness, and it will probably require a college education.

III

READING NOTES

E ven if you're someone who's lacked motivation in the past, it's possible to develop college-level reading skill quickly by becoming an aggressive notetaker. I ask people to think about this: "If you're not taking notes, then you're not reading." Many students do not read at the college level, because they do not read at the college level. Try to accept the circular wisdom of that comment. College is about reading and analyzing difficult books. You should make it a habit to use a notebook to record choices about facts, phrases, and quotes that seem interesting or important to you. Note-taking is part of active reading. It will help you concentrate, and it will keep you reading. Your notes become tangible evidence of the day's work. Your notes will usually lift out the really important ideas, making your notebooks a journal of discovery. This is very important to becoming an aggressive reader.

Good note-taking will provide documentation of your intellectual progress, while reducing the need to reread material. The real definition of speed reading is: READ IT ONCE. Also include a header about how you feel about studying on a given day: bored, happy, confused, depressed, motivated, "don't like reading difficult books," "I wish my instructor would discuss postfeminism," "I'm thinking about getting a new car instead of a diploma," "I need some alcohol to cope with my life." (Did you really write that?) Students have all kinds of attitudes toward learning. Over time, noting your moods can isolate psychological factors that may need to be addressed in order to improve intellectual concentration and focus.

In libraries, the time spent using books should always be accompanied by note-taking. Retracing your library reading is virtually hopeless without notes.

I prefer the 6 x 9 stenographer's notebook. It has good portability, can hold a pen in its spiral, and offers the opportunity to write at all times. It also doesn't require a large writing surface, is easy to hold, and provides a two-column page face. (Yes, I know you have technology, but do you understand Gandhi? "Writing is a form of meditation.")

IV

Lecture Notes

In addition to reading notes, you'll need to get into the habit of building good lecture notes in class. Staying awake during even the most boring lecture can be achieved by constructing lecture notes. Think about it: "If you're not taking notes, then you're not listening."

Get obsessed with the detail and accuracy of what is being presented and discussed. Studies show that the act of writing is also the key to remembering what took place in class. But, record notes selectively. You don't need to write down everything.

Create a chronological record of the ideas presented. When I attend talks at venues like the American Philosophical Association or the American Academy of Religion, I note what time it is about every fifteen minutes as a lecture unfolds (it may be time for sushi across the street from the San Francisco Hilton). I also do it online for important talks I can't attend. To be efficient, record nouns, verbs, adjectives, book titles, and names, rather than full sentences. Key aphorisms are the exception. Get those. But, catching everything is impossible. So, you need to be on the lookout for the main ideas and, especially, the book titles and maybe descriptive words that could provide clues about intellectual biases, presuppositions, and maybe the entertainment genius of a great speaker.

Use your pen or pencil to create boxes around specific ideas that represent a theme or theory that is emphasized. Other graphic techniques may also be useful. I have a colleague who draws excellent cartoon images about the lecture and the lecturer. Allow yourself the freedom to invent different ways to analyze

11

things while you build notes. Adding some personal artistic flair to note-taking can be energizing and may improve your recall about detail.

Also experiment with the **Cornell Note-Taking System**: This system breaks each page into two columns, with about 1/3 or 1/2 of each page left blank on the left. This blank margin can be filled in after class with further reflections, questions, and details about the lecture/discussion content. It may only take ten minutes to provide this kind of follow-up, but it's important to do it the same day since memory is fragile, and details will fade quickly by the day's end.

Recording Devices: I think the use of recording devices is overrated and may even lead to legal problems in some settings. Recordings are difficult to engage, since one has to go over the whole lecture to extract the key concepts. You're better off just getting into the habit of building notes during live presentations. After a few years, lectures in your discipline begin to sound so familiar that your notes will be very compact. Unless you're an FBI informant or a civil litigator, it can be a waste of time to collect recordings. Personally, I think that students who need to record everything are a little neurotic, and the lecturer may even need to be concerned about motives other than learning. To avoid disputes, ask a lecturer if recording is allowed. Try to enjoy lectures without the need to record. Try to relax into the purpose of a college education.

V

MINDFULNESS AND LISTENING

As a foundation for note-taking, listening is high on the list of skills. Zen Buddhist practices can improve our ability to listen. Even in the West, a relatively large number of psychotherapists have found the ancient spiritual practices of Zen Buddhism to be very effective for creating better focus, recall, and nonjudgmental awareness.

Mindfulness and nonjudgmental awareness provide a basis for better listening, because they foster intellectual tolerance and empathy. This state of mind is essential for consideration of philosophical arguments. Many people are very uncomfortable around ideas that challenge their unexamined biases and have an inherent defensiveness toward new theories that threaten their worldview. This is often a product of cultural conformity and bad philosophy. Mindfulness is the antitoxin that lowers the defenses of the ego through a specific orientation toward reality. The conversational format that Socratic thinking tries to cultivate can also be integrated with mindfulness training.

Mindfulness as listening connects us to content and the desire to understand. In terms of education, this is essential. Plato would argue that if one is not moving toward enlightenment, one is moving away from enlightenment. Mindfulness as concentration produces the awareness of detail that note-taking entails, because one is focused on the delivery of a stream of ideas. It is a movement toward enlightenment.

Listening as mindfulness also defines tolerance, often misrepresented as compliance. Tolerance does not require agreement or disagreement. It is more of a mental balance between self and world; subjective and objective reality.

Tolerance is a suspension of judgment, but it does not mean that we will let falsehoods prevail. It is a kind of etiquette that is accepted throughout academic culture. A limitation of tolerance is that it isn't going to get us to the heart of what is a good theory, concept, or argument. At some point, listening is replaced by rational analysis and criticism.

In cognitive terms, mindfulness makes us aware of our defensive avoidance. The automatic reaction to new ideas may incorporate a resistance that tries to block the anxiety associated with challenging concepts, theories, and arguments. In a state of defensive avoidance, a transfer of anger on to the philosophical speaker is likely. Though our culture claims to embrace diversity, this is not a genuine value. People seem to be less tolerant, more angry, and more neurotic about life's challenges.

What Buddhism calls *dukkha* (suffering) is a product of our desires and fears. In the case of judgmental listening, ideas may trigger feelings of denial or disavowal. We may want to reject, preemptively, the possibility of being harmed by new ideas. Philosophically challenging ideas perceived as dangers to the self may block the ability to listen objectively.

When we listen mindfully, we are waiting to receive the words another person has chosen to communicate. In an academic setting, there may be an egoistic desire to refute, engage, challenge, or doubt what is said. Instead of taking this judgmental stance during listening, we should practice nonjudgmental awareness. Let people say what they want to say. Let the words pass through the mind without contesting them or measuring them immediately. It is irritating for a speaker to be interrupted. Quietly note the points that are defining the message, theory, concept, or logic. For the moment, let the presentation stand. In letting it stand, quietly observe its strengths and weaknesses while recording the details. Mindful listening is an important preliminary practice to disputing ideas in the correct way. Mindful listening is part of empathy and gaining an undistorted understanding of a person's ideology. We need to stop our tendency to generate conflict, and we need to develop our ability to communicate through listening.

VI

THE CIRCLE METHOD

The Circle Method is an important habit to establish for building a good vocabulary. It incorporates a simple mechanical commitment to active reading.

When you are reading difficult material, keep a #2 pencil handy to circle each word whose meaning you are unsure of. Each circle is a warning that you aren't comprehending the material. So, if there are lots of circles, you need to stop and look up the circled words before continuing. If there are two or three per chapter in a difficult book, you are probably close to the level of reading you need to reach. In any case, do not erase circles unless you have looked up the definitions and committed them to memory.

Make it a habit to study with a good dictionary on your desk. Online dictionaries are okay, but some of them lack completeness. Looking up words is the core of your education, and the more focused you get on this habit the better your comprehension of difficult books will be. Using the Circle Method will help you catch every word you are unsure of and create a comprehension map.

VII

THE READ-AND-STOP METHOD

With this method, you will read until you reach the bottom of a page. When you reach the bottom, do not continue. STOP. Now THINK about what you just read. Did your mind wander? What were the main ideas? Do you recognize the topic sentence in each paragraph? After a little reflection, underline the statements that seem important. Do not underline everything, and do not underline as you go. READ – STOP – and – THINK about what you just read. Then underline. Make this a habit to improve your concentration while reading.

Underlining should also be accompanied by writing in the margins. Record any critical comments and questions that surface in your mind, while you are reading. Enter your own reminders about important premises and conclusions pertaining to the author's arguments.

If your mind wanders while reading, you'll want to keep an eye on this problem. If you want to get good at reading difficult books, your mind can't be drifting off toward fantasy or worries. There is a kind of emotional shift that takes place with the Read-and-Stop Method. You will feel a more powerful comprehension develop as your mind attacks each page in this way. It is, in effect, a kind of mindfulness training equivalent to Zen meditation.

Try it right now with a challenging book, and notice how you feel by making a deliberate effort to stop and review. You will notice a true shift in your awareness and concentration. Most people are surface learners until they try the Read-and-Stop Method. The act of reading this way shifts from a casual meandering to a deeper critical examination of the text. You should let this new feeling of control increase your comprehension, understanding, and enjoyment of reading. It will also add the discipline and focus necessary for dissecting arguments.

VIII

THE GENERAL NATURE AND SCOPE OF PHILOSOPHY

The dictionary definition of a philosopher is: "One who seeks wisdom or enlightenment; a reflective thinker, scholar, or investigator. One whose life is governed by reason; a person whose philosophical perspective enables him or her to meet trouble with equanimity."

Getting into philosophy can be rewarding on a number of levels, but remember, "Philosophy bakes no bread." Socrates was a stonemason, Saint Paul and Omar Khayyam were tentmakers, Spinoza was a lens grinder, Jesus was a *tekton* or woodworker; George Carlin, Jay Leno, and Jerry Seinfeld became professional comedians. George Soros became a skilled entrepreneur and investor. With such ostensive role models, I became a self-employed contract tradesman, entrepreneur, and itinerant instructor. Before earning a professorship in philosophy and religion, my trade skills supported me financially and psychologically. And, since the title of this book implies skills for *the life of reason*, I do not teach or advocate philosophy in a vacuum.

What is the existential meaning of philosophy itself? Among its various definitions, philosophy's literal meaning is "love of wisdom." This "love" has an existential component. The love of wisdom can involve spiritual practices implied by the Socratic maxim "know thyself." In fact, this was the core of ancient philosophy (Pierre Hadot). Philosophy was geared toward the moral development of the individual and advocated as a way of life (Pythagoras). The Academy and the Lyceum were founded by Plato and Aristotle to advance the philosophical way of life, especially by creating better citizens of the *polis*. So, today we should think of philosophy as a corollary for various career paths. The ability to debate, analyze, and dissect thought is an asset in any occupation. The guidance provided by virtue enables us to generate a more balanced life of body and soul.

According to Plato, wisdom is the cardinal virtue from which other virtues flow. And so, what is wisdom? It is a type of awareness. It alerts us to our best choices. It encourages us to plan for the long term as well as the short term. It reminds us to be vigilant against danger, and it can help us assess our own moral challenges and shortcomings. It is a product of our life experience, and it also emerges from a curiosity that looks into the "Big" questions.

To frame the "Big" questions, the study of philosophy proceeds along its Five Branches, which students can call MELEA—metaphysics, epistemology, logic, ethics, and aesthetics. Metaphysics asks, "What is ultimately real?" or "Why is there something rather than nothing?" (Friedrich Schelling). Epistemology asks, "How can we know that we know?" Logic asks, "What is correct vs. incorrect reasoning?" Ethics asks, "What is the right use of freedom?" Aesthetics asks, "What is the value, creation, and appreciation of beauty?"

IX

FOUR ASPECTS OF PHILOSOPHY

The utility of philosophy is something a little different from its branches of inquiry. This utility can be understood through four aspects, (KATS): knowledge, attitude, therapy, and skill.

1. **Philosophy is a body of knowledge:** Philosophy is the study of concepts, theories, and thinkers that compose the history of Western and Eastern thought. Philosophy as historical and ideological knowledge generates a comprehensive understanding of humanity's quest for enlightenment, whether that be the study of nature through science and cosmology, or the investigation of meaning in a more abstract sense. A knowledge of the history and problems of philosophy provides each practitioner a general competence to handle philosophy as a field of ideas. Many of these ideas have shaped history, from the pre-Socratics to Marxism in the West and from the Upanishads to Japanese religion in the East. This important knowledge "frees us from unconscious bondage to our own age" (Karl Jaspers).

2. **Philosophy is an attitude:** The attitude imparted by philosophy includes certain intellectual and moral virtues that add something to the personality or character of the individual philosopher. Philosophy as intellectual courage is typified in thinkers like Socrates, Lao-tzu, Boethius, Nietzsche, Marx, Darwin, Confucius, Patanjali, Tagore, Nagarjuna, and Jesus. This attitude embodies candor, intellectual honesty, the will to engage controversy, self-reliance, resistance to enculturation, and dynamic curiosity.

Each thinker's ego possesses an attitude toward the world. This attitude (protodoxy) underlies ideas and actions. It may also involve a creed that explains the choices people make in dealing with life. It can explain the presence or absence of the love of truth and influence the reasoning of the individual thinker or society. As such, an attitude may produce creative and/or destructive tendencies. Philosophy as attitude incorporates intellectual virtues that advance the rational selection of ideas, axioms, and proofs that make the final definition of reality a more carefully formulated presentation of truth.

3. **Philosophy is a therapy:** For the ancient philosophers, philosophy was considered psychagogic (teachings for the soul). It produced spiritual well-being for the practitioner. In historic times of great chaos this turning inward became a limitation (Stoicism). Yet generally, philosophy promoted self-knowledge and care of the soul (Pierre Hadot) through its various schools. This tended to set the individual apart from anxiety about fame, wealth, or political power, since there is a self-actualization that accompanies one's philosophical maturity. The ancient philosophers referred to this as *ataraxia* (peace of mind).

   Socrates was critical of his culture but also conventional. We see the same compliance-resistance in Buddha, Confucius, and Jesus. Each of them exhibited an alienation from their respective cultures. They presented ethical models that we recognize as inspirational and post moral. They did not seek the approval of people in power. They also rejected the naïve view that a meaningful life stems from uncritical conformity to one's culture and popular opinion. They often revealed a weird disinterest in worldliness, while accepting it as part of life (Lao-tzu). This is part of the therapeutic value of being "philosophical," of living a life free of worry (Seneca). It can generate self-confidence through its teachings about authentic life choices.

4. **Philosophy is a skill:** *"Thinking about thinking"* – Philosophy includes the specific critical ability that reason generates through the practice of skepticism, the application of logic, and the considerations of epistemology. Because philosophy's highest value is truth, skepticism expresses the demand that ideas be true. Skepticism checks the validity of beliefs and tests them with criticism. Because philosophy's

slogan is "reason alone," logic expresses the demand that ideas be factual, coherent, consistent, and correct in their deductive and inductive formation. Philosophy as a skill tests the merit, strength, and validity of ideas, laws, theories, and axioms. Philosophical thinking pushes us toward better insights through the objective application of critical reason.

By extension, philosophy as skill includes an understanding of rational methodology: the systematic analysis and organization of rational and experimental principles. This is important for empiricism and scientific inquiry (methodeutic). Generally, this entails six important philosophical steps that we can express compactly:

a. noting the exact object of inquiry
b. studying the object's origin, nature, and development
c. the formulation of accurate statements that describe the object
d. identification of the philosophical assumptions and presuppositions at work in thinking about the object
e. identification of the object's relationship to reality as a whole
f. identification of the way in which acquired knowledge of an object may be applied to the solution of problems

X

THE SOCRATIC METHOD

Socrates is recognized as the father of philosophy. His way of doing philosophy created a dialectical process and specific standards for critical thinking. This process is built upon the maxim that "the unexamined life is not worth living." The profession of ignorance was the Socratic Method's starting point, and the role of definition became its foundation. Thus, the Socratic Method, also called "intellectual midwifery," includes several important features:

- **Definition of terms:** Socrates continually peppered his companions with questions about what they meant. He took on the role of a teacher who drew ideas out of people based on what they claimed to know. For this reason he was also called "the gadfly."

- **Conversation:** Socrates wrote nothing. His entire philosophical life is recorded by Plato in the form of dialogues. Conversations between teacher and student characterized the "Socratic" approach. Today, this has become the standard way to do philosophy in the classrooms of universities and law schools.

- **Skepticism:** Socrates tried to raise the standard of truth by going after the answers people provided. The Oracle at Delphi had told Socrates that he was the wisest man, because he professed not to know. This self-professed condition was a product of his natural curiosity, his intellectual honesty, and his skepticism: doubt concerning the truth, facticity, or reality of claims, especially on philosophical grounds.

As per the Oracle, Socrates *knows that he does not know*. The use of skepticism or doubt is a way of being more careful and correct about beliefs. In being skeptical, we ask for deeper proof that a belief, theory, or concept is true.

- **Inductive reasoning:** the process of reasoning from a part to a whole or from several cases to all cases. This may be a mathematical or empirical application. For Socrates, he made this part of the test for truth, mainly by asking for examples of the things his companions were talking about. The more cases an argument presents in support of its conclusion, the stronger the argument becomes. Counterexamples usually cause corrections, weakening the inductive logic.

- **Deductive reasoning:** a process of reasoning, frequently defined as moving from a general truth to a particular truth, wherein the conclusion in an argument must be accepted, if the foregoing evidence is true and correctly arranged to show what is claimed. In modern logic, it includes rules of inference expressed as various kinds of syllogisms: deductive arguments that possess two premises and a conclusion.

XI

SCIENTIFIC REASONING: SOME BASIC POINTS

I n the essay "Is Google Making Us Stupid?," Nicholas Carr generates important criticism about our reliance on information technology. Besides noting that people are becoming surface readers, there is the added effect of unscientific thinking. From a philosophical standpoint this has a serious implication, because it may also mean we are becoming more dogmatic and less reflective.

Without going into the philosophical questions raised by this simple discussion of science, we can still be warned that unscientific thinking presents its ideas and explanations without consideration for causal factors. It is thinking that is based on subjective belief or naïve realism. The formula for unscientific thinking can be expressed compactly as, "Belief is the basis of truth." Thus, if one believes in Santa Claus, then Santa is real. If one believes that the theories of climate change are a hoax, then they are. Unscientific thinkers regard their ideas as infallible truths, self-evident due to an emotional element that creates a need for intellectual certainty and control. Call it the power of positive thinking taken to the realm of fantasy. Truth is traded down into other values.

There is no complete agreement among scientists as to what constitutes the right scientific method. Science emerged from philosophy. Over the centuries, many of its greatest minds were mavericks. We can, however, indicate some basic points and provide a broad outline of scientific thinking for better critical thinking.

Scientific thinking emphasizes the construction of theoretical proof and objective belief. The formula for scientific thinking can be expressed compactly as, "Truth is the basis of belief." Thus, if something is true it should be believed. This truth is a product of identifying data, laws, principles, and patterns that govern events in the natural world. Science usually refers to this as the quantitative and objective knowledge of events in nature. "Truth is the basis of belief" requires us to suspend our judgment and wait to see what the data of an investigation reveals.

Theoretical proof is based on careful and impartial observation of nature (inductive reasoning). This proof is also subject to revision and amendment, depending on the discovery of additional information. Methodologically, scientific thinking follows a number of recognized steps to create theoretical proof:

1. An event becomes the object of scientific investigation when there is no explanation for that event and it is important to have one. In setting up the investigation, scientific analysis tries to determine the causal factors that explain the existence of X. Every event X exists in a finite domain. Explaining the event will depend on a thorough investigation of its finite domain to identify causes.

    The study of weather may be just as important to an ancient sailor or hunter as it is to a modern meteorologist, but each has very different standards of scientific reflection for explaining weather events. The scope of an ancient shaman as scientist might work with flights of geese that coincide with past encounters of weather. Thus, by interpreting the flight patterns of geese, it might be possible to decide if it's a good time to embark on a voyage or hunt. But, unless it's just to lighten up a boring day at the lab, the modern meteorologist doesn't consult the flight patterns of geese. His or her conclusions are based on a vast set of technological extensions of sight that bring in the totality of facts relating to a weather event.

2. In deciding what a correct study of X will be, the scientist must select only relevant facts from the totality of facts in a domain. If there are too many facts to consider, it may obscure the discovery of causal relationships. Thus, the second step in causal analysis is the creation of a

preliminary study or hypothesis. This means gathering all the bare facts that seem to describe an event in the prescribed domain. This initial study may be incomplete and tentative, so the scientist should anticipate the emergence of new facts that will address contingency. Sometimes analysis starts with guesswork or what scientists call **the method of trial and error**.

3. To produce an understanding of event X, it is necessary to discover **an overall structure or chain of causes**. When the observation of an event reveals a structure for events going back in time, the hypothesis begins to move toward validation. The causal relationships in turn provide the opportunity to solve a problem or demystify the occurrence of an event. It is then possible to synthesize a collection of facts into a theoretical explanation.

4. Once the hypothesis defines how X occurs, **it is important to test correctness**. This entails setting up experiments that recreate the chain of causes and predict the outcome. Good causal reasoning increases the probability of predicting the event, based on the facts that support the hypothesis. The construction of good experiments that confirm beliefs provide opportunities to control an event X. These experiments are usually carried out in small-scale models. Here, if there is some unforeseen side effect or surprise, its potential to create unintended side effects is minimized.

In good experiments, the enterprise of testing moves up systematically to full-scale applications of the hypothesis. In bad experiments, the scientist is forced to reconsider the entire body of knowledge that is being used. Have you ever heard someone complain that something works in theory but not in practice? Well, if a theory doesn't work in practice, it's the wrong theory. Good theories work in practice. Common sense tells us to abandon theories that can't be practiced.

Reference: *How We Think*, John Dewey, Dover, 1997, pp. 145–156. Dewey covers the steps for empirical and scientific thinking in a pragmatic and straightforward style.

XII

THE PURPOSE OF ETHICS AND CITIZENSHIP IN THE *POLIS*

M any people seem to think that philosophical study of ethics is the endorsement of moral ambiguity, nihilism, and ethical relativism. These are subtopics in the field of ethics, but they are not its essence. There are not many big-name philosophers who endorse nihilism and relativism. They may note the prevalence of these conditions, but they are also looking for a way out.

Ethics is actually an essential component of personal sanity, capable of guiding the individual toward a viable life plan through the use of reason. This commitment to reason encourages the philosopher to exercise greater prudence than most people. This is exactly what Plato hoped for in arguing that societies will only experience the greater Good if philosophers become kings.

The attitude that philosophy encourages about truth becomes problematic in politics and modern society, where beliefs are often justified in ways that philosophy finds unacceptable. The biases inherent in society, and political institutions, project images and messages designed to appeal to the masses. Ethics is commonly compromised for practical and egoistic goals. At their worst, political systems take on totalitarian values.

> "Only the mob and the elite can be attracted by the movements of totalitarianism itself; the masses have to be won by propaganda...It was recognized early and has frequently been

asserted that in totalitarian countries propaganda and terror present two sides of the same coin…Wherever totalitarianism possesses absolute control, it replaces propaganda with indoctrination and uses violence not so much to frighten people as to realize constantly its ideological doctrines and its practical lies."

Hannah Arendt, *Totalitarianism*
(Part III of *The Origins of Totalitarianism*)

The wider social purpose of philosophy as a political monitor endorses the critical application of ethics. Through application of moral objectivism the use of lying, propaganda, misinformation, deliberate omission of facts, and distortion of events are exposed as destructive to the common good. The standards of belief that philosophy creates help us to understand the implications and consequences of decision making. Consequently, with moral objectivism we can argue that social philosophy should be guided by universal values. There are at least five such values that all people should use in daily life:

1. **Promote Flourishing:** It is important that some degree of wealth, or access to the necessities of life, be protected and kept within the reach of all people. So, our actions should support this aim through carefully reasoned solutions where flourishing is threatened. This may include a universal commitment to ecological factors, conservation of resources, alternatives to war, and solutions to civil disintegration or individual acts of egoism and violence. It may include the construction of social policies that can prevent the emergence of violent competition for the basic needs of life.

2. **Reduce Suffering:** The suffering of others, when it is not of their own doing, should be handled with empathy. This includes an awareness of when and where causes of suffering exist. Societies should use physical and professional resources to ameliorate suffering. The reduction of suffering may depend on our support of scientific, educational, psychological, and spiritual values that serve the interests of the planet and humanity.

3. **Assign Responsibility:** The use of freedom should be accompanied by the understanding that human actions represent motive, will, intention, and consequences. Holding ourselves and others accountable for unethical actions is an important part of justice and the common good. Accepting responsibility for action must include judgments of blame, reward, punishment, and praise. We should not try to evade responsibility for our actions through lying, deception, collusion, or sabotage of fair-minded interaction.

4. **Resolve Conflicts:** It is impossible to avoid disputes in life, but many disputes can be resolved through mediation and sincere adherence to negotiated agreements. It is important that reason guide the settlement of disputes, especially in conflicts where anger has escalated to dangerous levels. We acknowledge that conflict is part of every marriage, family, relationship, and community. The collision of interests and values generate conflicts that should be resolved by careful ethical reasoning about what is right, especially by the disputants. When necessary, parties should enlist the help of a neutral third-party mediator, trained in the process of dispute resolution. When people reason clearly with intellectual honesty and sincerity, a sense of fairness emerges. This will be true in all societies.

5. **Prevent Anarchy:** Justice must be created by a visible set of laws or rules that apply to all members of a society. In this sense, law and ethics should be integrated to prevent society from falling into a state of chaos. It isn't possible to achieve goodness, or the Good, in a society that doesn't commit itself to fair application and enforcement of its rules. It isn't possible to achieve a good standard of living in a society that is dangerous to live in.

An educated person should make use of his or her training in philosophy to advance these objective ethical values. In particular, individuals should be active in politics to ensure that power is not abused and self-interest is limited. Patriotism is the presentation of constructive criticism, and criticizing leaders is an important way of safeguarding liberty and justice.

PART TWO:

A PHILOSOPHER'S NOTEBOOK

A Philosopher's Notebook

" This book does not demand continuous reading; but at whatever place one opens it, one will find matter for reflection. The most useful books are those of which readers themselves compose half; they extend the thoughts of which the germ is presented to them."

– Voltaire, François-Marie Arouet (1694–1778), *Voltaire's Philosophical Dictionary*

This manuscript originated in my study and teaching of philosophy. It represents many of the lecture topics and material I have presented in the course of a career as a professor of philosophy and religion.

First, it was a synoptic set of graduate school notes shared with students. Then it went through some development in published classroom experiments, not very perfect, but useful in laying out a college vocabulary for undergraduates in philosophy. Students seemed to benefit quickly from the concentrated emphasis on vocabulary and an economical navigation of philosophy. This was an important benefit, because philosophy can present a confusing collage of ideologies that can overwhelm the beginning student.

This text is designed to act as a compilation and supplement for general learning and the study of philosophy. It presents philosophy in a simple dictionary format to aid the reader in getting quickly oriented about some ideology, concept, theory, or thinker. It usually presents the historical context, the key concepts, the key texts, and solid references pertaining to an entry. Perusing these ideas may trigger that "come to Jesus" moment or the "satori" encounter that you've been looking for. Make your favorite philosopher your guru for a while as you search for your own philosophy.

Many of the words scattered among the main entries are interesting nouns, verbs, and adjectives whose meanings are often forgotten due to their infrequent use. Placing them here creates opportunities to fine-tune our own conversations, reinforce our arguments, and improve our writing with special words we don't use often enough. Make use of your favorites and enjoy being questioned, "Where did you learn to think like that?"

I do not think of myself as having deep originality as a teaching philosopher, although my stubbornness might qualify on some level. I tend to agree with Karl Jaspers, "Communication is the aim of philosophy, and in communication all its other aims are ultimately rooted: awareness of being, illumination through love, attainment of peace." Thus, pedagogical techniques for advancing philosophy as therapy and self-actualization are my main professional interest, and deep originality in philosophy is a tall ambition that few can attain. In fact, few things are original, if they're not already synthetic. Almost everything we think of can be identified in some way with the past. We should be happy if we can achieve general competence and prevent mental erosion, especially in a culture where amusement is more important than knowledge, and where psychology is more important than ethics.

Take some time, while browsing, to add an idea to your own philosophy from the ideas provided here. New ideas can offer resistance to depression by adding perspective. They help to instill intellectual honesty and limit our egocentric nature. They can make us more socially versatile and politically astute. View each reference as a door to be opened. And, as I advise my students, "If you get a good education, when your mind loses efficiency, it will take people longer to notice."

Be reminded that the study of philosophy can generate a level of skepticism that becomes self-defeating. I felt a little better about philosophy when I was introduced to a certain perspective in John L. Austin (1911-1960). Austin was an important philosopher of language who criticized analytic philosophy for complicating the meaning of words when it isn't necessary. Austin argued that words should be used with their ordinary meaning in most cases. We should rely on the lexical definitions in order to improve our communication with one another. Lexical definitions have stood the test of generations, and they are likely to be more useful than the ones philosophers can invent in their armchairs (Austin). We should reserve philosophical skepticism for those cases in which disputes about what is true or false arise from a vagueness in describing the world with words. Many of the words in this book are presented with brief synonymous meanings to address the economics of space. Use a good dictionary to look up longer meanings. That is the starting point to ground our thoughts in ordinary definitions and to enhance communication and word selection.

Facts about philosophers have been cross-checked with *The Encyclopedia of Philosophy* (ed. Paul Edwards). I've included solid references for many entries throughout the text to provide back-up reading. Inflected forms, guide phrases, binomials, homographs, and other details aren't included. Some of the definitions have been criticized as subjective, but this is my preference for a better inventory with basic hints about deeper connotative meaning. As a thinker, you are responsible for assessing the merit of any ideology you encounter (see my argument sample under "logic" for immediate illumination).

PHILOSOPHY AND WORDS A-Z

Abelard, Peter (1079–1142) – a French philosopher and theologian. Abelard, the teacher, formed a romantic relationship with a beautiful student named Heloise (1101–1164). While acting as her tutor, he argued that her education would progress more effectively if he could move into her home, which was owned by her uncle, Canon Fulbert. This involved some nighttime instruction where the meaning of philosophy became more personal.

Abelard, the philosopher, debated the meaning of "universals" (words that refer to groups of things). E.g., "dog" refers to all (universal) dogs, whereas "Lassie," as a name, refers to one dog. He argued that a universal is a word and a concept based in some reality; that words are not a reality in themselves. Thus, Abelard opposed 1) the nominalist position that words are not real in the world or in the mind, and 2) a conceptualism that argued that words are a reality in themselves.

Abelard's critical reflections led to the theory of substitutions (*suppositio terminorum*). This idea generated a fresh intellectual climate, helping to undermine the dogmatic attitude toward knowledge, advocated by the Church. Abelard's criticism of Church doctrine was condemned by Pope Innocent II at the Council of Sens in 1141.

Principal works: *Yes and No* (1122), and *Theologia Christiana* (1124)

"By doubting we are led to inquire, by inquiring we are able to perceive the truth."

Peter Abelard, *Yes and No*

References: *Peter Abelard: His Place in History*, Kathleen M. Starnes; and *The School of Peter Abelard*, D. E. Luscombe

ab initio – adj. fr. Latin – from the beginning

ab irato – adj. fr. Latin – from an angry man (woman)

abreaction – n. catharsis or release; an aspect of Freudian therapy that resolves post-traumatic stress. Freud believed that traumatic events often account for a genesis of hysterical phenomena. The patient may be carrying an unconscious awareness of trauma into the course of daily life. It remains isolated and unrecognized but active in the sub-conscious.

Catharsis is supposed to resolve these traumas and takes place in a controlled setting. Through words and discovery, the patient is encouraged to remove the weight of events that have produced pathological complications in daily life.

References: *Studies on Hysteria* and *The Psychopathology of Everyday Life*, Sigmund Freud; *The Practice of Behavior Therapy*, Joseph Wolpe

abrogate – v. to terminate

abscond – v. to depart or escape, especially secretly

absit invidia – v. fr. Latin – (a salutation) let ill be absent

absonant – adj. without reason or logic

abstemious – adj. to be marked by moderation in eating and drinking; control of the mouth

abstinence, rule of – n. in psychology, the idea that the patient should abstain from important decision making until abstinence has created a separation from those psychological problems that lead to bad decisions. This abstinence includes restrictions on substitute satisfactions. The substitute satisfactions can block the resolution of psychological problems, reassigning them to new manifestations.

Detachment is an important practice in disconnecting the patient from pathological behavior, but suffering accompanies detachment. The rule of abstinence maintains that if this suffering is mitigated or compromised (substitute satisfactions), then the cause of difficulties will not be eliminated.

References: *Client-Centered Therapy*, Carl Rogers; *Handbook of Psychotherapy and Behavior Change*, A. E. Bergin and S. L. Garfield

absurd, the – n. a state of affairs that cannot be meaningful; associated with the concepts of nihilism and nothingness. Absurdity includes estrangement and disconnectedness between the members of society. This implies dehumanization that is caused by the effects of bureaucratic social organization, technology, overpopulation, and the decline of traditions, the family, and religion.

For Albert Camus, the absurd is thought about in connection with nihilism. Can we live effectively where a meaningful life is called into question? For Camus, this problem is resolved through moral heroism. Suicide is not a real option. Life is validated through personal resistance to cruelty and injustice. Life is made absurd by the evils of human society, thus each person is called upon to act against this condition.

Louis Lavelle (1883–1951) argues that *the feeling of the absurd* is caused by the absence of love. Love introduces a meaning to life that reduces the sometimes chronic feeling of forlornness. Love creates joy in the sense that it emphasizes the importance and meaning of "the other," and thus it conquers the absurd.

For William Barrett, as religion's decline created a sense of nihilism, it became necessary for mankind to invent a rational order to combat the feeling of the absurd. Barrett sees the death of the soul as a product of the decline of metaphysics in light of science and technology.

"Nothing is more real than nothing."

Samuel Beckett

References: *The Meaning of Holiness*, Louis Lavelle; *The Stranger, The Myth of Sisyphus*, and *Caligula*, Albert Camus; *Irrational Man*, William Barrett

abulia – n. the loss of will; pertaining to the inability to act or decide

abysmal – adj. like an abyss or chasm; also meaning "profound" or "immeasurable"

accinge – v. to bolster, prepare, or brace

acclivity – n. an upward slope; especially from the observer's point of view

accouter – v. to equip, furnish, or provide

accretion – n. an increase by natural process; growth, especially by addition to external parts

acosmic – adj. literally "not cosmic"; in philosophy, a reference to the unreality of the external world. Hegel advocated an idealism that was "acosmic"

act deontology – n. in ethics, with respect to duty, the agent must consider each act as a unique ethical situation in which to decide what is right or wrong. If an act possesses inherent goodness, it merits participation.

> References: *The Moral Point of View*, Kurt Baier; *Kant's Ethical Theory*, William D. Ross

act utilitarianism – n. in ethics, the view that an act is morally correct if and only if it provides as much good as any other available act. The act is judged for its effectiveness in getting to desirable consequences.

> References: *Consequentialism and Its Critics*, ed. Samuel Scheffler; *Utilitarian Ethics*, Anthony Quinton

adelphogamy – n. the practice of sharing a wife or wives between brothers

adephagous – adj. gluttonous; having a voracious appetite

adhesiveness of the ego or libido – n. in psychology, a reference to the way the libido adheres to an object or phase. Carl Jung used the term "psychic inertia" to mean the same thing. It recognizes limits in the effectiveness of counseling to free the individual from troubling psychic objects. This notion also sees problems in being too detached or mobile in one's interests. In such instances, the advice of counseling will not adhere.

> References: *Three Essays on the Theory of Sexuality*, Sigmund Freud; *The Portable Jung*, ed. Joseph Campbell

Adler, Alfred (1870–1937) – the namesake of Adlerian psychology. Adler's father was a Jewish grain merchant and his mother was a homemaker. Adler was trained at the University of Vienna as an MD. His medical training was supplemented by an interest in philosophy, which influenced conclusions he put forth in several important essays, including *Uber den nervosen Charakter* (*The Neurotic Character*) in 1912, and *Inferiority and Its Psychical Compensation* in 1927. Adler is classified as a Neo-Freudian.

A

As an opponent of psychological determinism, Adler argued that each person is born with feelings of inferiority and works to compensate for this by creating a life plan that will bring about a healthy adjustment to the external world. Adler tried to study the effects of factors like age-rank, excessive affection, neglect, and physical constitution in the understanding of personality development. Adler believed that exaggerated feelings of inferiority, which he termed the "inferiority complex," can lead to overcompensation in a pathological development of arrogance or "the superiority complex." Adler was confident of the power of creative reason to organize the life of the individual, and though influenced by some psychogenetic elements in Freud's philosophy, he believed most human problems stem from the incorrect development of a life plan. The problem lies in "guiding fictions" (life plans) that lack viability, perhaps a product of naïve realism or delusions.

Adler's theory of the "aggressive drive" is a derivation from Nietzsche's "will to power," but he regarded exaggerated drive as evidence of neurosis. The healthy individual finds a balanced way of creating a place in the world. This is validated by the social interests of the individual, especially the concern for social equality. The psychotic insists on making the fictions of the mind reality by attempting to make life fit the subjective images of one's inner world, simultaneously ignoring the social dimensions of life.

Adler's view is also called "individual psychology." Adler presupposed an optimistic personalism, claiming that each individual is unique. This uniqueness is often compressed by societal influences that can be destructive. Adler's analysis of human behavior studied the movement from inferiority to superiority. Society as a "superiority" presence can work against the "superiority" of the individual by corrupting the authentic life plan or "guiding fiction," as Adler calls it. Viability is important in the creation of the guiding fiction.

Principal works: *The Neurotic Character* (1912); *Practice and Theory* (1920); *Understanding Human Nature* (1927); and *Superiority and Social Interests* (1933–37)

"Anyone who wants to understand Individual Psychology correctly must orient himself by its clarification of the unitary purposefulness of thinking, willing, and acting of the unique individual. He will then recognize how the stand the individual takes and the life style, which is like an artistic creation, are the same in all situations of life, unalterable until the end—unless the individual recognizes what is erroneous, incorrect, or abnormal with regard to cooperation, and

attempts to correct it. This becomes possible only when he has comprehended his errors conceptually and subjected them to the critique of practical reason, the common sense—in other words, through convincing discussion."

Alfred Adler, *Superiority and Social Interests*

References: *The Individual Psychology of Alfred Adler*, eds. H. L. and R. R. Ansbacher; and *In Freud's Shadow: Adler in Context*, Paul E. Stepansky

adoptionism – n. in theology, the view that Jesus was the adopted son of God. It was offered as a Christology by Paul of Samosata, a bishop at Antioch (ca. 260 AD). Adoptionism denied the divinity of Christ and rejected the notion of unity among the three Persons of the Trinity.

Reference: *Manual of Patrology and History of Theology*, F. Cayre, trans. by H. Howitt

Adorno, Theodor Wiesengrund (1903–1969) – a German philosopher of music and society. He was a member of the Frankfurt School. He specialized in the philosophies of Hegel, Marx, and Kierkegaard. His most famous books were *The Authoritarian Personality* (1950) and *Philosophy of Modern Music* (1949). He was a political activist in West Germany until his death.

Adorno was a critic of fascism, and he identified certain traits as indicators of authoritarian personalities, including: conventionalism, projection, anti-intellectualism, "toughness," cynicism, and destructiveness. Adorno studied Husserl under the direction of Gilbert Ryle. He worked with Herbert Marcuse on a critique of capitalism, arguing that modern capitalism had successfully nullified the forces that might bring about a more humane society. Instead the West would experience a decline in the area of aesthetics and ethics.

Reference: *Adorno*, Martin Jay

adscititious – adj. supplemental, additional, or unessential

ad valorem – adj. fr. Latin meaning according to the value

Adventism – n. in religion, the views of William Miller (1782–1849). Miller tried to predict the Second Coming of Christ in 1843. Miller was wrong but revised his predictions several times. Near the end of his life, he was reluctant to make further predictions.

Modern Seventh-day Adventists find a basis in the views of William Miller. Adventists believe in the infallibility of Scripture and advocate a life of strict temperance; alcohol and tobacco are forbidden, while meat, tea, and coffee are discouraged. They believe in adult baptism.

Reference: *The Disappointed*, eds. R. L. Numbers and J. M. Butler

adventitious – adj. casually or accidentally acquired, especially in the sense of "good fortune"

aesthete – n. a lover of beautiful objects; one who appreciates the sensory qualities of physical objects

aesthetics – n. in philosophy, the study of beauty (Greek "aesthesis," meaning sensation). Process philosopher, Charles Hartshorne, observed that aesthetics is also the study of that which is ugly, for the study of the beautiful is conditioned by a knowledge of the ugly. Hartshorne noted that people are often just as interested to see the ugliest person in the world as they are to see the most beautiful person in the world.

Beauty is often connected with "value," and value is derived from scarcity versus interest. The scarcity of gold accounts for its value, combined with our interest in its appearance as a found substance.

In aesthetics there is an interest in the relationship between happiness and beauty (i.e., "Is it possible to be happy in an ugly world?"). We can think about the way appearances contribute to our own sense of order and harmony. Creative genius produces beauty in paintings, sculpture, architecture, landscapes, and various other mediums that are the products of individual and collective experimentation.

There is also the discussion of whether beauty is subjective or objective. The wide differences of opinion regarding the beautiful suggest a subjective basis. The Mojave Desert, for instance, is an objective reality. It would reveal different values to different observers, though a sunset in the Mojave Desert has a universal appeal.

"Beauty enters only the most awakened soul."

Friedrich Nietzsche, *Thus Spoke Zarathustra*

References: *Aesthetic Theory*, T. W. Adorno, trans. by G. Lenhardt; and *Feeling and Form*, Susanne K. Langer

agapism – n. fr. Greek *agape*, meaning love. In ethics, it is the view that love constitutes the highest virtue. Agape includes altruistic action.

> References: The Gospel of Matthew 22:36–40 and 24:12–13 and *Agape and Eros*, Anders Nygren

aggressive instinct – n. in the philosophy of Alfred Adler, the tendency of humans to act destructively rather than simply dropping a concern or interest that is not meeting the wishes of the ego. It is related to the "death instinct" and with the research into aggression. An underlying assumption is that all human behavior is in some fashion aggressive.

> Reference: *Superiority and Social Interest: A Collection of Later Writings*, A. Adler, 3rd rev., ed. H. L. and R. R. Ansbacher

agnosticism – n. a philosophical view emphasizing skepticism about the existence of God. Agnostics are sometimes said to be "sympathetic" to the idea of God but are unable to make a mental commitment to belief. Instead agnostics hold that all real knowledge can only be knowledge of a material world. The term "agnosticism" is attributed to Thomas Henry Huxley (1825–1895), and his *Man's Place in Nature* (1864) and *Essays upon Controversial Questions* (1889). Huxley believed consciousness to be epiphenomenal, a by-product of biological processes. He was an advocate of Darwinism and a rather strict form of empiricism, so belief in God was unsupportable on scientific grounds.

Technically, it is possible to equate agnosticism with atheism, since it is the failure to affirm a belief in God. It is often regarded as a turning point on the question of atheism. The agnostic's dilemma rests on the standards of evidence and reasoning used by theists, versus the standards of atheists.

> *"It is wrong for a man to say that he is certain of the objective truth of any proposition unless he can produce evidence which logically justifies that certainty. This is what Agnosticism asserts."*
>
> T. H. Huxley, *Essays upon Controversial Questions*

> References: *Naturalism and Agnosticism*, James Ward; *Dialogues Concerning Natural Religion*, David Hume

ahimsa – n. in Jainism, "nonviolence"; the prohibition against killing and injury

ajiva – n. in Jainism, nonliving things

Ajivakas – n. in Jainism, atheist ascetics who believe in determinism

alacrity – n. a state of being ready and cheerful with regard to required actions

alethic – adj. having a connection to fact or truth

algolagnia – n. pathological sexual enjoyment derived from the existence of pain. Passively, algolagnia is the sexual satisfaction in suffering pain (masochism). Actively, algolagnia is the sexual satisfaction derived from inflicting pain (sadism).

algophobia – n. a morbid, disproportionate fear of pain

allocentrism – n. the view that one should center interest and concern on other persons rather than one's self; contrasted with "egocentrism"

alloeroticism – n. making another person the object of sexual excitement, feeling, and action; as opposed to "auto-eroticism"

allopsychic – adj. characterized by being related mentally to the external world

allotheism – n. the adoration of gods outside a recognized theological system

alter ego – n. a second self; someone who is deeply trusted

altrigendristic – adj. being interested in the opposite sex without specific sexual goals or aims

altruism – n. the view that life should be lived intentionally for the well-being of others; a concern for others that overrides concern for one's self. In the West, Christ is the paradigm, causing Thich Nhat Hanh to call Jesus "the Buddha of the West."

Altruism appears in animals as well as humans. It has presented a puzzle in understanding individual self-preservation. Some philosophers argue that altruism is a disguised form of egoism and is enacted to produce advantages indirectly.

References: *Sociobiology*, E. O. Wilson; *Die Fröhliche Wissenschaft* (*The Gay Science*), Friedrich Nietzsche; *Complete Psychological Works of Sigmund Freud, The Economic Problem of Masochism*, vol. 19; *The Ego and the Mechanisms of Defense*, Anna Freud; *Beast and Man: The Roots of Human Nature*, Mary Midgley; *The Nature of Sympathy*, Max Scheler

ambisexual – n. or adj. having characteristics of both sexes; a hermaphrodite

a mensa et thoro – adj. in marital ethics, a reference to a conjugal relationship in which the man and woman are married but no longer sleep together

anaclitic depression – n. a downward turn in the psychic life of the child who is deprived of its mother after having a good relationship for the first six months of life. Manifestations include weight loss, changed facial expression, and withdrawal.

> References: *The First Year of Life*, Rene Spitz; *Introduction to the Work of Melanie Klein*, 2nd ed., Hanna Segal

anaclitic focus – n. a mental or libidinal dependence on a love object that represents infantile needs (e.g., the father or mother)

anagogic – adj. having a spiritual or uplifting effect; relating to inner psychic forces that move one toward lofty ideals. Referring to a universal ethical meaning, this term is contrasted with psychological analysis that points toward sexual meaning

anal character – n. a personality characterized by excessive devotion to neatness, self-discipline, pedantry, acquisitiveness, miserliness, and control. These are seen as the symbolic manifestations of anal eroticism.

anarchism – n. fr. the Greek *an* (without) and *archos* (head). In political philosophy, it is the view that organized government is the source of social injustice and the slaughter of liberty. Thus, anarchists typically call for the dissolution of the state. Anarchists come in violent and nonviolent varieties. Some, like William Godwin (1756–1836), author of *The Inquiry Concerning Political Justice* (1793), argue for its emergence through gradual moral progress, emphasizing a kind of evolution of society and confidence in the goodness of humanity. Others, like Max Stirner (1806–1856), author of *The Ego and One's Own* (1845), advocate radical individualism and open rebellion. In the case of Stirner, individual freedom, as a principle of virtue and a withdrawal into one's creativity, implies the respect of every other individual, and thus, it would not increase conflict. Still others, like Mikhail Bakunin (1814–1876), author of *The State and Anarchy* (1873), advocate a mission of destruction, because privileged society is depraved in heart and mind.

"The state is the sum of all the negations of the individual liberty of all its members . . . negation of the liberty of each in the name of the liberty of all or of the common right—that is the State. Thus, where the State begins, individual liberty ceases, and vice versa."

Mikhail Bakunin, *The State and Anarchy*

References: *Anarchist Portraits*, Paul Avrich; and *Action and Existence*, Pierre Guillet de Monthoux

anatta – n. in Buddhism, the unreality of the self; the "fetters" that block enlightenment

Anaxagoras (500–428 BC) – a pre-Socratic philosopher and friend of Pericles. Anaxagoras was trained in mathematics and astronomy. The main elements of his thought are left to us in a fragmented work entitled *On Nature*. Like Empedocles, Anaxagoras was interested to solve the puzzle of how and why things change. He disagreed with Empedocles about the existence of four basic elements: earth, air, fire, and water. Anaxagoras argued that there must be some absolute and unchangeable foundation to reality, but that this foundation was composed of more than four basic elements. Change was said to be the result of relative adjustments in the arrangement of the foundational elements. Consequently, Anaxagoras held the view that nothing comes into existence or passes away. Change is primarily a cosmetic reorganization of matter. The world is a product of Mind or *Nous*.

"It is the sun that endows the moon with its brilliance."

Anaxagoras, *On Nature*

References: *Beginning with the Pre-Socratics*, Merrill Ring, and *The Greek Philosophers*, W. K. C. Guthrie

Anaximander (611–546 BC) – a student of Thales. Anaximander was schooled in astronomy, geography, and cosmology. He held the belief that all living things evolved from the sea, including humanity. Consequently, he advocated a kind of alternation of worlds theory. This argued that all worlds recur in a cyclical fashion: a separation from and return to a primordial substance, a substance referred to by Anaximander as the "Boundless Indeterminate."

Reference: *Anaximander and the Origins of Greek Cosmology*, C. H. Kahn

Anaximenes (588–524 BC) – a pupil of Anaximander, Anaximenes was the last important natural philosopher of the Milesian school. His contribution to primitive science was an adjustment in the theories of his teacher. He proposed that "air" is the principal substance and that all changes are the result of rarefaction and condensation. Fire is a type of rarefaction, and stone, ice, water, and clouds are examples of condensation.

Reference: *The Greek Philosophers*, W. K. C. Guthrie

ancillary – n. or adj. subordinate

anicca – n. in Buddhism, impermanence; the transitory nature of all things

animism – n. the view that all matter has "soul." It stems from attempts to explain "change" in the physical world. In Greek philosophy this view was called "hylozoism"

anoesis – n. no thought; a vacant mental situation in which any content of the mind is not understood or coherently assimilated

anoia – n. idiocy; without mind

anomaly – n. outside of accepted notions; being out of place; a deviation

Anselm, St. (1033–1109) – a Christian philosopher and Archbishop of Canterbury, Anselm is known as the author of the ontological argument for God's existence. While *Monologium* contains a cosmological proof inherited from St. Augustine, *Proslogium* makes use of Platonic elements to show how one deduces the existence of God from the concept of God: God is that being greater than which nothing can be conceived.

The ontological argument uses the perfection of God to imply existence, especially a highest existence or being. This reasoning is achieved through the Platonic Theory of Forms: forms have existence apart from and superior to the existence of material objects. The effect of this argument on the wider thought of Anselm is obvious: to reveal the relationship between divine reality and physical reality. If lesser things have the property of existence, then greater things have the property of existence. A chair is a lesser thing whose existence is self-evident. Thus, God as a greater thing has all the properties of a lesser thing, including existence…Anselm reasoned that this has implications for human existence, especially human conduct. God is equated with the supreme Good, self-existent, eternal, and the source of absolute truth. Morality is based in a divine origin:

A

"It is one thing for an object to be in the understanding, and another to understand that the object exists…even the fool is convinced that something exists in the understanding, at least, than which nothing greater can be conceived. For when he hears of this, he understands it. And whatever is understood, exists in the understanding. And assuredly that, than which nothing greater can be conceived, cannot exist in the understanding alone. For, suppose it exists in the understanding alone: then it can be conceived to exist in reality; which is greater.

"Therefore, if that, than which nothing greater can be conceived, exists in the understanding alone, the very being, than which nothing greater can be conceived, is one, than which a greater being can be conceived. But obviously this is impossible. Hence, there is no doubt that there exists a being, than which nothing greater can be conceived, and it exists both in the understanding and in reality."

St. Anselm, *Proslogium*

References: *Anselm and a New Generation*, G. R. Evans; and *St. Anselm and His Critics*, John McIntyre

anthropomorphism – n. a view that attributes human qualities and characteristics to God or things that are not human. In logic, it is called the fallacy of reification.

anthropopathism – n. a view that projects human feelings on to nature, especially feelings of cruelty or sympathy. Think of the way it is particularly evident in the work of some poets, like Shelley and Tennyson. In logic, it is considered an error in reasoning, close to the fallacy of reification.

antithesis – n. counterargument. In epistemology, antithesis is central for the dialectical process. Without counterargument, there can be no real progress in the development of ideas. Ideas are attacked in order to be validated and pushed toward a higher degree of truth. Western thought is a history of antithesis.

aphanisis – n. the disappearance of sexual desire; the consequence of a deep fear. Reference: *Early Development of Female Sexuality*, Earl Jones (1927)

apologia – n. a defense, usually of a philosophical or theological position

a posteriori – adj. Latin meaning "from the latter"; this phrase refers to knowledge that comes after experience or the encounter with fact; connected to inductive reasoning

a priori – adj. Latin meaning "from before" or "from the preceding"; this phrase refers to statements that are true independent of experience; connected to deductive reasoning

Aquinas, Thomas (1224–1274) – an Italian philosopher and theologian, Aquinas became the dominant theological voice for Catholicism. Aquinas's thought reflects an Aristotelian influence, which he used to construct his theological conclusions.

For Aquinas, God is both pure actuality and pure form. A knowledge of God can be acquired by faith or reason, but God's existence is variously inferred from creation: a) everything has a cause, b) it is not necessary that natural objects exist; they exist because of some necessary ground, c) there are graded forms of being starting from a lowest to the highest, d) everything exists for a purpose, implying an intelligent designer, e) matter cannot create itself, thus God created it *ex nihilo* (out of nothing).

Aquinas defines man as pure spirit and substance, a higher being in the chain of being ascending toward God. The human soul is an immaterial and subsistent form. It possesses an eternal nature in that it is also actual form. So, it features an immortal condition that succeeds in the absence of the body. He argues that the union of body and soul is partial, with the soul retaining a type of independent destiny.

The highest good is the realization of the true self. This is accomplished by living a contemplative life, with God as the meditative object. Reason and faith contribute to an understanding of the best life in God, but it is finally a type of intuitive knowledge acquired in the afterlife that completes our understanding. Preparing for one's positive eternal destiny (salvation) requires a commitment to asceticism and ethical-spiritual development through the Sacraments of the Church and the message of the Gospels.

Principal works: *On Being and Essence (1243), On Truth (1259), Summa Contra Gentiles (1260),* and *Summa Theologica (1272)*

"A certain participation of Happiness can be had in this life, but perfect and true Happiness cannot be had in this life…Since happiness is a perfect and sufficient good, it excludes every evil, and fulfills every desire. But in this life every evil cannot be excluded. For this present life is subject to many unavoidable evils: to ignorance on the part of the intellect, to disordered affection on the part of the appetite, and to many penalties on the part of the body…Likewise neither can

the desire be satiated in this life. For man naturally desires the good which he has to be abiding. Now the goods of the present life pass away, since life itself passes away, which we naturally desire to have, and would wish to hold abidingly, for man naturally shrinks from death. Therefore, it is impossible to have true Happiness in this life. "

Thomas Aquinas, *Summa Theologica*

References: *Aquinas*, Frederick Copleston; *St. Thomas Aquinas*, Jacques Maritain; *The Philosophy of St. Thomas Aquinas*, Etienne Gilson

arahat – n. in Buddhism, an enlightened monk

ardhamagadhi – n. a North Indian language used in the canon of Jainism

aretaic ethics – n. the view that the character of the agent is an essential part of the measure of goodness. Thus, the concern with acts and duties becomes secondary to the personality or spiritual disposition (meaning character) of the agent. Derived from the Greek *arete*, meaning excellence.

argot – n. special vocabulary used to communicate privately

Aristotle (384–322 BC) – a student of Plato and the teacher of Alexander the Great. His father was a physician to the King of Macedonia. He was raised in the guild of Asclepiade, where he acquired his interest in biology. He entered Plato's Academy at seventeen years of age, when Plato had entered his "later" period: mathematics and natural science. After Plato's death, Aristotle accepted an invitation to work for King Hermeias near Troy. There he fell in love with the king's niece, Pythia, and married her. They had a daughter, but after Pythia died, he married a slave woman named Herpyllis and had a son, Nichomachus (Nichomachean Ethics). He traveled to Lesbos and eventually returned to Athens. Antipater, a Macedonian statesman, helped Aristotle found his school, the Lyceum, named after the sacred grove of trees for Apollo Lyceus. There he walked while teaching and his school earned the label "peripatetic." After the death of King Alexander, Aristotle fled to Chalcis. He died there of intestinal problems in 322 BC.

Aristotle invented the field of formal logic, including the starting points of reason, the syllogism, and the foundation of causal analysis for events in the natural world. Aristotle argued for substance as the primary essence of reality and deepened the Platonic reference to matter and form by showing their interdependence.

He developed his Doctrine of Categories for the description and organization of things. As a teleological thinker, Aristotle developed explanations of the potentiality of being vs. the actuality of being, including sophisticated arguments for design and the processes of change.

Aristotle explained the process of change: motion, growth, generation, decay, and corruptions. He identified four types of cause to understand a thing:

1) *formal cause* – the design of a thing
2) *material cause* – the substance from which a thing is made
3) *efficient cause* – the forces that bring a thing into empirical existence
4) *final cause* – the purpose or function for which a thing is created

He referred to the principle of motion as the Unmoved Mover.

Aristotle believed that all things possess a design, and this permeates all of reality, including psychology, ethics, biology, politics, physics, cosmology, and even art. For Aristotle, the problem of happiness and a successful life are dependent on how well each person is able to master and benefit from an understanding of the design of the cosmos. Man's purpose is to achieve a proper functioning of the soul. To achieve happiness, the rational part of the soul should control the irrational part.

Principal works: *Organon*; *On the Soul*; *The Metaphysics*; *Nicomachean Ethics*; and *Politics*

"All men by nature desire to know. An indication of this is the delight we take in our senses; for even apart from their usefulness they are loved for themselves; and above all others the sense of sight."

Aristotle, *Metaphysics*

"It is no easy task to be good. For in everything it is no easy task to find the middle, e.g. to find the middle of a circle is not for everyone but for him who knows; so, too, anyone can get angry—that is easy—or to give or spend money; but to do this to the right person, to the right extent, at the right time, with the right motive, and in the right way, 'that' is not for everyone, nor is it easy; therefore goodness is both rare and laudable and noble."

Aristotle, *Ethics*

A

References: *Aristotle*, Werner Jaeger; *A Portrait of Aristotle*, Marjorie Grene; *The Philosophy of Aristotle*, D. J. Allan; and *Practical Knowledge, Aristotle, and Weakness of Will*, N. O. Dahl

arriviste – n. one who has acquired success by dubious methods

arrogate – v. to seize without permission or the right to do so

asceticism – n. fr. the Greek *askesis*, meaning self-mastery or training. It refers to practices that aid self-mastery. It represents a moral science that seeks to eliminate vices and encourage personal excellence. In Eastern and Western religious traditions, it is a denial of body in order to keep the practitioner focused on spiritual goals. In Hinduism, asceticism is emphasized in the later stages of life with a renunciation of worldly interests. And, while Buddhism produced the "Middle Way," it retains certain ascetic practices as central requirements for proof of inner liberation from desire. In the West and the East, asceticism has sometimes been practiced to excess, leading away from enlightenment in a negative focus on the body, thus also deforming the spiritual life. Overall, the principles of asceticism are a path to renewed personal unity. Typical principles of asceticism include:

1) A commitment to nonviolence
2) Minimal contact with physical wealth
3) Simplicity of habitat, including only the possessions necessary for the most basic physical survival, e.g., a begging bowl, a razor, a robe, sandals, a candle, a cup, the simplest furniture (if any)
4) Noninvolvement in various kinds of sensual entertainment
5) Dietary laws: strict limits on how much and what one eats; often including no food after midafternoon
6) No use of intoxicants of any kind
7) Transcendence of sexual desires and activities
8) A daily routine of prayer, meditation, and simple but often demanding physical work
9) Progressive and continuous mastery of the Scriptures
10) The cultivation of universal love for humanity and one's community

"When strict with one's self, one rarely fails."

Confucius (551–479 BC), *The Analects*

"It is a great grace of God to practice self-examination. But, too much is as bad as too little."

St. Theresa of Avila (1515–1582), *The Interior Castle*

"Everyone should enjoy a quiet soul and be free from every type of passion.

Then will strength of character and self-control shine through in all their brilliance. But, when appetites are unleashed to run wild, either in desire or aversion, and are not reined by reason, they exceed all restraint and measure. They throw off obedience and leave it behind."

Marcus Tullius Cicero (106–43 BC), *On Duties*

References: *Yoga Sutras*, Patanjali; and *The Way of Ascetics*, Tito Colliander

ascribe – v. to attribute

ashram – n. in religions of India, a place to meditate; a religious retreat house

asomatous – adj. without body; incorporeal; a condition beyond lifelessness

asperity – n. roughness or sharpness, especially of manner

asperse – v. to slander or attack, especially with damaging claims or charges of moral wrong

asseverate – v. to affirm with sincerity and earnestness, especially with regard to truth

assiduous – adj. with regard to a project or business, the quality of paying very close attention; being persistent in the completion of work

assignation – n. an arrangement to meet; especially between secret lovers

assuage – v. to soften intensity

astatize – v. to make unstable or active

asthenic – adj. relating to or denoting a tall, lean build; a lightly muscled athletic physique

ataraxia – n. an ideal mental state; characterized by an almost euphoric sense of pleasure and calm with regard to the life of the philosopher

A

atavism – n. the view that one should go back to a more primitive lifestyle; the acquisition of an ancestor's skills. It can refer to a return to violence or pagan practices…In the venatic art, hunting with the bow is an example of atavism (Ortega y Gasset). In such an activity, one attempts to recover values and perceptions that may have contributed to an instinctive understanding of life (Eliade). Bowhunting, as atavism, affords the opportunity to examine the dynamic properties of man as a rational predator; the sensory awareness, the improvisation of needs, and the general spiritual and physical self-sufficiency that enhances the possibility of personal happiness through a wholistic immersion in nature.

> *"Thus the principle which inspires hunting for sport is of artificially perpetuating, as a possibility for man, a situation which is archaic in the highest degree: that early state in which, already human, he still lived within the orbit of animal existence."*

José Ortega y Gasset (1883–1955), *Meditations on Hunting*

> *"It is surprising to see the insistence with which all cultures, upon imagining a golden age, have placed it at the beginning of time, at the most primitive point.*
>
> *It was only a couple of centuries ago that the tendency to expect the best from the future began to compete with that retrospective illusion. Our heart vacillates between a yearning for novelties and a constant eagerness to turn back. But the latter predominates. Happiness has generally been thought to be simplicity and primitivism. How happy man feels when he dreams of stripping off the oppressive present and floating in a more tenuous and simpler element!"*

José Ortega y Gasset, *Meditations on Hunting*

References: *Man in the Landscape, The Tender Carnivore and the Sacred Game*, and *Thinking Animals*, Paul Shepard; *Meditations on Hunting*, José Ortega y Gasset

atelier – n. a craftsman's workshop; an artist's studio

atheism – n. the view that God does not exist. It is expressed in both secular and religious philosophies (e.g., Jainism and Buddhism vs. Marxism and Freud).

Hostility toward atheism has a long history. In fact, even certain theologies have been treated as atheism. Benedict Spinoza (1632–1677) claimed that God and nature are one, bringing about an assassination attempt, and making it clear that pantheism was considered atheism. This hostility exposes the emotional basis of belief in God, which, in philosophical terms, is evidence of irrational formulations and superstition at work.

Atheism has often been an expression of social protest. Take the example of Ludwig Feuerbach (1804–1872), who believed that the love of God often inspires a hatred of one's neighbor. Feuerbach abandoned his theological beginning, in part, as a protest against a seemingly hypocritical Christian society.

> *"Atheism is sometimes inspired by great-hearted dreams of justice and progress . . . and impatience with the mediocrity and self-seeking of so many contemporary social settings."*

Pope Paul VI, *Ecclesiam Suam* (1964)

Paul Tillich (1886–1965), author of *Shaking of the Foundations* (1948) and *The Dynamics of Faith* (1957), argued that atheism was a spiritual symptom, since it holds that life has no depth beyond a material scene. For Tillich, anyone who believes this must be an atheist, since only the reality of God provides the depth that is missing in the ontology of atheists. Tillich, however, did not embrace the traditional metaphysical definition of God, believing it to be too simplistic.

> *"Atheism can only mean the attempt to remove any ultimate concern, to remain unconcerned about the meaning of one's existence."*

Paul Tillich, *Dynamics of Faith*

In a simple way, the problem of evil has been an ancient argument for atheism. If God is good, why is there so much misery and suffering in this world? Where is the mercy and justice of God so commonly implied in the definition of God?

> *"Behold, I cry out, 'Violence!' but I am not answered; I call aloud, but there is no justice."*

The Book of Job, 19:7

The anthropomorphic view of God is sometimes attacked as a fallacy of reification. It is illogical to give attributes to God that are clearly a projection of human nature. The atheist argues that there is no verifiable evidence for an anthropomorphic theology.

A

"My atheism . . . is true piety towards the universe and denies only gods fashioned by men in their own image, to be servants of their human interests."

George Santayana (1863–1952), *Soliloquies*

The linguistic argument for atheism employs the verification principle. Language philosophers point out that sentences that talk about God are filled with pictures that have no external context, that God talk cannot be meaningful without a clear reference point.

"In its metaphysical use . . . the word 'God' refers to something beyond experience. The word is deliberately divested of its reference to a physical being or to a physical being that is immanent in the physical. And as it is not given a new meaning, it becomes meaningless. To be sure, it often looks as though the word 'God' had a meaning even in metaphysics. But the definitions which are set up prove upon closer inspection to be pseudo-definitions. They lead either to logically illegitimate combinations of words or to other metaphysical words (e.g. 'primordial basis,' 'the absolute,' 'the unconditioned,' 'the autonomous,' 'the self-independent,' and so forth), but in no case to the truth conditions of its elementary sentences. An elementary sentence would here have to be of the form 'x is a God'; yet, the metaphysician either rejects this form entirely without substituting another, or if he accepts it he neglects to indicate the syntactical category of the variable x."

Rudolf Carnap (1891–1970), *The Elimination of Metaphysics*

Freud regarded belief in God as an illusion and evidence of a neurotic temperament. God, in his view, is merely a conceptual refuge from reality. It allows the individual to escape from the problems of this life in a highly fantasized creation of an alternate reality.

"Religious phenomena are to be understood only on the model of the neurotic symptoms of the individual."

Sigmund Freud (1856–1939), *Moses and Monotheism*

References: *At the Origins of Modern Atheism*, Michael J. Buckley; *Ethics without God*, revised ed., Kai Nielsen

atman – n. in Hinduism, the soul; the essence of consciousness

atrabilious – adj. morose, gloomy, pessimistic, or sad

attenuate – v. to reduce in force or value; to threaten nonexistence

attrahent – adj. quality of drawing toward; attracting

audacity – n. a quality of great boldness; a condition of fearlessness, especially with regard to limiting authority

au fait – n. expert in something

augur – n. prophet; (the same in verb form) to prophesize

Augustine, St. (353–430 AD) – a Christian philosopher and Bishop of Hippo who wrote, "Understand in order that you may believe, believe in order that you may understand." Augustinian epistemology argues that no knowledge outside a knowledge of God and one's self is true knowing. Only knowledge of this kind can help the individual to secure a happy life. Ignorance is a restlessness or spiritual poverty. Beauty, truth, and goodness only come about in one's life as a result of the spiritual knowledge of God.

Augustine's philosophical energy seems to have been driven by his own guilt. His early love of pleasure, especially sexual pleasure, reached its final end when he was about thirty years of age. The psychological features of his transformation through Christian ideas can be found in his important autobiography, *The Confessions*. There one finds the personal basis of Augustine's rigorous commitment to spiritual change. Through Augustine's influence, this attitude was expressed in the official doctrinal position of Christianity for hundreds of years. This was as a consequence of Augustine's Neoplatonic influence on the Christian worldview.

In *The City of God* Augustine argues for a theory of salvation, dividing the human race into "reprobates" and "elect," the latter destined for the City of God and the former destined for the fires of hell. Other works, *On Free Will*, *On Christian Doctrine*, and *On the Trinity* fill out the main ideas of Augustine on psychology, history, theology, ethics, and the problem of evil.

Principal works: *Confessions*, *City of God*, *On Christian Doctrine*, and *The Trinity*

"I was in love with loving; and I hated security and a life with no snares for my feet. For within I was hungry, all for the want of that spiritual food which is Thyself, my God; yet I did not hunger for it: I had no desire for incorruptible food, not because I had it in abundance but the emptier I was, the more I hated the thought of it...My longing then was to love and be loved, but most when

I obtained the enjoyment of the body of the person who loved me...I wore my chains with bliss but with torment too, for I was scourged with red hot rods of jealousy, with suspicions and fears and tempers and quarrels."

St. Augustine, *Confessions, III*

"I in my great worthlessness . . . had begged You for chastity, saying 'Grant me chastity and continence, but not yet.' For I was afraid that You would hear my prayer too soon, and too soon would heal me from the sexual craving which I wanted satisfied rather than extinguished."

St. Augustine, *Confessions, VIII*

References: *Augustine*, Henry Chadwick; *Adam, Eve, and the Serpent*, Elaine Pagels; *Desire and Delight*, Margaret R. Miles; *The Essential Augustine*, Vernon Bourke

Aurobindo, Ghose (1872–1950) – also known as Sri Aurobindo; was a Hindu philosopher and political leader. Though naturally shy and relatively unknown as a professor at Baroda College in Bengal, he generated a following through his articles in the English-language weekly *Bande Mataram*. His father's choice to educate him in England from age seven until age twenty-one created a personal need to "renationalize" himself. His ideology reflects the influence of Ramakrishna, Vivekananda, and Bankim Chandra Chatterjee. It strives to liberate India and return the role of Hinduism in politics and national identity.

Aurobindo defended the view that reality is a graded spectrum of existence, beginning with matter and moving to the Absolute or Brahman. His system offers a bipolar movement: matter seeks Brahman and Brahman seeks matter, with Brahman guiding the overall dynamic as a kind of integral evolution of being. Aurobindo employed this metaphysic with ethical aims to call for a transformation of mind, life, and body. These principles were implemented in his political philosophy.

Principal works: *Essays on the Gita* (1926–44); *The Life Divine*, 2 vols. (1947); and *The Synthesis of Yoga* (1948)

"That which we call the Hindu religion is really the eternal religion, because it is the eternal religion which embraces all others. If a religion is not universal, it cannot be eternal. A narrow religion, a sectarian religion, an exclusive religion can only live

for a limited time and a limited purpose. This is the one religion that can triumph over materialism by including and anticipating the discoveries of science and the speculations of philosophy."

Sri Aurobindo, *Speeches*

Reference: *Aurobindo, Gandhi, and Roy*, Niranjan Dar

auspicious – adj. favorable

Austin, John Langshaw (1911–1960) – a philosopher of ordinary language. J. L. Austin was the son of an architect, attended Balliol College, Oxford, won the Gaisford Prize for Greek prose, and served in the British Intelligence Corps (M16) during WWII. He was responsible for intelligence logistics that saved many lives on D-Day.

After WWII, Austin became professor of moral philosophy at Oxford. He delivered the William James Lectures at Harvard University in 1955 and was president of the Aristotelian Society in 1956. Before his death, Austin became friends with Noam Chomsky. Austin died of lung cancer in 1960.

Austin separated himself from logical positivism by arguing that the way language is used ordinarily is important and helps to ground communication. He believed that skepticism does not need be applied to most words, and philosophers often make bad use of the English language. In *How to Do Things with Words*, he introduces "speech acts" and "performative utterances." These are statements that actually participate in doing things. For example, the statement, "I will sail this boat to San Francisco," is part of the act of sailing to San Francisco. Austin argued that "speech acts" are different from other statements that may describe what is done but are not part of the action.

Principal work: *How to Do Things with Words* (1955)

Reference: *Essays on J. L. Austin*, Isaiah Berlin

austral – adj. southern

autoeroticism – n. a term used by Havelock Ellis, a British sexologist. It refers to sexual pleasures that are created through daydreams, sexual arousal, nocturnal dreams, and masturbation. It is considered a breakup of a more natural sexual orientation due to deprivation in childhood.

autonomy thesis – n. in ethical theory, the view that moral principles and guidelines can be established without recourse to Divine revelation. Autonomy emphasizes self-rule (Immanuel Kant).

avarice – n. an excessive drive to acquire wealth

aver – v. to declare with confidence; to admit as valid or real

Averroes (1126–1198) – also known as Ibn Roshd; was a principal in the development of Arabic philosophy. Though a Spaniard, Averroes wrote in Arabic. His thought was modeled on the views of Aristotle, as Averroes believed that Aristotle was the perfect human being. His ideas also revealed strong Neoplatonic influences along with a modified Aristotelianism, including the emanation theory of reality and the concept of a universal mind as God. Averroes was important because he helped to preserve philosophy in an age of intellectual stagnation.

Principal work: *Commentaries on Aristotle*

Reference: *Averroes and the Metaphysics of Causation*, Barry S. Kogan

axiology – n. the study of worth or value, thus "value theory." It is the study of value in art, ethics, politics, logic, and the sciences. It produces more or less dyadic comparisons: right vs. wrong, good vs. bad, natural vs. non-natural, subjective vs. objective, absolute vs. relative, justifiable vs. unjustifiable, extrinsic vs. intrinsic, religious vs. nonreligious, rational vs. nonrational, scientific vs. nonscientific. George Santayana argued that interests are values.

Ayer, A. J. (1910–1989) – a leading figure in the school of logical positivism, Ayer was born to a wealthy family and attended the finest schools in England, including Christ Church College, Oxford. Ayer enjoyed sports, particularly rugby. He was married four times, the fourth being a remarriage to his second wife, Alberta Wells, with whom he earlier had a son. He became a member of the Welsh Guard during WWII and M16 (the British Secret Service). He was an honorary foreign member of the American Academy of Arts and Sciences. He was president of the British Humanist Association and a signer of the Humanist Manifesto. He was knighted in 1970.

Ayer was well connected throughout his life with academia, the establishment, and high society.

*According to biographer Ben Rogers, Ayer was invited to a party in 1987 by fashion designer Fernando Sanchez, where he met Mike Tyson. Tyson was trying to seduce a young model, Naomi Campbell, and Ayer asked him to stop. Tyson was said to reply: "Do you know who the fuck I am? I am the heavy-weight champion of the world." To which Ayer was heard to reply, "I am former Wykeham Professor of Logic. We are both preeminent in our field. I suggest we talk about this like rational men."

Ayer's most important book, *Language, Truth, and Logic*, went beyond atheism. Ayer argued that atheists are just as mistaken as theists, because statements about God's nonexistence are just as ridiculous as statements about God's existence. The atheist employs the same nonsense to prove God's nonexistence. In other words, the whole discussion about God is unverifiable. According to his "verification principle," statements themselves cannot equal factual content. Statements can only be meaningful if they have a verifiable scientific import.

> Principle works: *Language, Truth, and Logic* (1936); *The Problem of Knowledge* (1940); *Philosophical Essays* (1954); *Metaphysics and Common Sense* (1969); and *Probability and Evidence* (1972)

> *References: A. J. Ayer: A Life*, Ben Rogers

azharot – n. in Judaism, liturgical poems recommending obedience to the teachings of the Torah

Azrael – n. in Judaism and Islam, the angel of death who watches over the dying and separates the soul from the body

B

bacchant – n. one given to habits of drunkenness and uncontrolled conduct

Bacon, Francis (1561–1626) – an English philosopher and politician. Bacon's mother emphasized the importance of religious purity, while his father advocated worldly success. He became Lord Chancellor of the British Parliament, but was charged with accepting bribes and spent time in prison. He defended some of his political and moral vices by arguing that it was necessary to acquire power to effect good in the world.

Bacon argued that thinking is corrupted by "Idols of the Mind":

1) *Idols of the Den* – each person lives in a kind of den or cave, preferring his or her own ideas to the ideas of others. Bacon advocated careful scrutiny of the ideas one finds most satisfying in order to prevent the egoistic distortion of truth.
2) *Idols of the Tribe* – warns us of the tendency to measure all things by human standards. The human race has anthropomorphic tendencies. We fail to recognize the weaknesses of the senses in determining truth. Man is not the measure of all things.
3) *Idols of the Market* – refers to the likelihood of inferring from mere words that there are actual references in reality. In commerce, we discover that words are ambiguous and many disputes over truth arise from the careless use of language.

4) *Idols of the Theater* – observes the weaknesses of philosophical abstractions. Systems of ideas are like stage plays. They are often barely justified in representing reality.

Bacon was an amateur practitioner of the scientific method and died as the result of simple wintertime cryogenic experiments. Bacon tried to prove the preservative effects of snow, using a chicken. He contracted a fatal case of bronchitis…Bacon's understanding of the scientific method was flawed by an assumption that if one looked at facts in nature long enough a hypothesis would emerge. Modern scientists work it the other way: suggest a hypothesis, then look for evidence in nature to support it.

Principal works: *Novum Organum* (1620), *The Advancement of Learning* (1605), and *New Atlantis*(1623)

"If a child be bird-witted, that is, hath not the faculty of attention, the mathematics giveth a remedy thereunto; for in them, if the wit be caught but a moment, one is new to begin."

Francis Bacon, *The Advancement of Learning*

Reference: *Francis Bacon: Philosopher of Planned Science*, Benjamin Farrington

badinage – n. playfulness; good-natured wittiness

bagatelle – n. something of little or no value

bagnio – n. a place where women are available for pleasurable purposes; a brothel; a prison; a Turkish bath

baksheesh – n. a monetary gift, tip, or alms

balneology – n. the study of bathing, especially its therapeutic and hedonistic effects

banausic – adj. of practical use only; limited to "praxis"; also meaning vulgar and damaging with regard to mental finesse

barratry – n. fraudulent acts by a captain or crew of a ship at the owner's expense; also a reference to illegal traffic in ecclesiastical or state promotions of office

B

bathos – n. the sudden appearance of the vulgar or the ordinary in the midst of the sublime; a descent from the sublime to the ludicrous

battologize – v. to repeat words or phrases uselessly or to excess

Beauvoir, Simone de (1908–1986) – a French feminist philosopher, perhaps the most important voice for modern feminism. Raised in the Catholic faith by a devout mother, Francois Beauvoir (Brasseur), she had interest in becoming a nun. Instead she experienced a loss of faith at age fourteen and became a life-long atheist. She became a teacher after her philosophical training at the École Normal Supérieure, but lost her teaching license because of an affair with a female student. Though she was the common-law wife of Jean-Paul Sartre, whom she met during her philosophical studies, each of them took lovers during their life together. They worked together as political activists and writers until the death of Sartre in 1980.

In her writings, Beauvoir reflected on the role and destiny of women in ancient and modern times. Her philosophy of women is expressed in psychological and philosophical terms in *The Second Sex*. There, Beauvoir assembles the pieces to argue that woman is essentially preyed upon in a male world. She also outlines what she believes is necessary for liberating women from their past. She provides original insights into the nature of existence in its sexual manifestations.

She is often credited with broadening the rational psychology of Sartre. This included the introduction of social issues and the experiences of childhood as contributing factors in the formation of the individual.

Principal works: *The Ethics of Ambiguity* (1947) and *The Second Sex* (1949)

"One is not born, but rather becomes, a woman."

"It is not uncommon for the young girl's first experience to be a real rape and for the man to act in an odiously brutal manner; in the country and wherever manners are rough—half consenting, half revolted— the young girl loses her virginity in some ditch, in shame and fear. In any case, what very often happens in all circles and classes is for the virgin to be abruptly taken by an egoistic lover who is primarily interested in his own pleasure."

"Man has succeeded in enslaving woman; but in the same degree he has deprived her of what made her possession desirable. With woman integrated

in the family and in society, her magic is dissipated rather than transformed; reduced to the condition of servant, she is no longer that unconquered prey incarnating all the treasures of nature. Since the rise of chivalric love it is a commonplace that marriage kills love."

Simone de Beauvoir, *The Second Sex*

References: *The Philosophy of Simone de Beauvoir*, Debra Bergoffen; *Simone de Beauvoir: A Feminist Mandarin*, M. Evans; *Simone de Beauvoir and the Limits of Commitment*, Anne Whitmarsh; *Simone de Beauvoir: A Biography*, Dierdre Bair

bedizen – v. to dress vulgarly

bedlam – n. a scene or place of complete insanity, madness, or chaos

being – n. a reference to fundamental existence. "Being" stands in contrast to "becoming" and "nonbeing." In Plato, the material world implies a lesser state of being than the spiritual world. This is due to Parmenides's (fifth-sixth century BC) insistence that true being implies permanence. The material world, as a changing world, is not being or existence in the highest sense. The material world is closer to becoming and non-being. Absolute being is imperishable, thus it is realness in the highest sense. Much philosophy is an attempt to detail the definition of being, for it is believed that the successful investigation of being holds the key to solving the puzzle of death.

The puzzle of being is the basis of ontology. Ontology, the study of being, tries to discover ways to make sense out of reality as being. Ontology is then a central project of metaphysics, especially since there is no confidence in matter as ultimate reality. In the East and in the West, the search for a logic of being accounts for construction of all the various philosophies of life.

References: *Thaetetus* and *The Sophist*, Plato; *Being and Some Philosophers*, Etienne Gilson; *Mystery of Being*, Gabriel Marcel; *Being and Nothingness*, Jean-Paul Sartre; *Concerning Being and Essence*, Thomas Aquinas

belaud – v. to praise lavishly, especially to cause embarrassment

Bentham, Jeremy (1748–1832) – an English philosopher, jurist, and social reformer known as the coauthor of utilitarianism, a philosophical view that defines the highest moral principle as "the greatest happiness for the greatest number." Born into wealth, Bentham was a child prodigy who studied history and Latin at the age of three.

Bentham developed a novel calculus for the determination of right and wrong based on the pleasure-pain principle. This "hedonistic calculus" included seven criteria that are supposedly measured mathematically in plus (+) minus (-) fashion on a scale of, say, 1–10:

1) *intensity* – the acuteness of the pleasure
2) *duration* – the length of time the pleasure exists
3) *certainty* – the percentile regarding the pleasure's real occurrence when pursued
4) *propinquity* – the availability or nearness of the pleasurable experience
5) *fecundity* – the prospects of a pleasure leading to other pleasures
6) *purity* – the fractional existence of pleasure vs. pain and misery
7) *extent* – the number of people who will experience the pleasure

Bentham spent much of his life advocating the principle of utility to aristocratic society, which he perceived as an obstruction to the greatest happiness for the greatest number. He supported separation of Church and state, freedom of expression, the right to divorce, the end of the death penalty, the abolition of slavery, equality for women, prison reform, and the decriminalization of homosexuality. This made him a political radical.

Principal works: *Introduction to the Principles of Morals and Legislation* (1798), *A Plea for the Constitution* (1803), and *Catechism of Parliamentary Reform* (1809)

"The general object which all laws have . . . is to augment the total happiness of the community; and therefore, in the first place to exclude . . . everything that tends to subtract from that happiness . . ."

Jeremy Bentham, *The Principles of Morals and Legislation*

Reference: *Jeremy Bentham*, Bhikhu Parekh

Bergson, Henri-Louis (1859–1941) – a French philosopher of evolution. Bergson explained evolution as the result of a vital impulse, *elan vital*. This vital impulse operates as a creative force driving all living things toward more complex forms of being. In reasoning this way, Bergson worked against traditional philosophical systems, like Platonism, which defended fixed conceptual models of reality. Bergson emphasized the notion of "duration" (becoming) in a more rigorous way, pointing out that evolution has no set goal, that the future is open and truly dynamic.

Bergson was critical of science and its analytic emphasis, arguing that thought as analysis is unsympathetic and goes around things, falsifying the object of study. Instead he recommended thought as intuition. Intuition, argued Bergson, does not interrupt the processes that comprise things. Intuition is a sympathy toward things and sees movement or process as reality in itself. The accurate observation of things depends upon allowing the process of change in nature to proceed.

Bergson applied these concepts to moral philosophy, arguing that morality is also an aspiration toward higher forms of being in the Good. Moral and religious systems are of two general types: 1) *the static* – being closed, dogmatic, self-preservationist systems, and 2) *the dynamic* – being open, rational, novelty-oriented systems.

Principal works: *Laughter* (1900), *Introduction to Metaphysics* (1903), *Creative Evolution* (1907), and *Two Sources of Morality and Religion* (1932).

"If we could rid ourselves of all pride, if, to define our species, we kept strictly to what the prehistoric periods show us to be the constant characteristic of man and of intelligence, we should not say 'Homo Sapiens,' but 'Homo Faber.' In short, intelligence, considered is what seems to be its original feature, is the faculty of manufacturing artificial objects, especially tools to make tools, and of indefinitely varying the manufacture."

"If instinct is . . . the faculty of using an organized natural instrument, it must involve innate knowledge, both of its instrument and of the object to which it is applied. Instinct is therefore innate knowledge of a thing. But intelligence is the faculty of constructing unorganized, that is to say artificial, instruments... The essential function of intelligence is therefore to see the way out of a difficulty in any circumstances whatever, to find what is most suitable, what answers the best question asked."

Henri Bergson, *Creative Evolution*

Reference: *Bergson: Philosopher of Reflection*, I. W. Alexander

Berkeley, George (1685–1763) – a British philosopher, Bishop of Cloyne, and one of the principal authors of empiricism. "*Esse est percipi*" (To be is to be perceived) became the hallmark of his epistemology. Berkeley argued that nothing exists without being perceived. A necessary outcome of this logic is that mind or consciousness is primary and objects of perception are secondary in nature. To preserve the role and facticity of things, Berkeley introduces the Mind of God as the master viewer of the so-called objective world. If there isn't a human mind to perceive things and announce their existence, there is always the Mind of God to perceive all things in the absence of human perception. Thus, when a tree falls in the forest and there's no one there to hear it, God hears it. That's why things exist in the absence of our perceiving them. Things cannot exist independent of consciousness.

Principal works: *Treatise on the Principles of Human Knowledge* (1710), *Three Dialogues between Hylas and Philonus* (1713), and *Alciphron or the Minute Philosopher* (1733)

". . . all those bodies which compose the mighty frame of the world, have not any subsistence without a mind, that their being is to be perceived or known; that consequently so long as they are not actually perceived by me, or do not exist in my mind or that of any other created spirit, they must either have no existence at all, or else subsist in the mind of some Eternal Spirit—it being perfectly unintelligible, and involving all the absurdity of abstraction, to attribute to any single part of them an existence independent of a spirit."

George Berkeley, *Treatise on the Principles of Human Knowledge*

Reference: *Berkeley*, G. J. Warnock

binary – adj. having two parts or elements; in logic, the two-part design of logical functions, housing a statement on each side, as in disjunction, conjunction, and implication

bisexuality – n. the view that every human being is made up of both masculine and feminine characteristics. It represents material for determining conclusions about the conflicts people have in manifesting their own sex. Freud's use of the term was conditioned by the ideas of Wilhelm Fliess (1858–1928), who also argued for a theory he called "vital periodicity" and later linked to the idea of "biorhythms."

Reference: *Civilization and Its Discontents*, S. Freud

Bodhidharma – n. the legendary founder of Zen Buddhism, fifth century AD, who replied to a monarch's love of reading and good works with, "Reading is worthless, and good works gain no merit." Only real meditation admits one to the condition of enlightenment and sainthood.

According to one legend, when he was refused admission to a Shaolin monastery, he entered a cave to meditate alone. Bodhidharma was then called "the wall gazer," because he practiced meditation by staring at a blank wall for nine years. According to legend, Bodhidharma fell asleep in the seventh year and tore off his eyelids to prevent a lapse of concentration. When his eyelids hit the ground they grew into tea plants. Tea was then introduced to Zen practice as a stimulant to prevent sleepiness. After nine years, he is said to have become a teacher at the Shaolin monastery. He died sitting upright.

Reference: *The Bodhidharma Anthology: The Earliest Records of Zen*, Jeffrey Broughton

bodhisattva – n. in Buddhism, a person aspiring toward enlightenment; a Buddha-to-be; *sattva* meaning existence, and *bodhi* meaning wisdom. It refers to one who acquires *bodhichitta*, the spontaneous and compassionate desire to aid all sentient beings.

Bonhoeffer, Dietrich (1906–1945) – a German theologian, anti-Nazi dissident, and participant in the plot to assassinate Hitler. After his conviction in an SS courtroom, he was stripped naked and hanged in the concentration camp at Flossenburg, Germany, on the morning of April 9, 1945, along with other coconspirators.

Bonhoeffer was a founding member of the Confessing Church and the son of Karl Bonhoeffer, a psychiatrist. His anti-Hitler speeches began in 1933 and referred to Hitler as *Verfuhrer* (seducer/false leader). His teaching position at the University of Berlin was then revoked.

While teaching (1930) at Union Theological Seminary in New York, Bonhoeffer met Reinhold Niebuhr and Frank Fisher, a black seminarian who welcomed him to the Abyssinian Baptist Church in Harlem. His friendships there taught him to see life in a different way "from below." Bonhoeffer's thought is characterized by a concern with the nonreligious climate of the twentieth century. He advocated ecumenism and a departure from modern religious tradition to restore the primitive vitality of Biblical faith.

His views on revelation emphasized its connection to the life of the individual in community. He argued that revelation occurs in the spiritual communion of souls. His most important book, *The Cost of Discipleship*, developed a theology of "costly grace" vs. "cheap grace." "Costly grace" is the call to follow Christ in the battle against corrupt and criminal government institutions. He argued that secularization is the dilution of Christianity.

Principal works: *Die Nachfolge* (*The Cost of Discipleship*), published in 1937, *Ethics* (1947), and *Letters and Papers from Prison* (1953)

"Cheap grace is the preaching of forgiveness without requiring repentance, baptism without church discipline, communion without confession, absolution without personal confession. Cheap grace is grace without discipleship, grace without the cross, grace without Jesus Christ, living and incarnate.

"Costly grace is the treasure hidden in the field, for the sake of it a man will gladly go and sell all that he has...Such grace is costly because it calls us to follow Jesus Christ. It is costly because it costs a man his life. It is costly because it condemns sin, and grace because it justifies the sinner."

Dietrich Bonhoeffer, *The Cost of Discipleship*

Reference: *The Form of Christ in the World*, J. A. Phillips

Brahman – n. in Hinduism, a reference to the Absolute; a type of world-soul; the main character in the Hindu trinity (*trimurti*), along with Vishnu and Shiva. Brahman represents the creative principle, while Vishnu and Shiva stand for preservation and destruction. The concept of Brahman has an important cosmic and psycho-spiritual role in the harmony of reality.

"No one who seeks Brahman ever comes to an evil end."

Bhagavad Gita (ca. 500 BC)

"Meditate and you will realize that mind, matter, and Maya are but three aspects of Brahman, the one reality."

Svestasvatara Upanishad (ca. 600 BC)

bromide – n. a trite or platitudinous remark

brook – v. to put up with or tolerate

bruit – v. to spread a rumor

Buber, Martin (1878–1965) – a relative of Karl Marx and Helena Rubenstein, Buber was a Jewish existentialist born in Vienna. He experienced a break with religion in his youth, but became a religious existentialist through his philosophical study of Immanuel Kant, Søren Kierkegaard, and Friedrich Nietzsche.

Inspired by his grandfather's teaching of the Talmud, Buber also returned to religion through Hasidism. Hasidism filled his need to experience a deeper interpersonal life. This contributed to Buber's development of a special dialogic, leading to his existential articulation of relationships between persons. (Objects are It, and persons are Thou.) The possibility of treating persons as things, the I–It relationship, assumes a moral character that is the basis for evil. The I–It relationship does not produce genuine communion between persons and allows for the exploitation of the other. In the I–Thou setting, however, the person is seen in spiritual terms and in conjunction with God. Ontologically, there is a hierarchy of being that influences moral interaction.

> Principal works: *I and Thou* (1922), *Between Man and Man* (1947), and *Knowledge of Man* (1965)

> *"The capricious man does not believe and encounter. He does not know association; he only knows the feverish world out there and his desire to use it...And what he calls his destiny is merely an embellishment of and a sanction for his ability to use. In truth he has no destiny but is merely determined by things and drives; feels autocratic and is capricious."*

> Martin Buber, *I and Thou*

> *"Whoever pronounces the word God and really means You, addresses, no matter what his delusion, the true You of his life that cannot be restricted by any other and to whom he stands in a relationship that includes all others."*

> Martin Buber, *I and Thou*

> Reference: *Existence and Utopia: The Social and Political Thought of Martin Buber*, Bernard Susser

Buddhism – n. fr. "Buddha," which means "enlightened one." Buddhism is part of the family of Eastern religions including Hinduism, Taoism, and Jainism. Founded by Siddhartha Gautama (560–477 BC), it is a religion of worldly pessimism and spiritual meditation. Its psychological and spiritual orientation includes a denunciation of the utility of reason. Subsequently, it does not work out a rational or systematic metaphysics.

> *"What have I not elucidated? . . . I have not elucidated that the world is eternal; I have not elucidated that the world is not eternal. I have not elucidated that the world*

is finite; I have not elucidated that the world is infinite. I have not elucidated that the soul and the body are identical. I have not elucidated that the monk who has attained (the arahat) exists after death; I have not elucidated that the arahat does not exist after death. I have not elucidated that the arahat both exists and does not exist after death; I have not elucidated that the arahat (saint) neither exists nor does not exist after death. And why have I not elucidated this? Because this profits not, nor has to do with the fundamentals of religion; therefore I have not elucidated this."

"What have I elucidated? Misery have I elucidated. The origin of misery have I elucidated. The cessation of misery have I elucidated; and the path leading to the cessation of misery have I elucidated. And why have I elucidated this?

"Because this does profit, has to do with the fundamentals of religion, and tends to absence of passion, to knowledge, supreme wisdom, and Nirvana."

Gautama Buddha in H. Warren's *Buddhism in Translation* (1922)

Buddhism is opposed to the Vedas and the caste system. It preaches enlightenment by participation in the Three Treasures: the Buddha, the Dharma, and the Sangha. It has developed into two principal schools, Mahayana Buddhism and Hinayana Buddhism.

"Mahayana" means "great vehicle." It is compared to a raft upon which many people may cross the river of life to enlightenment. Mahayana Buddhism distinguishes itself with the institution of the *Bodhisattva*, an enlightened one who remains in this world to spread universal love for all beings. Some Mahayanists regard Bodhisattvahood as essential, requiring all to pass through its gates. Other Mahayanists regard it as optional.

"Hinayana" means "little vehicle." It is compared to a raft upon which one individual at a time crosses the river of life to enlightenment. Hinayana Buddhism emphasizes the absence of God, thus putting full responsibility upon the individual to achieve salvation…Buddhism is further divided under the following labels: Pure Land Buddhism, Nichiren Buddhism, Zen Buddhism, Tendai Buddhism, Tibetan Buddhism, and Shingon Buddhism.

The Dhammapada, a Buddhist text meaning "path of light," contains simple teachings of Buddhism intended to produce contact with nirvana. Its message is built on the Four Noble Truths: 1) life is suffering, 2) the cause of suffering is desire, 3) desire can be eliminated, 4) the elimination of desire is achieved through the Eightfold Path:

i   *Right Belief* – belief in the Four Noble Truths

ii   *Right Purpose* – the promise or vow to overcome a life of sensual desire

iii *Right Speech* – well-defined talk that is not hurtful or false

iv   *Right Conduct* – well-defined actions that bring only harmony to this world

v   *Right Livelihood* – choosing a subsistence that is right for one's talents and is consistent with the teachings of the Buddha

vi   *Right Effort* – striving in a way that preserves spiritual awareness of that which is wise and that which is foolish

vii *Right-Mindedness* – establishing good habits of thought and good topics of thought

viii *Right Meditation* – commitment to the advanced stage of enlightenment so that the soul is prepared for its encounter with *Nirvana*, the extinction of rebirth

"Better than a hundred years lived in vice, without contemplation, is one single day of life lived in virtue and in deep contemplation." (sutra 110)

The Dhammapada (500 BC)

"Neither in the sky, nor deep in the ocean, nor in a mountain cave, nor anywhere, can a person be free from the evil they have done." (127)

"Never speak harsh words, for once spoken they may return to you. Angry words are painful and there may be blows for blows." (133)

"But although a person may wear fine clothing, if one lives peacefully; and is good, self-possessed, has faith and is pure; and if one does not hurt any living thing, one is a holy Brahmin, a hermit of seclusion, a monk called a Bhikku." (142)

"Empty the boat of your life, O man; when empty it will sail swiftly. When empty of passions and harmful desires you are bound for the land of Nirvana." (369)

References: *An Introduction to Buddhist Thought*, A. L. Herman; *The Dhammapada*, trans. by Juan Mascaro; *Women in Buddhism*, Diana Paul; *A History of Indian Buddhism: From Sakyamuni to Mahayana*, Hirakawa Akira

Bultmann, Rudolf (1884–1976) – Bultmann was the son of Arthur K. Bultmann, a Lutheran minister. Bultmann became a professor of theology at the University of Marburg, where he befriended a colleague, Martin Heidegger. Bultmann's students included Günther Bornkamm and Hannah Arendt. Heidegger's existentialism influenced Bultmann's theological reasoning. As a liberal German theologian, Bultmann offered a modern Christology focused on the quest for the "Historical Jesus." He argued that the essence of Jesus lay in the message and that Christianity was the most radical form of existentialism. In *The History of the Synoptic Tradition* (1921), Bultmann argued (in "form criticism") that the real life of Jesus was buried under several oral traditions detectable in the Gospels of Mark, Matthew, and Luke. Bultmann demonstrated the Greek or Hellenistic influence on Christianity, resulting in a specific communal existence with its own myths and culture.

Bultmann argued that one should not speak about God in the past tense, since it implied a limited revelation in a particular epoch. Bultmann taught that a coherent theology should refer to God as an eternal power, capable of revelation in the present. Owing to the cogency of Heidegger's existentialism, he denied the preexistence of Christ.

Bultmann criticized the secularization of Christianity through higher education, while admitting the validity of modern science. He argued that secularization reduced Christianity and the life of faith to worldly interests: a biological essence, commitment to a career, and over-involvement in the secular institutions of the state. In this context, he protested the Nazi mistreatment of Jews and the emergence of tyranny. To Bultmann, secularization was a betrayal of the theological meaning of eschatology. For, in spite of science, humanity is lost without Christian theology.

Principal works: *The History of the Synoptic Tradition* (1921), *Jesus and the Word* (1934), *Theology of the New Testament* (1951), *Primitive Christianity* (1957), and *Faith and Understanding* (1969)

"Every human being knows or can know about its limitedness, for—consciously or unconsciously—it is driven to an fro by its limitedness, as long as it exists... Mankind has no power over the temporal and the eternal. The power which has power over the temporal and eternal is God."

"Many a life is poor in friendship and in love, many another rich, but even the rich life is aware of a final solitude into which it is driven... The power which drives mankind into this final solitude is God."

Rudolf Bultmann, *Essays: Philosophical and Theological* (1952)

References: *The Future of Our Religious Past: Essays in Honor of Rudolf Bultmann*, James M. Robinson; *Christ without Myth*, Schubert Ogden; *Rudolf Bultmann: Interpreting Faith for the Modern Era*, ed. Roger A. Johnson

bumptious – adj. being excessively self-assertive

bunkum – n. speechmaking by a politician that is deceitful, calculated to impress constituents

Bushido – n. in the Shinto religion of Japan, "the way of the warrior." Bushido reflected a code of ideal conduct incorporating eight dispositions of the superior warrior: honor, reserve, politeness, truthfulness, justice, loyalty, gratitude, and courage.

Reference: *Warriors of Japan: As Portrayed in the War Tales*, Paul Varley

C

cabal – n. a small group of persons engaged in secret plotting against a political body

cachinnate – v. to laugh without restraint

cacodemon – n. a spirit possessing evil character and influence

cadastral – adj. of or relating to boundaries

cadre – n. a group of skilled people who train others in an expanding organization

caducity – n. fr. the Latin *caducus*, meaning perishable; also a reference to senility

cafard – n. a mood of sadness, melancholy, or severe depression

caitiff – n. or adj. a person who is cowardly, despicable, and worthy of contempt

calcify – v. to become inflexible and changeless; to harden

callet – n. a frivolous person; in medieval times, a court fool, and perhaps a prostitute

callow – adj. lacking in maturity

calumniate – v. to accuse without proof

campy – adj. exaggerated in speech or gesture; homosexual

Camus, Albert (1913–1960) – a French philosopher of existentialism, though Camus himself denied the label "existentialist." Camus's parents lived in poverty. His father was a field laborer, and his mother was an uneducated house cleaner. Camus's father was killed at the Battle of the Marne in 1914. He lived in ascetic circumstances with his mother and was a bright student. Eventually, he entered the University of Algiers. He associated with a French anarchist group in 1937, and continued to identify with the ideological values of anarchy into the 1950s. He preferred the label "anarchist" over "existentialist," complaining that it was a case of mistaken identity because of his relationship with Jean-Paul Sartre. He received the Nobel Prize in Literature in 1957.

Camus became famous through his literary work and his association with Sartre in producing the underground periodical *Combat*. Through the experience of WWII and the general character of the twentieth century, Camus focused on the absurdity of the human condition, in particular the way being is not given any definitive rational support. The absence of clear definitive meaning in life is the experience of the Absurd. He did not equate this with anarchism. Anarchism acknowledges that the life of humanity is tragic, seems lost in infinite moral choice, and is dominated by institutional organization that is not truly geared toward democratic economic progress. He interpreted Nazism as an exaggerated and desperate reaction to nihilism but devoid of any authentic social solidarity. In his final years, Camus expressed the view that life is simply a case of choosing moral heroism in which one tries to preserve innocence while combating evil. In *The Rebel*, Camus affirms the importance of rebellion and revolution as forms of moral heroism.

Principal works: *The Stranger* (1946), *The Plague* (1948), *The Rebel* (1954), *The Fall* (1957), and *The Myth of Sysiphus* (1955)

"Obscenity is a form of despair."

"What a man thinks, that does he become."

"Politics, and the fate of mankind, are shaped by men without ideals and without greatness. Men who have greatness don't go in for politics."

"One can, with no romanticism, feel nostalgic for lost poverty. A certain number of years lived without money are enough to create a whole sensibility."

Albert Camus, *Notebooks* (1935–1942)

C

References: *Camus* by Germaine Bree, and *The Ethical Pragmatism of Albert Camus* by Dean Vasil

canny – adj. cautious, clever, or shrewd

captious – adj. characterized by a tendency to find fault; difficult to please

carking – adj. anxious, worried; also stingy or miserly

Carnap, Rudolf (1891–1970) – a German philosopher of logic. Carnap was a member of the Vienna Circle, a group of philosophers committed to elevating the status and influence of philosophy through the improvement of methods in science and mathematics.

In 1935, Carnap moved to the United States because of Nazism's threats to free thinking and began teaching at the University of Chicago. Later, after the death of Hans Reichenbach, Carnap assumed the chair of philosophy at UCLA. He was associated with UCLA until his death in 1970.

Carnap's philosophical work was influenced by Ludwig Wittgenstein, especially his views on metaphysics. Carnap concluded that any real progress in the use of language would require the removal of metaphysical expressions. Instead language must be guided by scientific observation and methods of logic.

Principal works: *The Logical Construction of the World* (1928), *The Unity of Science* (1932), *Foundations of Logic and Mathematics* (1939), and *Introduction to Semantics* (1942)

"Logical analysis . . . pronounces the verdict of meaninglessness on any alleged knowledge that pretends to reach above or behind experience. This verdict hits, in the first place any speculative metaphysics, any alleged knowledge by 'pure thinking' or by 'pure intuition' that pretends to be able to do without experience.

"Perhaps we may assume that metaphysics originated from mythology. The child is angry at the 'wicked table' which hurt him. Primitive man endeavors to conciliate the threatening demon of earthquakes, or he worships the deity of the fertile rains in gratitude. Here we confront personifications of natural phenomena, which are the quasi-poetic expression of man's emotional relationship to his environment. The heritage of mythology is bequeathed on the

one hand to poetry, which produces and intensifies the effects of mythology on life in a deliberate way; on the other hand, it is handed down to theology, which develops mythology into a system."

Rudolf Carnap, *The Elimination of Metaphysics*

Reference: *The Philosophy of Rudolf Carnap*, ed. Paul A. Schilpp

carp – v. to find fault unreasonably; to emphasize minor flaws

carpe diem – n. Latin meaning "to enjoy the day"; getting the most out of life in the present without serious regard for the future

Caso, Antonio (1883–1946) – a Mexican philosopher important to Latin American philosophy. Initially a positivist, and an avid researcher into German philosophy (Kant, Husserl, Scheler, Hartmann, Nietzsche, and Heidegger), Caso adopted a type of process philosophy through the study of Henri Bergson. His Christian inspiration was Blaise Pascal, and he combined various philosophical arguments into a critique of Mexican government.

Caso concluded that life is dynamic and resistant to purely scientific and logical description. Consciousness is the projection of freely designed structures on to sensory experience. Caso develops this assumption within a metaphysics of freedom and spirit. True life is experienced ethically and aesthetically. Ethically, the life of humanity is involved with two triads of choice, which Caso also calls "levels of being":

1) things, individuals, and persons
2) economics, disinterest, and love

Things are objects without specific value, in spiritual terms. Their existence is ordered economically as elements of utility. Humanity is perpetually entangled in the demands of utility and things. The challenge of existence is to move beyond the purely economic view of life into a type of creative spiritual altruism. Disinterest in the world fosters a value for love and persons over things and impersonal society. Thus, in Caso one also witnesses an existentialism that adopts a Christian metaphysical outlook.

Principal works: *The Philosophy of Intuition* (1914), *Existence as Economy, Disinterest, and Love* (1919), *The Problem of Mexico and the National Ideology*

C

(1924), *Principles of Aesthetics* (1925), and *The Human Person and the Totalitarian State* (1941)

"The purely psychical nature of man is not sufficient for defining the concept of a person. Over and above the psychical is the spiritual. Man is not only a psychical being, he is also a spiritual being. He is a 'creator of values,' as Nietzsche says so well...

"The error of (de-spiritualized) individualism and socialism are very much alike because in their extreme forms both . . . ignore the superior nature of the human being, they ignore the quality of his spiritual reality...

"The recognition of the personality of human beings obliges society to accept their real inequality rather than an impossible uniformity."

Antonio Caso, *The Human Person and the Totalitarian State*

References: *Latin American Philosophy in the Twentieth Century*, Jorge J. E. Gracia; *Philosophical Analysis in Latin America*, eds. J. J. E. Gracia, E. Rabossi, E. Villanueva, and M. Dascal; and *The Revolt of Unreason: Miguel de Unamuno and Antonio Caso on the Crisis of Modernity*, Michael Candelaria

cassation – n. cancellation

castigate – v. to punish, chastise, or reprove severely

casualism – n. a philosophical doctrine holding that events occur by chance

casuist – n. one skilled in the application of general moral rules to specific cases; also meaning one who reasons dishonestly

casus belli – n. Latin, meaning an event that justifies war or conflict

catamite – n. a young boy kept for homosexual gratification; the love object of a pederast

cataphasia – n. a speech disorder wherein there is a constant repetition of a word or phrase (e.g., excessive use of the same obscenity)

categorical imperative – n. in the philosophy of Immanuel Kant (1724–1804), a principle for deciding what is right and wrong. It is expressed in two ways:

1) Act as if the maxim of thy act were to become by thy will a universal law of nature.

2) Treat every man as an end in himself, and never only as a means.

References: *The Foundations of the Metaphysics of Morals*, Immanuel Kant; and *The Development of Kant's Views of Ethics*, Keith Ward

catena (plural, **catenae**) – n. extracts from the writings of the early fathers of the Church

catenate – v. to connect or link together in a series

caudal – adj. situated near the tail; cowardliness

causerie – n. a nonformal discussion; casual conversation

caveat – n. a legal notice to temporarily halt proceedings

cavil – v. to raise unimportant or trivial objections; to quibble

celerity – n. speed; rapidity

cenacle – n. fr. the Latin *cenaculum*, meaning retreat house or dining room; also a reference to the room where Jesus held the Last Supper

cenobite – n. a member of a religious group living in a commune setting

cenogenesis – n. philosophy of evolution; the introduction of characteristics not found in ancestors; differentiation from earlier phylogeny in a race or breed

cenotaph – n. a tomb erected as a memorial to a person buried somewhere else

cephalic – adj. relating to the head

cession – n. fr. Latin *cessus*, meaning to withdraw; to yield to another

chagrin – n. disappointment

charily – adv. carefully; from "chary," meaning discretion

charismatic – n. in Christianity, a person who views the validation of faith by experiences of religious ecstasy. Included in the meaning is the belief that special powers or healing flow from divine grace.

chevy – v. to run after; to be anxious; to nag or harass

C

chiliasm – n. the view that Christ will return to earth to reign one thousand years; connected to millenarianism. Justification lies with the Book of Revelation, Ch. 20: 1–5.

chimera – n. fr. Greek "chimaera." She-goat; imaginary monster; an illusion of the mind, often a frightening manifestation

choplogic – n. crude reasoning; complicated reasoning; specious thought

chouse – v. to cheat or swindle

Christianity – n. monotheistic faith based on the teachings of Jesus, who left no writings. It has roots in Judaism, as Jesus was a Jew and was often called "rabbi." It was influenced by Greek philosophical traditions (Plato/Augustine) and has become part of the Western canon, including the notion of technical and scientific progress (Max Weber), the ethical ideals of meliorism, the ideal spiritual value of love and nonviolence, and the linear view of time. Its religious views are rooted in the (Torah) Old and New Testaments. The New Testament contains the new religious challenge for humanity: love your enemies. In both spiritual and psychological terms, Christianity represents the first major elevation of women and outcasts of society. This has had a major impact on the moral and legal codes of the Western world.

Christianity tries to effect the reunification of humanity with God, based on the alienation (Broken Covenant) of the Fall. Sinfulness stems from the ego or self-consciousness. As alienation, sin is cured by faith in the teaching of Christ through the Gospels. Grace, faith, and the sacraments represent the theological means to receive salvation (soteriology).

Christianity teaches that love is the highest virtue from which all other virtues flow. The theological dynamic of love is represented in God as "three Persons," with the Son of God being sent to bear the suffering of this world in an act of Divine altruism, specifically the Crucifixion of Jesus. (See the entry on "Christology" below as part of the definition of Christianity.)

"Christianity, which ordains that men should love each other, would have every nation blest with the best civil, the best political laws; because these, next to this religion, are the greatest good that men can give and receive."

Charles L. Montesquieu (1689–1755), *The Spirit of Laws*

"In Christianity we discern a transition from the religion of the cult to the prophetic religion of pure morals, from the religion of law to the religion of love, from the religion of priests to the religion of individual prayer and inward life, from the national God to the universal God."

Sarvepalli Radhakrishnan (1888–1975), *The Philosophy of Radhakrishnan*, ed. Paul Schlipp

References: *The Foundations of Christian Faith*, Karl Rahner; *Early Christian Doctrines*, J. N. D. Kelly; and *The Christian Tradition*, 4 vols., Jaroslav Pelikan

Christology – n. in Christian theology, the study of Jesus the Person of Christ (Quest for the Historical Jesus). Christology tries to uncover the Christocentric implications of the New Testament, especially the Gospel accounts that point to Christ as both God and man. Pauline (St. Paul) references to the "preexistence" of Christ are the beginning of the Apostolic Age and the argument that only a complete devotion to the Son of God establishes salvation (soteriology)...To the Apostles, Christ is at least an agent of revelation from God. Additionally, Christ is seen as the manifestation of being in ultimate form. Christology takes into account the many perspectives on Jesus. This includes the view that he was a member of the human race. It also evaluates his historical presence, that he was perceived by some, say Romans and Jews, as a teacher and even a rebel.

The different interpretations of Christ's nature are categorized as either "high Christology," emphasizing the Divinity of Christ Jesus, or "low Christology," emphasizing the humanity of Christ. The rational and positivistic approach to modern Christology that one finds in some theological work is connected to the research of the nineteenth century, where theologians tried to untangle Christ from the accumulated effects of almost two thousand years of speculation and ritual. Adolf Harnack (1851–1930), author of *What Is Christianity?* (1901), was responsible for revealing the Hellenistic influences on Christian theology. David F. Strauss (1808–1874), author of *Life of Jesus* (1836), created a shock wave with the thesis that the supernatural elements were introduced between the death of Jesus and the appearance of the Gospels in written form. Ernest Renan (1823–1892), author of *Life of Jesus* (1863), also argued against the supernatural identity of Jesus. Renan pictured Christ as an effective and friendly Galilean minister, even downplaying the ethical impact of Christ. Renan was rewarded with a dismissal from his position as professor of Hebrew at the College of France. Later, Renan softened his theological views on Christ.

C

"The son of God is unique. To appear for a moment, to flash forth a sympathetic but piercing radiance, to die very young, that is the life of a God."

Ernest Renan, *St. Paul* (1869)

The modern controversies about the nature and essence of Christ have their basis in theological arguments of the past, the most important of which include:

Arianism – the views of Arius (250–336 AD) were primarily preserved in songs called the Thaleia, as he wrote very little. His effectiveness as a priest and preacher popularized the idea that the Logos (word or reason) was an "ex nihilo" product of God, with the implication that Christ is a separate non-eternal phenomenon. Christ is the Son of God as all men are the sons of God through a spiritual adoption and because of his supreme righteousness. The Council of Nicaea (325 AD) was the site of the first dispute over its theological correctness.

Monarchianism – (second century) was a reaction to the idea of the Trinity. Monarchians argued that there is no separateness in Christ, that God is a set of "modes" represented as Father, Son, and Holy Spirit. These theologians sought to preserve the unity or monotheism of God by rejecting the theological emphasis on three Persons in God.

References: *Jesus*, Edward Schillebeeckx; *Jesus and the Word*, Rudolf Bultmann; *Jesus Christ and Mythology*, Rudolf Bultmann; *The Original Jesus*, N. T. Wright; *The Crucifixion of Jesus*, Gerard S. Sloyan; and *Meeting Jesus Again for the First Time*, Marcus Borg

chutzpa – n. insolence; extreme self-confidence

cicisbeism – n. practice of keeping a cicisbeo (the lover of a married woman)

cincture – n. something that encircles, like a belt or girdle

circadian – adj. referring to a twenty-four-hour period or cycle

circumjacent – adj. lying all around

circumvent – v. to avoid, evade, or outwit

civil death – n. the legal status of a person, as in punishment, so as to be deprived of civil rights

civil disobedience – n. a means of protesting laws by nonviolent refusal to obey those laws, especially laws contradicting what is morally good

> References: *Political Violence and Civil Disobedience*, Ernest van den Haag; *Civil Disobedience: Theory and Practice*, ed. Hugo A. Bedau; and *Disobedience and Democracy: Nine Fallacies on Law and Order*, Howard Zinn

civil liberty – n. a reference to the freedom of assembly, speech, thought, press, and religious belief. These are considered rights that governments cannot override and are defined as natural and inalienable. Civil liberties include the right to privacy and security, the right to a fair trial, the right to own property, the right not to be tortured, the right to defend one's self against bodily harm, and the right to due process.

> Reference: *Civil Rights: Rhetoric or Reality*, Thomas Sowell

clamant – adj. important or demanding notice; noisy

clastic – adj. fr. Greek *klastos*, meaning broken; disintegrating into fragments

clement – adj. gentle; merciful; mild

clerisy – n. the clergy; the intellectual class

clique – n. a group with identical interests; a narrowly defined group, exclusive in nature

coadjutant – n. an assistant; adj. – providing assistance

coaptation – n. a fitting together of independent parts

codicil – n. a legal supplement or appendix

coercion – n. fr. Latin *coertio*, meaning nullification or domination. To compel the other to submit through the use of threats or other sources of fear. A person is not considered morally responsible for acts that are the result of coercion. The moral issue revolves around finding out what actually constitutes coercion. When does a person actually have no other choice but to submit to proposals that are coercive?

> Reference: *Coercion*, Alan Wertheimer

coetaneous – adj. being of the same age

coeval – adj. at the same time; contemporary

cogito, ergo sum – Latin meaning "I think, therefore I am." In Cartesian philosophy (the views of René Descartes), this is the foundational truth upon which other truths are to be built, since no degree of doubt can refute it.

Descartes argued that no matter how deceived one is about knowing truth, one has to exist to have any kind of belief. Thus, knowledge of one's existence is a fact, no matter what else one thinks (*Meditations*, 1641).

cognomen – n. surname; family name; also, nickname

cognoscenti – n. the wise; those who are well informed on a particular subject

cognoscible – adj. capable of being known

cognoscitive – adj. having the ability to know

Coherence Theory of Truth – n. in philosophy, a theory of truth advocated by rationalist thinkers (e.g., G. W. F. Hegel, Benedict Spinoza, F. H. Bradley, Otto Neurath, and Carl Hempel). A system of thought is said to be true on the basis that any judgments (statements) in the system logically imply other judgments (statements) in the same system, usually by various applications of the rules of inference. Some definitions of the theory hold that any judgment in a system must imply any other judgment in the system, so that it becomes impossible to accommodate belief in judgments from other systems. For instance, a scientific atheist cannot somehow also hold the belief that God exists. The coherence theory tends to force admission of the prevailing rational interpretation of nature (i.e., reality), and the rejection of thought systems outside that model.

References: *The Coherence Theory of Truth*, Nicholas Rescher; and *The Coherence Theory of Truth*, Ralph C. S. Walker

collectanea – n. a collection of literary works

colligate – v. to bind together; gather under a general heading

collimate – v. to make parallel; to bring into alignment

collocate – v. to arrange or set in order; to emphasize a proper order

collocation – n. the correct placement of words in a sentence

colloquy – n. a serious conversation or dialogue; a conference

collude – v. to cooperate by secret agreement for deceptive or dishonest ends; to plot; to conspire

colophon – n. symbol or inscription at the end of a book, detailing the printer, author, publisher, and place of publication; an identifying emblem

colporteur – n. one who peddles books, especially religious books

comity – n. a courteous manner of behavior; a friendly quality

commensal – adj. taking meals together, especially as a regular routine

comminate – v. to threaten, especially with divine involvement; vengeance through God; to denounce

comminute – v. to pulverize

commove – v. to agitate violently; to cause intense feelings

commutation – n. an act of substitution or replacement. In logic, an expression of logical equality. It allows the rearrangement of statement components in both disjunctive and conjunctive statements: $a + b = b + a$.

comparative psychology – n. the study of animal behavior under controlled conditions as compared to the study of animal behavior in the wilderness. This type of research looks for evidence that can be extrapolated from animals to humans in order to understand human behavior. The theory of evolution, and especially the study of primate behavior, inspired the emergence of comparative psychology.

> References: *Comparative Psychology in the Twentieth Century*, D. A. Dewsbury; *Animal Thinking*, D. R. Griffin; *The Moral Animal*, Robert Wright; *The Bonobo and the Atheist*, Frans de Waal

compathy – n. the sharing of feelings with others

compeer – n. one having equal rank, position, or ability

compendious – adj. concise; expressing in a brief form the basic substance of a topic

C

complex question – n. in logic, a fallacy in which a question is posed in such a way as to force the acceptance of a conclusion embedded within that question (e.g., "Have you stopped stealing cars?"). Answering either "yes" or "no" would imply one's involvement in car theft.

complot – n. a conspiracy; v. to conspire

composition – n. in logic, a fallacy in which the characteristics of the part(s) of a respective whole are said to be the characteristics of the whole itself: "The tires on this vehicle are in excellent condition, so the whole car is in excellent condition."

Comte, Auguste (1798–1857) – a French philosopher who attempted to reorganize society around a positivist philosophy for a new elite. The goal was to develop the emerging influence of science and technology, reorient the intellectual climate of his time, and then to extend the effects of the Scientific Revolution into social, political, moral, and religious spheres. Through his work, he was recognized as the founder of a new field of study, sociology.

Comte argued that thought moves through three stages in the quest for truth: 1) *the theological* – here phenomena are causally explained as the result of divine influence; included are superstitious beliefs and irrational prejudices; 2) *the metaphysical* – here phenomena are calculated to be extensions of impersonal, abstract forces; included are claims devoid of any observable facticity; and 3) *the positivistic* – here the natural world is viewed strictly through the lens of rational science and references to the previous stages are abandoned. According to Comte, the last stage holds the greatest prospect for coordinating a peaceful society, because it establishes knowledge in a public or verifiable way, reducing the opportunity for arbitrary disagreement. Comte was particularly optimistic about the influence of science on the moral development of humanity.

Principal works: *The Positive Philosophy*, 6 vols. (1830–1842), *A System of Political Positivism*, 4 vols. (1851–1854), and *Catechism of Positivism* (1852)

". . . each branch of our knowledge passes successively through three different theoretical conditions: the Theological or fictitious; the Metaphysical, or abstract; and the Scientific, or positive."

Auguste Comte, *The Positive Philosophy*

"In regard to morals, I think it is indisputable that the gradual development of humanity favors a growing preponderance of the noblest tendencies of our nature... The lower instincts continue to manifest themselves in modified action, but their less sustained and more repressed exercise must tend to debilitate them by degrees; and their increasing regulation certainly brings them into involuntary concurrence in the maintenance of a good social economy."

Auguste Comte, *The Positive Philosophy*

References: *The Philosophy of Auguste Comte*, Lucien Lévy-Bruhl; *August Comte*, Kenneth Thompson; and *August Comte and Positivism: The Essential Writings*, ed. Gertrud Lenzer

conatus – n. a natural impulse or striving

concatenate – v. to unite in a series; to link in a chain

concinnity – n. harmony and elegance of design

concinnous – adj. harmonious; fitting

concrescence – n. a growing together as in plants or cellular development; a favorite Whiteheadian term

concupiscence – n. sexual desire; the internal pressure to find sexual relief

condign – adj. appropriate; well deserved

Condillac, Étienne Bonnet de (1715–1780) – a French philosopher of knowledge and experience (empiricism). Condillac was born at Grenoble and ordained a priest in Paris. He was a friend of Jean-Jacques Rousseau. He became the Abbott of Mureau and is important as a psychologist-philosopher. He went a step further than Locke. While Locke believed knowledge is rooted in sense experience, Condillac believed that the faculties of the mind are themselves based in experience.

The linguistic views of Condillac were influential for the philosophy of Jacques Derrida. Condillac argued that language is an organizer of sensation, accounting for the higher faculties of the mind.

Principal works: *Essay on the Origin of Human Knowledge* (1746) and *Treatise on Sensations* (1754)

C

Reference: *The Archaeology of the Frivolous*, J. Derrida, trans. by J. P. Leavey Jr.

condolent – adj. showing sorrow

conduce – v. tending to produce a particular result

confabulation – n. an informal discussion or conversation

conflation – n. the combining of two texts into one

confluent – adj. uniting into one

Confucius (551–479 BC) – a Chinese humanist philosopher whose moral views shaped Chinese culture and character.

Confucius rejected metaphysical concerns in favor of social and political interests. Social harmony was more important to him than discovering the foundations of reality, because Confucius was unimpressed with the results of such reflection. He outlined the virtues necessary for the creation of a stable and prosperous nation.

Li refers to the sense of propriety and the external presentation of acceptable habits and manners toward others. Filial respect is the beginning of social harmony, and *Li* is useful to the formation of character. It is also a method of avoiding social disgrace, since it is often only by good habits that we avoid expressing our primitive feelings in stressful settings.

Jen refers to the inner qualities of a person: truthfulness, sincerity, respect, love, loyalty, generosity, mental excellence, and discipline. *Jen* reveals the level to which a person has mastered the *Tao* or Way. Along with *Li*, *Jen* provides the basis for strong families and thus, a strong nation. Rulers and parents dictate the nature and future of society.

In *The World's Religions*, historian of religion, Huston Smith, asks the question whether Confucianism is a religion or merely an ethic. This is due to the absence of metaphysical questions (e.g., "What is death?" and "What is ultimate reality?").

For Confucius, devotion to family life is a rendering of the *Tao* and the central place for the practice of *ren*: the will to seek the good of others. As the family goes, so goes society.

Principal work: *The Analects*

"The great man is sparing in words and prodigal in deeds."

Confucius, *Analects*

References: *The Wisdom of Confucius*, Lin Yutang; *Confucius and the Chinese Way*, Herrlee G. Creel; *Confucius: The Secular as Sacred*, Herbert Fingarette

congruous – adj. showing harmony in character or makeup

conjugal – adj. relating to marriage or the married state

connate – adj. inborn, innate; associated in origin

connotation – n. in logic, that part of the theory of definition that refers to the meaning conveyed by a word apart from the thing named or described. It stands in conjunction with denotation, which refers to the set of things named by a word.

consanguineous – adj. descended from the same ancestor; related by blood

consciousness – n. according to Freud, a transient property that identifies internal and external perceptions apart from other psychical events. In philosophy, it refers to self-knowledge, introspection, intention, subjectivity, and awareness. This is tied to phenomenology (Husserl) and thinking about thinking.

Modern psychoanalysis has tried to show that some thinking takes place without conscious awareness because of repression. Philosophers like Gilbert Ryle argue against this privacy theory, claiming that mind or consciousness is a collection of observable behaviors (or observable in behavior).

Zen Buddhist psychology defines consciousness as "mindfulness." Then consciousness is a deep awareness of responses to the outside world as well as the inner world of mind. Awareness of sensory events is seen as a set of distractions from an unchanging underlying reality. When one connects with the underlying reality of all things, one is truly conscious.

References: *The Concept of Mind*, Gilbert Ryle; *Consciousness*, William G. Lycan; and *Consciousness in Contemporary Science*, eds. A. J. Marcel and E. Bisiach

C

consilience – n. the concurrence of generalizations from separate classes of facts in logical inductions so that one set of inductive laws is found to be in agreement with another set

Consistency Theory of Truth – n. in epistemology and logic, the view that the truth of statements is measured by their ability to stand together in a system of thought. Also referred to as the coherence theory, for consistency is a judgment on the way statements are part of a collection of statements that fit together. Critics point out that one can have a coherent set of statements that are false.

consternate – v. to dismay or terrify

conterminous – adj. adjacent; enclosed within a common boundary; bordering

contexture – n. framework; structure

contiguous – adj. adjoining; being in actual contact; touching

contradistinguish – v. to make distinct, especially by contrasting or different qualities

contraposition – n. in logic, categorical propositions, a valid type of immediate inference. A contrapositive is formed when the subject term is replaced by the complement of the predicate term in a categorical proposition. For example, the contrapositive of "All Marxists are Hegelians" is "All non-Hegelians are non-Marxists."

contravene – v. to oppose; to act against or contrary to

contrite – adj. full of sorrow; moved by deep remorse

contumacious – adj. forcefully disobedient

contumely – n. insulting or rude language; also insulting behavior by words or deeds

convenance – n. propriety, suitability

conventual – adj. appropriate to monastic or convent life

convive – n. a companion, especially at meals

convivial – adj. relating to feasting, good times, eating and drinking joyfully

convoluted – adj. distorted, twisted, or complicated

copacetic – adj. wonderful; excellent; very satisfactory

coquette – n. a flirtatious woman, especially one lacking sincere affection; a woman who seeks advantage through feigned love

Correspondence Theory of Truth – n. the view that beliefs must correspond to fact. The theory argues that there must be a relation between a system of thought and objective reality. There is an assumption that reality is external to mind, that sensory experience is the organization of data into a picture of reality. It is the mental picture, as a system of beliefs, that must be mated to external reality for truth to exist. Truth or falsity depend on external conditions and not belief. Verification of correspondence is achieved, in part, through the application of ideas to action, which seems to lead on to the pragmatic theory of truth.

The correspondence theory has gone through a long history of evaluation. There are Platonic-Aristotelian versions of the theory, Scholastic versions, the Realist versions, and the meta-linguistic versions expressed through the thoughts of G. E. Moore, Bertrand Russell, Ludwig Wittgenstein, and Alfred Tarski.

> References: "The Correspondence Theory of Truth," D. W. Hamlyn, in *Philosophical Quarterly* 12: 193–205 (1962); and "The Correspondence Theory of Truth," H. B. Acton, in *Proceedings of the Aristotelian Society*, 35: 177–194

corrigendum – n. a note regarding an error in a printed book

corroborant – adj. confirming

corybantic – adj. wild; frenzied; out of control; from the Greek *Korybas*, a priest of Cybele known for wild orgiastic processions and rituals

cosset – n. a pet lamb; one who is a favorite; a spoiled, pampered individual

coterie – n. an intimate and exclusive group

countervail – v. to act in opposition with equivalent power and force

coup de foudre – n. Fr., overwhelming love at first sight; an astonishing event

coup de grace –n. Fr., meaning "a death blow"; mercy killing

coup d'état – n. the sudden removal of government personnel with concentrated force

courtesan – n. a royal prostitute; a sex professional for the upper classes

cozen – v. to cheat or fool shrewdly; to beguile; to defraud

credendum – n. that which must be believed; an article of faith

criminal – n. one who lives against the values of society; one who commits errors in acting according to the social standards of the time. As per Nietzsche's sardonic wit:

> *"The criminal type is the type of strong human being under unfavourable conditions, a strong human being made sick. What he lacks is the wilderness, a certain freer and more perilous nature and form of existence in which all that is attack and defense in the instinct of the strong human being comes into its own. His 'virtues' have been excommunicated by society; the liveliest drives within him forwith blend with the depressive emotions, with suspicion, fear, dishonor. But this is the recipe for physiological degeneration. He who has to do in secret what he does best and most likes to do, with protracted tension, caution, slyness, becomes anemic; and because he has never harvested anything from his instincts but danger, persecution, disaster, his feelings too turn against these instincts . . . he feels them to be a fatality. It is society . . . tame, mediocre, gelded society, in which a human being raised in nature, who comes from the mountains or from adventures of the sea, necessarily degenerates into a criminal."*

Friedrich Nietzsche (1844–1900), *Twilight of the Idols*

crisis theology – n. a Neo-orthodox view often connected with the ideas of Karl Barth (1886–1968). Barth argued for a philosophical theology proving the utter transcendence of God, which included the complete and infinite superiority of God, especially when compared to any human striving and creativity. All worldly achievements are rooted in egoism and represent the final worthlessness of reason. All human institutions are fractured by the inevitable contradictions of human reason, creating despair in the possibility of control. Thus, human existence without God is doomed to crisis and failure. Crisis theology attempts to lead humanity away from the positivism of science toward the spiritual power of divine revelation, grace, and faith.

Reference: *The Theology of Karl Barth*, H. Hartwell

cumbrance – n. a source of trouble

cybernetics – n. fr. Greek *kybernete*, meaning steersman. The term "cybernetics" was first coined by Norbert Wiener (1894–1964), a mathematician and author of *Cybernetics: Control and Communication in the Animal and the Machine* (1948). It is the theoretical field that studies feedback systems and self-regulatory systems. Thus, the history of cybernetics dates back to the earliest devices used to produce self-regulating actions, such as automatic outflow systems on reservoirs (ca. 1000 BC). Cybernetics is connected to mechanical engineering: from windmills to steam engines to modern industrial equipment.

There are roughly four categories or stages of cybernetic engineering: 1) *basic tools* – human action is augmented by a specific implement such as an ax. Judgment remains with the human user. 2) *Tools plus energy* – human effort is reduced but judgment is still required for the machine to operate successfully according to its designed task, such as a chainsaw. 3) *Machine plus energy and control* – human judgment is deeply augmented by automatic machine functions, as in modern logging machines that are programmed to remove the tree, de-bark it, cut it for length, and stack it. Immediate control is with the machine. Human judgment controls the goal. 4) *Machines plus energy plus control plus autonomy of judgment* – the machine is developed to the extent that it determines its own history. Human judgment is virtually eliminated. This is the stage we are working on today. The machine construction/design achieves virtually full operational parity with humans, or it surpasses human capability and reaches complete autonomy.

References: *Spiritual Machines*, Ray Kurzweil; and *Foundations of Cybernetics*, ed. Stuart Umpleby

Cynicism – the views of philosophers called "cynics." From the Greek *kynikos*, meaning "doglike." Cynics, like Diogenes of Sinope, taught that virtue is the only good. They developed a strong opposition to the values of civilization and taught that the love of reputation, wealth, and pleasure led to indulgences that ruined human happiness.

In essence, the Cynics were ascetic monks who spent their days hardening the body and tempering the mind. At its peak in the fourth century BC, they saw themselves as the "watchdogs" of morality and ethics. Largely individualistic and antisocial, the Cynics also stood against intellectuals whose pedantic character disqualified them as spiritual leaders.

C

According to legend, Diogenes lived in a large oak barrel, slept on straw, ate lentils, and kept dogs for companions. Diogenes is reputed to have scolded Alexander the Great for "blocking the sun" when Alexander rode up on his horse to speak with Diogenes about being a court philosopher. Plato referred to him as "Socrates gone mad," because of his unsparing criticism of society. Diogenes created a culture of beggar preachers dressed in cloaks, shoulder purses, and walking sticks.

Cynicism had an influence on the Stoic philosophers of the first century AD and found parallels in the East, especially the Indian *fakir*. Mahavira, the founder of Jainism, was a notable example.

Reference: *The Greek Cynics*, F. Sayre

cynosure – n. a center of attention

D

Daedalian – adj. having great skill; like Daedalus; from *Daedalus*, a mythical craftsman of ancient Greece, remembered for building a labyrinth to trap the Minotaur and for his construction of wings to escape imprisonment. According to myth, his wax wings melted as he flew close to the sun

daft – adj. silly, foolish, or stupid; also out of one's mind

daimon – n. in ancient philosophy, a spirit inhabitant or mentor. Socrates claimed to be guided by such a spirit, which he viewed as a source of inspiration and moral guidance

Dalai Lama – n. in Tibetan Buddhism, "the measureless and superior one," the official spiritual leader of that faith

dalliance – n. amorous conduct, foreplay, or spiritual preparation

damming up of the libido – n. in psychology, the "economic" process that accounts for a person's fall into a neurotic or psychotic condition. In psychoanalysis, the process signals underlying collections of energy, believed to be of a sexual type, and which are deprived of release.

Dao – n. (Tao) in Daoism (Taoism), a reference to the eternal principle present in all things. It lacks obvious characteristics and cannot be named, yet it supports *yin* and *yang*.

darsana – n. in Hinduism, a reference to "seeing the truth." It includes the notion that people must do more than believe in religious and philosophical principles. They must also understand them in order to realize the best spiritual life.

Darwinism – n. the views and theories of Charles Darwin (1809–1882), author of *The Origin of Species* (1859) and *The Descent of Man* (1871). Darwinism argues that all living things come into being biologically, undergo change through environmental pressure, and sometimes go extinct.

Biological reproduction increases in any progeny such that, if unchecked, it would dominate the earth. Multiplication is checked by competition, both within and outside a species, creating a dynamic struggle in which the best survive. Variation exists in biological entities as to their quality and function. These are passed on to succeeding generations. Favorable variations are preserved and passed on and unfavorable ones are eliminated. These observations apply to the human species as well, which Darwin considered an advanced primate. In later years, Darwin began to make a greater assessment of the environment's impact on evolution.

> *"When I view all beings not as special creations, but as the lineal descendants of some few beings which lived long before the first bed of the Cambrian system was deposited, they seem to me to become ennobled. Judging from the past, we may safely infer that not one living species will transmit its unaltered likeness to a distant futurity. And of the species now living very few will transmit progeny of any kind to a far distant futurity; for the manner in which all organic beings are grouped, shows that the greater number of species in each genus, and all the species in many genera, have left no descendants, but have become utterly extinct."*

> Charles Darwin, *The Descent of Man*

> References: *The Moral Animal*, Robert Wright; and *Charles Darwin: A Scientific Biography*, Gavin De Beer

deanthropomorphism – n. a philosophical view emphasizing the removal of human characteristics or beliefs

debauchery – n. excessive involvement in sexuality; orgiastic activity; a conversion from virtue to vice through actions that reduce inhibitions

D

deduction – n. in logic, one of two types of argument; the other is induction

A deductive argument contains evidence that, when correctly arranged, forms the basis for one conclusion, a necessary conclusion. If the arrangement of evidence is correct then the argument is said to be valid; if the arrangement is incorrect, it is invalid.

The nine fundamental arguments forms, or rules of inference are: modus ponens, modus tollens, disjunctive syllogism, pure hypothetical syllogism, constructive dilemma, absorption, simplification, conjunction, and addition. These forms provide the foundation for modern logic and its symbolic language.

Another way of understanding deduction, as distinguished from induction, focuses on the relative generality of their premises and conclusions. Deductive arguments tend to reason from the general to the particular, while inductive arguments tend to reason from the particular to the general (Whewell).

The classical example is:

All humans are mortal.
Socrates is human.
So, Socrates is mortal."

defense – n. in psychology, an action of the ego designed to push back threats to its interests and fantasies. Responses designed to reduce or eliminate changes in the biopsychological constitution of the individual. Instinct is believed to underlie "defenses" and account for their compulsive appearance.

Reference: *The Ego and the Mechanisms of Defense*, Anna Freud

defloration – n. the end of a person's virginity

deicide – n. the killing of a god

deictic – adj. in logic, serving to prove directly

deism – n. belief in a God who created this world but does not relate to or intervene in its functions. Deism does not support belief in miracles or revelation.

Pierre Viret, a Calvinist, first used the term in 1564 to refer to believers who accepted God as creator but rejected belief in Christ. Historically, deism marked the rise of rationalism, secularism, and modern theology. Thus, it also advanced the ethics of tolerance, since it became less and less permissible to dogmatically attack differences of belief.

References: *Reasonableness of Christianity*, John Locke; *Deism*, Peter Gay; and *Deism in Eighteenth Century America*, H. M. Morais

deleterious – adj. harmful, especially in an obscure or unexpected way

delict – n. an offense; a violation of law

delitescent – adj. concealed; hidden from view

delphic – adj. (relating to the Delphic Oracle) obscure; ambiguous

demimondaine – n. a woman who has a reputation for indiscreet behavior; especially one acquainted with wealthy lovers

demirep – n. ("demi" from Latin, "demidiare," meaning to halve) a person with a reputation for associating with reprobates

Democritus (460–370 BC) – a Greek pre-Socratic philosopher famous for his defense of a primitive theory of atomism. Democritus believed in a hard, irreducible type of atomic matter that explained the existence of all things through various combinations and processes of formation and disintegration. This assumption was extended into his understanding of family life, economics, politics, and every area of human activity.

"Violent desire for one thing blinds the soul to all others."

Democritus, *Fragments*

"The old man has been young; but the young man cannot know if he will reach old age. Thus, the perfected good is better than the uncertain future."

Democritus, *Fragments*

Reference: *The Greek Cosmologists*, David Furley

demos – n. the population, people, viewed as a political unit

demotic – adj. of the people

demur – v. to delay, hesitate, object or protest; to take exception

D

demure – adj. shy, modest, reserved

denizen – n. a creature or inhabitant of a particular locale

denouement – n. the climax of a dramatic or literary plot; the outcome of a complex sequence of events

Deontological ethics – n. in ethical theory, views that focus on the importance of duty. Thus, some moral acts are considered obligatory due to the relationship or nature of other acts or entities. Goodness is said to reside in the act itself rather than some other reward or consequence, thus the "obligatory" nature of the act.

> References: *Ethics*, William Frankena; and *The Theory of Morality*, Alan Donagan

depone – v. to declare under oath; to put down critically; to testify

depredate – v. to attack; to plunder or lay waste to

depurate – v. to make pure

depute – v. to appoint as a representative or agent

deracinate – v. to rip out; to eradicate

dereism – n. the tendency to see life through daydreams and unrealistic fantasy; a viewpoint or condition where there is little regard for reality

Derrida, Jacques (1930–2004) – an Algerian-French philosopher of language and culture. Considered the avant-garde leader of deconstructionism and postmodernism. Derrida was born into a Sephardic Jewish family in French Algeria. He experienced anti-Semitism as a youth in Algiers. This probably shaped some of his thinking in later life. It is also easier to understand Derrida's deconstruction philosophy if one considers his interest in Edmund Husserl, Friedrich Nietzsche, Martin Heidegger, Ferdinand de Saussure, Sigmund Freud, Jacques Lacan, Louis Althusser, and Paul Ricoeur. To some degree, he argued against all these thinkers in the spirit of deconstruction.

Derrida married Margeurite Aucouturier, a psychoanalyst, in 1957 and they had two sons. He became a full professor at the École des Haute Études en Science Sociales (School for Advanced Studies in Social Sciences). He had a third son with Sylviane Agacinski, a feminist philosopher, in 1985. Derrida was a visiting professor at Yale

University, Johns Hopkins University, New York University, and The New School for Social Research. In 1986, he began teaching at the University of California–Irvine until his death in 2004. Derrida died of pancreatic cancer.

Derrida's criticism of Western language, philosophy, psychology, and culture defines his postmodern position and sets the tone for deconstruction. Along with other research topics, Derrida's creative exegetical work selected certain moral puzzles or paradoxes (aporia) for analysis. Hospitality, mourning, forgiveness, and gift giving are subjects that he selected under deconstruction in order to illustrate impasses (aporia). In each case, Derrida engages exploration of these acts to find internal meanings that are not obvious without deconstruction. In this context, understanding the mission of deconstruction is as challenging as the dilemmas (aporia) themselves. Deconstruction follows a linguistic skepticism initiated by logical positivism and analytic philosophy.

> Principal works: *Of Grammatology* (1976), *Writing and Difference* (1978), *Spurs: Nietzsche's Styles* (1979), *The Archeology of the Frivolous: Reading Condillac* (1980), *Dissemination* (1981), *Positions* (1981), and *Aporias* (1993)

> References: *Jacques Derrida*, Geoffrey Bennington; *Deconstruction in a Nutshell: A Conversation with Jacques Derrida*, ed. John D. Caputo; *Derrida: A Biography*, Benoit Peeters

Descartes, René (1596–1650) – a French philosopher and tutor of Queen Christina of Sweden, often called the "father of modern philosophy." Descartes is known for his great contributions to the school of Rationalism.

Descartes completed most of his philosophical work in the Netherlands, where a climate of intellectual tolerance allowed the presentation of his ideas. He was intimidated by authority and feared retribution for ideas that trampled on popular religious notions (recalling Copernicus). He made important contributions in mathematics (Cartesian geometry) and developed a method of reflection (hyperbolic doubt) that became a standard for the application of skepticism. This became the famous formulation: "*Cogito, ergo sum*" / "I think, therefore I am."

Descartes argued that even the most demanding skepticism will not refute the proposition "I think, therefore I am," because one must exist in order to be deceived. Descartes tested this with his examination of problems of sensation, including mistaken judgments, hallucinations, illusions, and the proposal that God is an evil genius who deceives his subjects.

D

The general direction of Descartes's philosophy produced the rational view that the best understanding is not acquired through sense perception; rather it is the result of innate ideas, ideas that are formed by logical principles, including the existence of God and the external world.

Principal works: *Discourse on Method* (1637), *Meditations on First Philosophy* (1641), *Principles of Philosophy* (1644), and *The Passions of the Soul* (1649)

"Rule I: We must occupy ourselves only with those objects that our intellectual powers appear competent to know certainly and indubitably.

"Rule III: As regards any subject we propose to investigate, we must inquire not what other people have thought, or what we ourselves conjecture, but what we can clearly and manifestly perceive by intuition or deduce with certainty. For there is no other way of acquiring knowledge.

"Rule VIII: If in a series of subjects to be examined we come to a subject of which our intellect cannot gain a good enough intuition, we must stop there; and we must not examine the other matters that follow, but must refrain from futile toil."

René Descartes, *Rules for the Direction of the Mind*

References: *Descartes: Philosophical Writings*, ed. G. E. M. Anscombe and P. T. Geach; *Descartes*, Marjorie Grene; and *The Method of Descartes*, L. J. Beck

desiccate – v. fr. Latin *desiccare*, meaning to dry up; also meaning to exhaust emotional or intellectual strength; to eliminate vitality

desiderate – v. to wish for; to desire or want

desideratum – n. something regarded as essential

despond – v. to lose heart; to lose courage

desultory – adj. casual, disconnected; lacking method and order

determinism – n. the view that everything happens as a result of events in the past. Determinism denies the validity of freedom and will. It assumes that an uncaused event is impossible. It makes use of scientific evidence to support its presuppositions.

Determinism gets divided into "hard determinism" and "soft determinism." In psychological behaviorism, there is a hard form that argues for reducing all events to causally determined events. Sociobiology and neuropsychology have added to the belief in hard determinism.

Soft determinism finds room for freedom and chance amid the natural laws that govern events. It assumes that freedom can act as an antecedent to events.

References: *Causality and Determinism*, G. H. von Wright; *Determinism and Freedom in the Age of Modern Science*, ed. Sidney Hook

detrital – adj. made up of trash or debris; composed of "detritus"

detrivorous – adj. surviving or feeding on organic debris; trash-eating

detrude – v. to force down or away

deus ex machina – n. literally "god out of the machine"; reference to a god who intervenes and sorts out solutions in otherwise irresolvable entanglements

deuterogamy – n. a second marriage

devolution – n. a condition of biological degeneration

Dewey, John (1859–1952) – an American philosopher of pragmatism, education, and social reform. Like other pragmatists, Dewey argued that the consequences of ideas are very important to their truth value. His version of pragmatism became known as "instrumentalism." Dewey rejected the rationalist position that the rules of logic are "a priori" principles, arguing that the truth of propositions is more dependent upon consequences. This concern about consequences carries over into his sense of what liberal democracy should advocate. Human progress hinges on a pragmatic philosophy of meliorism. He believed in the moral call to develop and improve the world, so this required a philosophy of meliorism, were action is thoughtfully designed to aid progress beyond what nature will provide.

Dewey also developed a psychological outlook called "functionalism." Functionalism argues that past experiences improve the coordination of present experiences. This perspective reinforced the pragmatic emphasis on action as a measurement of truth.

As an educational reformer, Dewey disputed the educational value of school in American society. He argued that schools should prepare the student for actual success in the world they would enter. Education should impart knowledge that can be useful to forming a way of life. He argued that a student could not excel in life, if his or her interests were not addressed by the educational system. They would be forced into a compromised mediocrity and lose the opportunities to develop their natural talents. Students are different in their curiosity and interests. Curiosity is the cause of real thinking, thus an educational program that discourages curiosity also prevents real thinking.

Principal works: *How We Think* (1910), *Human Nature and Conduct* (1922), *Experience and Nature* (1925), and *The Teacher and Society* (1937)

"For ordinary purposes, that is for practical purposes, the truth and the realness of things are synonymous."

John Dewey, *The Practical Character of Reality*

"Happiness is fundamental in morality only because happiness is not something to be sought after, but is something now attained, even in the midst of pain and trouble, whenever recognition of our ties with nature and with fellow men releases and informs our action."

John Dewey, *Human Nature and Conduct*

References: *New Studies in the Philosophy of John Dewey*, ed. S. M. Cahn; and *The Life and Mind of John Dewey*, G. Dykhuizen

dextral – adj. a reference to right-handedness; right-sidedness

dharma – n. in Buddhism, natural law, especially with regard to the world's essence; also a reference to the ideal qualities in one's own nature, conformity to which produces spiritual harmony. Dharma is one of the brief minute appearances of which the existence of any object is made up (Hinayana). In terms of Buddhahood, understanding Dharma is the best way to remove suffering. Posed as an ethical principle, Dharma involves recognition of the Four Noble Truths (see "Buddhism"). In Jainism, it is the uncreated eternal substance that is a necessary condition for the movement of matter and souls.

"In this world, aspirants may find enlightenment by two different paths. For the contemplative is the path of knowledge. For the active one is the path of selfless action."

Bhagavad Gita

dharna – n. (India) a type of protest-fasting designed to exact justice from an offending party; fasting at the door of the one who has offended the protestor

dialectic – n. in philosophy, a reference to the exchange of ideas. It includes the examination of logical conclusions, criticism of data, and the presentation of counterargument. It is an integral feature of healthy skepticism and one of the main ingredients in the general testing of theories and ideas.

dialogic – adj. relating or pertaining to dialogue, verbal or written

dianetics – n. the theory that one's personality can be understood in terms of an individual's experiences before birth. This is a principal assumption in the religious views of Scientology (L. Ron Hubbard).

dianoetic – adj. pertaining to discursive reasoning (reasoning that passes from one topic to another)

dianoia – n. faculty used in discursive reasoning; a capacity for logically ordered reflection

diarchy – n. government by two leaders or authorities

diatribe – n. a seemingly endless speech; writing or speech that is abusive, including criticism that is satirical

Dibelius, Martin (1883–1947) – a German theologian. Dibelius specialized in New Testament theology and argued for the use of *Formgeschichte* (Form Criticism).

He divided the oral traditions of early Christianity into five basic types: short stories, exhortations, paradigms, legends, and myths. Along with Rudolf Bultmann, he argued that the historicity of Jesus could not be detailed. He also argued that the ethical standards presented by Jesus in the Sermon on the Mount could not be realized in modern society.

Reference: *From Tradition to Gospel*, Martin Dibelius

didactic – adj. designed to teach; also, that which is entertaining and pleasurable as well as instructional

didymous – adj. fr. the Greek *didymos*, meaning "twin"; the quality of growing in pairs

diffidence – n. a lack of self-confidence; a failure to be self-assertive; hesitance

diffluence – n. a flowing away or apart

digamy – n. marriage to two people

dilemma – n. in logic, a complex argument form in which two conclusions are forced, both of which may be undesirable. It is typically constructed of two modus ponens arguments, side by side, united by the logical functions of conjunction and disjunction:

$$P{\to}Q, \ P{\vdash}Q$$

If I announce my philosophical views, I will be attacked and if I remain silent, I will lose my self-respect. I will either announce my philosophical views or I will remain silent. So, I will either be attacked or I will lose my self-respect.

dimerous – adj. having two parts

diplopia – n. a condition of sight in which a single object appears as two

dipsomania – n. an uncontrollable craving for drink, especially alcoholic liquors

discept – v. to argue, debate, or dispute

dispiteous – adj. mean-minded, cruel, and vicious

disputatious – adj. provoking controversy; quarrelsome

disquiet – n. anxiety; disturbance

distrait – adj. weak attention or absentmindedness due to worries

ditheism – n. belief in two gods

divagate – v. to wander about aimlessly

divine command theory – n. the view that all moral guidelines should appeal to the will of God. The theory includes God's communication of divine will (i.e., revelation)

dormient – adj. sleeping

Dostoevsky, Fyodor (1821–1881) – a Russian writer-philosopher who is an important figure in existentialist thought. His novels explore the psychological, social, and political problems of life in nineteenth-century Russia.

Dostoevsky was the son of a doctor, and the family lived near the grounds of the hospital where his father worked, the Marinsky Hospital for the Poor. While playing as a child, Dostoevsky encountered the lower social classes on the outskirts of Moscow. This environment led to an accidental horror when young Dostoevsky witnessed the rape of a nine-year-old girl by an older man. Although he ran to get his father's help for the girl, this tragic event haunted him for the rest of his life, and it found its way into some of Dostoevsky's novels (*Brothers Karamazov*). All his novels seemed to develop on this autobiographical basis, including the years he spent doing hard labor in prison for being an intellectual dissident.

Though it may not seem so, Dostoevsky was also a religious personality. Throughout his life he maintained a private interest in the message of Christ. Russian Orthodox Christianity was the tradition he followed on a sporadic basis. At the end of his life, he was candid about his attachment to a simple religious faith.

Dostoevsky's stories frequently address the challenges of freedom. He notes the pressures of modern society, with its moral expectations and confinements. The social, economic, religious, and legal forces around his characters require moral, spiritual, and psychological decisions for a variety of moral dilemmas.

Dostoevsky's novels suggest certain terrifying possibilities, especially the specter of nihilism: perhaps there is no God and no preset values. If humanity is totally free, then there are no guidelines for life. This is the meaning of "total freedom." Moral truth as something reliable disappears in this philosophy of freedom. Yet, the supreme truth is that people are free to redeem themselves with positive moral outcomes if they choose.

Dostoevsky's novels portray characters who are enmeshed in the anguish of choice, lives damaged by bad decisions. In *The Idiot*, Prince Myshkin is portrayed as an ideal man who is eventually dragged down by the depravity of his society. This makes the point that being a good person is no better than being an idiot. In *Crime and Punishment*, the main character is Raskolnikov. He rationalizes his right to kill an old woman whose wealth he wants to acquire. The effects of this act follow him. He wants to confess and receive redemption, but he cannot. His moral anguish becomes his punishment. In *The Brothers Karamazov*, brother Dimitri represents the man who is guided by sensual pleasure. Brother Ivan represents an intellectual whose rationality is a source of depression. Alyosha, as the third brother, represents an ideal man who is gentle, intelligent, and practical. In *Notes from Underground*, the main character is used to attack utopianism and socialist philosophy. The "Underground Man" encounters various social challenges. His encounter with a police officer is a portrait of obsession. His attendance of a dinner party with friends narrates relationship disaster. His encounter with a prostitute examines complicated sexual events.

Principal works: *Notes from Underground* (1864), *Crime and Punishment* (1866), *The Idiot* (1869), *The Possessed* (1872), and *The Brothers Karamozov* (1880)

"Grand Inquisitor: . . . The most painful secrets of their conscience, all, all they will bring to us, and we shall have an answer for all. And they will be glad to believe our answer, for it will save them from the great anxiety and terrible agony they endure at present in making a free decision for themselves."

Fyodor Dostoevsky, *The Brothers Karamazov*

References: *The White Monk: An Essay on Dostoevsky and Melville*, F. D. Reeve; *Critical Essays on Dostoevsky*, ed. R. F. Miller; and *Fyodor Dostoevsky*, Harold Bloom

dotage – n. weakness or lack of mental poise due to aging

dukkha – n. in Buddhism, a reference to the sorrow present in the endless cycle of birth, growth, decay, and death. This sorrow stems from the impermanence (*anicca*) that characterizes everything and of which mind is acutely aware. The self (*anatta*) is unable to find peace in a life that requires perpetual striving.

dulcify – v. to appease; mollify; to make agreeable or sweet

dulcinea – n. secret lover, especially a mistress

dulocracy – n. a government by former slaves

Durkheim, Émile (1858–1917) – a French philosopher of society, Durkheim developed a science of society. As a professor and editor, he constructed views on ethics as science and a philosophy of social policy. Among his more original ideas was the notion of a "collective conscience." Durkheim believed that group psychology is external to the individual and often has a coercive effect on the individual.

In his theory of social types, Durkheim was influenced by Darwinian thought. Durkheim concluded that "normal" social types exhibit objective characteristics that are advantageous for the survival of human beings. Whereas "pathological" social types work against the overall well-being of society. With a focus on organic solidarity (*sui generis*), Durkheim believed that pathological behavior, such as suicide, could and should be offset by healthy influences pressed on to the life of the individual by his or her specific occupational group. He believed that things like marital divorce demonstrated the pathological existence of "anomie."

Social crisis, caused by economic uncertainty and the loss of holistic intellectual development via specialization, becomes a destructive fact in the life of individuals. Anomie, or lawlessness, is related to a society's failure to affirm values and plans that enhance survival through solidarity. Without a communal structure, the individual is more and more left to his or her own devices to establish a sense of order, thus lessening the possibility of moral harmony within the group.

For Durkheim, the social group's inner values constitute the "social milieu." This provides a ground of being to understand the conduct of individuals. Concerns of this sort led to questions regarding sociology and religion. Here Durkheim simply extends his thesis that the specific content of a religion is secondary to its social role: to produce solidarity within the group. In totemism, for example, Durkheim argues that the totem symbolizes a clan and a god, never just a god.

In his work on suicide, Durkheim argued that there is a relationship between individualism, intellectual development, and voluntary death. The attempt to be self-sufficient is ultimately doomed. Durkheim, however, points out that movement beyond the visions of one's group is unidirectional. Belief systems that are ruined or "carried away by the current of affairs" can only be successfully transcended through reason. Reason must find new premises for solidarity in order to avoid anomie, self-hatred, and suicidal reactions.

Principal works: *The Division of Labor in Society* (1893), *The Rules of Sociological Method* (1895), *Suicide* (1897), *The Elementary Forms of Religious Life* (1912), and *Moral Education* (1925)

"Man seeks to learn and man kills himself because of the loss of cohesion in his religious society; he does not kill himself because of his learning. It is certainly not the learning he acquires that disorganizes religion; but the desire for knowledge wakens because religion becomes disorganized. Knowledge is not sought as a

means to destroy accepted opinions but because their destruction has commenced. To be sure, once knowledge exists, it may battle in its own name and in its own cause, and set up as an antagonist to traditional sentiments. But its attacks would be ineffective if these sentiments still possessed vitality; or rather, would not even take place. Faith is not uprooted by dialectical proof; it must already be deeply shaken by the causes to be unable to withstand the shock of argument."

Émile Durkheim, *Suicide*

". . . if the Jew manages to be both well instructed and very disinclined to suicide, it is because of the special origin of his desire for knowledge. . . .Religious minorities, in order to protect themselves better against the hate to which they are exposed or merely through a sort of emulation, try to surpass in knowledge the populations surrounding them...The Jew, therefore, seeks to learn, not in order to replace his collective prejudices by reflective thought, but merely to be better armed for the struggle. For him it is a means of offsetting the unfavorable position imposed on him by opinion and sometimes by law. And since knowledge by itself has no influence upon a tradition in full vigor, he superimposes this intellectual life upon his habitual routine with no effect of the former on the latter. This is the reason for the complexity he presents. Primitive in certain respects, in others he is an intellectual and a man of culture. He thus combines the advantages of the severe discipline characteristic of small ancient groups with the benefits of the intense culture enjoyed by our great societies. He has all the intelligence of modern man without sharing his despair."

Émile Durkheim, *Suicide*

References: *Émile Durkheim and the Reformation of Sociology*, S. G. Mestrovic; and *The Radical Durkheim*, F. Pearce

dysgenic – adj. causing inferiority or degeneration in biological descendants

dysgnosia – n. an impairment of intellectual capacity to acquire knowledge

dysphoria – n. a condition of deep dissatisfaction; anxiety; excessive concern marked by unhappiness

dysteleology – n. a philosophical doctrine that refutes the possibility of a final or ultimate cause of existence

dysthemia – n. a condition of severe despondency or dejection

E

ebullience – n. the quality of energy and enthusiasm, especially in the expression of ideas

ecdemic – adj. originating outside of the place where found

ecdysiast – n. a creature that sheds its skin; one who changes outward identity; a stripteaser

Eckhart, Johannes (1260–1327) – a German Dominican priest, philosopher, mystic, and theologian. Eckhart is sometimes compared to Sankara (788–820 AD). His influence is evident in the views of Jan van Ruysbroeck, Nicholas of Cusa, and Heinrich Suso.

Officially condemned by the papacy, Eckhart argued for four levels of the soul's operation:

1) the bodily existence: sensations
2) the emotional existence: anger, joy, desire, etc.
3) the rational existence: higher intellectual understanding of the world
4) the Divine existence: abstract knowledge of God

Eckhart's theology incorporated Neoplatonic ideas. He argued that enlightenment is an experience in which the subjective and objective states of consciousness become one. He maintained that the goal of contemplative life is to transcend the notion of God and reach the Godhead itself. The experience of faith and salvation requires the believer to practice detachment from the world, so that God may enter the soul. God's "ebullience" enters the detached soul in the form of love.

Much of his work was believed to have been destroyed during the Inquisition and by his Franciscan critics. In 1960, a set of writings belonging to Eckhart were found in a Carthusian monastery. His ideas also circulated among philosophers of the nineteenth century.

Principal work: *Treatises and Sermons*

"The life of work is necessary and the life of contemplation is good. In service one gathers the harvest that has been sown in contemplation."

Meister Eckhart, *Sermons*

"The less theorizing one does about God, the more receptive one is to his inpouring."

Meister Eckhart, *Sermons*

Reference: *Master Eckhart and the Rhineland Mystics*, J. Ancelet-Hustache

echolalia – n. the involuntary repetition of someone else's words immediately after they have been spoken

echopraxia – n. the abnormal copying of another person's actions

éclat – n. brilliant reputation

eclecticism – n. a philosophical position that collects what appears to be the best in various doctrines, methods, or techniques

ectad – adj. outward from the inside

ectal – adj. exterior; outside

ectomorphic – adj. having a thin, muscular body (e.g., Jesus Christ)

ectopic – adj. occurring in an unusual position

ectype – n. a copy, as contrasted with an original or prototype

edacious – adj. relating to voraciousness or appetite; devouring

E

edacity – n. voraciousness

edify – v. fr. the Latin *aedificare*, meaning to instruct spiritually; thus to instruct or improve morally or spiritually

effable – adj. possible to express or communicate (reference to the adequacy of language in describing phenomena). Compare with "ineffable," the impossibility of describing.

efferent – adj. carrying outward or away from

effrontery – n. boldness marked by lack of concern; shamelessness; insolence

effuse – v. to pour out

egoism – n. the view that the ego is the cause of the acts and intentions of the agent. *Psychological egoism* argues that people will only act in their own self-interest. Even altruism is self-gratifying, if only for its spiritual benefits. *Ethical egoism* is the prescriptive view that all people *ought* to act in their own self-interest, making selfishness a normative ethic.

> References: *Egomania and the Psychology of Contemporary Man*, M. Nordau; *The Ego and Its Destiny*, Louis Lavelle; *The Virtue of Selfishness*, Ayn Rand

egregious – adj. extremely bad; flagrant (mistake)

egress – n. an act of leaving

eidetic – adj. of or pertaining to complete visual experience; strong visual recall; accuracy; a concern with essences

eidolon – n. a visual illusion; apparition

eidos – n. the essence of a culture; the basic philosophical assumptions a culture uses to interpret experience and relate to reality

eisegesis – n. a biased interpretation, especially of a written manuscript; a reading into

élan – n. a spirit of vitality; vigorous enthusiasm; panache

elate – v. to make happy

eldritch – adj. weird; unusual; uncanny

Electra complex – n. in the views of Carl Jung, the female equivalent of the Oedipus complex, wherein the girl expresses an attachment toward the father or father figure... *Electra* was the Greek mythological personage who urged her brother Orestes to slay their mother Clytemnestra in revenge for her murder of their father, Agamemnon.

Reference: *The Theory of Psychoanalysis*, Carl Jung

elegiac – adj. suitable for use as a lamentation; of or relating to an elegy

elegy – n. a poem or song expressing sorrow; melancholy

elenchus – n. a logical refutation.

Eleusinians – n. devotees of Demeter and Persephone; a mystery religion of ancient Greece modeling its philosophy of personal growth and rebirth on the succession of seasons, especially spring.

Reference: *Eleusis and The Eleusinian Mysteries*, George Mylonas

Eliade, Mircea (1901–1986) – a Romanian philosopher of religion. Eliade was an expert on myth and symbolism in religion. He was associated with certain fascist groups in the 1930s, and this eventually resurfaced as criticism when he was a professor of religion at the University of Chicago. Nonetheless, his books enjoyed commercial success, and he flourished as a result of his writing. His final years were complicated by his political activism in Romania before WWII.

His childhood was marked by certain formative experiences, such as witnessing the WWI bombing of Bucharest by German zeppelins. Although he read passionately, his adolescence was marked by problems with the educational system in Romania. His state of mind was affected by feelings of alienation toward the discipline required in the Romanian school system.* At one point, he was failing in most subjects. He tried to increase his willpower and motivation by forcing himself to eat insects and sleep less than six hours per night. If he could do that, it would demonstrate an improvement in self-control. His reading included the philosophy of Socrates and Epictetus.

While his life was marked by episodes of melancholy, he often mastered these feelings by meditating on times in his childhood that were spectacular moments of spiritual epiphany. They had a mythic influence on his mind. This interesting fact seems to coincide with Eliade's research into religion, myth, the sacred, and the eternal return.

Eliade traveled widely in search of the central meaning of religion, including travels to India and study at the University of Calcutta. There he acquired the knowledge of yoga that would make him an expert on the subject.

He believed that myth represented pure religious meaning. He introduced the concept of "heirophanies" as the basis of religious experience: the separation of reality into the sacred and the profane. The sacred represents the "origin" of things, and in connecting with it, a person acquires a connection to a celestial archetype. The profane represents a lost state: limited to the meaning of a secular life. The spiritual content of the sacred is not present in the profane. The profane is a more limited and superficial type of meaning leading to a different kind of ethical orientation, where worldly values predominate.

Eliade combined his theory of the sacred and the profane with the idea of the "eternal return": a belief by the practitioner that it is possible to return to the original experience of a myth and bring it forward for a contemporary meaning and application. Eliade argued that all traditional societies have a longing to return to the origins, the cosmogony, and the values of the mythical age. Their rituals are the vehicles for reaching back to the onto-mythical origins of life. For Eliade, myth was an important basis for true religious enlightenment. Eliade believed that modern man's anxiety was a product of lost mythological consciousness, plus immersion in nonreligious culture and what he termed "the terror of history." Modern man's secularization represents a lost condition, which includes an obsession with linear history and, thus, "the terror of history."

Principal works: *The Myth of the Eternal Return* (1949), *Patterns of Comparative Religion* (1949), and *The Sacred and the Profane: The Nature of Religion* (1957)

Reference: *Imagination and Meaning: The Scholarly and Literary Works of Mircea Eliade*, eds. Mac L. Ricketts and Norman Girardot; *from "Mircea Eliade's Second Life" by Silviu Mahai in *Cotidianul* (Romanian newspaper), July 31, 2007

elicit – v. to draw forth

ellipsis – n. an omission of a word or phrase from a sentence, especially one that makes the construction logically incomplete

elliptical – adj. extreme economy of speech or writing; obscure

elocution – n. voice control; effective public speaking

eloign – v. to conceal; to move away to an obscure location; to keep at a distance

elutriate – v. to purify by rinsing in water, especially in a current

embrangle – v. to cause confusion or perplexity

emend – v. to edit or censure; to remove mistakes

emesis – n. an instance of vomiting; the unexpected purging of foreign substances

emolument – n. payment for a service; salary

empathize – v. to communicate; to participate in another's feelings

empathy – n. identification with the feelings of another person

Empedocles (ca. 490–430 BC) – a pre-Socratic philosopher, known primarily for his theory that matter is composed of four basic elements: earth, air, fire, and water. Change is explained as the outcome of dynamic properties within these elements, which foster separation and combination. This view of physics and cosmology dominated the Western view up to the Renaissance period.

Empedocles was considered to have supernatural powers. Many sought out his advice and healing powers. He proclaimed himself a "deathless god."

Principal works: *On the Nature of Things* and *Purifications*

"The intelligence of man grows toward the material that is present."

Empedocles, *On Nature*

Reference: *Empedocles: The Extant Fragments*, M. R. Wright

emperean – n. the most exalted heavenly state

empiricism – n. a theory of knowledge developed principally by John Locke (1632–1704), George Berkeley (1685–1753), and David Hume (1711–1776). At the center of empiricism is the claim that all knowledge originates in sense experience. Reason, in contrast, operates as an organizing mental property.

Empiricism has roots in Aristotle, whose epistemology was inductive, concentrating on the observation of cases in nature. Other thinkers such as Copernicus

(1473–1543), Kepler (1571–1630), and Galileo (1564–1642), also defended the importance of empiricism and physical cosmology.

Empiricism is skepticism with a positive result. By noting the nature and content of sensation, concerns about the limits of sensation produced a technology of extended and refined sensation (e.g., telescopes and microscopes). In this sense, it is surprising that Spinoza, a lens maker, was not more interested in the potential of sensation to yield knowledge. The push for empirical knowledge is the parent of other extensions of sensation such as radar, infrared vision, X-ray vision, auditory detection devices, tactile instrumentation, CAT scans, MRIs, electron microscopes, linear accelerators, the Hubble telescope, and the Haldron collider.

In pragmatism, empiricism became an important model of truth. There empiricism is the philosophical willingness to limit and control the role of abstract reasoning. This emphasis, in pragmatism, is the empirical concern with the consequences of actions. The utility of knowledge is important in the attempts to improve life.

In the twentieth century, empiricism influenced the logical positivist movement. Truth of statements is contingent on empirical verification. Empirical observation, which is the principle tool of scientists, motivated philosophers to value the correspondence theory of truth.

References: *These Last Four Centuries*, C. C. Faille; and *The Empiricists*, R. S. Woolhouse

empyreal – adj. belonging to the highest heaven in ancient cosmology

emulous – adj. having the desire or wish to equal or imitate

enchiridion – n. handbook

encomiast – n. one who praises; eulogist

endemic – adj. restricted to a certain locale; native

endogamy – n. marriage within a social group

endomorphic – adj. having a heavy, round, and soft body build, especially with a tendency to become and remain fat; massiveness, especially of digestive viscera; the fat Buddha

endophasia – n. speech that is internalized and inaudible

energumen – n. someone possessed by an evil spirit, especially a fanatic

enervate – v. to make weak, especially in the sense of mental or moral strength; to reduce vigor

Engels, Friedrich (1820–1895) – a German socialist and poet, Engels was the lifelong coworker and supporter of Karl Marx.

Raised in a wealthy family, Engels acquired the Protestant view of work and society. He rejected both his faith and the capitalist affections of Protestantism due to the influence of Hegelianism and his personal encounter with starving textile workers. Engels developed the view (like Marx) that economics determines social form. Yet, social forms are not without effect on economics. This was an implication of Hegelian dialectics.

> Principal works: *Economic and Philosophic Manuscripts of 1844* (1844), *Anti-Duhring* (1878), *Socialism: Utopian and Scientific* (1883), *The Origin of the Family, Private Property, and the State* (1884), *Ludwig Feuerbach and the Outcome of Classical German Philosophy* (1888), *Principles of Communism* (1919), and *The Dialectics of Nature* (1925).

> *"The proletarian is . . . in law and in fact, the slave of the bourgeoisie, which can decree his life or death. It offers him the means of living, but only for an 'equivalent' for his work. It even lets him have the appearance of acting from a free choice, of making a contract with free unconstrained consent, as a responsible agent who has attained his majority.*

> *"Fine freedom, where the proletarian has no other choice than that of either accepting the conditions which the bourgeoisie offers him, or of starving, of freezing to death, of sleeping naked among the beasts of the forests! A fine 'equivalent' valued at pleasure by the bourgeoisie. And if one proletarian is such a fool as to starve rather than to agree to the equitable propositions of the bourgeoisie, his 'natural superiors,' another is easily found in his place; there are proletarians enough in the world, and not all so insane as to prefer dying to living."*

> Friedrich Engels, *Manuscripts of 1844*

Reference: *Engels*, T. Carver

engender – v. to cause to exist or develop; to bring about

enigma – n. something that cannot be explained

enjoin – v. to command or proscribe; to direct by authoritative request; also, to prohibit

enmity – n. typically mutual hatred or ill will, especially active hatred

ennui – n. boredom, especially as in weariness or dissatisfaction

enosis – n. union, especially political

enounce – v. to declare or enunciate

ensconce – v. to settle in; to shelter; to conceal or make safe

ensorcell – v. to put under a spell

entelechy – n. an actualization by form-giving cause; a manifestation; contrasted with mere potentiality (Aristotle)

entente – n. an agreement between nations outlining a common course of action

enthetic – adj. brought in from the outside

entourage – n. one's surroundings, especially including one's servants

entre nous – adj. Fr., meaning just between the two of us; secretly

entropy – n. the decline of matter and energy in the universe until a uniform level is reached

enucleate – v. to remove the center or nucleus

eonism – n. the adoption of female attitudes and habits by a male

epeiric – adj. reaching toward the interior, especially with regard to land

ephemera – n. something lasting only a short time; transience

epicene – adj. reflecting male and female characteristics; inter-sexual; effeminate; also weak or feeble

epicrisis – n. a minor disturbance following a major one

epicritic – adj. the ability to respond to small differences in sensation, including temperature; accurate discrimination

Epictetus (50–130 AD) – the slave-philosopher and the most important member of the Stoic school. He was owned by Epaphroditos, a wealthy secretary to Nero. Epaphroditos allowed Epictetus access to a library, where he studied Stoic philosophy. Through his experience as a slave, Epictetus developed the view that the ability to absorb suffering and misery is part of happiness. This attitude is at the center of Stoicism, which adopts a fatalistic view of life's events. E. V. Arnold and Simplicius depict Epictetus as a generous man who lived simply. In his old age he adopted a friend's child who was left to die. He raised the child with the aid of a woman whom he may have married. He was loved by his disciples and admired by Emperor Hadrian. According to Diogenes Laertius, he died of kidney stones.

Epictetus's philosophy became the inspiration for Rational Emotive Behavior Therapy, developed by Albert Ellis (1913–2007). This a psychotherapy that argues that the attitude of the individual toward adversity, as much as the adversity itself, can play a role in the creation of misery. Learning to control irrational and unrealistic thoughts about events can lessen the incidence of depression and anxiety.

Principal works: *Enchiridion* and *Discourses*

"Once a child is born, it is no longer in our power not to love it."

Epictetus, *Discourses*

"Remember that you are an actor in a play, which is as the playwright wants it to be: short if he wants it short, long if he wants it long. If he wants you to play a beggar, play even this part skillfully, or a cripple, or a public official, or a private citizen. What is yours is to play the assigned part well. But to choose it belongs to someone else."

Epictetus, *Enchiridion*

"Let death and exile and everything terrible appear before your eyes every day, especially death; and you will never have anything contemptible in your thoughts or crave anything excessively."

Epictetus, *Enchiridion*

Reference: *Roman Stoicism*, E. V. Arnold; *Commentary on the Enchiridion of Epictetus*, Simplicius of Celicia (sixth century)

E

Epicureanism – n. the philosophy of Epicurus (341–270 BC). He wrote *Letter to Menoeceus* and *Principal Doctrines*. He argued that the goal of life is happiness. He accepted the physics of Democritus, who argued that reality is composed of atoms. This contributed to his observation that fear, which is a cause of human misery, is often unfounded. Fear of the gods is irrational, since gods do not control the events of this world, and every natural event is explained as an effect of atomic action. Fear of death is also irrational, since death is the cessation of all feeling. One can have a painful life, but one cannot have a painful death. Epicurus advocated a balanced hedonism, because psychic misery is connected to sensual abandon. Happiness is *ataraxia* (intellectual tranquility or peace).

Epicurus had little confidence in the possibility of wide social happiness, arguing that the life of the average person is a complex tangle of needs and problems that tend to have negative social effects. The best life is to be found by developing a few good friendships that can provide simple physical and intellectual satisfaction.

> *"Death is nothing to us: for that which is dissolved is without sensation; and that which lacks sensation is nothing to us."* (II, *Principal Doctrines*)

> *"No pleasure is a bad thing in itself: but the means which produce some pleasures bring with them disturbances many times greater than the pleasures."* (*VII*)

> *"The most unalloyed source of protection from men, which is secured to some extent by a certain force of expulsion, is in fact the immunity which results from a quiet life and retirement from the world."* (*XIV*)

> *"The wealth demanded by nature is both limited and easily procured; that demanded by idle imaginings stretches on to infinity."* (*XV*)

> *"Of desires, all that do not lead to a sense of pain, if they are not satisfied, are not necessary, but involve a craving which is easily dispelled, when the object is hard to procure or they seem likely to produce harm."* (*XXVI*)

> *"Of all the things which wisdom acquires to produce the blessedness of a complete life, far the greatest is the possession of friendship."* (*XXVII*)

> References: *Epicurus' Ethical Theory*, P. Mitsis; and *Epicurus: An Introduction*, J. M. Rist

epigone – n. an imitator, especially of a famous writer; an inferior follower

epigram – n. a witty, cryptic, or pointed remark; a paradoxical saying, especially one that reveals a surprising turn of insight

epigraph – n. a quotation at the beginning of a written work

Epiphany – n. fr. Greek *epiphaneia*, meaning a divine appearance or manifestation. In Christianity it marks the last day of the twelve days of Christmas on January 6.

In Christian theology, it refers to a moment of spiritual illumination. This is associated with the joy of seeing the enlightened infant Jesus.

epiphenomenalism – n. the doctrine that mental processes (mind/consciousness) are the effect of complex foundational substances (i.e., bio-matter). It is one of the proposed solutions to the mind-body problem (René Descartes). The mind-body problem is a puzzle about the relationship between the dissimilar entities of mind and body. How do these dissimilar "things" exist together? What is their connection? Since epiphenomenalism argues that mind is merely the effect of complex biochemical arrangements, one should think of mind as smoke rising from a fire.

epistemology – n. the study of the sources, nature, and validity of knowledge. Theories of knowledge fall into two general categories—1) empiricism: reliance on sense data, and 2) rationalism: reliance on innate ideas and the power of reason.

Empiricism is partially defined through the views of John Locke (1632–1704), in his *Essay Concerning Human Understanding* (1690). Locke argued that the mind is a *tabula rasa* or blank slate, and that all our ideas derive from experience. Locke's philosophy is assisted by the work of David Hume (1711–1776) in *An Inquiry Concerning Human Understanding* (1748). Hume argued that one does not understand beyond one's experience. His radical advocacy of empiricism proposed that causality itself is not strictly defensible, since "causality" is simply a prediction based on past experience. There can be no strict predictions of anything that will take place in the future. All statements of "fact" are contingent upon careful observation, and observation, no matter how careful, cannot capture every detail.

Rationalism is mainly associated with the views of René Descartes (1596–1650), author of *Discourse on Method* (1637) and *Meditations* (1641). Descartes called for a scrapping of all past ideas and insisted on a fresh deployment of skepticism to discover rational principles that stand *a priori* (of necessity, self-evident). The foundation of his viewpoint is self-consciousness, "*Cogito, ergo sum*" (I think, therefore I am), for no matter what sort of deception or errors exist, the awareness of self cannot be a deception. In order to be deceived one must exist. Thus, self-consciousness is beyond any type of skepticism. From here Descartes moves to the existence of God as the first "clear and distinct" idea and then to the veracity of other ideas through the existence and goodness of God.

"My question is, what can we hope to achieve with reason, when all the material and assistance of experience are taken away?"

Immanuel Kant (1724–1804), *The Critique of Pure Reason*

References: *Epistemology and Cognition*, Alvin Goldman; *Theory of Knowledge*, Roderick M. Chisholm; *The Inquiring Mind: An Introduction to Epistemology*, George Boas; *The Degrees of Knowledge*, Jacques Maritain

epistolary – n. a series of letters (as in correspondence)

epithet – n. a word (or words) ascribing an attribute to someone or something

epitome – n. a summary: an ideal example

epitomize – v. to show what is typical

eponym – n. a person, real or not, whose name is adopted as the description of something

epuration – n. a cleansing or purge; elimination

equable – adj. unvarying, uniform; marked by a lack of extreme difference

equanimity – n. a state of composure; serenity

equinox – n. the solar time when night and day are of equal length everywhere; occurring about March 21 and September 22

equipose – n. balance; equality of force

Erasmus, Desiderius (1467–1536) – a Dutch philosopher and theologian, Erasmus advocated a theological humanism and opposed the evangelistic efforts of Martin Luther. Both Luther and Erasmus were ordained priests but with very different solutions to the problems of the Reformation Period. Erasmus advocated internal moral renewal, claiming that establishment of other Christian churches outside the mainstream of Catholicism would permanently damage the unity of Christendom.

Principal works: *The Contempt of the World* (1490), *In Praise of Folly* (1509), and *The Epicurean* (1533)

"Formerly monasteries were nothing other than retreats where good men betook themselves when they were weary of pleasure and vice, or feared the moral contamination when pagans lived with Christians; or else they dreaded the cruel persecutions then raging, and betook themselves to the neighboring mountains, where they lived . . . in prayer and meditation. After laboring with their hands and living on the coarsest food, they spent the rest of their time reciting the psalms, or in pious reading or conversation, in prayer or works of charity, such as helping the sick and needy... To be a monk in those days was simply to be a Christian... Control over others was conspicuous by its absence, since all were only too eager to advance towards perfection, and there was more need of the bit than the spur... Now, alas, many monasteries are tinged with the follies of the world...In these there is such a lack of discipline that they are nothing but schools of impiety, in which no one can be pure or good ."

Erasmus, *Contempt of the World*

References: *Erasmus and the Age of Reformation*, Johan Huizinga; *The Spirituality of Erasmus of Rotterdam*, ed. Richard DeMolen

ergomania – n. ceaseless devotion to work, possibly evidence of mental illness

ergophobia – n. unnatural aversion to work; fear of effort

eristic – adj. controversial; characterized by disputatious or questionable reasoning

Eros – n. There are conflicting accounts about the lineage of Eros. In Greek mythology, the god of physical love is described as the son of Aphrodite; though correctly interpreted to mean sexual love, the term also means a general love of physical life. Eros, as love, gave birth to the world. The absence of Eros results in destruction. In artwork, Eros is depicted with wings and a quiver of arrows. Parmenides regarded Eros as the first god to enter the world. According to one legend, Eros married Psyche, and they gave birth to Hedone (pleasure). In Roman mythology, Eros is Cupid.

In Hadot, Eros is identified as the son of Poros (resourcefulness) and Penia (poverty). His account is based on Plato's *Symposium*.

References: *The Greek Myths*, Robert Graves; *What Is Ancient Philosophy?*, Pierre Hadot

erotica – n. literary and artistic materials that have explicit sexual themes.

Generally, works that have aesthetic merit are considered erotica. Whereas, cheap and artistically worthless creations are considered pornography.

References: *A History of Pornography*, H. Montgomery Hyde; *Porneia: On Desire and the Body in Antiquity*, Aline Rousselle

ersatz – adj. being a superficial or inferior substitute

erudition – n. extensive knowledge acquired primarily from books and lacking a basis in experience

escalate – v. to increase

escharotic – adj. caustic

Eschatology – n. in theology, the study of the end of the world; the doctrine of the last things. It speculates on the nature and meaning of immortality, the resurrection, death, the Second Coming of Christ, and the notion of a last judgment. Thus, it has a meaning on two levels. One is a reference to the personal destiny of each person after his or her death. The other is a reference to the purpose (*telos*) of society in history.

Reference: *Eschatology and the New Testament*, ed. W. H. Gloer

eschew – v. to avoid or shun

esne – n. laborer

esoteric – adj. understood by those who are specially initiated; knowledge restricted to a small group

esperance – n. hope; expectation

espial – n. act of observing or spying

espionage – n. the practice of gathering sensitive information in order to undermine an opponent or competitor. It is practiced by corporations and governments. Agents of espionage are usually engaged, wholly or partially, in the life of the spy, depending on the tactical advantages of working directly or discreetly.

The ethics of espionage center around the justification of stealing, forging, buying, killing, wiretapping, cyber attacking, misrepresenting, seducing, and any other creative activities that can be used to get the desired results.

References: *The Dictionary of Espionage*, H. S. Becket; and *The Second Oldest Profession*, Phillip Knightley

estivate – v. to pass the summer, as in a certain place

esurient – adj. greedy or voracious

Eternal Return or Recurrence – n. the belief that all events will happen again in their exact and specific details over and over. It is a cyclical view of time vs. the linear view of history. A finite universe in an infinite expanse of time logically implies the recurrence of any configurations now present. This cyclical view of time and reality is present in ancient and modern philosophy: Pythagoras, Plato, Aristotle, and Nietzsche. The theory depends on viewing matter as a constant (i.e., atoms of the classical type). The theory is generally rejected by philosophers who emphasize the notions of becoming, novelty, and immortal past-time. (Not the same idea one finds in Mircea Eliade, where it is a reference to the desire to return to the mythical past.)

ethereal – adj. delicate, tenuous; also spiritual

ethical relativism – n. in ethical theory, the view that values are subjective. Thus, each person or each culture makes its own values. As a theory, it is antagonistic toward absolutism, universalism, and objectivism. For example, if values are relative, then the values of Adolf Hitler have the same moral validity as the values of Mother Teresa or Gandhi.

Reference: *Ethical Relativism*, ed. John Ladd

ethics – n. fr. the Greek *ethos*, meaning character. Ethics is the study of action, freedom, responsibility, and decision making, for individuals but also in groups. The concern with practical action is aimed at uncovering "right" (good) and "wrong" (bad) decisions. In some theories (utilitarianism), decisions are theoretically connected to creating happiness. Producing happiness socially and individually defines the utilitarian achievement of goodness.

The study of ethics is often divided into the following theories:

E

1) *Theocentric Ethics or Divine Command Theory* – the view that rules and principles of judgment derive from God or the Divine. Thus, ethical values are linked to metaphysical and religious sources (i.e., the will of God, scripture, the Divine).

2) *Utilitarianism* – the view that the good is decided by producing the "greatest happiness for the greatest number." Though evident in the philosophies of Thomas Hobbes and David Hume, this theory was popularized by John Stuart Mill (1806–1873), author of *Utilitarianism* (1863). Mill's view included pleasure as a source of happiness but avoided raw hedonism: "Better to be a Socrates dissatisfied than a pig satisfied." He argued that rational beings discern the quality of their experiences as well as the quantity.

3) *Deontology* – the study of duty or obligation. It includes the observation that duty is more important than personal happiness, as that happiness is secondary to a true achievement of "the Good." Performing good deeds for rewards is an inferior motive compared with having a "good will." Immanuel Kant (1724–1804) did the most to advance deontology.
"The majesty of duty has nothing to do with the enjoyment of life."

I. Kant, *Critique of Practical Reason*

"Nothing can possibly be conceived in the world, or even out of it, which can be called good, without qualification, except a good will."

I. Kant, *Critique of Practical Reason*

"There is therefore but one categorical imperative, namely this: act only on that maxim whereby thou canst at the same time will that it should become a universal law."

I. Kant, *The Metaphysics of Morals*

4) *Aretaic Ethics* – concerns itself with the pursuit of *arête* (excellence). It is also called "virtue-based ethics." It emphasizes the importance of character traits over rules and principles of judgment (Aristotle).

5) *Hedonism* – the view that the highest good is the pursuit of pleasure (Aristippus, Epicurus).

"The scent of flowers does not travel against the wind, nor that of sandalwood . . . but the fragrance of good people travels even against wind; a good person influences every place."

The Dhammapada, 500 BC

"I have found little that is 'good' about human beings on the whole. In my experience most of them are trash, no matter whether they subscribe to this or that ethical doctrine or to none at all."

Sigmund Freud, *Psychoanalysis and Faith*

"Goodness is a product of the ethical and spiritual artistry of individuals; it cannot be mass-produced."

Aldous Huxley (1894–1963), *Grey Eminence*

References: *Ethics: Theory and Practice*, Jacques P. Thiroux; *The Methods of Ethics*, Henry Sidgwick; *Ethics*, 2nd ed., William K. Frankena; *History of Ethics*, 2 vols., Vernon J. Bourke; *Ethics: Discovering Right and Wrong*, Louis Pojman and James Fieser

ethnocentrism – n. a view that promotes the social, cultural, and political values of one ethnic group; also the fallacy or habit of judging other ethnic groups by the standards and practices of one's own ethnic group (e.g., Nazism, Reconquista, black nationalism, etc.). In practice, ethnocentric groups view other ethnicities with disfavor and may include a denial of evidence that obligates the admission of error. Call this "the history of humanity" (Schopenhauer). It includes the inverted genetic argument that the beliefs, rights, and tastes of one ethnic group are superior to those of other ethnic groups. It seeks correct ethnic representation in employment and politics propelled by discrimination, wherein one or more races receive preferential treatment over the racial complement. Typically, the race comprising the majority are the oppressors, and the race comprising the minority are the oppressed, in a never-ending cycle of bigotry, discrimination, and hatred. This argument is also supported by primate studies, the results of which can be extrapolated on to human populations (Frans de Waal).

Ethnocentrism becomes more of a problem when competition for survival increases (Darwin). Ethnic groups see "security" in their own racial type, and they may naïvely assume that ethnic identity is the key to safety and flourishing.

This fallacy is countered by "Hobbesian" (Thomas Hobbes) realities that often betray the delusion of "safety in one's group" (group psychology).

Reference: *Nationalism, Ethnocentrism, and Personality*, Hugh D. Forbes

ethnogeny – n. the ordering of distinctive groups or races

ethnology – n. the study of the origin of races

ethos – n. the distinguishing character of a person or group, especially its moral nature

etiology – n. a branch of epistemology (knowledge) dealing with causes; in medicine, the study of the causes of disease

eudaemonia – n. happiness; literally, a good spirit

eudaemonism – n. the study of happiness or spiritual well-being, especially as a consequence of a life committed to reason. Aristotle (384–322 BC) was the first strong advocate of this view. He believed in a connection between reason and self-fulfillment. Reason guides us to the most beneficial pleasures that are an added touch to the balanced, contemplative life.

> *"True happiness flows from the possession of wisdom and virtue and not from the possession of external goods."*

> Aristotle, *Politics*

With Plato, happiness is not equated with pleasure, as pleasure is a consequence of *eputhemia* (desire). Desire is perceived as a natural element of the soul, but its fulfillment should be guided by reason. Unhappiness stems from the reversal of this hierarchy. As desire grows, the need for satisfaction grows. Going beyond natural limits introduces various kinds of evil, since desire as justification is not always consistent with good judgment (Lacan).

The problematic expansion of choices due to increased desire can be analyzed in the experience of hunger. As the desire for food grows, so does the range of choices. In starvation, what was once outside the individual's moral boundaries becomes a means of satisfying the craving for food (e.g., cannibalism). This example provides reasons for limiting (repression vs. sublimation) desire in its various manifestations. Desire, when allowed or encouraged to grow, produces a willingness to participate in acts that are more extreme and perhaps dangerous (vices). Moreover, "excess" desire produces a narrowing of experience and thus, a narrowing of life. In eudaemonism, which includes the understanding that happiness is "flourishing," it is important to flourish through reason. According to Plato, a rational or creative life is essentially more fulfilling than a pleasurable one. The former involves the life of the mind and the body, and the latter involves the life of the body alone.

"Happiness is gained by a use, and right use, of the things of life, and the right use of them, and good fortune in the use of them is given by knowledge."

Plato (428–348 BC), *Euthydemus*

Reference: *Nichomachean Ethics*, Aristotle; *The History of Sexuality: The Use of Pleasure*, vol. 2, Michel Foucault

eulogize – v. to provide high praise

eunomy – n. good social order due to just government and laws

Eusebius of Caesarea (ca. 260—ca. 340 AD) – an important historian of the early Christian Church. Eusebius wrote *Ecclesiastical History* (324 AD). This became the principle source of early theology and politics. Eusebius was a pro-Arian thinker but backed the Athanasian position on Christology at the request of Emperor Constantine.

Reference: *Eusebius as Church Historian*, Robert M. Grant

euthanasia – n. the practice of killing people (or animals) who are hopelessly sick as an act of mercy. (See *thanatos* – god of death)

euthenics – n. the science of improving the human condition by improving human surroundings

eversible – adj. having the ability to be turned inside out

evert – v. to turn to the outside; to upset

evitable – adj. avoidable

excide – v. to cut out

excogitate – v. to think out

excoriate – v. to censure without mercy

excruciation – n. the act of providing great pain or anguish

excursive – adj. to be digressive in speech and thought

execrable – adj. detestable; horrible; also, *execrate* – v. to hate

ex facie – adj. fr. the face of; apparently; presumable (as in a legal document)

exigent – adj. demanding or urgent

exiguous – adj. small, scanty, meager, or inadequate

eximious – adj. outstanding, excellent; eminent.

existentialism – n. philosophy of existence; concerned with the individual person in mass society and the nature of freedom. Existentialism is tied to phenomenology in its investigative technique, especially with regard to the presence or absence of meaning for the individual. It is also concerned with the nature of being. Existentialism is committed to ontological observations, including the analysis of life in a technological culture.

Karl Jaspers (1883–1969) author of *General Psychopathology* (1913), *Existence Philosophy* (1938), and *The Way to Wisdom* (1950), was a key figure in the development of existential thought. He used existentialism to criticize deterministic scientific psychology. According to Jaspers, a psychiatrist, it is wrong to treat actual outcomes in a person's life as the necessary outcomes. Freedom of choice is not revealed by examining the past. Freedom and the true self are only observable in "boundary situations" (*Grenzsituationen*). These are situations in which real awareness of self is also an awareness of suffering, struggle, despair, urgency, guilt, anxiety, and death. These mental situations are circumstances for recognizing pure responsibility and freedom. Courage protects the self in "boundary situations," so it can choose effectively against personal annihilation.

For existentialists, the essence of being human is to be creative. Creativity is an inner choice to produce meaning in thought and action. This is accomplished by the development of authentic personal interests. This development, this fulfillment of personal curiosity, is perpetually in danger of being lost in the bureaucratic and mechanistic organization of modern life. The point of all existentialism is to attack this tendency through preserving the natural existence of freedom, and cultivating an awareness of dynamic choice over the corrupting influence of life in a mass culture. Though existentialists are about evenly divided into theistic, atheistic, and agnostic polarities, the issue of God is technically a separate philosophical consideration from the true interests of existentialism.

Key figures include: Fyodor Dostoevsky (1821–1881), Jean-Paul Sartre (1905–1980), Søren Kierkegaard (1813–1855), Friedrich Nietzsche (1844–1900), Martin Buber (1878–1965), Paul Tillich (1886–1965), Gabriel Marcel (1889–1973), Martin Heidegger (1884–1976), Albert Camus (1913–1960), Rudolf Bultmann (1884–1976), and Maurice Merleau-Ponty (1908–1961).

References: *Existentialism from Dostoevsky to Sartre*, ed. Walter Kaufmann; *Introduction to Existentialism*, Marjorie Grene; *From Rationalism to Existentialism*, Robert Solomon

ex officio – adj. in the capacity of official position

exogamy – n. marriage outside a specific group

exogenous – adj. with an external origin

exorable – adj. persuadable

exorcism – n. the practice of expelling evil spirits. Practiced in many religions, including Islam, Judaism, Japanese Buddhism, and Catholicism. It is based on the belief that evil spirits are the cause of illness, emotional instability, and even death. The degree of possession is considered complete once it occurs, and thus, it requires exorcism.

Reference: *Unclean Spirits*, D. P. Walker

exoteric – adj. appropriate for general distribution (public use)

ex parte – adj. from one side only, as in a dispute

expatiate – v. to enlarge upon; to move about freely

expiate – v. to make amends; to atone

expletive – n. an exclamatory word or phrase, especially one that is obscene; words without real meaning but placed for emphasis

E

ex post facto – adj. Latin for "after the fact."

expugnable – adj. vulnerable to elimination and defeat

extenuate – v. to prove an offense less serious; to lessen the effect of; to mitigate

extirpate – v. to destroy totally; to uproot; to exterminate

extrapolate – v. to deduce from a known; to project from given fact

extrinsic – adj. from the outside

extrusile – adj. to be able to be pushed or forced out

eyre – n. a periodic journey made in a circuit

fabulist – n. a liar

facetious – adj. amusing but somewhat inappropriate

facile – adj. easily accomplished; dexterous; fluent

facinorous – adj. excessively wicked

factitious – adj. artificial; produced by human rather than natural forces

facture – n. the act of making something

facultative – adj. granting a special privilege; having permission or authority

fainague – v. to cheat or deceive

fainéant – adj. idle or lazy.

faith – n. fr. the Latin *fidere*, meaning to trust. In theology, faith is the principal of three theological virtues: faith, hope, and charity. Theologically, faith is a response to the Divine truth, measured in the words of Jesus as the "childlike acceptance" of the Kingdom of God. Faith is God's action in the soul. This action is considered impossible without the existential entry into a theocentric life, wherein the individual also comes to a full acceptance of the self as whole and sufficient in spiritual terms. Faith then is also an ontological measurement of being and Being. It is the elimination of self-estrangement.

"Faith is the acceptance of the 'kerygma' (Christ's teaching) not as mere cognizance of it and agreement with it but as genuine obedience to it which includes a new understanding of one's self."

Rudolf Bultmann (1884–1976), *Theology of the New Testament*

"Faith means being grasped by a power that is greater than we are, a power that shakes us and turns us, and transforms and heals us. Surrender to this power is faith."

Paul Tillich (1886–1965), *The New Being*

"The faith of a Christian . . . is trust in God, in a good God who created a good world, though the world is not now good; in a good God, powerful and good enough finally to destroy the evil that humanity does and redeem them of their sins."

Reinhold Niebuhr (1892–1971), *Beyond Tragedy*

"Faith is a gift of God; do not believe that we said it was a gift of reasoning."

Blaise Pascal (1623–1662), *Pensées*

References: *The Phenomenon of Religion*; Ninian Smart; *Faith and Belief*, Wilfred Cantwell Smith; *Dynamics of Faith*; Paul Tillich

fallacy – n. an error in reasoning. Fallacies are divided into two general categories, formal and informal. Formal fallacies break accepted structural arrangement or form in deductive argumentation. Informal fallacies are rational errors or deceptions in the linguistic presentation of an argument. Common fallacies used in everyday thinking include:

1) *Accent* – by placing emphasis on a word or phrase, it is possible to create extra meanings that confuse the issue or introduce unwarranted conclusions. Advertising strategies often employ this tactic to attract people: "Free" followed by an asterisk, the asterisk footnoting a requirement that must be met before something is received for "free."

2) *Argumentum ad hominem* – attacking a person or institution in an abusive manner in order to discredit them, thus evading an argument or critique.

3) *Syntactical Ambiguity* – errors in the use of grammar, thus introducing multiple meanings: "All the cars Jack owns are worth at least $25,000 dollars."

The careless use of "all" makes it difficult to know whether they are $25k each or $25k total.

4) *Semantical Ambiguity* – confusion introduced through words that carry multiple meanings. "Few of us ever test our powers of deduction, except when filling out our income tax forms."

5) *Apriorism* – refusal to consider evidence that counts against one's own thinking (e.g., "I don't care what studies show, pornographic material does not have an effect on the thoughts of mature adults.")

6) *Fallacy of the Continuum* – arguing that small differences are not real or important differences, thus ignoring the need for standardization of limits. "What's the big deal, so the average temperature of the earth rose two degrees in five years. It's only two degrees. The temperature around here in the Mojave Desert changes up to fifty or sixty degrees in a single day." Another example: "If you buy this car on payments, it will only cost you $5 per day." This kind of reasoning allows further incremental changes to be accepted without concern for the real and cumulative effect.

7) *Hypothesis Contrary to Fact* – reasoning how things might have turned out if different steps were taken in the past. It is also called "Monday-morning quarterbacking." Reasoning of this sort is pointless, because the changes cannot be produced.

8) *Distinction without a Difference* – using language to rename or redescribe an event or entity without any real difference being involved. "I'm not a bad driver, I'm a practical driver. I get more done if I write or read while driving."

9) *Fallacy of Fake Precision* – using mathematical claims that cannot be proven. Statistical facts are often asserted in such a way that they distort the truth. "73 percent of the American population believes in the moral correctness of capital punishment." It is impossible to document the opinion of every person in the United States regarding capital punishment.

10) *Gambler's Fallacy* – occurs when one believes that the probability of winning is influenced by the number of times one participates in a game situation. If a betting arrangement produces a 25 to 1 probability of losing, that ratio holds in every betting act. It does not change to 5 to 1 because one has lost in twenty betting acts.

11) *Appeal to Humor* – is sometimes used to avoid a logical defense, especially if the evidence in a defense is weak or unavailable. Humor tends to sidetrack poorly trained minds. Humor is an evasive tactic.

12) *Inference from a Label* – assuming that the name brand or title of something provides sufficient information to form solid conclusions about product service or institutional integrity. "World's finest chocolate" does not guarantee that it is indeed the best chocolate in the world. "Department of Defense" does not guarantee that the activities and experiments of the Defense Department are in fact good for or protecting the best interests of civilians and soldiers.

13) *Complex Question* – a question designed to direct the individual to a specific choice or conclusion. "Have you stopped beating your spouse?" presupposes that the beating is or has taken place. To answer yes or no would imply responsibility.

14) *Appeal to Novelty* – arguing that something is better because it is "new."

15) *Rationalization* – coming up with plausible but false justification for a position that one is unwilling to defend on another and less acceptable basis.

Reference: *Attacking Faulty Reasoning*, T. Edward Damer

famacide – n. a slanderer; the death of a reputation

famulus – n. an assistant, especially of a scholar and, at one time, a medieval sorcerer

fanfaron – n. a boaster; empty bragger; also *fanfaronade* – n. boastful talk

Faraday, Michael (1791–1867) – a British philosopher of science, whose story in chemistry and physics is an inspirational achievement in the history of experimental science.

Coming from a very poor family and having no formal training beyond elementary school, Faraday possessed a natural curiosity about chemistry and electricity. At age fourteen, Faraday's future changed when he acquired an apprenticeship with a bookbinder-seller, George Riebau. This gave him access to a library and free education. He was especially influenced by Isaac Watts's *The Improvement of the Mind*. He used many of Watts's principles in his research. In 1831, Faraday's endless tinkering uncovered the secrets of electromagnetic induction, with which, in later experiments, he identified the role of friction in the creation of electric power. Part of his success is due, strangely enough, to the fact that he was not trained in the mathematics of his day. This allowed (forced) him to find his own theoretical explanations for the way electricity works. His chemical experiments, equally representative of his strong independent curiosity, yielded the knowledge for liquefaction of chlorine gas.

F

"I am persuaded that all persons may find in natural things an admirable school for self-instruction, and a field for the necessary mental exercise; that they may easily apply their habits of thought, thus formed, to a social use; and that they ought to do this, as a duty to themselves and their generation."

Michael Faraday, *Observations on Mental Education*

Reference: *Faraday Rediscovered*, eds. F. A. James and David Gooding

farraginous – adj. made of mixed materials

fascism – n. a twentieth-century political philosophy originating in Italy and associated with Nazism. Fascism emphasizes strong authoritarian leadership, extreme nationalism, and militarism to achieve its social objectives. These objectives include regulation of a minimum wage, confiscation of property belonging to religious institutions, governance through a single-party state, and state control of values and pedagogies in educational systems.

Fascism is built on social Darwinian values that promote purification of a people through elimination of biologically weak and degenerate individuals. Fascism advocates dictatorial action, propaganda, and violence to bring about the creation of a perfect society. It forbids political dissent, and thus, it restricts freedom of speech, intellectual freedom, and freedom of the press.

Fascism has been promoted to various degrees in various forms and includes historical proponents in Giovanni Gentile, Benito Mussolini, Adolf Hitler, and Francisco Franco.

References: *The Mass Psychology of Fascism*, Wilhelm Reich; *The Doctrine of Fascism*, Giovanni Gentile

fastidious – adj. having high and sometimes capricious standards; difficult to please

fastuous – adj. overbearing, haughty, arrogant

fatidic – adj. relating to prophecy or divination

fatuitous – adj. foolish; possessing poor judgment; also *fatuity* – n. stupidity; marked inability to honor fact

faute de mieux – n. fr. French, meaning "for lack of anything better"

149

faze – v. to frighten; to cause to feel disconcerted; to cause discomposure

fealty – n. loyalty

fear – n. an emotional response to threats; the desire to flee. It is distinguished philosophically from cowardice, which is a moral weakness attended by fear. Fear is part of the cognitive process and is the conscious identification of danger. This is its rational form. In its irrational form, fear that is out of proportion to the respective cause is labeled a phobia. Beyond the level of phobias, persistent fear constitutes paranoia.

Gavin de Becker argues that fear is a virtue. As a forensic psychologist who specialized in the homicides of women, de Becker claimed that all the female homicides he investigated had "warning signs for the victim." The failure of the victim to act on fear and withdraw from dangerous relationships where warning signs were present, ended in the death of the victim.

> References: *The Psychology of Fear and Stress*, Jeffrey Gray; *The Anxious Self: Diagnosis and Treatment of Fears and Phobias*, Ronald A. Kleinknecht; *Children of Crisis: A Study of Courage and Fear*, vol. 1, Robert Coles; *The Gift of Fear*, Gavin de Becker

fecit – v. from the Latin, meaning "made by"

fecund – adj. fruitful, abundant, prolific

felicity – n. happiness

feminism – n. in philosophy and other academic disciplines, it is the concern with the rights of women compared with their historical subordination in societies throughout the world. Feminism now works on a number of issues connected with the second-class status of women, including the psychological, intellectual, and biological differences between men and women.

As in other fields, there is disagreement among feminists as to the nature and goals of feminist thought, especially in detailing the foundation of feminism as ethics. Obvious concerns begin with the criticism of Western thinkers like Aristotle, whose depreciation of domestic life contributed to a lack of appreciation for woman's spiritual and intellectual life. But, feminists themselves debate what values and principles should be used in defining feminism.

In the Netherlands, one finds the emergence of "postfeminism"; the consolidation of rights and dialogue for both women and men. This feminist view tries to move past the conflict model of feminism, seeking a completion of the transformation of woman's role in modern society. Sylviane Agacinski, Derrida's lover and mother of Derrida's third son, is a feminist philosopher who argues that women should retain the right to seduce or be seduced.

> References: *In a Different Voice: Psychological Theory and Woman's Development*, Carol Gilligan; *Third World Women and the Politics of Feminism*, eds. A. Mohanty, A. Russo, and L. Torres; *The Woman Beneath the Skin*, B. Duden

ferial – adj. pertaining to a holiday

ferine – adj. fr. "feral," meaning wild or untamed

ferity – n. fr. the Latin *feritas*, meaning "the condition of being wild"

fervent – adj. having warm or deep feeling; passionate; hot

Festschrift – n. fr. the German *fest*, meaning festival; plus *schrift*, meaning writing. It is a collection of articles contributed and published in honor of a writer or scholar

fetid – adj. stinking or rotten

fiasco – n. a complete failure

Fichte, Johann Gottlieb (1762–1814) – a German philosopher, influenced by Kant and recognized as the founder of German Idealism. Fichte argued for the priority of practical reason over theoretical reason. Fichte believed moral will to be the basis of idealism.

Fichte explained, prior to Hegel, that thinking is started on assumptions, realizes counterpoints, and synthesizes the conflict of ideas to achieve a new basis. Thus, the progress of thought is dialectical and formulated as: *Thesis + Antithesis = Synthesis*.

After meeting Kant, Fichte wrote *Versuch einer Kritik aller Offenbarung* (1792). It was mistakenly published without his name. Readers assumed it was the work of Kant. Critics praised the book. Kant stepped forward to explain it wasn't his work. Fichte's reputation was secure, and the book placed him alongside Kant.

Fichte adjusted Kant's view of "things-in-themselves." Kant had argued that things exist but are ultimately unknowable. Fichte argued that knowledge of existence is a knowledge of things and that one could move on from there. It is more correct to say, "one thinks one sees an object" than to say, "one sees an object." Awareness is an awareness of self and the world. The self and the world are assumptions upon which we work in a teleological and dialectical sense. This dialectical pursuit of knowledge has a moral objective: to increase our virtue through successful interaction with the world.

The moral focus of Fichte's epistemology characterizes his idealism. The human vocation is to exercise our duties in preserving freedom and protecting the rights of every person. This moral order is then identified with God as the *logos* in the world.

> Principal works: *An Attempt at a Critique of All Revelation* (*Versuch einer Kritik aller Offenbarung*), pub. 1792; *The Basis of All Theory of Science* (1794); *The Foundation of Natural Rights* (1796); *A System of Ethics* (1798); *The Vocation of Man* (1800); and *Way to a Blessed Life* (1806)
>
> *"There is nothing real, lasting, imperishable in me, but these two elements: the voice of conscience and my free obedience."*
>
> J. G. Fichte, *The Vocation of Man*
>
> Reference: *The Fundamental Principles of Fichte's Philosophy*, E. B. Talbot

filicide – n. the killing of a son or daughter; the act of

flaccid – adj. lacking firmness; without vigor

flagitious – adj. heinous; terrible

flaneur – n. a person without aims or goals; an intellectual fake

foible – n. a weakness of will

foist – v. to force another to accept by deceptive means

foment – v. to instigate; rouse

forensic – adj. suitable to public discussion or debate

forfend – v. to protect

forte – n. strength or skill

fortitudinous – adj. marked by strength

fortuity – n. chance; luck

Foucault, Michel (1926–1984) – a French philosopher of society. Foucault broke new ground in his interesting and disturbing books. He was interested in understanding the forces of domination and exclusion within societies, especially the manner in which definitions are used to marginalize those who do not conform to the theories of order mandated by societies. Reminiscent of the work of R. D. Laing, Foucault noted the social divisions created by labeling people "sane" or "insane." His moral writing analyzed why people are accepted or rejected by others. He called his encounter with Nietzsche "an inspiration."

Foucault's personal life seemed to generate his research: "fragments of an autobiography." His biographer, Didier Eribon, described his personality: "under one mask there is always another." Foucault wrote about the damaging psychological effects of institutions and political movements, with a seemingly personal knowledge and a deep command of historical facts. The attack on the well-being of the individual is an ongoing theme in his arguments.

Some of his most popular books addressed the challenge of sexuality and self-mastery. *The History of Sexuality* is an important book for anyone to read. Yet, while examining "self-mastery" in Greek philosophy, he seemed, according to Eribon, to depend on drugs, alcohol, and promiscuous homosexual behavior to escape from a pessimistic vision of society.

Foucault is the kind of philosopher who shocks and enlightens with adventurous and dark assessments of society's organizational structure. In this respect, and in death, he seems to be like Nietzsche; never quite able to get to the belief that life can become a happy experience (redemption).

Principal works: *Madness and Civilization* (1961); *The Order of Things* (1966); *Discipline and Punish: The Birth of the Prison* (1975); *The History of Sexuality*, vols. 1–3 (1976).

References: *Foucault*, Gilles Deleuze, trans. by Sean Hand; *The Foucault Reader*, ed. Paul Rabinow; *Michel Foucault*, Didier Eribon

fractious – adj. irritable

frangible – adj. breakable

fratricide – n. the act of killing a brother

Frege, Gottlob (1848–1925) – a German philosopher of logic and mathematics, Frege is recognized as the founder of modern mathematical logic. He was successful in showing that all mathematical work owes its structural order to the principles of logic.

Frege placed logic at the front of all philosophical investigations by showing that all branches of philosophy must progress with the tools of logic. Without a correct understanding of logic, all subsequent efforts to construct knowledge must be flawed. Frege had a direct influence on the work of Edmund Husserl, Bertrand Russell, and Ludwig Wittgenstein. The modern use of variables and the notion of quantifiers (to handle the problem of generality) are stock elements in symbolic logic.

Frege was successful in overturning the views of psychologism: the theory that the meanings of words must be accounted for in terms of mental processes that supposedly hold the true sense of a word.

> Principal works: *Begriffschrift* (1879); *Die Grundlagen der Arithmetik* (*The Foundations of Arithmetic*), pub. 1884; *Function and Concept* (1891); and *Grundgesetze der Arithmetik* (*The Basic Laws of Arithmetic*), pub. 1903.

> *"A definition of a concept must be complete; it must unambiguously determine, as regards any object, whether or not it falls under the concept. Thus there must not be any object as regards which the definition leaves in doubt whether it falls under the concept; though for us men, with our defective knowledge, the question may not always be decidable."*

> Gottlob Frege, *Grundgesetze der Arithmetik*

> Reference: *Frege and the Philosophy of Mathematics*, Michael Resnik

Freud, Sigmund (1856–1939) – an Austrian, Freud developed the general architecture of modern psychoanalysis. Through the influence of Jean-Martin Charcot (1825–1893) and Joseph Breuer (1842-1925), Freud discovered the basis of psychoanalytic practices. Freud became interested in the role of fantasies and the method of catharsis developed by Breuer. He made use of Breuer's hypnotic techniques, which developed into the theory of free association. Charcot, likewise, gave Freud important lessons in the use of hypnosis. Freud moved beyond simple hypnosis on the suspicion that neurosis included clever defenses, called repression, which prevented the analysis of causal factors. He proposed that sexuality played an important role in the development of the self. It was especially important, in Freud's view, to note the interaction between children and their parents in understanding the psychosexual self.

In *Three Contributions to the Theory of Sex* (1906), Freud presented ideas that influenced modern theories of personality development. And, during a period of self-analysis, Freud developed notions on the importance of dreams and their role in understanding the subconscious self. This led to publication of *The Interpretation of Dreams* in 1900, which is still considered an important work.

Principal works: *The Psychopathology of Everyday Life* (1904), *Wit and Its Relation to the Unconscious* (1905), *Lectures on Psychoanalysis* (1922), *Beyond the Pleasure Principle* (1922), *The Ego and the Id* (1923), *New Lectures on Psychoanalysis* (1933), and *Inhibitions, Symptoms, and Anxiety* (1936)

"In psychoanalytic treatment nothing happens but an exchange of words between the patient and the physician... Words and magic were in the beginning one and the same thing, and even today words retain much of their magical power. By words each of us can give to another the greatest happiness or bring about utter despair; by words the teacher imparts knowledge to the student; by words the orator sweeps his audience with him and determines its judgments and decisions. Words call forth emotions and are universally the means by which we influence our fellow creatures."

Sigmund Freud, *Introduction to Psychoanalysis*

References: *Psychoanalysis: Freud's Cognitive Psychology*, M. Erdelyi; *The Scientific Evaluation of Freud's Theories and Therapy: A Book of Readings*, eds. Roger Greenberg and Seymour Fisher

fugacious – adj. fleeting, temporary

fulgent – adj. very bright; dazzling

fulminate – v. to explode; to utter with denunciation; to put down in rank

funest – adj. sinister; fatal

furibund – adj. being furious or frenzied

fustigate – v. to beat with a stick; to criticize mercilessly

G

gaffe – n. a careless remark; a social blunder

galvanize – v. to coat with zinc; to make resistant to wear; also, to excite or motivate

Gandhi, Mohandas (1869–1948) – an Indian philosopher, lawyer, and social reformer, Gandhi extolled the ideological and spiritual values of Hinduism, Jainism, and Christianity (the Sermon on the Mount in the Gospel of Matthew). He utilized principles from Jainism, an appreciation of which he acquired through his mother's contact with Jain monks.

Gandhi's work advanced the use of pacifism and nonviolence as tools for conflict resolution and political protest. He argued for religious pluralism. He hoped that Hindus and Muslims would live side by side in India. This couldn't be achieved, and India separated itself into Muslim Pakistan and Hindu India in 1947. Gandhi held "fasts unto death" to force the acceptance of religious tolerance. Riots and killing followed in Punjab and Bengal. He was assassinated in 1948 by a Hindu nationalist named Nathuram Godse.

Gandhism emphasizes the use of "passive resistance" to counteract institutional forms of injustice. The title "*mahatma*" (great souled) was bestowed on him by the millions of Hindus who perceived him as a saint and holy man. He was singularly responsible for the expulsion of British rule in India.

Principal work: *Indian Home Rule* (1919)

"Passive resistance is a method of securing rights by personal suffering; it is the reverse of resistance by arms. When I refuse to do a thing that is repugnant to my conscience, I use soul-force. For instance, the government of the day has passed a law which is applicable to me. I do not like it. If, by using violence, I force the government to repeal the law, I am employing what may be termed body-force. If I do not obey the law, and accept the penalty for its breach, I use soul-force. It involves sacrifice of self."

Gandhi, *Indian Home Rule*

References: *Life of Mahatma Gandhi*, Louis Fischer; *Gandhi and Non-Violence*, William Borman

garrulous – adj. pointlessly talkative; excessive chatter; loquacious or wordy

gauche – adj. tactless; crude; lacking social skill or grace

geomancy – n. divination by throwing a handful of earth at random; also by drawing lines in the dirt

germane – adj. relevant; logically connected

gerontocracy – n. government by the old

Gestalt – n. fr. German meaning "a unified whole" that cannot be derived from the sum of its parts; Gestalt has importance for a philosophy of being. In psychotherapy, it has modified the philosophy of treatment for inner crisis to emphasize a balanced awareness of mind and body. Moreover, in emphasizing the person as a whole, it recommends a strong recognition of personal responsibility while resisting the interpretive or intrusive techniques of traditional psychoanalysis.

The development of Gestalt therapy was undertaken by several important thinkers, including Max Wertheimer (1880–1943), Wolfgang Kohler (1887–1967), and Kurt Koffka (1886–1941). Their work laid the foundation for the psychology of Fritz Perls (1893–1970). Perls used his talents to use, promote, and prove the value of Gestalt therapy.

Gestalt's holistic approach works on the individual's awareness, especially of his or her self in relation to the external world. Perls called Gestalt therapy "psychology of the obvious," training people to see what was happening in the present. Achieving wholeness demands a certain independence from authority models and the damaging effects of the superego. Balancing this objective with certain virtues like discipline has presented challenges to the theory. Removing obstacles to successful development does not eliminate the need for desirable character traits that can often help the individual move through obstacles. One of the differences between Gestalt therapy and traditional psychoanalytic work is the greater autonomy of the patient. Whereas psychoanalysis may encourage greater passivity and alienation from one's own rational power, Gestalt therapy creates a continual self-reference to thoughts and perceptions, with the therapist offering limited forms of guidance.

> *"Fortunately men believe in their will, and even if they are philosophically convinced of determinism, they will not make use of it in actual situations."*

Max Wertheimer, *Freedom: Its Meaning*, ed. Ruth Nanda Anshen (1940)

References: *Principles of Gestalt Psychology*, Kurt Koffka; *The Task of Gestalt Psychology*, Wolfgang Kohler; and *Gestalt Therapy Verbatim*, Frederick Perls, et al.

gesticulate – v. communicating with the use of gestures, in addition to words

gnathonic – adj. obsequious; servile

gnome – n. (not the same as the deformed dwarf creature of folklore who lives in the earth as the guardian of treasures) aphorism; a short but meaningful saying; also *gnomist* – n. writer of maxims; and *gnomology* – n. the study of maxims; also the collecting of

gnosticism – n. fr. the term *gnosis*, meaning knowledge. Gnosticism was originally a non-Christian sect. It became a Christian sect in the second century, claiming to have a mystical understanding and the only genuine knowledge of the meaning of Christ.

It was led by Valentine and Saturninus, who argued that Judaism was a corruption of religion, and the Old Testament was an invalid document. Gnosticism argued that Jesus was a human whose body was used by a supreme Divine Being. Christ had a stature beneath God and angels, but is linked to a demiurge and provides a connection to this supreme and unknowable Divine Being. Christ possesses a seed or spark of the Divine Being. This spark is "gnosis" and can be shared temporarily through Jesus.

References: *The Gnostic Religion*, Hans Jonas; and *The Gnostic Gospels*, Elaine Pagels

God – n. the supreme or ultimate reality; the Deity variously conceived in philosophy, theology, and religion as the holy, infinite reality expressed in the Bible. In Hebrew theology, God is a personal Divine Being who carries out his purpose as creator, judge, sovereign, and redeemer of the world.

"Why is there something rather than nothing?" (Schelling). God is an answer to this question. The idea of God is historically rooted in Judaism and Greek philosophy. In philosophy, the idea of God is open to definition. In theology, God is a presupposition, even a natural idea (Descartes). In popular religion God is Mind, Soul, Truth, Love, the Eternal Spirit, Life, All-knowing, and All-powerful.

Philosophy relies on reason alone in the investigation of God. Theology sees the idea of God as reason and the experience of God as faith. This faith is an intuitive recognition of God and an affirmation of his personal nature. Worship is an aspect of faith. In the Judeo-Christian model of God, the story of the Fall represents an alienation from God through reason. In the myth of the Fall, humanity is estranged from God through reason's creation of self-reliance. The relationship with God is compromised by eating the "forbidden fruit" (knowledge of good and evil). And, reason acquires the reputation of atheism, the Broken Covenant.

The debate about the nature and existence of God is the history of philosophy and religion in the West. The traditional proofs for the existence of God are:

1) *Cosmological Argument* – employed by both philosophers and theologians, the argument is presented with the following sorts of premises:

   a. Everything has a cause.
   b. Nothing is the cause of itself.
   c. The universe is a thing.
   d. The universe is not the cause of itself.

The conclusion, that God is the cause of the universe, also states that God is independent of causality, because God is the source of causality.

In Aristotle's presentation of the argument, God is called the "Unmoved Mover." It is important here to accept the functional differences between metaphysical causation and physical causation.

2) *Teleological Argument* – employs the concept of "design" (*telos* meaning design or purpose). It argues that nature reveals designs and patterns of almost infinite complexity, especially with regard to life forms. These designs and patterns reveal a type of logical architecture that is not the product of chance. If anything, the chance that there is a Designer is infinitely greater than the alternative.

William Paley (1745–1805) advanced this reasoning as the "Watchmaker Argument." If one finds a watch on a deserted island, the inductive conclusion that there is or was a human visitor is very strong. The watch implies a watchmaker. In the case of God, even if God no longer has a relationship to Creation (deism), God's history is tied up with the existence of a world.

3) *Ontological Argument* – St. Anselm of Canterbury (1033–1109); it plays on the observation that God is a being of the highest rank. A being of the highest rank cannot be lacking in a basic feature, meaning existence. St. Anselm avoided the problems of further definition in the formulation: "God is that being greater than which nothing can be conceived."

4) *Moral Argument* – employed by Immanuel Kant (1724–1804); this argument proposes the existence of moral consciousness as *a priori* (necessary). The source of this moral consciousness is God, the highest moral consciousness. The possibility of true goodness and justice does not lie with humanity. Ultimate justice is defined by the metaphysical properties of the soul and immortality. Only a universe where there is a God can be a morally sensible universe. Without God, the soul, and immortality, good and evil are nullified in death.

References: *God the Problem*, Gordon Kaufman; *Theological Investigations*, 22 vols., Karl Rahner; *Systematic Theology*, 2 vols., Wolfhart Pannenberg; *Naming the Whirlwind*, Langdon Gilkey; *Existence of God*, John H. Hick; *The Ontological Argument*, ed. Alvin Plantinga

Gödel, Kurt (1906–1978) – a Czech mathematician and logician who introduced undecidability theorems that came to be known as Gödel's Proof (1931). Gödel undermined deeply held assumptions about axiomatic methods in mathematics. Understanding Gödel's reasoning assumes an advanced understanding of mathematics (Nagel). Some of his theoretical contributions were used to develop geometric models for Einstein's theory of relativity. His work opened a new direction for mathematics and logic in the twentieth century.

As a youth, Gödel excelled at mathematics, linguistics, and religion. He was a devout theist all his life, professing belief in a personal God. He met and befriended Einstein in the 1930s and was a member of the Vienna Circle.

Gödel emigrated to the United States in 1940. He was a professor at the Institute for Advanced Study in Princeton, New Jersey, from 1953 until 1978. He died of malnutrition in 1978, as a result of persistent fear of being poisoned.

> References: *Gödel's Proof*, Ernest Nagel and James Newman; *Logical Dilemmas: The Life and Work of Kurt Gödel*, John W. Dawson

Good, the – n. an ideal fulfillment of morality or virtue. It implies values of prosperity, peace, the welfare of others, the elimination of suffering, and the production of happiness. It is a moral order in society. It is promotion of success in life and the possession of particular advantages. In Aristotle, it is honor, friendship, wisdom, character, health, courage, temperance, justice, and pleasure.

In the concept of *eudaemonia*, happiness, spiritual well-being, and flourishing represent the Good. The Good is also identified as something to be sought for its own sake and represents a duty (Kant).

Gorgias (483–380 BC) – a Sophist and the main character in Plato's dialogue *Gorgias*. He argued that knowledge is impossible. He summed up his position with three claims: (1) nothing exists; (2) even if something exists, we cannot know it due to the difference between thoughts and things; (3) even if things exist and we could know them, we could not really communicate knowledge due to the unbridgeable gap between minds.

According to Guthrie, Gorgias taught his students to tailor their words to the audience and the situation. Gorgias generated a good income as a teacher and public speaker. Plato ridiculed Gorgias as a fake in a dialogue by that name (eponym), as Gorgias did not respect the importance of truth and argued that only the art of persuasion has value.

> Principal work: *On Nature or the Non-existent*

> References: *A History of Greek Philosophy*, vol. 3, W. K. C. Guthrie; *Gorgias*, Plato

gorgonize – v. to hypnotize

G

grace – n. fr. Latin *gratus*, meaning beloved. In theology, grace is a reference to super-natural assistance God may grant to a believer aimed at sanctification. It is also virtue or moral excellence coming from God.

In the theology of St. Paul, grace refers to the favor God shows toward those who may appear undeserving or ungrateful but needful of God's redemptive presence. According to Paul, faith is connected to the reception of grace (Rom. 4:13–16, Eph. 2:5–8). In the theology of St. Augustine (354–430 AD), grace is connected to salvation and deemed necessary due to the Fall. Later, grace was attached to participation in the sacraments (i.e., sacramental grace). Sacramental grace became the mechanism of inner grace:

1) *Sanctifying grace* – the presence of God that enables persons to perform noble acts. This grace arrives through authentic participation in the Sacraments.
2) *Actual grace* – the general presence of God in persons, even the unbaptized, for the production of some specific act of goodness.
3) *Prevenient grace* – the spiritual influence that inspires a movement toward the soul's sanctification without involvement in the Sacraments. This grace is said to be gratuitous and unmerited.

In Greek mythology, the name Grace refers to three sister goddesses: Thalia (Grace of Blossom), Euphrosyne (Grace of Beauty), and Aglaia (Grace of Delight). They were daughters of Zeus and the Oceanid Eurynome. They attended to Aphrodite, Eros, and Dionysus.

References: *The Concept of Grace*, Philip Watson; *Divine Grace and Man*, Peter Fransen, trans. George Dupont; *The Dictionary of Classical Mythology*, Pierre Grimal

gramary – n. the lore of sorcery

gray eminence – n. power behind the throne or political position; a person who holds power but wields it through another

group therapy – n. a social approach to psychological counseling. Group therapy has many applications and uses, from psychotherapy to meditation. Therapy groups are comprised of five to fifteen people to facilitate meaningful personal dialogue.

In group therapy individuals try to accomplish a number of things: 1) experimen-tation with improved behavior; 2) emotional support and understanding from those with similar goals or problems; 3) the acquisition of new philosophies of life that aid the individual in reforming his or her own thoughts and values; and 4) the creation of affordable, yet effective counseling.

References: *Principles of Group Treatment*, Eric Berne; *Basic Approaches to Group Psychotherapy and Group Counseling*, ed. George Gazda

Guevara, Che (1928–1967) – an Argentine doctor who became a social activist and Communist guerilla. Guevara achieved fame through his paramilitary actions and his association with Fidel Castro. He worked closely with Castro in the early days of Castro's dictatorship, where he was given important leadership opportunities. He adopted a Marxist-Leninist philosophy while acting as a physician for the poor. He witnessed poverty, starvation, and disease, all of which radicalized his social activism. He blamed unregulated capitalism and political corruption for the problems of the poor, and he argued that violence was necessary to produce authentic change.

Guevara's heroic actions and ideology brought him into personal contact with Jean-Paul Sartre, Simone de Beauvoir, Ernest Hemingway, and world leaders of the time.

In 1965, Guevara left Cuba and traveled to Bolivia to organize a resistance force. His skills as a guerilla fighter were too advanced for the regular Bolivian army to counter, but he had difficulty recruiting a large force to overthrow the government. He was disappointed to learn that many of the Bolivian peasants he was fighting for had turned against him and become informants. Two years later, his guerilla force was annihilated in a confrontation with a Bolivian military force that had been trained by international experts. It is believed that the US government, the CIA, and US Special Forces played a role in the capture that led to his execution.

Principal works: *Guerilla Warfare* (1961); and *Guerilla Warfare: A Method* (1966)

References: *Che's Guerilla War*, Regis Debray; *The Black Beret: The Life and Meaning of Che Guevara*, Marvin Resnik; *Che Guevara, Paulo Freire, and the Pedagogy of Revolution*, Peter McLaren

gynarchy – n. government by women

gyrovague – n. itinerant monk, especially one who travels between monasteries

habitude – n. usual state of mind; disposition

haecceity – n. the quality that gives something its individuality

hagiocracy – n. government by those deemed holy or spiritually enlightened

hagiolatry – n. the worship of saints

hajj – n. annual pilgrimage to Mecca

halcyon – adj. bearing calmness, peace, happiness, and prosperity

Hammarskjöld, Dag (1905–1961) – a Swedish moral philosopher, Lutheran Christian, and international leader. Hammarskjöld served as secretary general of the United Nations from 1953–1961. He received the Nobel Peace Prize posthumously in 1961. Suspicious circumstances surrounded his death. At the time, he was being criticized by the USSR for sending a peacekeeping force to the Congo. He was killed in a plane crash in the Congo. The accident was never fully investigated. Two theories emerged, that the plane was either shot down, or it was brought down by an act of mechanical sabotage.

Hammarskjöld's only book, *Markings*, became a modern classic on personal spirituality. It reflects the influence of Meister Eckhart and Jan van Ruysbroeck. Some of the poems are written in haiku form.

Principal work: *Markings*, trans. by Leif Sjoberg and W. H. Auden (1964)

"Tired and lonely, so tired the heart aches.
Meltwater trickles down the rocks, the fingers are numb, the knees tremble.
It is now, now, that you must not give in."
"On the path of the others are resting places, places in the sun where they meet.
But this is your path, and it is now, now that you must not fail."
"Weep if you can, weep, but do not complain. The way chose you—and you
must be thankful."

July 6, 1961, Dag Hammarskjöld, *Markings*

Reference: *Dag Hammarskjöld Revisited*, ed. Robert S. Jordan

hapax legomenon – n. Gr. meaning a word or group of words of which there is only one recorded use

haplography – n. a copying error by which a letter(s) that should be repeated is omitted (e.g., "repition" for "repetition")

Harnack, Adolf von (1851–1930) – a German theologian and the main advocate of liberal theology in the nineteenth century, Harnack taught Karl Barth and Dietrich Bonhoeffer. For Harnack, liberal theology meant a complete commitment to reason and faith. It meant that theology had to become more than moral philosophy defended on Divine authority. Harnack defended "doubt" as the essence of intellectual honesty, a kind of sequel to Cartesianism necessary for good theology.

Harnack advocated unrestricted investigation into the historical Jesus, criticized liberal and orthodox theology, argued that the miracles of Jesus did not happen, and that Christian theology contained a Greek influence that confused the meaning of dogma. All this produced the question, "How can we know who Jesus is, when he is buried beneath two thousand years of interpretation and speculation?"

Principal works: *What Is Christianity?* (1901), *History of Dogma* (1897), *Essays on the Social Gospel* (1907), and *Christianity and History* (1896)

References: *Harnack and Troeltsch: Two Historical Theologians*, Wilhelm Pauck; *The Reality of Christianity: A Study of Adolf von Harnack as Historian and Theologian*, G. Wayne Glick

H

hebephrenia – n. a type of split personality disorder, allied to puberty; characterized by childish emotional responses

hebetate – v. to make dull or inert. Also "hebetude" – n. the state of being dull or lethargic

hedonism – n. the philosophy of pleasure. Hedonism is studied under the related concerns of ethics and psychology. Ethical hedonism argues that we "ought" to pursue a life that makes the greatest use of pleasure. Psychological hedonism argues that we must, as a type of nature instinct, act from a motive to derive pleasure. The later view incorporates behavioristic assumptions about human life and diminishes the role of free choice.

Aristippus the Cyrenaic, a student of Socrates, argued that the virtues of pleasure are self-evident. People should use pleasure as their principal source of happiness. Pleasure should be maximized to outweigh pain. Pain is another self-evident fact that supports the value of hedonism.

Epicurus argued that happiness is a state of tranquility. The goal of life is to maximize enjoyment and use pleasure wisely. He warned that some pleasures lead to great pain, so they should be avoided. Fear is not an enjoyment, so it needs to be countered by courage. He argued that people are often unhappy, because they experience anxiety about death, or they are worried about what the gods may be plotting.

Foucault argued that people are led away from the pursuit of pleasure to make them docile and practical servants of the status quo. He viewed hedonism as proof of autonomy. He found communitarian living distasteful and confining. Individuals should define their own purpose and avoid universal morality (Nietzsche), because it causes a kind of slavery. The enjoyment of life becomes difficult in organized society. Foucault's defense of hedonism as autonomy sets a trend for postmodernism.

Critics of hedonism, on the other hand, point to its narcissistic values and how they may be destructive of higher moral values, including the welfare of spouses, children, and families.

References: *The Use of Pleasure*, Michel Foucault; and *Pleasure and Desire*, Justin C. B. Gosling

Hegel, George Wilhelm Friedrich (1770–1831) – a German idealist philosopher, Hegel influenced Karl Marx and, thus, helped to shape the philosophy of dialectical materialism (communism). Hegel viewed life as an organic process infused with a spiritual Absolute. He attempted to stay between materialism and pantheism, arguing that while there is unity in reality, it is a complex arrangement.

The hallmark of Hegel's philosophy is the special definition he provides for "dialectic." Becoming is a consequence or result of triadic movement explained as *thesis + antithesis = synthesis* (Fichte). Each synthetic conclusion becomes a new thesis. This understanding uses the assumption that all of reality is rationality or thought. Absolute Spirit or Thought acts as a kind of polarity that draws forth the organic process.

Hegel's views are influenced by the philosophies of Kant and Fichte. Philosophers influenced by Hegel include Kierkegaard, von Clausewitz, Feuerbach, Engels, Marx, Merleau-Ponty, and Foucault. Hegel's writings became part of the Marxist canon and dialectical materialism.

> Principal works: *The Phenomenology of Mind* (1807); *Philosophy of Right* (1821); and *Philosophy of History* (1837)
>
> *"The history of the world begins with its general aim, the realization of the idea of spirit, only in an implicit form, that is, as nature; a hidden, most profoundly hidden, unconscious instinct; and the whole process of history is directed toward rendering this unconscious impulse a conscious one."*
>
> G. W. F. Hegel, *Philosophy of History*
>
> References: *Reason and Revolution: Hegel and the Rise of Social Theory*, Herbert Marcuse; *Hegel: Texts and Commentary*, Walter Kaufman; *The Religious Dimension in Hegel's Thought*, E. L. Fackenheim; *Hegel: A Re-examination*, J. N. Findlay

hegira – n. a journey undertaken to escape from a dangerous or undesirable life

Heidegger, Martin (1884–1976) – a German philosopher and one of the main representatives of existentialism. Heidegger is also known for his early support of Hitler, probably the consequence of a naïve anticipation of Nietzsche's views in German politics and unpleasant features of his own personality. This circumstantial *ad hominem* notwithstanding, Heidegger's analysis of existence also exhibits the influence of Edmund Husserl, his teacher. By 1935, he had become academically critical of the Nazi use of Nietzsche's thought as propaganda, but found it hard to take back his missteps. Though he sought the support of Karl Jaspers after WWII, Jaspers refused to exonerate Heidegger.

Favorite themes in Heidegger's thought include the notions of *Angst* (anxiety), *Dasein* (being), and *Sorge* (concern). Anxiety includes a recognition of one's finitude and thus, the issue of one's death or non-being. *Dasein* issues in the notion of authentic existence, which is linked to *Sorge*. The individual who lacks authentic concern regarding being is unable to discover one's self, unable to produce originality of thought, and is submissive to the crowd. In reflection, one becomes aware of nothingness or non-being and, thus, also being. Heidegger tries to uncover the relationship between being and nothingness. The work of reflection must also, then, comprehend the role of time in existence.

Dasein involves three aspects:

1) *understanding* – seeing the purpose and interconnectedness of things
2) *mood* – describes our attitude toward Being. It will lie somewhere between the attitude of joy and exuberance on the one hand, and despair on the other hand. It reflects the way in which the world appears and exists for us.
3) *discourse* – the formulation of a language to express what it is that we understand and experience

In nearly all of Heidegger's thought there is a push into ontological reflection. His works are an important resource for speculations on metaphysics and mysticism, and they are considered a logical extension of Husserl's phenomenology.

Principal works: *Being and Time* (1927), *The Basic Problems of Phenomenology* (1928), *What Is Metaphysics?* (1929), *What Is Thinking?* (1954), and *Phenomenology and Theology* (1970)

References: *The Philosophy of Martin Heidegger*, J. L. Mehta; *Martin Heidegger*, John MacQuarrie; *Heidegger and Nazism*, Victor Farias, trans. by P. Burrell and G. R. Ricci; *The Mystical Element in Heidegger's Thought*, John D. Caputo

heliolatry – n. worship of the sun

henotheism – n. recognizing several gods but the worship of one

heortology – n. the study of religious festivals

Heraclitus (540–475 BC) – a Greek pre-Socratic philosopher, Heraclitus was often called "the dark philosopher," as he was pessimistic about religion and democratic politics.

As an ancient forerunner to process philosophy, Heraclitus focused on the problem of "change." His observation that everything changes led him to suppose that the underlying reality is fire (logos). In fire one finds constant transformation or "flux." Furthermore, the changes one witnesses in nature are not random, so there must be some ordering and universal *logos* (God). This universal logos or fire, in turn, implies that everything is one in a pantheistic sense.

Heraclitus viewed the various types of strife as part of the full definition of reality. Change or flux requires a constant conflict of opposites. Good and evil, war and peace, are simply extensions of reality that should be viewed as normal features and not as calamities that can be prevented. What appears to be chaotic is actually part of a larger order and harmony.

Principal work: *Fragments of Heraclitus*

"War is both king of all and father of all, and it has revealed some as gods, others as men; some it has made slaves, others free."

"To God, all things are beautiful, good and just; but men have assumed some things to be unjust, others just."

"It is hard to fight against impulse; whatever it wishes, it buys at the expense of the soul."

"Men who love wisdom must be inquirers into very many things indeed."

Heraclitus, *Fragments*

Reference: *The Art and Thought of Heraclitus*, ed. C. H. Kahn

heresiology – n. the study of heresies (deviations from religious doctrine)

hermaphrodite – n. one having male and female sex organs; a homosexual; a person possessing or exhibiting male and female qualities

hermeneutics – n. the science of interpretation; methods of interpretation, especially with regard to religious manuscripts such as the Bible. It stems from the Greek *hermeneutikos*, meaning interpretation.

1) In philosophy, hermeneutics advances research by systematic evaluation and observation of phenomena, the interpretation of what exists. Martin Heidegger's (1884–1976) work in phenomenology employed some of the techniques recommended by Friedrich Schleiermacher (1768–1834), especially on miracles and the hermeneutical work in theology. Eduard Spranger (1882–1963) also depended upon hermeneutical technique to explore ideal human types. He was the author of *Forms of Life: A Sketch* (1914), and *Problems of Cultural Morphology* (1936).

2) In theology, hermeneutics is embedded within the aims of Scriptural exegesis. Exegesis is the work of explaining textual meaning. Hermeneutics is the construction of procedures for validating interpretations. For one thing, it works on the awareness of ambiguity in sacred texts. This concern is an outcome of the many theological disagreements that arise from the study of sacred texts. The work of Wilhelm Dilthey (1833–1911), author of *Types of World View* (1911) and *Studies on the Foundations of the Spirit* (1905), helped to show the limitations of historical analysis of reality through hermeneutical sensitivity, believing history and philosophy to be relative to specific times. The pure meaningfulness of each age is essentially lost in history-keeping. According to Dilthey, this limits the interpretational power of both cultural and spiritual sciences (*Geisteswissenschaften*) to make clear the real nature of spiritual life in the past.

References: *An Introduction to the New Hermeneutic*, Paul J. Achtemeier; *Pattern and Meaning in History*, Wilhelm Dilthey; *Contemporary New Testament Interpretation*, William G. Doty; *Existence and Faith* and *Jesus Christ and Mythology*, Rudolf Bultmann; and *Word and Faith*, Gerhard Ebeling

Hesperian – adj. fr. the Greek *hesperos*, meaning evening, thus western. Also *Hesperus* – n. evening star; Venus

hetaera – n. a cultured courtesan in ancient Greece; demimondaine; female companion. Also, *hetaerism* – n. a social system wherein women are common property.

Reference: *Goddesses, Whores, Wives, and Slaves: Women in Classical Antiquity*, S. Pomeroy

heuristic – adj. exploratory

hiatus – n. a gap or break, especially in a sequence

hieratic – adj. pertaining to sacred things

hierocracy – n. government by priests

Hinduism – n. the original religion of India. "Hindu" means "person of the Indus Valley." Hinduism contains a range of ideas from determinism to existentialism. Hindu beliefs are contained in two primary sources, the Upanishads and the Bhagavad Gita.

A central theme is that reality is always changing but never changing. This logical paradox is subsumed under the term "Brahman." Only Brahman is reality. Everything else, including souls and things, is a manifestation of Brahman.

"Atman" is the Hindu concept of soul or self. The atman, as the true self, is connected with Brahman. The empirical world is a set of appearances or illusions, depending on Brahman. The self or atman is Brahman appearing in limited form.

Hinduism recognizes four primary values: *Kama, Artha, Dharma,* and *Moksha.* Kama is the base value and refers to pleasure. Artha means status and wealth. Dharma is higher and represents law and the duty toward its enactment. And, Moksha is enlightenment and the highest value. These values correspond roughly to stages of life, with Moksha generally occurring with age.

The law of *karma* provides for the positive or negative destiny of souls, though no soul in Hinduism is eternally lost. Karma is a belief in strict cause and effect within the framework of moral life. The existence one experiences is an outcome of moral choices that influence the spiritual well-being of the individual. The philosophy of karma is the source of the caste system: Brahmans (rulers), Kshatriyas (warriors), Vaishys (merchants, skilled artisans, farmers), and Shudras (untouchables).

The stages of life that correspond roughly to the four values are called *ashramas.* These stages point the individual to spiritual liberation. First, from 0–25 years the practitioner is a student. Second, from about 25–50 years the practitioner is expected to marry and become a parent. Third, from 55–70 years, roughly, is a period of reflection, generativity, and meditation. And, in the fourth ashrama the practitioner seeks full union with Brahman by means of self-mastery, aspiring to reach liberation from this world: *moksha*.

Yoga is a special type of physical and spiritual training that seeks to unify atman and Brahman. Traditional yoga is practiced under a master or *guru*. Training is closely supervised and demands the elimination of all material distractions. In folk yoga, training is not as rigorous and is carried out in a group. Folk yoga is more ritualistic with its use of such aids as incense and animal sacrifice. Both forms of yoga claim to strive toward enlightenment and liberation. Together, there are four types of yoga: Jnana (knowledge of being itself), Bhakti (practice of love), Karma (practice of work), and Raja (movement through four layers of the self: the body, conscious mind, subconscious mind, and deep mind, or Being itself).

References: *The Indian Way*, John M. Koller; *A Critical Study of Hinduism*, Sarasvati Chennakesavaan; *A Survey of Hinduism*, Klaus K. Klostermaier

historicism – n. the theory that events are predetermined; history as a standard of value; events are unaffected by human action and thought

histrionics – n. exaggerated, insincere speech or conduct

Hobbes, Thomas (1588–1679) – a British political philosopher, best known for the phrase, "Man is a wolf to his fellow man." With the quality of mathematical thought, Hobbes hoped to create similar quality in the construction of political, psychological, and social theory.

Hobbes is known as the father of totalitarianism, because of his preferences in the social contract between rulers and their subjects. Hobbes held a pessimistic view of life in the state of nature. There, "Life is solitary, poor, nasty, brutish, and short," and "Man is a wolf to his fellow man." He believed that the way to tame the vicious character of the human race was through the establishment of his strict "social contract" weighted toward the ruler.

In nature, there is a "right of all to all." There is a type of brutal equality. One takes what one can, and does what one can, to pursue one's own self-interest. Hobbes believed that in nature the pervading mood is fear, especially fear of a violent death. His psychological behaviorism explained human action under a set of "aversions" and "appetites." Combine this with egotistical human behavior and the result is anarchy.

The social contract was a way out of the natural condition of anarchy: "I authorize and give up my right of governing myself, to this man, or to this assembly of men, on this condition, that thou give up thy right to him, and authorize all his actions in like manner." One of the provisions of this contract, according to Hobbes, is that there can be no "unjust law." This is because justice and law begin with a sovereign. Justice, for Hobbes, means the universal application of law and universal obedience to that law.

> Principal works: *The Citizen* (1642), *Concerning Body* (1655), *Concerning Man* (1658), and *Leviathan* (1651)

> *"If the essential rights of sovereignty . . . be taken away, the Commonwealth is thereby dissolved, and every man returneth into the condition and calamity of a war with every other man, which is the greatest evil that can happen in this life."*

> Thomas Hobbes, *Leviathan*

> References: *Thomas Hobbes and Political Theory*, ed. M. G. Dietz; *Hobbes's System of Ideas*, J. W. N. Watkins

holism – n. a philosophical theory that natural phenomena are entities, more than the sum of different parts

holophrasis – n. the use of a single word to express ideas contained in a whole sentence or phrase

homocentric – adj. having the same center

homomorphism – n. likeness in form

homothetic – adj. similarly positioned

hormic – adj. purposeful; teleological

Horney, Karen (1885–1952) – born Karen Danielson, she was a German psychologist and dean of the American Institute of Psychoanalysis (1941). She attended the University of Freiburg, University of Göttingen, and the University of Berlin in spite of her father's disapproval. Her father was a ship's captain who was an aloof disciplinarian. Although he tried to compensate for his hardness by bringing Karen gifts from faraway countries, a good father-daughter relationship did not develop. During medical school, she married Oskar Horney, with whom she had three daughters. Oskar Horney was also a disciplinarian. The stress this created almost caused Karen Horney to kill herself by swimming out to sea. She eventually separated from Oskar Horney and moved to the United States with her three daughters in 1930. She was quickly recognized as a gifted teacher and psychoanalyst.

Horney's work provided important criticism of Freud's theories, and she is classified as Neo-Freudian. She pointed out Freud's male-biased view with regard to the mental life of women. She argued that sexual needs and aggressive interests are not as significant as the achievement of inner security and peace. She also believed it is important to downplay deterministic psychology in favor of models that demonstrate the creative opportunities for change and improvement. She argued that the differences between men and women are not significant but are mostly the result of social and cultural influences. She became interested in the work of Alfred Adler, Erich Fromm, and Abraham Maslow. She had a failed personal relationship with Fromm. Karen Horney's approach to neurosis identified certain "needs" as causes.

These causes of neurosis include: need for approval, need for a life partner, need for power, need to exploit and dominate others, need for prestige, need for personal achievement, need for recognition, need for self-sufficiency and autonomy, need for solitude and distance from others, and need for perfection. Not all these causes have to be active to produce neurosis. Delays in the fulfillment of these needs generate neurosis. At the same time, attempting to fulfill these needs may create contradictions that also foster neurosis. She extended this definition to other mental conditions, such as narcissism, which she saw as unnatural but a by-product of a certain upbringing.

Each individual, according to Horney, seeks self-idealization based in his or her achievements. The narcissist wants indulgence and does not seek self-idealization built on achievements. The narcissist probably desires omnipotence, but is guilty of a facade.

Solutions to neurosis are achieved in three ways: expansive solutions—perfectionism and aggressive-vindictive behavior; self-effacement solutions—submission to others and abandonment of self-idealization; and resignation solutions—detachment from others.

Principal works: *Neurosis and Human Growth* (1950); *New Ways in Psychoanalysis* (1939); *The Neurotic Personality of Our Time* (1937)

References: *The Feminist Legacy of Karen Horney*, Marcia Westkott; *Karen Horney: A Psychoanalyst's Search for Self-understanding*, Bernard J. Paris; *A Mind of Her Own: The Life of Karen Horney*, Susan Quinn

hortatory – adj. the characteristic of urging or exhorting

human condition – n. in philosophy, the object of study for purposes of defining the nature and destiny of humanity. Existentially, it is awareness of the finitude of life in the context of the infinite. It is also a study of the perils of life; the constants and fatalisms that exist in every life.

> *"Nothing can be meaner than the anxiety to live on, to live on anyhow and in any shape; a spirit with any honor is not willing to live except in its own way."*

George Santayana (1863–1952), *Winds of Doctrine*

> *"Human life must be some kind of mistake."*

Arthur Schopenhauer (1788–1860), *Vanity of Existence*

> *"To have contemplated human life for forty years is the same as to have contemplated it for ten thousand years."*

Marcus Aurelius (121–180 AD), *Meditations*

> *"Let us imagine a number of men in chains and all condemned to death, where some are killed each day in the sight of the others, and those who remain see their own fate in that of their fellows and wait their turn, looking at each other sorrowfully and without hope. It is an image of the condition of humanity."*

Blaise Pascal (1623–1662), *Pensées*

> *"My wish for myself and for those whom I love is to be successful now, and now to meet with a check; thus passing through life amid alternate good and ill, rather than with perpetual good fortune. For never yet did I hear of anyone succeeding in all his undertakings, who did not meet with calamity at last, and come to utter ruin."*

Herodotus (ca. 500 BC), *History*

H

Hume, David (1711–1776) – a Scottish philosopher and contributor to epistemology. Hume concluded that all knowledge is the result of sensory impressions. Inward impressions are the emotions (e.g., love, hate, anger, and patience). Outward impressions are the experiences of the senses themselves (e.g., color, taste, sound, tactility, and auditory experiences). These experiences are the basis of all ideas. The ideas themselves hang together in a type of order called "association of ideas." Association is made possible by principles such as resemblance between experiences, contiguity in time, and observation of cause and effect.

Hume's analysis of causality utilizes an inductive process of reasoning. A cause *x* does not necessarily entail an effect *y*. Causal relationships are contingent relationships. Contingency varies from one phenomenon to the next. Thus, there is always a "probability factor" in causal explanations. Custom, repetition of experience, or habit incline us to expect certain effects, but there is no logical necessity that permits us to predict with certainty what will occur among events. The anticipation of certain effects is merely a psychological anticipation based on prior experience.

Ultimately, Hume is pessimistic about knowledge outside the domain of experience. Ideas about God and cosmology are never really justified in any logical sense, since these represent notions beyond the ground warranted by experience. But, it is natural for the human mind to seek out higher and higher explanations of design and order, so the notion of God and a cosmology are too tempting for most people to discard in the absence of other explanations.

Principal works: *Treatise on Human Nature* (1739), *An Inquiry Concerning Human Understanding* (1748), and *Dialogues Concerning Natural Religion* (1779)

". . . while the body is confined to one planet, along which it creeps with pain and difficulty, the thought can in an instant transport us into the most distant regions of the universe; or even beyond the universe, into the unbounded chaos, where nature is supposed to lie in total confusion. What never was seen, or heard of, may yet be conceived; nor is anything beyond the power of thought, except what implies an absolute contradiction.

"But though our thought seems to possess this unbounded liberty, we shall find, upon a nearer examination, that it is really confined within very narrow limits, and that all this creative power of the mind amounts to no more than the faculty of compounding, transposing, augmenting, or diminishing the materials afforded us by the senses and experience...[A]ll the materials of thinking are derived either

from outward or inward sentiment: the mixture and composition of these belongs alone to the mind and will. Or, to express myself in philosophical language, all our ideas or more feeble perceptions are copies of our impressions or more lively ones."

David Hume, *An Inquiry Concerning Human Understanding*

References: *The Skeptical Realism of David Hume*, J. P. Wright; *David Hume*, Antony Flew; *Hume's Philosophy of the Mind*, J. Bricke

Husserl, Edmund (1859–1938) – a German philosopher, educated at the University of Vienna and the founder of phenomenology.

A phenomenon is any appearance of basic reality; it is the subject's confrontation with an experience. Phenomenology, for Husserl, is the science of description of subjective processes. Thus, it takes a Cartesian approach in analyzing the ego and its presentations. Phenomenology is fundamental to psychology, because it asserts the importance of logic in its methodology. Rational inquiry is a type of analysis of relational factors in one's experience of phenomena. Psychology oversteps the necessary establishment of logical principles in its analysis of the mind, since it is primarily an empirical science. Phenomenology is defined by the requirements of logic. Logic, like mathematics, is the study of necessary truths rather than contingent truths. Consciousness is seen as a collection or stream of intentional awareness, wherein mental objects point to other mental objects. Consciousness is always consciousness of phenomena. Logic is necessary to evaluate the coherence of relationships between ideas (mental objects) of phenomena.

Principal works: *Logical Investigations*, 2 vols. (1900); *Ideas on a Pure Phenomenology and Phenomenological Philosophy* (1913), and *The Crisis of European Science and Transcendental Phenomenology* (1936)

"If . . . we disregard any metaphysical purpose of the critique of cognition and confine ourselves purely to the task of clarifying the essence of cognition and of being an object of cognition, then this will be phenomenology of cognition and of being an object of cognition and will be the first and principal part of phenomenology as a whole."

Edmund Husserl, *The Idea of Phenomenology*

References: *Edmund Husserl's Project of Phenomenology in Ideas*, Erazim Kohak; *Edmund Husserl: Philosopher of Infinite Tasks*, Maurice Natanson

H

Huxley, Aldous Leonard (1894–1963) – an English philosopher of social themes and a critic of modern life. Huxley feared the abolition of religion, art, and philosophy through the evolution of technology. He sought truth through various mystical philosophies and experiences, including brief experimentation with alternative types of meditation. Huxley was repulsed by the conformity and superficiality of modern life, and he eventually transcended his own suffering through a philosophical awakening at Ramakrishna Monastery in Trabuco Canyon, California.

> Principal works: *Point Counter Point* (1928); *Brave New World* (1932); *The Doors of Perception* (1954); and *Heaven and Hell* (1956)

> References: *Aldous Huxley's Quest for Values*, Milton Birnbaum; *The End of Utopia*, Peter Firchow; *Huxley on God*, ed. Jacqueline H. Bridgeman

hydromancy – n. divination by means of water (e.g., baptism, holy water)

Hygeia – n. goddess of health in Greek mythology; thus, "hygiene"

hylomorphic – adj. made up of corporeal and spiritual matter. Also, "hylomorphism" – n. the view that real existence occurs only in material forms

hylotheism – n. the view that gods and matter are intimately related

hylozoism – n. the view that all matter is animated; a doctrine held by early Greek philosophers to account for "change"

hyperbole – n. deliberate exaggeration; as in René Descartes

hyperdulia – n. worship of the Virgin Mary above all other divine references

hypocorism – n. the use of pet names

hypostasis – n. in science, the condition of settling to the bottom, especially by a substance in a fluid. In theology, a reference to the fundamental divine substance of God as trinity. Thus, in metaphysical terms, an essential transcendent entity: also *logos*, world soul, or *nous* (mind).

hypothecate – v. to pledge something as security without giving up title or possession

hysteron proteron – n. a reversal of a rational or causal order; a logical fallacy in which the premise holds what is yet to be proved

I

iatric – adj. relating to medicine

id – n. in psychoanalysis, the source of primitive instinctual urges and drives; the directive force toward amoral, immediate gratifications. In the philosophy of Freud, the id represents the unconscious. In theory, it holds that the dynamic and often illogical properties of the psychosexual self are active. The id often influences human choice without regard for the external realities of life. The destructive potential of the unrestricted action of the id, through the pleasure principle, explains much of the suffering of humanity.

> References: *Essays on Ego Psychology*, Heinz Hartmann; *How Does Analysis Cure?*, Heinz Kohut; *Treating the Self*, Ernest Wolf

idealism – n. any system of thought that organizes itself and reality around the Greek term "idea," meaning "vision" or "contemplation." Idealism denies the material primacy of reality. Thus, if the world is not principally matter, idealism is also suspicious of knowledge built exclusively on the observation of matter. Laws of thought are more important to idealists than empirical data. Logical-spiritual approaches to reality are the key to discerning order and harmony. Idealism implies that views of the universe are dependent upon mind. Still, commitment to idealism varies from thinker to thinker:

1) *Subjective idealism* – holds that ideas alone exist. What appear to be objects are only perceptions. Perceptions are the only material to work with in the view of subjective idealism. The philosophy of George Berkeley (1685–1753), referred to as *immaterialism*, maintained that nothing ever exists without its being perceived. "To be is to be perceived" (*Esse est percipi*). In subjective idealism the knower, the subject mind, is seen as the center of the issue. There is nothing to say or think about so-called "things" if they are not perceived. Thus, it is argued that matter is a creation of mind. As a system of thought, subjective idealism is easily attacked due to its skepticism regarding the external world.

2) *Objective idealism* – does not deny the existence of an objective reality. Instead objective idealists maximize the existence of order and designs within nature to produce a philosophical mirror of that order and design. Objective idealism frequently works toward the identification of some Absolute source and remains committed to developing theory about the foundations of being. However, it does not allow self or subjectivity to override the dynamic flow of its logic, which involves an honoring of external reality. William Ernest Hocking (1873–1966) developed a type of objective idealism in *The Meaning of God in Human Experience* (1912). Hocking believed in the real, the pragmatic, and the ideal. He blended these assumptions into an effective analysis of human life and the relationship to God.

References: *The Idealist Tradition: From Berkeley to Blanshard*, ed. A. C. Ewing; and *Idealism: A Critical Survey*, 3rd ed., A. C. Ewing

idioglossia – n. speech invented for private communication; also, speech that is unintelligible, a consequence of mental pathology

illation – n. a deduction; a conclusion inferred

Imam – n. in Islam, a reference to a leader or guide. An imam is any person who is morally respected and has the competence to lead others in prayer and instruction. Among Sunnites, the imam is a successor of Muhammad. Among Shiities, the imam must have blood ties to Ali, the son-in-law of Mohammad.

Reference: *Islam*, Fazlur Rahman.

imbrute – v. to degrade to the level of a primitive animal

immolate – v. to kill or destroy by sacrificial practice

impanation – n. the doctrine that Christ is physically present in bread after consecration

impeccant – adj. without faults; perfect

impedimenta – n. objects that hinder progress

impercipient – adj. not perceiving

impetrate – v. to obtain by request

impolitical – adj. unwise; foolish

importune – v. to demand urgently; to solicit persistently to the point of being troublesome

imprecate – v. to curse; to invoke evil upon

improbity – n. lack of principle

impudicity – n. lack of shame

impugn – v. to attack or assault by argument

impuissant – adj. feeble; powerless

imputrescible – adj. incorruptible

in absentia – fr. Latin, meaning "in the absence of"

inchoate – adj. incomplete; having just begun

incondite – adj. unpolished; ill-composed

indigent – adj. poor; needy; without self-sufficiency

in flagrante delicto – n. fr. Latin, meaning "the very act of committing an offense"

infra dignitatem – adj. fr. Latin, meaning "beneath one's dignity"

ingeminate – v. to repeat, reiterate

innocuous – adj. harmless

insalubrious – adj. unhealthy

insentient – adj. without feeling or sensation

insidious – adj. seductively harmful; having a slow effect

insipid – adj. lacking in qualities that stimulate; also, tasteless

insouciance – n. lighthearted indifference

instinct – n. in psychology, a behavior that is peculiar and common to a species. It signifies a behavior that occurs on a timeline that seems similar in all members of the species. An action that is resistant to change or elimination and seems to be part of a design within the creature. Instinct includes hereditary and unalterable responses to environmental stimuli.

> References: *The Study of Instinct*, Nikolaas Tinbergen; *Animal Behavior: A Synthesis of Ethology and Comparative Psychology*, 2nd ed., Robert A. Hinde

intellection – n. the process of understanding

interdict – v. prohibit; prevent

interlocutory – adj. intermediate; not decisive

internecine – adj. mutually destructive; characterized by slaughter

intransigent – adj. unyielding; immovable; not to be influenced

inure – v. to condition the acceptance of something undesirable

invective – n. an abusive denunciation

inveigh – v. to attack verbally

invidious – adj. causing dislike

involuted – adj. complex

iracund – adj. angry; passionate

irascible – adj. easily angered

irrecusable – adj. not to be refused or turned down

irrefragable – adj. not to be denied; impossible to refute

irremeable – adj. offering no possibility of return; irreversible (e.g., a life history)

Islam – n. a Middle Eastern religion, *Islam* is translated as "peace." *Muslim* is trans-lated to mean "one who submits." Islam was founded by Mohammed (570–629 AD), the last in a line of prophets including Jesus. Mohammed was known for his honesty, generosity, spirituality, and ability to reconcile conflicts. Upon his marriage to a widow named Khadija, he began a process of meditation and is said to have received Divine revelations, which are recorded in the Koran.

Mohammed's concern for the poor and the politically weak became the basis of his social work. After much persecution, he established a successful community in Medina. This community became the nucleus for the eventual spread of Islam throughout the world.

Koran means "recitation." Other than the Koran, there is no central authority in Islam. It is the word of Allah, eternal and unchangeable. Thus, no translations from Arabic are considered valid. Muslims seek to memorize the full text in Arabic. It offers guidelines for daily existence, especially individual and social morality. It recommends five practices or pillars: the profession of faith, prayer five times each day, almsgiving, fasting during the month of Ramadan, and the holy pilgrimage to Mecca. Though the Five Pillars are also pre-Islamic, the religious manuscripts of Zoroastrianism, Judaism, and Christianity are considered corrupt and theologically useless for a correct understanding of the will of God.

The Five Pillars have their roots in Judaism and Christianity. As such, they are not original creations of Islam, rather Islam emerges from these traditions as a new form of monotheism (Hans Küng). Küng reminds us that Judaism and Christianity also possess the Five Pillars: profession of faith, prayer, almsgiving, fasting, and pilgrimage to the Holy Land.

There are three principal sects in Islam: Sunnites, Shiites, and Sufis. Sunna means "way" and Sunnites follow the way of Mohammed without the possibility of further interpretations or revelations. Shiites (from *Shia*, meaning "party") believe in valid successors of Mohammed, called *imams*. Sufis (*sufi* meaning "wool-clad") emphasize the inward path to salvation through meditation and asceticism. Sufism is apolitical and does not engage the use of jihad to spread Islam.

References: *Islam*, Fazlur Rahman; *What Is Sufism?*, Martin Lings; *Sacred Rage*, R. Wright; and *Islam: Past, Present and Future*, Hans Küng

Islamic philosophy – n. the views and thought of the Arab world. Islamic philosophy holds an interesting place in the transmission of Greek philosophy. As Greece declined, the Arab world provided the main advances in science, mathematics, medicine, literature, and philosophy. Greek-based Islamic thought played a major role in maintaining the momentum of discovery. Its principal philosophers included Al-Farabi (ca. 875–950), Al-Ghazali (1058–1111), Averroes (1126–1198), and Avicenna (980–1037). Through their work, the preservation of Aristotelian and Platonic writings and ideas at Alexandria became the basis for educating Europe in the twelfth and thirteenth centuries.

isocracy – n. government in which all people have an equal amount of power

isodynamic – adj. characterized by equality or uniformity of force

isomorphism – n. equal form; similarity of structure. Two groups of entities can be said to be isomorphic when a one-to-one correspondence can be established between members of one group and the members of another group.

jactation – n. self-congratulation; boasting

Jainism – n. an Indian religion that teaches a type of pluralistic realism. Embracing the notion of karma, Jainism teaches that the soul is enmeshed in a body as a result of physical attachments. Liberation is dependent upon the three jewels (*triratna*):

1) right belief or faith (*samyag-darsana*) in Jainist teachings
2) right knowledge (*samyag-jnana*) of nature as it is found, and
3) right conduct (*samyag-caritra*) by the values of truthfulness, detachment from things, chastity, and nonviolence. Jainism is atheistic but reserves a kind of divine status for liberated souls, who are then both immortal and omniscient.

The central document of Jainism is the Yagur Veda. Mahavira (598–527 BC) was the last great teacher of Jainism. Jainism survives today in isolated portions of India and also in Southern California.

> *"I renounce all killing of living beings, whether movable or immovable. Nor shall I myself kill living beings, nor cause others to do it, nor consent to it. As long as I live I confess, and blame, and exempt myself of these sins, in mind, speech, and body."*

> *"I renounce all vices of lying speech arising from anger or greed or fear or mirth."*

"I renounce all taking of anything not given, either in a village or a town or wood, either a little or much, of great or small, of living or lifeless."

"I renounce all sexual pleasure. I shall not give way to sensuality, nor cause others to do so, nor consent to their doing so."

Mahavira (attributed)

References: *The Jaina Path of Purification*, Padmanabh Jaini; *Outlines of Jaina Philosophy: The Essentials of Jaina Ontology, Epistemology, and Ethics*, Mohan L. Mehta

James, William (1842–1910) – an American philosopher of pragmatism, James was an advocate of philosophy for the average person. This meant that the value of philosophy lay in its potential to implement improvements in daily life. This might not occur without the development and application of critical reason. So, knowledge is for the sake of life. We should want to know things in order to improve our situation. James argued that this was a valid presupposition to thinking.

Since James was also a physician, his views reveal the functional and biological concerns of a man of medicine. His pragmatism emphasized truth or falsity of statements according to their ability to fulfill and satisfy our biological and emotional needs. True propositions lead to success and false propositions lead to failure. Expedience and practicality distinguish the thinking of James. As with the Greek term *pragmatikos*, James saw "acts" or "deeds" as the focal point of human understanding. True ideas are corroborated in actions. Verification of the merit of ideas comes from their practical application. They should be socially and individually effective.

In the characteristic of novelty, James saw proof of a pluralistic universe. Successful problem solving recognizes the existence of variety and multiplicity of choice. A universe that is monistic, absolutist, and undifferentiated would paralyze the will. Freedom to live intelligently requires options of thought and action.

Reason itself is secondary to experience. Reality is experience. Reason supplements this reality experience. Life is presented in pure sensual form, in a type of uncorrupted encounter before reason occurs. It is always somewhat beyond our rational comprehension for this reason.

Theologically, James advocated a type of cocreator theism. He perceived God as a companion, both morally and spiritually. As such, God is also limited in influence. God as finite cannot be a guarantor of a purely good world. God requires the assistance of humanity to produce good in this world.

Principal works: *Psychology*, 2 vols. (1890), *The Will to Believe* (1897), *Varieties of Religious Experience* (1902), *Pragmatism* (1907), and *The Meaning of Truth* (1909)

"The whole function of philosophy ought to be to find out what definite difference it will make to you and me, at definite instants of our life, if this world formula or that world formula be the true one."

William James, *Pragmatism*

"My experience is what I agree to attend to. Only those items which I 'notice' shape my mind—without selective interest, experience is an utter chaos. Interest alone gives accent and emphasis, light and shade, background and foreground—intelligible perspective, in a word. It varies in every creature, but without it the consciousness of every creature would be a gray chaotic indiscriminateness, impossible for us even to conceive."

William James, *Psychology*

"Outside of their own business, the ideas gained by men before they are twenty-five are practically the only ideas they shall have in their lives. They cannot get anything new. Disinterested curiosity is past, the mental grooves and channels set, the power of assimilation gone. If by chance we ever do learn anything about some entirely new topic we are afflicted with a strange sense of insecurity, and we fear to advance a resolute opinion. But with things learned in the plastic days of instinctive curiosity we never lose entirely our sense of being at home. There remains a kinship, a sentiment of intimate acquaintance, which, even when we know we have failed to keep abreast of the subject, flatters us with a sense of power over it, and makes us feel not altogether out of the pale."

William James, *Psychology*

References: *Introduction to William James*, A. J. Reck; *The Thought and Character of William James*, Ralph B. Perry

jejune – adj. uninteresting; lacking significance

Jehovah's Witnesses – n. an American-Christian sect. It was founded around 1870 by Charles Taze Russell (1852–1916). Jehovah's Witnesses believe in the literal existence of God's kingdom, and that this kingdom will be reestablished on earth. They maintain an apolitical stance by rejecting the secular world, including the refusal to salute any flag. They believe that the Bible is the complete and infallible Word of God. They anticipate the occurrence of Armageddon as presented in the Bible.

The Watchtower is the main publication of the Jehovah's Witnesses. It was heavily promoted by Joseph F. Rutherford (1869–1941), a partner to Russell. Jehovah's Witnesses launched an open attack on Catholicism and other institutions. Both Russell and Rutherford generated ethical controversies with their management style, but the Jehovah's Witnesses remains a sect that continues to attract many followers. It is appealing to many people due to its simplicity, especially its non-scientific explanations of the universe, nature, society, and culture.

According to JW, secular society is corrupt and in the grip of Satan. This secularization is highlighted by organizations like the United Nations. Thus, Jehovah's Witnesses do not recognize nations, salute the flag, or participate in war. They believe the world is faced with Armageddon and only God will change this. God is not Trinitarian but will be involved in the end time. Those who "witness" shall be saved in the final cataclysmic destruction and replacement of the current world order.

Reference: *Faith on the March*, A. H. Macmillan

jihad – n. Muslim holy war; originally signifying the inner struggle or war of the soul within the individual disciple of Islam. *Jihad* gradually became a reference to political militance and conflict with modernity. Jihadists are religious fundamentalists, and as such, they are committed to the elimination of all other religions, because they are manifestations of Satan.

jinn – n. Islamic spirit or angel

jocose – adj. inclined to joking; wittiness

Judaism – n. a Middle Eastern religion, whose origins go back to about 1800 BC. It represents the first religion to clearly adopt a theology of monotheism.

J

Judaism emphasizes God's creation of the world out of nothing, the selective preference for "the Chosen People of God," the finitude of humanity and its dependence on God, the linear nature of time in which God is seen as a supernatural influence, and a theology of hope: that God will reestablish his "Covenant" through the coming of a Messiah. The Decalogue (Ten Commandments) establishes the necessary limitations in daily life and guides the community in the establishment of a justice-based society.

Judaism relies heavily on its traditions and rituals to separate itself from the Gentile world, which it views as a consequence of the alienation from God. The survival of Judaism has been spiritually masterminded through the metaphysics of suffering, wherein suffering is seen as a natural feature of this world and a type of crisis turned to advantage in the assumption that Divine justice will prevail.

Traditional social divisions include:

1) Sadducees – those who saw Judaism primarily through its written traditions, particularly the Torah (Genesis, Exodus, Leviticus, and Deuteronomy) and Jewish theology in general
2) Pharisees – a rabbinic element who saw the oral traditions as equally important with written law
3) Essenes – a monastic element that emphasized spirituality and ascetic practices to be the true core of Judaism. These divisions have played an important role in the subsequent theology of Judaism.

"Rabbi" means teacher of the Torah. The Talmud contains the rabbinical commentaries on the meaning of the Torah. It is sometimes humorously noted that, "If you don't like the advice of your rabbi, then see another rabbi."

References: *Old Testament Theology*, 2 vols., Gerhard von Rad; *The History of Israel*, Martin Noth; *Prophetic Faith*, Martin Buber; *The Essence of Judaism*, Leo Baeck; and *The Way of Torah: An Introduction to Judaism*, Jacob Neusner

Julian of Norwich (1342–1413) – a female English philosopher and mystic. She used her religious experiences as the basis of spiritual meditations on the meaning of life. Influenced by Neoplatonism and St. John of the Cross, she reasoned that faith, prayer, and the love of God are central influences on the correct formation of the personality. She claimed that the absence of Divine reality and presence of evil is cured by the spiritual effects of Divine Love.

Principal work: *The Sixteen Revelations of Divine Love* (1385)

Reference: *The Penguin Dictionary of Saints*, Donald Atwater

Jung, Carl Gustav (1875–1961) – a Swiss psychologist and once an associate of Freud. Jung moved away from Freudian thinking into more metaphysical concerns regarding the nature of the self. Jung developed important ideas about the extrovert and introvert personality types, the notion of archetypes and their relation to the unconscious, and the way in which archetypes are found in religion, myth, and art. His ideas about personality types became the basis of the Myers-Briggs Type Indicator, a psychometric personality test.

Jung's views were the result of his own religious and moral searching. He never resolved the issue of God's existence, though he made progress in a book entitled *Answer to Job* (1952). During this part of his life he used painting to explore the meaning of symbols and was attracted to the Eastern use of *mandalas*, symbols having four parts to represent self-unity. Jung understood *mandalas* to be connected with the struggle of the conscious and unconscious. He also saw them as a means to resolving discordant parts of the personality, especially as a means of avoiding personal disintegration. Within its archetypal symbolism, God the Father is a projection of the self in its most idealistic form.

Jung developed a new interpretation of Freud's death wish. For Jung, an archetype he called the Shadow represented the hidden tendency to self-destruct. The Shadow archetype was used to explain the often disastrous choices people make in bringing misfortune onto themselves.

Principal works: *Psychological Types* (1921), *In Search of a Soul* (1933), *The Structure and Dynamics of the Psyche* (1940), *Archetypes and the Collective Unconscious* (1950), *The Practice of Psychotherapy* (1966), and *The Development of Personality* (1967).

> *"Freud has unfortunately overlooked the fact that man has never been able single-handedly to hold his own against the powers of darkness, that is, of the unconscious. Man has always stood in need of the spiritual help which each individual's own religion held out to him. It is religion which lifts him out of his distress."*

J

Carl Jung, *In Search of a Soul*

References: *C. G. Jung: The Haunted Prophet*, Paul J. Stern; *A Primer of Jungian Psychology*, Calvin S. Hall and Vernon J. Nordby

junta – n. fr. Spanish, meaning committee or council. It is a reference to group rule established by revolutionary seizure of power. *Juntas* govern by decree and automatically introduce barriers to democratic rule.

Reference: *Military Institutions and Coercion in Developing Nations*, 2nd ed., Morris Janowitz

juration – n. the administration of an oath

juvenescence – n. the state of being young or growing young

Kaaba – n. fr. Arabic, meaning square structure. In Islam, it is the pilgrimage shrine located in the courtyard of the Great Mosque at Mecca. The Kaaba contains the Black Stone, a meteorite believed to be a stone that fell from heaven during the life of Adam. Thus, by location and history, the Kaaba is the most sacred sanctuary in the Muslim world.

Once a site for pagan worship, Mohammad removed the pagan symbols and rededicated the site as the shrine of Allah. During the five daily prayers, all Muslims kneel in the direction of the Kaaba.

> References: *History of the Arabs*, Philip K. Hitti; and *Islam in Modern History*, Wilfred Cantwell Smith

Kafka, Franz (1883–1924) – a Czech literary figure on the border of philosophy, per se. He was of Jewish ancestry and felt that anti-Semitism did not apply to his life. Kafka supported himself as an attorney by day, so he could work as a writer by night. His novels are about people who are tormented by modernity and authoritarianism. His writing inspired the term "kafkaesque."

Kafka wrote for himself and asked Max Brod, his friend and publisher, to destroy his writings at his death. Instead, Brod published them. Dora Diamant, a kindergarten teacher who lived with Kafka, also kept letters and notebooks. These were confiscated by the Gestapo in 1943…His writings reflect the troubled relationship with his parents, especially his father, but also the problems of bureaucracy and legal systems. In *Brief an den Vader* (*Letter to the Father*), Kafka details the problems of living with a parent who was self-centered, authoritarian, and overbearing. This tension created the motivation for many of his stories. His themes focus on the problems of anxiety, fear, absurdity of certain situations, physical brutality, and the prevalence of anomie. He is often included in discussions about the meaning of existentialism.

In spite of Kafka's poor health (tuberculosis) and personal problems in his relationships with women, he managed to create an interesting social life with other important writers like Max Brod. He also loved sports, especially swimming, cycling, rowing, and hiking.

> Principal works: *The Metamorphosis* (1915); *The Trial* (1925); *The Castle* (1926); *Amerika* (1927)

> References: *Franz Kafka*, Max Brod; *Kafka and the Contemporary Critical Performance*, ed. Alan Udoff

kainophobia – n. fear of that which is new

kakistocracy – n. government by the worst people in society; rule by criminals

Kant, Immanuel (1724–1804) – a German philosopher, whose work exercised an important influence on modern philosophy, because Kant was able to form a reconciliation of empiricism and rationalism. He argued that knowledge is derived from experience but it is organized according to innate *a priori* rational principles. This distinction in turn divides judgments into a) analytic and b) synthetic.

Analytic judgments are logically complete. These are judgments (statements) that possess a type of necessary connection between the nouns they contain (e.g., "All carpenters are craftsmen."). Whereas, synthetic judgments are logically contingent. These are judgments (statements) that lack a necessary connection between the nouns they contain (e.g., "All carpenters have ten fingers."). Analytic judgments are *a priori* (necessary), while synthetic judgments are *a posteriori* (probable). From this, Kant derives a sentential hybrid called a *synthetic a priori*. The synthetic a priori is a judgment (statement) necessarily true but whose nouns are separately incapable of producing the inherent necessity of truth that the synthetic judgment asserts (e.g., "7 plus 5 gives us 12."). Separately, 7 or 5 do not automatically imply 12.

Kant agreed with Hume that experience brings something to the mind, but Kant also argued that the mind does something with experiences. Mind organizes experience. This is referred to as "Kant's Copernican Revolution."

Kant's concern with the "moral law within" produced a duty-based moral theory, deontological ethics. Good is defined as a good will, a will guided by what one "ought" to do. Kant's "categorical imperative" emphasizes the role of duty toward the good; good for its own sake. Good is more important than happiness. This is where duty plays a role, since the pursuit of happiness may not coincide with the creation of goodness. In fact, the pursuit of happiness may produce evil.

Principal works: *Critique of Pure Reason* (1781), *Foundations of the Metaphysics of Morals* (1785), *Critique of Practical Reason* (1788), and *Critique of Judgment* (1790)

"*A good will is good not because of what it performs or effects, not by its aptness for the attainment of some proposed end, but simply by virtue of the volition; that is, it is good in itself, and considered by itself is to be esteemed much higher than all that can be brought about by it in favour of any inclination.*"

Immanuel Kant, *Foundations of the Metaphysics of Morals*

"*There is . . . but one categorical imperative, namely this: Act only on that maxim whereby thou canst at the same time will that it should become a universal law.*"

Immanuel Kant, *Foundations of the Metaphysics of Morals*

"*Reason never has an immediate relation to an object; it relates immediately to the understanding alone. It is only through the understanding that it can be employed in the field of experience. It does not form conceptions of objects, it merely arranges them and gives them that unity which they are capable of possessing when the sphere of their application has been extended as widely as possible.*"

Immanuel Kant, *Critique of Pure Reason*

References: *Kant*, Karl Jaspers; *A Short Commentary on Kant's Critique of Pure Reason*, A. C. Ewing

kathenotheism – n. in religion, a reference to Vedic monotheism. The spectrum of gods is structured so that one god is honored at a time, without entailing nonbelief of the other gods who are, in a way, regarded as dormant. The term "kathenotheism" was coined by Friedrich Max Müller (1823-1900). Muller was a comparative philologist at Oxford with a special interest in Eastern religions.

Principal works: *History of Ancient Sanskrit Literature* (1859), *The Sacred Books of the East* (1875), and *The Origin and Growth of Religion* (1878)

Keynes, John Maynard (1883–1946) – an English logician and economist, Keynes was at home in a number of fields: journalism, business, and philosophy. Keynes revolutionized economic philosophy after 1930. Economic theorists prior to Keynes argued for the quantity theory of money (Say's Law) and the flexibility of wages, holding that unemployment can be countered by lower wages with the same quantity of money in circulation. In Keynesian theory, full employment is the exception in a normal economy. So, government stimulation of jobs is necessary to a degree. Keynes argued for policies that control inflationary pressure.

Keynes did not embrace Marxist theory and viewed it as a threat to individualism. He sought adjustments in capitalism to ensure full employment and create price stability, but he did not have confidence in strong forms of socialism, due primarily to the psychological egoism in human nature. Human interrelationships are impossible to control and predict beyond certain general principles. The egoism that is often manifested in primitive capitalism is just as real in advanced forms of socialism and can only be countered by a rational-legal model of competition.

Principal works: *A Treatise on Probability* (1921), and *General Theory of Employment, Interest, and Money* (1936)

"Money . . . serves two principal purposes. By acting as a money of account, it facilitates exchanges without its being necessary that it should ever itself come into the picture as a substantive object. In this respect it is a convenience which is devoid of significance or real influence. In the second place, it is a store of wealth. So we are told, without a smile on the face. But in the world of classical economy, what an insane use to which to put it! For it is a recognized characteristic of money as a store of wealth that it is barren; whereas practically every other form of storing wealth yields some interest or profit. Why should anyone outside a lunatic asylum wish to use money as a store of wealth?"

K

"The owner of wealth, who has been induced not to hold his wealth in the shape of hoarded money, still has two alternatives between which to choose. He can lend his money at the current rate of money-interest or he can purchase some kind of capital-asset. Clearly in equilibrium these two alternatives must offer an equal advantage to the marginal investor in each of them. This is brought about by shifts in the money-prices of capital-assets relative to the price of money loans. The prices of capital-assets move until, having regard to their prospective yields and account being taken of all those elements of doubt and uncertainty, interested and disinterested advice, fashion, convention, and what else you will, which affect the mind of the investor, they offer an equal apparent advantage to the marginal investor who is wavering between one kind of investment and another."

John Keynes, *General Theory*

References: *Keynes's Relevance Today*, F. Vicarelli; *Keynes's Impact on Monetary Economics*, J. C. Gilbert; and *Essays on John Maynard Keynes*, ed. Milo Keynes

Kierkegaard, Søren (1813–1855) – a Danish philosopher of existentialism, Kierkegaard reacted against the systematic idealism of G. W. F. Hegel, emphasizing the subjective nature of truth. Truth is particular to each person's frame of reference. What is universal alone is the necessity of choice. Each person is confronted with choosing a life, a commitment that is objectively uncertain. In this special irrationalist stance, Kierkegaard argues that reason does not offer us the kinds of security we seek. People who are well educated, work hard, and think rationally may still be quite unlucky, unhappy, and unsuccessful.

Kierkegaard believed in three stages of being: the aesthetic, the ethical, and the religious. The aesthetic stage is a life of impulse and emotion; the individual has no specific moral or religious beliefs and exercises no limits over questions of sensual life. The aesthetic stage denies spirit, eventually producing a feeling of despair and anxiety. The individual is then confronted with a continuation of this emptiness or a choice is made to go beyond it to the ethical stage ("either/or" is the term Kierkegaard uses to describe this crisis of choice). In abandoning the sensual life, the individual accepts moral and legal limits to action. Choices like marriage exhibit the essence of this stage. There is a commitment to moral direction and completeness. But moral self-sufficiency, too, has limited meaning. In fact, living up to moral self-sufficiency is too difficult and ushers in feelings of guilt, which Kierkegaard sees as the onset of another crisis of meaning. The individual is again confronted by a feeling of emptiness that can only be transcended by entering the religious stage. This is a personal encounter with God. In the personal, subjective encounter with God the individual encounters true self-fulfillment.

Principal works: *The Concept of Irony* (1841), *Either/Or* (1843), *Fear and Trembling* (1843), *Philosophical Fragments* (1844), *The Present Age* (1847), *Works of Love* (1848), and *Sickness unto Death* (1849)

"Faith is the highest passion in a man. There are perhaps many in every generation who do not even reach it, but no one gets further."

Søren Kierkegaard, *Fear and Trembling*

References: *The Mind of Kierkegaard*, James Collins; *A Short Life of Kierkegaard*, Walter Lowrie

kinetic – adj. dynamic; active; having to do with the energy and motion of material bodies

King, Martin Luther (1929–1968) – an activist-philosopher of ethics and social reform who was the principal leader of the civil rights movement in the United States from 1960–1968. He received the Nobel Peace Prize in 1964 for his social activism, including peaceful protests of the Vietnam War and organized nonviolent civil disobedience for the civil rights movement. His philosophy garnered bad feelings from both blacks and whites, and he was assassinated in 1968.

His thinking was influenced by Gandhi, especially his commitment to *ahimsa* (nonviolence), and the philosophy of Christ in the Sermon on the Mount. King spent time during his doctoral research investigating the theology of Alfred North Whitehead and came to accept the importance of process philosophy. The confluence of these different ideas contributed to the activist theology of Martin Luther King.

Principal works: *Stride Toward Freedom* (1958), *Why We Can't Wait* (1964), and *Where Do We Go from Here: Chaos or Community?* (1967)

"Power properly understood is the ability to achieve purpose. It is the strength required to bring about social, political, or economic changes. In this sense power is not only desirable but necessary to implement the demands of love and justice.

K

One of the greatest problems of history is that the concepts of love and power are usually contrasted as polar opposites. Love is identified with a resignation of power and power with a denial of love. It was this misinterpretation that caused Nietzsche, the philosopher of the 'will to power,' to reject the Christian concept of love. It was the same misinterpretation which induced Christian theologians to reject Nietzsche's philosophy of the 'will to power' in the name of the Christian idea of love. What is needed is a realization that power without love is reckless and abusive and that love without power is sentimental and anemic. Power at its best is love implementing the demands of justice. Justice at its best is love correcting everything that stands against love."

> Martin Luther King Jr., *Where Do We Go from Here: Chaos or Community?*

> References: *Bearing the Cross: Martin Luther King, Jr., and the Southern Christian Leadership Conference*, D. Garrow; *Martin Luther King, Jr.: Nonviolent Strategies and Tactics for Social Change*, J. J. Ansbro

kitsch – n. writing of shallow, popular appeal

kleptomania – n. a compulsive need to steal. It is classified as a neurosis. Psychological theory suggests that kleptomaniacs are reacting to emotional disturbances in childhood, in particular, problems of deprivation. Since they often steal things that are neither desired nor necessary, this kind of theft fits the analytic description.

The moral question as to the responsibility and guilt of the kleptomaniac is problematic. Neurosis is defined as behavior that is self-defeating and repetitive, thus it is a maladaptation. To what extent is a person morally responsible for neurotic behavior?

> Reference: *Freud's Early Psychology of the Neuroses: A Historical Perspective*, K. Levin

koan – n. a Zen Buddhist puzzle designed to reduce attachment to reason and bring about intuitive enlightenment. There are more than one thousand koans in the history of Zen.

Koan studies are part of Soto and Rinzai Zen. The goal of koan exercises is to bring the student to an understanding of non-duality and into *satori*. Zen masters will ask the student or disciple to explain their answers to koan questions. Responses are checks on the progress toward *satori* and "Pure Consciousness."

"What was the appearance of your face before your ancestors were born?"

Zen koan

References: *The Zen Koan*, Isshu Miura and Ruth Sasaki; *Sitting with Koans: Essential Writings on Zen; Koan Introspection*, John Daido Loori; *Secrets of the Blue Cliff Record*, trans. Thomas Cleary

Krishna – in Hinduism, a god possessing a complex and sometimes confusing set of characteristics. On the one hand, the Mahabarata (Bhagavad Gita) depicts Krishna as a very powerful war hero, full of force and determination. On the other hand, Krishna is depicted as a playful and mischievous wonder worker. Then he is portrayed as an amorous cowherder, playing a melodious flute to win the attention of the *gopis* (milkmaids). There are portraits of Krishna stealing the clothes of *gopis* while they are bathing. Each girl comes to Krishna with palms folded to ask for her clothing. The nudity of these girls is said to symbolize the transparency required of the believer to be accepted by God, as God knows all secrets and has no respect for adornment and possessions. Thus, the love of Krishna is spiritual rather than carnal.

Reference: *The Loves of Krishna in Indian Painting and Poetry*, William G. Archer

kshatriya – n. in Hinduism, an individual of an upper caste, especially one in government or military leadership

kudo – n. award, honor, praise

kyudo – n. in Japanese Zen philosophy, the practice of archery as a means of physical, spiritual, and moral development. In *kyudo*, it is believed that three elements guide the soul: truth, goodness, and beauty. Truth is modeled in *kyudo* as right-mindedness. The archer must have the correct mental outlook (*seishahichu*) as well as great skill (*noshahichu*) in handling his or her equipment. A perfect shot lying in the center of the target, *tekichu*, must be achieved in the correct way.

Goodness is the second element of *kyudo*. The arrow's flight is spoiled by destructive emotions. The sound made by the bowstring (*tsurune*) reveals the level of tension in the body of the archer. The good archer is a person whose emotions are balanced; the mind is calm and well disciplined. This state of being is called *heijoshin*, ordinary mind. Moreover, the archer's relation to other archers is marked by courtesy and compassion.

Beauty is the third element of *kyudo*. Without the first two elements *kyudo* cannot be beautiful, but beauty is also extended to the appearance of the bow, the arrows themselves, and the attire of the archer. The actions of the archer are marked by correct etiquette, and the archery range (*kyudojo*) is maintained with attention to the general themes of grace, dignity, and tranquility.

The origins of *kyudo* go back to about 7000 BC in the hunting life of the earliest known inhabitants of the Japanese islands, the *Jomon* people. Through time it came under the influence of tribal warfare, advanced military use, and most of all Zen. Zen emphasized the importance of balanced effort, the working of the spirit, and the discovery of self-mastery through a rigorous daily regimen of meditation and action.

References: *Kyudo: The Essence and Practice of Japanese Archery*, Dan and Jackie De Prospero, with Hideharu Onuma; *Zen in the Art of Archery*, Eugen Herrigel

labefaction – n. weakening or downfall

labile – adj. readily open to change; unstable

labyrinth – n. a place full of intricate passageways and blind alleys

Lacan, Jacques (1901–1981) – a psychiatrist who brought back the ideas of Sigmund Freud, arguing that psychology could not be considered genuine without the conclusions and personality theories that Freud built. Lacan's work became a support for postmodernism. He used Plato, Kant, Hegel, and Heidegger to bolster the argument that some "psychoses" are legitimate philosophical positions rather than illness.

Lacan argued that looking into "desire" should be the central interest of psychoanalysis, since desire and the unconscious represent a continuous reality of the mind (e.g., a person has a desire to be the object of another's—the other's—desire). Desire is seen as lack (in the soul—Plato), and Lacan argues that desire cannot be totally captured or defined with words. Words are the investigative tools to understand desire, but words will leave a "surplus" out of the analysis. Understanding human relationships requires a discussion of what the desire is. Lacan does not allow desire to be identified as a "drive," since he argues that drives are many and desire is one. If allowed to be connected with desire, Lacan argues that drives are limited manifestations of desire. Desire is reaching toward something that is missing but deemed necessary. We do not desire what is possessed.

Principal works: *The Four Fundamental Concepts of Psychoanalysis* (1964); *The Ethics of Psychoanalysis* (1960)

References: *How to Read Lacan*, Slavoj Zizek; *Key Concepts of Lacanian Psychoanalysis*, ed. Dany Nobus

laconic – adj. brief or concise; a reference to Laconia (Sparta), thus speaking or writing with Spartan brevity

lacuna – n. a gap or missing portion

Lakota, Oglala – n. a Native American religion, especially the spiritual traditions of the Sioux. The principal symbolic features of Lakota philosophy are found with the circle and its center. The circle represents the cosmos, and thus, the camp is laid in the fashion of the sacred hoop, with its entrance facing the east. The Lakota home, *tipi*, also embodies the spirituality of the circle and its center. Inherent within its meaning is the principal of unity— tribally, individually, and ecologically.

Another element is the sacred pipe or *chanunpa wakan*, the most valued holy object of the Lakota. Its use promotes a spiritual union of the Lakota people with the surrounding universe. As sacred smoke rises and drifts, it is part of praying for and with everything.

Hanblecheya ("crying for a vision") is a ritual catharsis. The individual participant seeks purification through fasting for three to four days. During this ascetic practice, the individual awaits a vision. The vision resembles the advice of sacred animals or thunder spirits, bestowing holiness and spiritual wisdom.

Upon the death of a Lakota, the soul may be kept, *wanagi yuhapi*, for a time to mark the spiritual significance of death. The deceased's hair is cut and placed with a sacred pipe in a deerskin sleeve, then rolled into a bundle and kept in its own *tipi*. This ritual is concluded by a great feast to mark the release of the soul, with possessions being given away to honor the spiritual nature of the Lakotas' nomadic life.

Inikagapi is the practice of the sweat lodge, symbolizing "renewed life." Constructed of willow branches and buffalo skins, a dome is created, representing the universe. Participants in this purification process leave behind their impure habits and meditate on who they really are, emptying their egotistical tendencies in favor of humility toward Mother Earth.

References: *Black Elk: The Sacred Ways of a Lakota*, Wallace Black Elk and William Lyon; *Lame Deer, Seeker of Visions*, John Lame Deer; *How to Take Part in Lakota Ceremonies*, William Stolzman, SJ

lallation – n. infantile babbling; the repetition of sounds without logical structure

lalophobia – n. fear of speaking

lam – n. sudden or hurried flight, especially from the law

lama – n. in Tibetan Buddhism, "superior one"; a reference to a spiritual preceptor or monk

lambent – adj. a surface effect; having soft radiance; dealing softly and expertly with a topic

lamia – n. a female demon or vampire; a woman of a particularly vicious character

lampoon – n. light ridicule

languid – adj. weak, sluggish, or listless

languor – n. weakness, especially of body and mind; weariness

Lao-tzu (ca. 500 BC) – Chinese philosopher and the founder of Taoism. While Confucius attempted to heal the problems of China with an emphasis on etiquette and moral goodness, Lao-tzu emphasized a spiritual connection with the natural world…Be like water. Water is forceful yet gentle. Meditation can act like water: *"Muddy water let stand becomes clear."* A still mind removes turmoil, bringing about insight and understanding of the *Tao*.

The *Tao* is a power that provides a spiritual path. People must use their mind to discern the workings of the *Tao* in their life. Things work toward perfection naturally. The problems of human existence stem from a resistance to the natural flow of reality. So, Lao-tzu taught the following points:

1) Desire seems to rule the life of humanity. It is the motive behind most human action.
2) The strife of society is caused by competing for the things that desire seeks.
3) Morality is a tool to promote harmony in society and to put checks on desire.

4) Morality is useless, since the guidelines of moral philosophies do not prevent evil individuals from working the world to their own satisfaction. Plus, the principles of morality seem to change with the passage of time.

5) It is necessary to go beyond morality in order to find true harmony and happiness.

6) Going beyond morality can only be achieved by abandoning the desires that necessitate the creation of moral philosophies.

7) Transcending desire requires an acceptance of the Tao.

8) The creation of a better society rests upon the education of the people in the way of the *Tao*.

Principal work: *Tao-Te Ching* (*The Way and Its Power*)

"Who is rich in character is like a child.
No poisonous insects sting him,
No wild beasts attack him,
And no birds of prey pounce upon him.
His bones are soft, his sinews tender, yet his grip is strong.
Not knowing the union of male and female, yet his organs are complete, which means his vigor is unspoiled.
Crying the whole day, yet his voice never runs hoarse, which means his natural harmony is perfect.
To know harmony is to be in accord with the eternal, and to know eternity is called discerning. But to improve upon life is called an ill-omen; to let go the emotions through impulse is called assertiveness. For things age after reaching their prime; that assertiveness would be against Tao. He who is against Tao perishes young."

Lao-tzu, *Tao-Te Ching*

References: *Lao Tzu and Taoism*, Max Kaltenmark, trans. by Robert Greaves; and *Taoism: The Parting of the Way*, Welch Holmes

lapactic – adj. aperient; causing a purge

lapidate – v. to stone to death

largesse – n. ample giving of money or gifts; innate generosity of mind and spirit; sometimes ostentatious giving, as if to an inferior

lascivious – adj. wanton; lustful

latent – adj. existing but not yet manifest

latitudinarian – n. one who is liberal and open in religious belief and conduct

Law, William (1686–1761) – an English theologian and mystic philosopher. Law defined knowledge as a communion between the one who knows and that which is known. His ideas were conveyed in the example of divine self-communication as love. His philosophical and theological work was devoted to establishing the importance of Christian life and maintaining the validity of faith as opposed to strict rationalism. Law insisted that God and reality are more complex than rationalism allows, and that spiritual intuitive knowledge is necessary for a real understanding of life.

> Principal works: *Christian Perfection* (1726), *A Serious Call to a Devout and Holy Life* (1728), and *The Spirit of Prayer* (1749)

> *"The Spirit of Prayer is a pressing forth of the soul out of this earthly life. It is a stretching with all its desire after the life of God."*

> William Law, *The Spirit of Prayer*

> *"The one who has learned to pray has learned the greatest secret of a holy and happy life."*

> William Law, *Christian Perfection*

> Reference: *The Mysticism of William Law*, George Clarkson

Laws of thought – n. in traditional logic, three foundational principles (axiomatic rules) regarded as a basis to all logical reasoning:

1) Law of Identity – "Whatever is, is" or "A is A"
2) Law of Noncontradiction – "Contradictories cannot both be true" or "A is not not-A"
3) Law of the Excluded Middle – "Contradictories cannot both be false" or "Everything is either A or not A."

In modern logic these traditional suppositions are often regarded as tautologies, a formal way of declaring them nonsense (*tautology*: needless or meaningless repetition of a word, phrase, or statement).

Reference: *The Development of Logic*, W. Kneale and M. Kneale

lebensraum – n. fr. German, meaning the space necessary for life, growth, and self-sufficiency

lectionary – n. a book of lessons, or daily meditations, for an entire church year

left field – n. a source of the unexpected or illogical; far from the mainstream

legalese – n. the specialized language of lawyers

Leibniz, Gottfried Wilhelm (1646–1716) – a German philosopher of the rationalist school. Leibniz presented a theory of matter similar to twentieth-century notions of physics. According to Leibniz, the universe is composed of "monads," which he described as a type of eternal energy without shape or size. Each monad is an independent entity with its own created purpose. Leibniz intended monads to operate as metaphysical elements at the foundation of empirical reality.

Leibniz saw problems with the notion of freedom and found it difficult to rid his system of its deterministic features. The idea of built-in or created purposes was partly countered with the idea of self-development, which was described as change that is free of forces applied from without.

For Leibniz, the problem of evil is defined as the absence of perfection. God created the best possible world, not the best world. Creation is made of limited objects, thus the existence of imperfection is a necessary consequence of such objects. Evil or imperfection is not incompatible with a loving God. It is necessary for the moral requirements of the universe that evil exist.

God is a perfect monad and represents the source of general harmony throughout the universe. Humanity, being limited and imperfect, suffers from limited understandings. God, however, as the perfect and highest being, transcends all monads.

Leibniz's view of knowledge argues that universal and necessary truth is based solely on logical principles and cannot be derived from experience. The universe is primarily built on a logical-mathematical model.

Principal works: *Meditations on Knowledge, Truth, and Ideas* (1664), *Discourse on Metaphysics* (1686), *On the Origin of Things* (1696), and *Monadology* (1714)

There are two kinds of truth: *"[T]hose of reasoning and those of fact. Truths of reasoning are necessary and their opposite is impossible: truths of fact are contingent and their opposite is possible. When a truth is necessary, its reason can be found by analysis, resolving it into more simple ideas and truths, until we come to those which are primary."*

G. W. Leibniz, *Monadology*

References: *Leibniz: A Collection of Critical Essays*, ed. Harry G. Frankfurt; *The Philosophy of Leibniz and the Modern World*, ed. Ivor Leclerc

leitmotiv – n. a dominant or recurring theme

lemma – n. the starting point in a proof; a statement allowed as "true" to begin argumentation

Lenin, Vladimir Ilyich (1870–1924) – a Russian Marxist philosopher and political leader whose real name was V. I. Ulyanov. As early as 1887 Lenin began to establish a reputation for strong-willed resistance to authority, probably the direct result of the arrest and hanging of his brother, Aleksandr, when he was convicted of plotting against the Czar. V. I. Lenin's philosophical development produced loyalty to the ideas of Karl Marx and Friedrich Engels. The Marxist ideology fit well with his upbringing, which emphasized deep concern for the welfare of others. He led the Bolsheviks from 1903, and after the revolution of 1917, he headed the Soviet Union until his death.

Lenin's influence on modern communism produced the label "Marxism-Leninism." Ideologically, Lenin was a Hegelian who, like Marx, saw no contradiction in using the idea of "dialectic" along with a materialist position. In fact, Lenin believed there was no difference between dialectic, logic, and epistemology.

Lenin went beyond Marx's theory of social reconstruction, especially in his commitment to establish a "dictatorship of the proletariat." This entailed the destruction of the bourgeois state machinery. This directive emerged from the "oppositional" nature of dialectical thought, which meant the destruction of the thesis by the antithesis. Lenin's political emphasis was "from each according to his ability, and to each according to his need." In constructing his strongest version of Marxism, Lenin envisioned a withering away of the state and creation of the pure classless society outlined by Marx.

Principal work: *State and Revolution*, 1917

"The teaching of Marx and Engels regarding the inevitability of a violent revolution refers to the bourgeois state. It cannot be replaced by the proletarian state through 'withering away,' but as a general rule, only through a violent revolution... The replacement of the bourgeois by the proletariat state is impossible without a violent revolution. The abolition of the proletarian state, i.e. of all states, is only possible through 'withering away.'"

Lenin, *State and Revolution*

References: *Lenin's Childhood*, Isaac Deutscher; *The Life of Lenin*, Louis Fischer; *Lenin: Notes for a Biographer*, Leon Trotsky

Lesbos, Sappho of – (630–570 BC) a poet and leader of the homosexual band of females on the Island of Lesbos, thus referred to as Lesbians

lethe – n. oblivion, forgetfulness

levity – n. lack of seriousness; also frivolity

lexiphanic – adj. after Lucian's character, Lexiphanes, in the dialogue *Lexiphanes*; meaning pretentious, showy, or bombastic, especially with speech and words

lex talionis – n. fr. Latin, meaning law of retaliation

li – n. in Confucianism, a reference to propriety and etiquette; external forms of order and ceremony that serve to cover the possible roughness of inner tendencies

liberation theology – n. a religious political philosophy in Latin America that combines Marxist and Christian ideologies of social justice; Jesuit social activists

libertarian – n. one who holds that unrestricted free will, esp. of thought and action, is a right

libertine – n. one who is unrestrained by conventions and morality; one who lives a dissolute existence

libidinous – adj. lustful; referring to "pressure" to act out sexual desires.

libido – n. in psychoanalysis, the unconscious energy through which life instincts (the sex drive) perform their function. For Jung, the libido represents life energy or psychic energy. For Freud, the libido represents energy stemming from the sexual instinct, manifested in three areas of behavior:

1) displacement of cathexes (objects of sexual craving)
2) sublimation (nonsexual behavior used to soften the pressure of sexual craving), and
3) the erotic parts of the body (the somatic evidence of stimulation, attended by a mental awareness of erotogenic zones).

References: *Three Essays on the Theory of Sexuality* and *Group Psychology and the Analysis of the Ego*, Sigmund Freud; also *Anatomy of the Psyche*, E. Edinger; and "Two Essays on Analytical Psychology," *Collected Works*, vol. 7, C. G. Jung

licentious – adj. lacking legal or moral restraint, especially sexual; marked disregard for rules and correctness

litany – n. a prayer consisting of invocations and supplications by the leader with responses by the congregation; also, a long, monotonous narration

lithe – adj. characterized by grace and flexibility

loath – adj. unwilling; disinclined to act against one's interests

loathe – v. to show disgust; to detest

Locke, John (1632–1704) – an English philosopher of empiricism. Locke is an advocate of the view that mind is a *tabula rasa* or blank slate. Locke rejects the rationalist view that ideas are innate, since reflection only follows sensation. All ideas stem from experience. If there were innate ideas such as "God" or "numbers," Locke argued, it wouldn't be necessary to introduce these ideas to children.

Locke's epistemology divides ideas into simple and complex types. Simple ideas are those received passively through the senses or originating with elementary reflection on experience. Complex ideas are those actively synthesized by analysis. An extension of this distinction moved on to the identification of primary and secondary qualities. A primary quality of an object is one that is inherent in the object, such as shape and size. Secondary qualities are sensory qualities, such as color, taste, and sound. Philosophers have disputed these distinctions as lacking precision, and Locke's work on perception uses theories of nature commonly circulated in 17th Century philosophy.

Locke's political thought starts with observations on the state of nature, arguing somewhat optimistically that peace and self-restraint are natural boundaries of action, since violating the welfare of others leads to open conflict and thus, self-harm. Still, the crude conditions of a natural state require some refinement, made possible by civil government. The state acts as guarantor of life, freedom, and property. If governments should be dissolved through revolution, it would be with the aim of perfecting or improving upon the quality of sovereignty.

Locke was a theist and accepted the divinity of Christ, the principal virtues of faith, charity, and love, as well as the concept of God as a father. He believed in the theological validity of the New Testament and argued that it was consonant with human rationality.

Principal works: *On Toleration* (1689), *Two Treatises on Government* (1689), *Essay Concerning Human Understanding* (1690), and *Thoughts on Education* (1693)

". . . [S]uppose the mind to be, as we say, white paper, void of all characters, without any ideas: How comes it to be furnished? Whence comes it by that vast store which the busy and boundless fancy of man has painted on it with almost endless variety? . . . To this I answer, in one word, 'experience.' In that all knowledge is founded; and from that it ultimately derives itself. Our observation employed either, about external sensible objects, or about the internal operations of our minds perceived and reflected on by ourselves, is that which supplies our understanding with all the materials of thinking."

John Locke, *Essay Concerning Human Understanding*

"The great skill of a teacher is to get and keep the attention of his scholar; whilst he has that, he is sure to advance as fast as the learner's abilities will carry him; and without that, all his bustle and pother will be to little or no purpose. To attain this, he should make the child comprehend, as much as may be, the usefulness of what he teaches him, and let him see, by what he has learned, that he can do something which he could not do before; something which gives him some power *and real advantage above others who are ignorant of it. To this he should add sweetness in all his instructions, and by a certain tenderness in his whole carriage make the child sensible that he loves and designs nothing but his good, the only way to beget love in the child, which will make him hearken to his lessons. . . ."*

John Locke, *Concerning Education*

References: *John Locke*, Richard Aaron; *The British Empiricists: Locke, Berkeley, Hume*, James D. Collins

logic – n. a branch of philosophy that studies the difference between correct and incorrect reasoning. It recognizes two kinds of argumentation, a) deduction – the use of sentential arrangements (correctly stacked statements of evidence) or forms that force the acceptance of the conclusion, and b) induction – which is the use of case examples to provide partial support for conclusions. Deductive arguments are judged "valid" or "invalid," while inductive arguments are judged somewhere between "strong" and "weak." Arguments are not judged "true" or "false." These values are applied only to statements. Thus, it is technically wrong to regard arguments as true or false, even though the average person proclaims, "Argument X is true," or "Argument X is false."

Examples of valid deductive arguments:

> *Terrorists are a danger to society.*
> *John is a terrorist.*
> *So, John is a danger to society.*

> *If college students do not think critically, they will be brainwashed by their professors.*
> *Regina is a college student who does not think critically.*
> *Therefore, Regina will be brainwashed by her professors.*

An example of a moderately strong inductive argument:

> *Five thousand rats on a diet of aspartame (NutraSweet) showed no ill effects over a five-year period. So, aspartame is safe for human consumption.*

Most philosophers regard logic as the most important branch of philosophy, since the other branches, as well as other disciplines, are dependent upon its principles and methods to test their research. Logic includes the study of definition, language, formal and informal fallacies, conflict resolution, rules of inference, axiomatic reasoning, probability, quantification theory, predicate calculus, metalogic, modal logic, Greek logic, scientific hypothesis, and general proof theory.

References: *Introduction to Logic*, Irving Copi and Carl Cohen; *Theory of Formal Systems* and *First-Order Logic*, Raymond Smullyan; *Symbolic Logic*, Irving Copi; *The Development of Logic*, Martha and William Kneale

logion – n. proverb, adage; sayings attributed to Christ

logomachy – n. a dispute over words; controversy marked by verbal entanglement

logorrhea – n. unnecessary and incoherent chatter; excessive talkativeness

longanimity – n. patience

loquacious – adj. talkative; garrulous; inability to remain silent

lucent – adj. glowing, especially with light; marked by clarity

lucid – adj. being easily understood

lucubration – n. night study or night work; laborious involvement

luculent – adj. convincing thought or expression; clear

luetic – adj. diseased; morally decadent

lugubrious – adj. morbid, gloomy; seemingly permanent state of mourning

luminous – adj. enlightened, intelligent

lurch – v. to move about secretly; loiter; steal

lurdane – n. a dull, ignorant fool

lurid – adj. invoking terror; gruesome

Luther, Martin (1483–1546) – a Christian monk and theologian who led the Protestant Reformation. Luther was influenced by William of Ockham and St. Augustine. It was through Augustine that Luther received inspiration to attack reason and philosophy, calling philosophy "the Devil's whore."

Luther initiated the Reformation of Christianity with his famous posting of "Ninety-Five Theses" at Wittenberg Cathedral. This document disputed the validity of Roman Catholicism and denounced nepotism, usury, the sale of indulgences, and other forms of corruption, including the sale of religious office. By marrying Katharina von Bora, Luther ended the practice of celibacy for priests. Besides his contempt for the papacy, Luther also denounced Jews and called for the confiscation of their wealth, the burning of synagogues, and restrictions on their freedom. He viewed Muslims as agents of the apocalypse sent to punish false believers.

Luther's theology was affected by his personal struggle to correct the unprecedented decay in the ecclesiastical structure of the Church, manifested in his literary style. (Luther struggled with nightmares of his childhood, brought on by the vicious and bloody attacks of his father and mother, who believed that all children are born as demons and require frequent whippings.) His charismatic influence also manifested itself through his command of language and public speaking. Unfortunately, his religious pessimism about this world led straight to the condemnation of human efforts to succeed without God.

Luther's personal quest for a relationship with God led to the doctrine of salvation by faith alone (*sola fide*). According to Luther, without a Christo-centric orientation humanity is influenced by evil and utterly lost in vanity and hopelessness. The theology of Luther is also described as a Pauline theology (St. Paul of Tarsus).

Luther's reformation theology emphasized the "priesthood of all believers."

This in itself pleased many who had a pure contempt for the Vatican. Now each person could be a ministerial follower of Christ.

Principal work: *Luthers Werke—Kritische Gesamtausgabe* (1883)

"The world is a drunken peasant. If you lift him into the saddle on one side, he will fall off on the other side. One can't help him no matter how one tries. He wants to be the devil's."

Martin Luther, *Table Talk*

"To him that believeth not in Christ, not only all his sins are damnable, but even his good works are also his sins."

Martin Luther, *Commentary on Galatians*

References: *The Theology of Martin Luther*, Paul Althaus; *Young Man Luther*, Erik Erikson.

lycanthrope – n. a werewolf (a human who transforms into a wolf at night to eat people). The belief originated in European forest mythology. The werewolf must take a human form at the end of each night by removing its skin and concealing it. Finding and destroying the skin of a werewolf kills the werewolf. It is a pet belief of children and a certain distinguished logician, Raymond Smullyan.

lycanthropy – n. a state of insanity in which the individual believes one's self to be a wolf

lyssophobia – n. fr. the Greek *lyssa*, meaning madness; fear of going insane

macerate – v. to reduce or waste away, especially by fasting; reminiscent of the Jain practice of fasting unto death (*itvara*)

Machiavelli, Niccolò (1469–1527) – an Italian political philosopher, famous for the phrase, "The end justifies the means." Machiavelli detailed a type of political egoism on the assumption that every successful political leader develops a double standard of operation in order to acquire power: one for rulers and one for the ruled. Princes or rulers should give people the impression that they are sincere, religious, moral, and concerned about the interests of the population. Then, they should enact another agenda for personal control, one that is built upon craftiness and the calculated deployment of power. It is important to notice that pagans rule the world because they are fierce, unlike Christians, who are meek, humble, and thus, unsuccessful.

Machiavelli believed people are not loyal to one master and change loyalties with their own best interests. Rulers should know this. Rulers should also watch carefully those closest to them, for they are often the source of treachery, being interested in their own advancement at the expense of others. While a ruler should feign virtue, ruthlessness must sometimes be used, for it is better to be feared than loved. Public executions are useful to ensure security of the state, for it is important for people to see the consequences of disloyalty and helps them take the ruler seriously. A ruler should also maintain a powerful, well-disciplined military force to preserve independence.

Principal works: *The Prince* (1513), *The Art of War* (1520), *Mandragola* (1524), and *Discourses* (1532)

"A prince need not actually have all the qualities I have enumerated, but it is absolutely necessary that he seem to have them. Indeed, I shall even venture to assert that there is a danger in having those qualities and always respecting them. It is useful to seem, and actually to be, compassionate, faithful, humane, frank, and pious. Yet a prince's mind should be so enlightened that when you do not need to have these qualities, you have the knowledge and the ability to become the opposite."

N. Machiavelli, *The Prince*

References: *Thoughts on Machiavelli*, Leo Strauss; *The Statecraft of Machiavelli*, Herbert Butterfield

machismo – n. excessive masculinity; the polar opposite of homosexual femininity. According to Erich Fromm in *The Art of Loving*, "Very often if the masculine character traits of a man are weakened because emotionally he has remained a child, he will try to compensate for this lack by the exclusive emphasis on his male role in sex."

macro – adj. a Greek prefix meaning large

macula – n. spot or blemish; imperfection

maelstrom – n. a powerful streaming force, capable of sucking in objects coming near it; reference to any destructive turbulence

maenad – n. a female participant in Dionysian rituals; an unnaturally frenzied or lustful woman

magnanimity – n. the quality of being generous and understanding, especially in the way of sacrifices and bearing trouble patiently

magnum opus – n. a literary work of great importance: an artist's greatest achievement

maieutics – n. the Socratic method of instruction; drawing ideas from ideas; stemming from the Greek *maia* (midwife)

Malcolm X (1925–1965) – a black political activist whose real name was Malcolm Little. After the murder of his father in 1931, Little became a social rebel. Yet, he was an excellent student in his youth. Later his family moved to Harlem, where he was hooked into the underworld. In 1946, he served time for burglary. While in prison, he converted to the Nation of Islam. At that time, he preached a philosophy of black supremacy.

In 1952, he changed his name to Malcolm X. He read widely during his imprisonment and embraced the philosophy of Elijah Muhammad, father of the Nation of Islam.

In 1964, Malcolm X traveled to the Middle East to study the roots of his spiritual beliefs and make a pilgrimage to Mecca. His travels in Africa and the Middle East softened his political stance on racism. He broke his affiliation with the Nation of Islam and converted to Sunni theology. He began to advocate racial socialism for whites and blacks, preaching an ideology of reconciliation. As he was beginning to promote his new ideology for black nationalism, he angered members of the black Muslim faith. He was assassinated in 1965.

References: *The Victims of Democracy: Malcom X and the Black Revolution*, E. V. Wolfenstein; and *The Death and Life of Malcolm X*, 2nd ed., Peter Goldman

malediction – n. a curse

malefaction – n. an evil act

maleficence – n. harm

malevolence – n. the desire to harm

Malthus, Thomas Robert (1776–1834) – an English moral philosopher and economist, whose work had an influence on John M. Keynes. Malthus was concerned about population growth in the absence of natural checks. The progress of science threatened natural population leveling, which would eventually intensify survival requirements through overpopulation, resulting in catastrophe. According to Malthus, overpopulation is a cause of misery and vice.

Darwin expressed his views with Malthusian conclusions, as it was Malthus who coined the term "struggle for existence." Though many viewed Malthus's theories as overly pessimistic, others like Keynes described his outlook as "prosaic sanity."

Malthus posed a moral question in asking what checks "ought" to be active in a population: "Positive checks" are natural causes of premature death. "Preventive checks" are natural limits on the birthrate. "Moral checks" are limits voluntarily enacted to control population.

Principal works: *An Essay on the Principle of Population* (1798), and *The Second Essay on Principle of Population* (1803)

"A laborer who marries without being able to support a family may in some respects be considered as an enemy to all his fellow laborers."

"The power of population is indefinitely greater than the power in the earth to produce subsistence for man."

Thomas Malthus, *An Essay on the Principle of Population*

References: *Malthus and Lauderdale: The Anti-Ricardian Tradition*, Morton Paglin; *Malthus and His Work*, James Bonar

Mandaeans – n. the only known remnant of the ancient gnostic community. They live in remote regions of southwest Iran, with some living also in Iraq, while numbering less than fifty thousand. Their gnostic philosophy takes ideas from Judaism, Christianity, and Islam, but they don't identify with these religions. They still speak a form of Aramaic and draw their inspiration from a scripture called The Sidra Rabbah (Great Book) and the Qolasta, a book of rituals.

Reference: *Gnostic Ethics and Mandaean Origins*, E. M. Yamauchi

Mandala – n. fr. Sanskrit, *mandala* means magic circle. In Hinduism, Buddhism, and Jainism, it is a symbol used to meditate on inner peace. Carl Jung noted its importance in Navajo religion, which depicts the Great Hunter as a mandala to restore health for the sick. The Lakota Sioux also use the "circle" to emphasize a spiritual consciousness. And then, there is also King Arthur's roundtable, said to resemble the table of the Last Supper.

Jung discovered that mandala images also occur in dreams, and that they are a universal pattern for being. Thus, Jung saw the mandala as an archetypical symbol of the self.

References: *Man and His Symbols*, Carl Jung; and *Mandala: Literature for Critical Analysis*, Wilfred L. Guerin.

Manichaeism – n. in philosophy, the views of Mani, a Persian noble who lived from 215–276 AD. For a time, Manichaeism was the philosophy of St. Augustine. It was an innovative moralistic religious cult, which claimed God was present in prior ages with Buddha and Zoroaster. It argued: After primal man, humanity is a servant of Satan acting to limit the light of God. Christ is the messenger of warning, especially with regard to the dangers of sensual life.

Reference: *The Religion of the Manichees*, F. C. Burkitt

manifest – adj. easily perceived by the senses

manifest content – n. in psychoanalysis, a reference to the psychological material to be studied and interpreted. It assumes the role of phenomenology in the interpretational work on dreams. Freud coined the term in *The Interpretation of Dreams*. There, it has to do with the subject of a dream before it receives analytic consideration. Freud considered the possibility that there is more than one meaning in a dream.

Reference: *The Interpretation of Dreams*, Sigmund Freud

manism – n. ancestor worship

mansuetude – n. gentleness

Mantra – n. Sanskrit for "tool of meditation." The sound "*om*" is regarded as the perfect sound for meditating on the harmony of the universe, especially in *mantra yoga*. In both Hinduism and Buddhism, devotional and ritualistic use of sounds are important to producing contact with the architecture of ultimate reality. The use of mantras involves correct body position, correct setting, and correct mental focus. In the Vedas, mantras are part of the prayers and poetry of enlightenment.

Reference: *The Vedas: A Critical Study*, C. K. Raja

manumission – n. liberation, especially from slavery

Marcel, Gabriel (1889–1973) – a French existentialist philosopher who argued for a theistic model of existentialism, largely in opposition to Jean-Paul Sartre's atheistic existentialism. He labeled mankind *Homo Viator* (Man the Wanderer) to highlight the spiritual homelessness of life in mass society.

In his epistemology, Marcel distinguished two kinds of reflection: primary and secondary. Primary reflection is thought organized around criteria of the objective, the verifiable, and the analytic. This kind of reflection deals with the problematic issues of life. It entails specific empirical solutions to its difficulties, which tend to center on scientific and technological topics. Whereas, secondary reflection is concerned with ontology and the mystery of being. This kind of reflection deals with the spiritual issues of life, including the presence of God, the development of virtue, and the notion of personhood as it relates to transcendence and spiritual availability.

Marcel used the term "broken world" to describe the impersonal nature of modern society. He criticized the absence of fellowship and love. He also noted the relationship between absurdity and a world that is spiritually impoverished. Marcel was also critical of technological salvation vs. moral social excellence.

Marcel observed the warnings of Friedrich Nietzsche regarding nihilism. Marcel emphasized an existentialism in which the individual chooses to go beyond egocentricity toward an appreciation of other selves in determining the quality of one's life. For Marcel, the essence of life is always "to be in a situation," specifically a situation of choice.

Principal works: *Metaphysical Journal* (1927), *Being and Having* (1935), *Creative Fidelity* (1940), *The Philosophy of Existence* (1949), *The Mystery of Being*, 2 vols. (1950), *Men Against Humanity* (1951), and *The Existential Background of Human Dignity* (1963)

"*Egocentrism . . . is possible only in a being which has not properly mastered its own experience, which has not really assimilated it. It is worth devoting our attention to this for a few moments, for it has an important bearing on the rest of our inquiry.*

Insofar as I am obsessed by an ego-centric preoccupation, that preoccupation acts as a barrier between me and others; and by others must be understood in this connection the life and experience of others. But let us suppose this barrier has been overthrown. The paradox is that at the same time it is also my own personal experience that I rediscover in some way, for in reality my experience is in a real communion with other experiences."

Gabriel Marcel, *Mystery of Being*, vol. 2

References: *The Philosophy of Gabriel Marcel*, Kenneth Gallagher; *Gabriel Marcel*, Sam M. Keen

Marcus Aurelius (121–180) – a Roman philosopher who acted as emperor from 161–180 AD. In practicing Stoicism, Marcus Aurelius lived by the principles of this philosophy and endowed the major schools of philosophy at Athens with financial support. His only book, *Meditations*, was written between 170–180 AD while on military campaigns. He is known as the "Philosopher-King."

Marcus Aurelius was a personal leader and king for his warriors and worried about their survival in battle. He felt morally obligated as emperor to generate a good life for all Romans. During his rule, the persecution of Christians continued. Historians dispute his role in these persecutions. However, as an emperor he accepted the duty of destroying enemies of the empire.

Principal work: *Meditations*

"Receive wealth or prosperity without arrogance; and be prepared to let it go."

Marcus Aurelius, *Meditations*

Reference: *Marcus Aurelius, His Life and His World*, Arthur Farguharson, ed. D. A. Rees

Marcuse, Herbert (1898–1979) – a German social philosopher. Marcuse was an important social activist in the 1960s, during his professorship at UC–San Diego. He was the teacher of Angela Davis, a black activist who initiated a radical philosophy of civil disobedience and public protest.

Marcuse was critical of repressive social orders and drew from the philosophies of Marx, Hegel, and Freud. He advocated a philosophy of nonconformity toward the contemporary social framework, which he saw as a direct threat to human freedom. For Marcuse, people who are sexually promiscuous are repressed and uncritical. He termed this condition "desublimation." He argued that it is evidence of "objectification" and a "one-dimensional" existence.

Because people identify with the commodities they consume, they are alienated from the deeper self. Modern capitalist culture creates false needs and a false consciousness. Technology, through corporate profits, generates a power over people's lives. In most instances, the alienation is so complete that critical awareness of manipulation, exploitation, and deception is no longer possible. The alienated and "one-dimensional" life is seen as a normative set of values. Thus, Marcuse concluded that the working class could not be a subversive political force. It could not save itself from a life of empty materialism.

Principal works: *Eros and Civilization* (1955); and *One-Dimensional Man* (1964)

Reference: *Marcuse and Freedom*, Peter Lind

martinet – n. a very strict disciplinarian; one who insists on rigid adherence to details and rules

Marx, Karl (1818–1883) – a German economist, philosopher, and the founder of modern communism. Having had the widest social impact of any modern philosopher, Marx's views blend the dialectical theory of G. W. F. Hegel (1770–1831) with the atheistic materialism of Ludwig Feuerbach (1804–1872) in what is called "dialectical materialism."

Marx collaborated throughout his life with Friedrich Engels (1820–1895), whose literary skills gave expression to Marx's economic and political theory. In *Das Kapital*, Marx argues that the wealth of the capitalist class is produced through the exploitation of the proletariat or working class. The concept of *surplus value* (value that does not go to the worker) is used to show how capitalists acquire wealth and power over workers and smaller competition.

Marx argued that the central problem of society is class struggle, outlined through five major historical epochs: 1) primitive communalism, 2) slave society, 3) feudal society, 4) capitalist society, and 5) communist-socialist society. Moreover, class struggle is exhibited in religious, philosophic, and ethical ideals, which are often used to control the lower classes, supplementing the economic plans of the capitalist class. Along these lines, Marx as pragmatist, preferred the validity of action over the theoretical claims of philosophy.

Principal works: *Economic and Philosophic Manuscripts of 1844*, *The German Ideology* (1846), *The Communist Manifesto* (1848), and *Das Kapital* (1867)

"Philosophy and the study of the actual world have the same relationship to one another as masturbation and sexual love."

Karl Marx and Friedrich Engels, *German Ideology*

"Let the ruling classes tremble at a Communist revolution. The proletarians have nothing to lose but their chains."

Marx and Engels, *The Communist Manifesto*

Reference: *Karl Marx: His Life and Environment*, Isaiah Berlin

Maslow, Abraham (1908–1970) – an American psychologist who promoted humanistic psychology as an alternative to psychoanalysis and behaviorism. Maslow believed that it makes more sense to study people who are successful and well adjusted in life than to study sick individuals. Thus, humanistic psychology studies healthy personalities and the ways these people achieved their good self. Seeking a knowledge of inner resources, identity choices, and the creation of goals after basic needs have been met, is the individual's best approach to gaining a healthy psychological outlook.

Maslow defined man as a "wanting animal." As desires are satisfied, new desires take their place. In healthy persons there is an order and harmony in the successive desires. Self-actualized persons maintain a realistic outlook and tend to accept life openly. For Maslow, awareness and joy accompany true self-actualization. He illustrated this in his "hierarchy of needs." The interpretations of Maslow's writings have created a set of levels to illustrate his theory of motivation:

Self-actualization – art, music, personal ideals, spontaneity, creativity, acceptance of reason and facts, lack of prejudice

Esteem – self-respect, achievements, self-worth, confidence

Love – friendship, family, sexual intimacy, and marriage

Safety – money, family, health, security for the body and property

Physiology – water, food, shelter, clothing, sleep, homeostasis

Principal works: *The Psychology of Science* (1966); *Toward a Psychology of Being* (1962); *Motivation and Personality* (1951)

References: *A Third Force: The Psychology of Abraham Maslow*, Frank G. Goble; *Profile of Three Theories: Erikson, Maslow, Piaget*, Carol Tribe

masochism – n. in psychoanalysis, the subjective experience of pain or humiliation as a type of sexual perversion. Named after Leopold von Sacher-Masoch (1836–1895), a writer who suffered from this condition. It is often linked to feminine psychic elements and psychopathology. The term *masochism* was officially introduced by psychiatrist Richard F. von Krafft-Ebing in 1886.

Erotogenic masochism is the voluntary participation in sexual pain. *Moral masochism* expresses unconscious guilt and exhibits the individual as a victim without any necessary connection to sexual pleasure. *Feminine masochism* is seen in the subject's willingness to tolerate suffering and can occur in both men and women. In all these forms, aggressiveness is turned on the self in some manner. Masochism is the psychological opposite of sadism.

Theories on masochism indicate that it is connected with feelings of shame and confusion regarding sexuality, wherein subjects may treat pain as punishment for sexual desires. Some subjects also use pain to gain attention. So, masochism also has nonsexual application to explain pleasure from being punished or dominated.

References: *The Anatomy of Human Destructiveness*, Erich Fromm; *Masochism in Sex and Society*, Theodor Reik; *Self-Destructive Behavior*, Albert Roberts; *Psychopathia Sexualis*, Richard von Krafft-Ebing

materialism – n. in philosophy, any doctrine that rejects spirituality and spiritual factors and focuses on the primacy of matter. Materialism includes epiphenomenalism. It logically presupposes that any and all so-called spiritual details of life are merely effects of the primary material basis of reality.

Materialism has a long tradition. In Eastern philosophy, the doctrine of Charvaka (materialism) was evident about 590 BC. This system of materialism has some basis in the Rig Veda. It maintained the existence of four elements: earth, air, fire, and water. It emphasized a decidedly empirical approach to knowledge, arguing that what cannot be perceived does not exist. It held that pleasure and pain regulate the life of humanity. It proposed that spiritual afterlife is the result of faulty thinking. It criticized religious priests as charlatans, reducing them to creators of an ingenious plan for free subsistence at the expense of others.

In ancient Greece, Democritus (460–370 BC), the father of atomism, theorized that all experience has a measurable material basis. Atoms, as hard irreducible elements, provide the clues to any kind of phenomena. The strongest modern consequences to the school of materialism are found in the philosophy of Karl Marx (1818–1883), whose work in economics and political philosophy is magnified by the proposed bankruptcy of theological or spiritual philosophy.

References: *In the Tracks of Historical Materialism*, Perry Anderson; *A Materialist Theory of Mind*, David M. Armstrong; *The German Ideology*, Karl Marx and Friedrich Engels

matriliny – n. female lineage; ancestry through the mother's side

mawkish – adj. having an unpleasant taste; also, pathetic sentimentality

maya – n. fr. Sanskrit *maya*, meaning a cosmic force that creates the illusion that the phenomenal world is real. In Hinduism, it is the concept that the manifestation of Brahman creates problems of discernment. To say that the world is *maya* implies the existence of illusions in the mind of the perceiver. The challenge of *maya* is to see what is real vs. what appears to be real.

mea culpa – n. fr. Latin, meaning "my own fault"

meditation – n. fr. the Latin *meditio*, meaning center. Meditation refers to the contemplative practice of focusing on God, reality, or the self with the goal of improving the inner self. It characterizes the activity of many Eastern religions, such as Buddhism, Taoism, and Hinduism, which are seen as religions of meditation.

Meditation can be practiced in the repetition of a prayer, word, sound, or phrase. The somatic effects of meditation as a spiritual exercise are manifested in specific bodily changes such as lowered heart rate and metabolism. Scientific studies have confirmed meditation's effect on brain waves and respiration to be the opposite of those created by stress. Stress-related diseases are therapeutically controlled by regular meditation. Participants in yoga begin to experience significant mental changes after six weeks of daily practice.

"Mindfulness" is a contemporary term for meditation. It teaches people how to discover enjoyment in existence itself. Mindfulness, as a psychosomatic focus, produces healing effects for persons suffering from anxiety, depression, hypertension, insomnia, and even cancer and infertility. This has been an operating axiom in the emphasis on healing through spiritual praxis. Medical research has validated the meditative practices of East and West and promoted the use of these techniques as a supplement to physiological treatments of human suffering.

References: *Light Within: The Inner Path of Meditation*, Laurence Freeman; *The Heart of Buddhist Meditation*, Nayanaponika Thera; *Zen in the Art of Archery*, Eugene Herrigel; *Sadhana: A Way to God*, Anthony de Mello; and *Total Liberation: Zen Spirituality*, Ruben Habito

megalomania – n. excessive pride in one's self and one's achievements

meiosis – n. representation of a thing as less than it really is

melancholy – n. a state of mental or spiritual unhappiness; sadness

mélange – n. a collection or set of unrelated elements; a mess

meliorate – v. to improve

meliorism – n. fr. the Latin *melior*, meaning better. Meliorism is the belief that human action, while limited and imperfect, can improve the world. It was a hope of William James (1842–1910) in his work on pragmatism. James was a pluralist and defended the openness of the universe and its future against monistic and deterministic interpretations of reality. He believed that mind and matter are separate sources of organization, with mind having a clear power over the material order.

> *"The world is not yet with them, so they seem often in the midst of the world's affairs to be preposterous. Yet they are impregnators of the world, vivifiers and animators of potentialities of goodness which but for them would lie forever dormant."*

> William James, *Varieties of Religious Experience*

ménage à trois – n. a household of three, made up of a married pair and a lover of one of the spouses

mendacious – adj. untruthful; given to deception

mendacity – n. a lie

mendicant – n. a member of a religious order who practices both monastic life and outside religious work

mensal – adj. monthly

mentalism – n. also called *psychic monism*; the philosophical view that mind is ultimate reality and that the physical realm is a derivative

mercurial – adj. having the qualities of Mercury, star of Hermes and Greek messenger of the gods; eloquence, ingenuity, and thievishness; also, unpredictable

meritricious – adj. attractive in a false way; tawdry; also, relating to prostitution

Merleau-Ponty, Maurice (1908–1961) – a French philosopher of phenomenology and existentialism whose philosophical work contributed much to the broadening of both fields. Merleau-Ponty taught at the College of France and occasionally worked with Jean-Paul Sartre and Simone de Beauvoir.

Merleau-Ponty was influenced by Descartes and Husserl. He spent most of his life working out original re-interpretations of their thoughts. Idealism, in his view, was subject to problems stemming from fractures in the unity of consciousness and the world. Purely logical systems of the explanation of experience failed to produce complete understanding of human existence.

From Husserl, Merleau-Ponty acquired the means to provide a descriptive account of the design of consciousness. He also borrowed from Gestalt theory to build a theory of the person as consciousness. Consciousness is an awareness of objects and the perpetual "perspectiveness" that characterizes one's consciousness of objects. Thus, the world is always an experience of incompleteness. This condition is a requirement for consciousness to work and includes situations in which a person chooses courses of action among objects. Moral being is an implicit part of the creative nature of existence among objects.

Merleau-Ponty was also interested in the role of language in human consciousness. Language is the only tool that allows each person to create connections with other persons as perceiving subjects. Children present special opportunities to learn how language becomes part of being. The body itself is a continuous engagement with experience. The primacy of perception, corporeity, language, and art form the material for an adequate phenomenology of experience.

Principal works: *The Structure of Behavior* (1942), *Phenomenology of Perception* (1945), *Humanism and Terror* (1947), *In Praise of Philosophy* (1953), *Signs* (1960), *The Primacy of Perception* (1964), and *The Visible and the Invisible* (1964)

"The world is not an object such that I have in my possession the law of its making; it is the natural setting of, and field for, all my thoughts and all my

explicit perceptions. Truth does not 'inhabit' only the 'inner man,' or more accurately, there is no inner man, man is in the world, and only in the world does he know himself."

Maurice Merleau-Ponty, *Phenomenology of Perception*

Reference: *Merleau-Ponty's Philosophy*, Samuel B. Mallin

Mesmer, Franz Anton (1734–1815) – a Viennese doctor of medicine, Mesmer's name is the root of the word mesmerism, which is associated with his therapeutic methods. Mesmer believed in the existence of "animal magnetism," a fluid force much like gravity that permeates the universe and living creatures. He believed that this force could contribute to healing in individuals if properly channeled. Though often connected with theories of hypnotism, mesmerism is now classified with such arts as faith healing. Mesmer's theories never received wide scientific support.

References: *Anton Mesmer*, D. M. Walmsley, and *Hypnotism: Its History, Practice and Theory*, J. M. Bramwell

metaethics – n. the philosophical inquiry into the logical integrity of statements in the formulation of ethical systems. It is a separate kind of skepticism regarding the efficacy of the words themselves to convey strict and reliable meanings. This separate skepticism is called "second-order" inquiry and has its beginnings in language philosophy. Metaethics is a concern with the logical and epistemological quality of ethical statements. Historically, the work of G. E. Moore, *Principia Ethica* (1903), represents the shift over to this kind of concern.

References: *Ethics and Language*, C. L. Stevenson; *Ethical Theory: The Problems of Normative and Critical Ethics*, Richard B. Brandt; *The Language of Morals*, R. M. Hare; *Morals by Agreement*, David Gauthier

metaphor – n. a figure of speech in which a word belonging to a particular object is carried over to another object. It is the use of analogy to clarify meaning through a comparison; to suggest a likeness (e.g., "God the Father").

metaphysics – n. fr. the Greek *meta + physics*, meaning after physics. In philosophy it is the study of reality: its foundations, origins, and nature. Metaphysics is subdivided into *cosmology* (the study of the universe: its origin, nature, and development) and *ontology* (the study of being, including non-being). A. N. Whitehead

(1861–1947) regarded the conclusions of all metaphysical investigations to be only probable and never certain. In his view metaphysics must draw from the cumulative data of all disciplines to propose answers to the deepest questions humans can ask. Henri Bergson (1859–1941) believed that intuition was necessary to break past the natural world and the limited power of reason. Topics like God, death, the soul, time, space, and immortality are classical metaphysical concerns.

Anti-metaphysical philosophy has persisted since the time of Buddha. Buddha believed metaphysical reflection to be a waste of effort. Socrates also abandoned serious metaphysics, leaving that work to Plato and Aristotle. Thus, the philosophy of Western metaphysics is mainly defined through Platonism and Aristotelianism.

"Metaphysics has for the real object of its investigation three ideas only: God, Freedom, and Immortality."

Immanuel Kant, *The Critique of Pure Reason*

References: *Metaphysics*, W. H. Walsh; *Appearance and Reality*, F. H. Bradley; *An Introduction to Metaphysics*, Henri Bergson; *Metaphysics*, Aristotle

metapsychology – n. in psychology, a reference to Freud's hope of finding conceptual theories that would stand apart but support explanations of empirical psychic reality. Freud tried to show that metapsychology is an improvement of metaphysics.

It considers three points of view:

1) *dynamic* – psychical events are the result of conflicts and combinational forces that create pressures in the individual
2) *economic* – psychic movements and states consists of different quantifiable energy that can increase, decrease, or stabilize, and
3) *topographic* – the reference to levels or areas of investigation, as if to comprise "spaces" where psychic entities are found (e.g., the unconscious, the conscious, and the preconscious)

References: *Studies on Hysteria* and *Beyond the Pleasure Principle*, Sigmund Freud

metempirics – n. philosophy dealing with issues outside empiricism

metempsychosis – n. migration of the soul after death, especially to another body, whether human or animal. It is a feature of most Indian religions including Hinduism, Jainism, and Buddhism. Transmigration of souls is due to one's failure to reach spiritual completion and thus liberation from rebirth.

> *"The spiritual perfection which opens before man is the crown of long, patient, millennial outflowering of the Spirit in life and nature. The belief in a gradual spiritual progress and evolution is the secret of the almost universal Indian acceptance of the truth of reincarnation."*

> Sri Aurobindo (1872–1950), *Silver Jubilee Commemorative Volume of the Indian Philosophical Congress* (1950)

Aurobindo (1872–1950) advocated a metempsychosis strikingly similar to Neoplatonism. He believed that reality was a graded or staged hierarchy, starting with matter and ascending to Brahman or the Absolute. In his philosophy, Brahman is connected to the finite world through a type of dynamic spiritual force. This power influences the finite to work toward the infinite as well. In nature, it is a struggle from lower to higher evolutionary forms. In humanity, it is the quest to move from the physical to the mental to the spiritual-divine life. Aurobindo called the passage process "integral yoga," creating a transformation of being in life, mind, and body.

Among Greek philosophers, Pythagoras claimed a theory of metempsychosis, arguing that memories of past lives constitute proof.

References: *Six Pillars*, R. McDermott; and *The Synthesis of Yoga*, Sri Aurobindo

metonymy – n. the substitution of a characteristic or related concept for the thing meant (e.g., "the bottle" vs. "drink"); one word for another that it may be expected to suggest

miasma – n. a pervasive influence that corrupts or destroys; the putrid-smelling gases that arise from swamps, marshes, and ponds (metaphor)

micromania – n. depreciation of the self

millenarianism – n. (also with "millennialism") a feature of many religious prophecies, including Islam and Zorastrianism; in Christianity, the literal interpretation of chapter twenty in the Book of Revelation that Christ will rule the earth for one thousand years before the resurrection of the dead. Millenarianism has strong connections to apocalyptic teachings. It argues that there will be penultimate conflict with Satan's worldly manifestations. It is popular with Mormons, Anabaptists, Jehovah's Witnesses, Adventists, and other Christian fundamentalist theologies.

Mill, John Stuart (1806–1873) – an English philosopher. His fame rests on his construction of utilitarianism: goodness is the achievement of "the greatest happiness for the greatest number."

Influenced by the empiricist philosophers, Mill regarded inductive reasoning as the actual and productive use of logic. Mill noticed that all deductive arguments have an inductive basis, so experience rather than deductive processes provide ultimate confidence in conclusions. The causal connections one is able to make are experienced rather than thought. Mill developed a set of devices known as Mill's Methods to organize inductive conclusions.

Mill advocated democratic government, but only if there was a commitment to the education of its population. As a safeguard, educated people should have more influence than the uneducated.

> Principal works: *A System of Logic*, 2 vols. (1843), *On Liberty* (1859), *Utilitarianism* (1863), *The Subjection of Women* (1869), and *Three Essays on Religion* (1874)

> *"It is better to be a human being dissatisfied than a pig satisfied; better to be a Socrates dissatisfied than a fool satisfied. And if the fool, or the pig, is of a different opinion, it is because they only know their side of the question."*

> J. S. Mill, *Utilitarianism*

> References: *John Stuart Mill: A Mind at Large*, ed. Eugene August; *Happiness, Justice, and Freedom: The Moral and Political Philosophy of John Stuart Mill*, Fred R. Berger

minacious – adj. threatening.

Mind-Body Problem – n. in philosophy, the concern with the puzzling relationship of two very dissimilar entities (mind as nonmaterial and body as material) and how they might be explained to coexist with each other in the body. The main historical antecedent is René Descartes. Theories include:

1) *Interactionsim* – holds that the mind influences the body and that the body can act upon the mind. Examples are found in illness and depression, happiness and health.

2) *Parallelism* – argues that the mind and body do not interact. Their actions are independent and run parallel in time and space.

3) *Epiphenomenalism* – argues that mind is an effect of complex material arrangements; biological design. Mind derives from complex physical processes just as smoke rises from fire.

4) *Psychic monism* – argues that matter is illusory and that mind is primary. Matter or the body is the consequence of a spiritual primacy or foundation in the universe.

5) *Double-aspect theory* – argues that mind and body are aspects of a third, unidentified entity X that accounts for their coexistence.

6) *Functionalism* – seems to be an attempt to provide X. It argues that mind is a set of states (e.g., experiencing pleasure, pain, and/or desires) that are attached to certain behaviors or functions. This theory includes computerization. Functionalists like Hilary Putnam argue that mind can exist in machines. Ned Block, a critic of functionalism, finds the definition of "consciousness" to be an obstacle to equating mind with machines.

References: *Body and Mind*, K. K. Campbell; *Phaedo*, Plato; *The Mind and Its Place in Nature*, Charles D. Broad; *The Concept of Mind*, Gilbert Ryle; *Introduction to the Philosophy of Mind*, ed. Harold Morick

mirabile dictu – adj. fr. Latin, meaning "wonderful to relate," including "strange to tell"

Mirror Phase – n. in psychology, a phase between six and eighteen months when the child's encounter with the mirror reflection of itself is a source of fascination. Theory focuses on the relationship of the mirror reflection with development of the ego. Accordingly, the child supposedly anticipates mastery of its body perceived; related to narcissistic identification (René Spitz).

misanthrope – n. one who hates humanity

miscegenation – n. a marriage or cohabitation between persons of different races

miscreance – n. inauthentic religious faith; heresy; from *miscreate*—badly made.

miserabilism – n. a philosophy of pessimism. Fr. the Latin *miser*, meaning a wretched, grasping person; to live uncomfortably in order to generate wealth

misgiving – n. feeling of doubt or suspicion

misogamy – n. hatred of marriage

misogyny – n. hatred of women

misology – n. hatred of logic; an aversion to rational discourse

misoneism – n. hatred of change or innovation

misopedia – n. hatred of children

misprision – n. contempt; also, wrongful performance of duty, especially governmental duty

misprize – v. to hold in contempt or to undervalue

Mithraism – n. Mithras was a Persian sun god. Belief in this god was popular with the soldiers of Alexander the Great. Monuments to the god are very common at the old frontier boundaries of the Roman Empire. Mithras's slaying of a great bull and the spilling of its blood were said to produce vegetable life on earth, thus this mythos is commemorated in worship and the sacrifice of bulls is supposedly a basis for immortality. Therein lies the appeal of Mithraism to men in combat. Initiation was elaborate, limited to men, and involved passage through seven stages symbolizing movement through the cosmology of the seven heavens. Bullfighting has roots in Mithraism.

Reference: *Mithraic Studies*, 2 vols., ed. J. R. Hinnells

mnemonics – n. the study and art of memory. In Greek mythology, Mnemosyne was the goddess of memory. She slept with Zeus for nine nights and gave birth to the nine Muses.

Mnemonics are mental techniques for remembering things that can be hard to recall. It was emphasized as part of learning by the Greek Sophists, Plato, and Aristotle. For instance, to recall the days in each month, children are taught a mnemonic poem: "Thirty days hath September, April, June, and November. All the rest have thirty-one; except February alone, which has twenty-eight days clear, and twenty-nine in each leap year." To remember the colors of the rainbow use the phrase, "Richard of York Gave Battle in Vain" = Red, Orange, Yellow, Green, Blue, Indigo, Violet.

References: *The Memory Book*, Jerry Lucas and Harry Lorayne; *Ars Memoriae*, Giordano Bruno

mobocracy – n. rule by the irrational mob

modality – n. in logic, the classification of logical propositions, according to which they are modes (mannäer of taking effect) distinguished as asserting or denying the possibility, impossibility, contingency, or necessity of their content. What is the likelihood or probability of relationship to exist? Is a relation possible, impossible, contingent, or necessary?

modiste – n. one who sells what is fashionable, especially for women

mogigraphia – n. writer's cramp

mogilalia – n. any defect in the ability to speak; difficulty in speaking

moiety – n. one of two; half; fraction; small portion

moil – n. hard work; also, confusion

moira – n. in Greek philosophy, a reference to fate; what is allotted; representing forces that influence the life of the individual, simultaneously announcing the limits of the power of the gods. These forces are represented in the fates' names—Terror, Strife, Rumor, Death, Chaos, and Blind Vanity. Moira obtains a primary role in the type of life lived and refers to elements that cannot be realistically objected to. This point was reinforced by the recognition of limits with the gods themselves.

Reference: *Ethics and Human Action in Early Stoicism*, Brad Inwood

moksha – n. in Indian philosophy, Sanskrit for "deliverance." The term appears in the Upanishads as well as the Bhagavad Gita. It holds slightly different meanings for Hindus, Buddhists, and Jains. Primarily it suggests autonomy and self-control.

"Not going naked, nor matted hair, nor dirt, nor fasting, nor sleeping on the ground, nor rolling in the dust, nor sitting motionless can purify the one who has not overcome desire."

The Dhammapada, 500 BC

M

"When all desires of the heart cease, then one becomes immortal; then one attains to union with absolute being."

Katha Upanishad, ca. 600 BC

mollify – v. appease; pacify; conciliate

monandry – n. the practice of having one husband at a time

monasticism – n. fr. the Greek *monazein*, meaning to be alone. Monasticism is important in both Eastern and Western traditions. It focuses on self-mastery through contemplative life, withdrawal from urban influences, and a commitment to work, meditation, and physical simplicity. Typically, although there is a focus on being alone, monastic life usually means community membership with established rules of community life. In the West, St. Antony of Egypt (251–356 AD) created the first monasteries in the desert. For St. Antony the aims of the monk's life are centered on personal sanctification, especially through the vows of chastity, poverty, and obedience. Later St. Benedict of Nursia (481–548 AD) became the chief influence on monastic philosophy in the West (i.e., the Benedictines).

> References: *One Yet Two: Monastic Tradition, East and West*, ed. Basil M. Pennington; *The Silent Life*, Thomas Merton; *The Sufi Orders in Islam*, J. S. Trimingham; *Patrology*, J. Quasten

monition – n. warning; indication of danger

monocarpic – adj. bearing fruit once, resulting in death

monocracy – n. government or rule by one person

monoecious – adj. having both male and female sex organs; hermaphrodite

monology – n. the practice or act of a person speaking to one's self

monophobia – n. the fear of being alone

monotheism – n. in theology, the belief in one God and typically represented by the theological views found in Judaism, Christianity, and Islam.

> References: *Philosophers Speak of God*, C. Hartshorne and W. Reese; *From the Stone Age to Christianity*, W. F. Albright.

Montaigne, Michel de (1533–1592) – a French philosopher of skepticism. Montaigne criticized almost every known system of philosophy, religion, and science, casting doubt on any possibility of certainty. Strangely enough, he also served as mayor of Bordeaux and was a member of the local parliament.

As a cynical skeptic, Montaigne held that people do not know or value truth and goodness. Human beings are basically vain and immoral, especially in their "civilized" state. People who live in primitive settings are actually much more dignified. Even the life of animals seems better than the degraded existence of modern man. So, Montaigne advocated a simple and natural existence to reduce the ambition and egoism that are so destructive to personal peace and happiness.

These views led Montaigne to advocate the role of faith and a version of Christianity. He abandoned the pretense that human reason can decipher reality and thought all rational puzzles pointed eventually to the acceptance of faith.

Principal work: *Essays*, 3 vols. (1588)

"*Wonder is the foundation of all philosophy, inquiry its progress, ignorance its end…Ignorance that knows itself, that judges itself and condemns itself, is not complete ignorance: to be that, it must be ignorant of itself.*"

Michel de Montaigne, *Essays*

References: *Montaigne*, Donald M. Frame; *The Essays of Montaigne: A Critical Exploration*, R. A. Sayce

montane – adj. being mountainous; eminent

Moore, George Edward (1873–1958) – an English philosopher sometimes labeled a realist, Moore was raised in a religious home but had a very degrading experience at the age of twelve. He was forced to spread the word of Jesus. This caused him much personal torment and destroyed his interest in religion. Subsequently, Moore's philosophical interests were directed toward a construction of realist philosophy at the expense of idealism.

Moore was noted for his work in ethical theory and argued that the fundamental purpose of ethics is to identify one object: the good. Central to his definition of the good were the roles of human affection and aesthetic enjoyment.

Moore's work is important for meta-ethics. His attention to philosophical detail led him to argue that "good" is indefinable. Moore offered to explain "good" under the theme of "ethical intuitionism."

Moore's Paradox: involves the logical absurdity of saying, "It is raining, but I don't believe it is raining." Moore argued that the absurdity is superficial, and that if one thinks about it, it's possible that it is raining, while believing that it is not raining.

Principal works: *Principia Ethica* (1903), *Ethics* (1912), and *Philosophical Papers* (1959)

"No one, probably, who has asked himself the question has ever doubted that personal affection and the appreciation of what is beautiful in Art or Nature, are good in themselves; nor, if we consider strictly what things are worth having 'purely for their own sakes,' does it appear probable that anyone will think that anything else has nearly so great a value as the things which are included under these two heads."

G. E. Moore, *Principia Ethica*

Reference: *G.E. Moore and the Cambridge Apostles*, Paul Levy

moral fatigue – n. in ethics, the observation that moral and ethical philosophies in the life of the individual and society may undergo sustained pressure and, thus, exhibit a weakening of will, collectively or individually.

Moral fatigue is the slackening of commitment and the loss of spiritual strength in upholding certain moral positions. This fatigue may be the sign that a revision of ethics is necessary in the life of the state or the individual. Or, it may indicate that the original inspiration and vision of moral goals need to be revitalized.

moralism – n. the practice of morality as distinct from religion; religion reduced to morality, implying a narrow attitude

morbific – adj. producing disease

mordacious – adj. the tendency to bite; a biting quality of speech

mordant – adj. being sarcastic or harsh in manner; from *mordancy* – n. sharply critical thoughts or speech

moribund – adj. being in death throes; near death

morpheme – n. in language, the smallest syntactically meaningful element, as in the use of "s" to show plurality; also described as a feature of language showing the relations between nouns, verbs, adjectives, and concrete adverbs (as an affix, a preposition, or a conjunction)

mortiferous – adj. having the power to cause death

mortify – v. to bring about the death of something; to eliminate vitality

mukti – n. in Hinduism, a reference to "liberation." It is the final release from worldly existence.

mundify – v. to set free, especially from noxious or irritating concerns (matter); cleanse

munificent – adj. generous; very giving, even lavish

myopia – n. the condition of lacking breadth of understanding; the absence of foresight; defective vision, especially an inability to see laterally

mysophilia – n. the love of filth; including indifference to cleanliness

mysophobia – n. extreme fear of dirt or infective bacteria

mystagogue – n. a teacher of mystical doctrines; one who initiates novices into esoteric practices; a cult leader

mystery cult or religion – n. any religion or cult that uses secret rites for admission. As a general term, it does not include some of the ancient cults of Egypt and Greece. Still, all these religions provide esoteric knowledge that is not publicly shared, and the implication of special blessings for the devotees is strong.

mysticism – n. in philosophy, the term refers to any ideology that is centered on the spiritual realm more than the ordinary world. Generally, mysticism tries to find a union or mental oneness with the foundation of experienced reality, be it God or the Divine, Brahman or Truth. It employs intuitive reason more than discursive processes, banking heavily on the emotional affirmation of core spirituality in persons and things. In fact, mysticism in both Eastern and Western traditions is suspicious of purely rational explanations of reality.

M

"The estate of Divine union consists in the total transformation of the will into the will of God, in such a way that every movement of the will shall be always the movement of the will of God."

St. John of the Cross (1542–1591), *Ascent of Mt. Carmel*

References: *Mysticism in the World's Religions*, Geoffrey Parrinder; *Mysticism*, Robert Zaehner; *Mysticism: Christian and Buddhist*, Daisetz T. Suzuki

mythomania – n. an extreme need to lie or exaggerate the ordinary

nadir – n. the lowest point beneath the earth; the point of the celestial sphere that is directly opposite its zenith; the time of greatest depression

Nagarjuna (100–200 AD) – in Buddhism, the philosophical founder of the Middle Way School, related ideologically to Zen principles. Nagarjuna's way to nirvana was to apply rigorous criticism to all rational philosophies. Implicit within this strategy was the assumption that all words and ideas bind us down, trapping us in constructs of reality that actually manage to blind us.

Sunyata is the notion of "emptiness." Nagarjuna argued that *sunyata* is a riddance of this world's entrapments. Of course, encased within this strategy of emptiness lies a paradox, for it is a concept to be grasped and the grasping of concepts is wrong for the goal of liberation. Even *nirvana* is an illusion. There is nothing more important in the thrust of Zen Buddhism than transcendence of illusions.

To accommodate the paradox of knowing, Nagarjuna held a two-tiered epistemology: a high level of philosophical discourse, where knowledge is somewhat misleading, and a lower level of discourse employing common sense for success in daily life.

Principal works: *Twenty Verses on the Great Vehicle* and *Treatise on the Middle Doctrine*

References: *Nagarjuna's Philosophy*, K. Venkata Ramanan; *Empty Logic: Madhyamika Buddhism from Chinese Sources*, Hsueh-li Cheng

Nag Hammadi Papyri – n. manuscripts found near Chenoboskia (Nag Hammadi), Egypt, in 1945. They reveal details of gnostic philosophy and testify to the importance of gnosticism in the Judeo-Christian worldview in twelve volumes.

Reference: *Nag Hammadi Library*, James M. Robinson

naïve realism – n. "naïve" meaning childlike; the view that what one sees and experiences is the sum total of reality. Basically, it represents a failure of critical reason. Naïve realism underestimates the complexity and mystery of the objective world. It involves an exaggerated confidence in common sense. It is the philosophy of children and adults who do not see a need to think about things.

naology – n. study of ancient temples, especially their edifices

naos – n. temple

narcissism – n. fr. Narcissus, exclusive love of one's self, to the detriment of social effectiveness. Narcissus was unable to resist admiring his reflection whenever possible.

In Freud, narcissism explains the object-choice in homosexuals, who see themselves and each other as the correct sexual object. Narcissism as "autoeroticism" finds its parallel in the homosexual or lesbian who seeks lovers who resemble his or her self.

The healthy development of love, which is a turning toward living things in the human environment, is reversed in the pathological individual. This theory carries us to further insights on the development of love. Psychoanalysis, thus, poses the distinction between "primary" and "secondary" narcissism.

References: *Three Essays on the Theory of Sexuality*, S. Freud; "Le Stade du Miroir comme Formateur de la Fonction du Je," Jacques Lacan (Trans. as "The Mirror-Phase," *New Left Review*, 1968, 51, 71–77); *The Art of Loving*, Erich Fromm

narcolepsy – n. a strong need to sleep; sleep beyond normal biological demands

narcomania – n. an uncontrollable desire for drugs that soothe the body and relieve pain **narcosis** – n. a state of unconsciousness caused by chemicals (e.g., LSD and opium)

narcosynthesis – n. treatment of mental pathology with the use of drugs

nascent – adj. the quality of beginning; coming into being

natant – adj. floating

naturalism – n. in philosophy, the view that reality has no supernatural order. Nature is the whole of reality, and any explanations about reality must be connected to the natural world. Reference to objects and events must be limited to space-time references in order to be valid. Non-natural orders are fictions of the mind.

natural theology – n. pursuit of a knowledge of God independent of traditional revelation; use of nature as a paradigm for an understanding of God. It emphasizes the designs in nature as evidence of a Designer. Natural theology in the philosophy of William Paley occurs as the Watchmaker Argument: if one finds a watch, then one concludes there is a watchmaker. Thomas Malthus also defended a natural theology.

necrolatry – n. worship of the dead

necromancy – n. witchcraft, especially in relation to communication with the dead; sorcery work with the dead, often with the goal of promoting evil; magic and fortune-telling based on knowledge that the dead possess regarding this world and the next

necromimesis – n. the subjective belief that one is dead

necrophilia – n. fascination with the dead; sexual attraction to corpses of the recently deceased; erotic feelings toward the dead; psychopathology; the love of death

necrophobia – n. an extreme fear of death

need for punishment – n. in psychology, behavior that turns out to be the quest for unpleasant or humiliating experiences, from which a pathological enjoyment is derived. It raises metapsychological problems of interpretation, but it is generally connected with the death instinct. It is sometimes included in personality portraits where melancholia exists. Then too, some theoretical treatments include suicide as "need for punishment."

Reference: *The Ego and the Id*, Sigmund Freud; *Neurosis and Human Growth*, Karen Danielson-Horney

nefarious – adj. being particularly evil, wicked, or mean; having flagrant disregard for goodness

nemesis – n. fr. the Greek *nemein*, meaning "to give what is due"; a goddess of ancient Greece, identified with forests and fertility and the personification of divine revenge. Nemesis was especially opposed to human arrogance and its associated moral consequences: temerity (recklessness), excess, insolence, and the failure to live up to one's duties.

The holy ground of Nemesis was called *nemos* (a clearing in the woods), a place where mortals could not encroach. Thus, *adyton*, the notion of trespassing, was connected to her realm of being as a moral aspect of her coexistence with mortals. Over time, she was associated with *nomos* (law), because the Greeks recognized the ability of humans to lose shame for satisfying their irrational desires. Without shame, punishment became an essential deterrent to human wrongdoing. Nemesis operates as the balance in human affairs, the protectress of that which is good and holy over and above the *hubris* (pride) of mortals, through her power to inflict suffering for moral evil. Her punishments were complex and manifested themselves in the spiritual lives of immoral individuals by deeper and deeper feelings of isolation and unhappiness.

Reference: *Paideia: Ideals of Greek Culture*, Werner Jaeger

neologism – n. a word or phrase that is new and perhaps crude or inappropriate

Neoplatonism – n. the philosophical views of Plotinus (204–270 AD). As the name implies, it is a reformation of Platonism, a "new Platonism." It had a formative impact on the metaphysics of Christianity through St. Augustine. Plotinus argued that all of reality is a series of emanations from the One (God). Near the center is the first emanation, *nous* (mind). The second emanation is *psyche* (soul). At the outer edges of reality one finds matter. Beyond matter there is only nothingness. The theocentric nature of Neoplatonism suggests as things become more intelligible, they become more spiritual. Reason and spirituality are mixed together, as are matter and chaos. Matter derives its structure from the higher emanations.

"The One is perfect because it seeks for nothing, and possesses nothing, and has need of nothing; and being perfect, it overflows, and this its superabundance provides an Other."

Plotinus, *Enneads*, vol. 2, 1

References: *Plotinus: The Road to Reality*, John Rist; *The Cambridge History of Later Greek and Early Medieval Philosophy*, ed. A. H. Armstrong

neoteric – adj. novel; recently begun

nepenthe – n. something that removes suffering, grief, etc.

nepotism – n. rule by family; bestowal of office or position on the basis of family ties rather than competence and merit

nescience – n. a state of ignorance

Nestorianism – n. the Christological views of Nestorius (d. ca. 451 AD). It argues that there were two separate Persons in Christ, one being God and the other being human. This view stands opposed to the traditional view that Christ was one single Person having the attributes of both God and humanity. In modern times, Nestorianism has survived in the mountains of Kurdistan among descendants of the original Nestorian communities as Assyrian Christians.

> *"I have learned from Scripture that God passed through the Virgin Mother of Christ; that God was born of her I have never learned."*

> Nestorius, *Reply to Proclus* (429 AD)

> Reference: *Nestorius and His Place in the History of Christian Doctrine,* Friedrich Loofs

Neurath, Otto (1882–1945) – an Austrian philosopher and sociologist, Neurath made important contributions to the field of linguistic analysis. He was also very interested in social and political problems, working hard to make improvements in education and government. One of Neurath's beliefs was that education was the key to social harmony and that it could be made more effective by the development of a visual learning process. This was funded on the assumption that there is a materialist basis of knowing.

For Neurath, a principal obstacle to learning was the ambiguity and uncertainty of meaning in language. He sought a way of using only pictorial signs, his "Vienna Method," to provide acquisition of knowledge that was stripped of encumbrances and easily remembered. Neurath promoted an educational approach that was simple, encyclopedist, and general. He believed that an excellent instructor could simplify the most complex theories and focus clearly on the most important ideas.

> Principal works: *Scientific World View* (1929), *Empirical Sociology* (1931), and *Foundations of the Social Sciences* (1944)

"We are like sailors who must rebuild their ship on the open sea, never able to dismantle it in dry-dock and to reconstruct it there out of the best materials... Vague linguistic conglomerations always remain in one way or another as components of the ship."

Otto Neurath, "Protocol Sentences" in *Logical Positivism*, A. J. Ayer

Reference: *Otto Neurath*, eds. F. Stadler and E. Nemeth

nexal – adj. of, or relating to

nexus – n. link; connection

nidification – n. the act of nest building; the process of providing a secret or protected place

nidulus – n. center

nidus – n. a breeding place; nest or home

Niebuhr, Reinhold (1892–1971) – an American philosopher-theologian born in Wright City, Missouri, Niebuhr gained an important place in public debates of the forties and fifties. His expertise ranged from philosophy to economics to social policy and psychology. Lacking a doctorate, he humored himself as a "mongrel among thoroughbreds," a Midwesterner among Easterners, a master's prepared intellectual among doctorates.

Labeled a "Christian Realist," Niebuhr interpreted this as theological realism, measured against spiritual and idealistic facts, especially as found in the ethics of Jesus. His idea of "vertical dialectic" emphasized the creative and self-transcendent properties of mankind along with a finite, contingent creatureliness.

In *Moral Man and Immoral Society*, Niebuhr outlines the uses of power in social groups, the manner in which it corrupts individuals striving to be good, and the way in which idealism runs into trouble when reality presents morally ambiguous situations, situations that cannot be toppled by mere intellectual desire for social justice.

Niebuhr's "Serenity Prayer" is a profession of faith for Alcoholics Anonymous.

Principal works: *Moral Man and Immoral Society* (1932), *Reflections on the End of an Era* (1934), *Christianity and Power Politics* (1940), *The Nature and Destiny of Man*, 2 vols. (1941–43), and *The Irony of American History* (1952)

"Nothing that is worth doing can be achieved in our lifetime; therefore we must be saved by hope. Nothing which is true or beautiful or good makes complete sense in any immediate context of history; therefore we must be saved by faith.

"Nothing we do, however virtuous, can be accomplished alone; therefore we are saved by love. No virtuous act is quite as virtuous from the standpoint of our friend or foe as it is from our standpoint. Therefore we must be saved by the final form of love which is forgiveness."

Reinhold Niebuhr, *The Irony of American History*

References: *Reinhold Niebuhr*, Richard Fox; *Reinhold Niebuhr: His Religious, Social, and Political Thought*, eds. R. W. Bretall and C. W. Kegley

Nietzsche, Friedrich W. (1844–1900) – a German existentialist philosopher and forerunner for postmodernism. Nietzsche's social and self-criticism produced interesting interpretations of human existence. Sometimes called "the father of existentialism," Nietzsche introduced cultural criticism as philosophy. He made rich use of metaphors, aphorisms, and contradiction throughout his writings, especially in *Thus Spoke Zarathustra*.

Nietzsche's analysis of human problems discerned three levels of crises: the physical, the psychological, and the ontological. For modern humanity, the central crisis is ontological. People are uncomfortable with existence itself. The absence of apparent ontological meaning and purpose in people's lives leads them to construct cheap substitutions of meaning in the areas of physical and psychological existence (e.g., sensual hedonism and identification with the state).

An antagonist and creator of psychology, Nietzsche characterized modern life as the era of nihilism and psychology rather than reason and morality. Moreover, insanity, which is the domain of psychology, has self-deepening features because it does not recognize the legitimacy of ontological reflection. Psychologically, all human beings seek power (Will to Power) over their domain and other persons. Life is about power relationships. This may be a consequence of anxiety regarding the security of life, but Nietzsche calls it the will…Having missed the essential signs directing life toward an authentic ontological meaning, people seek power only in obvious but unsatisfying forms (i.e., physical achievements, property, domination of others, and hedonistic abandon). For many, modern life produces feelings of emptiness that generate frustration, cruelty, violence, despair, and drunkenness (Dionysus).

Nietzsche makes use of nihilism to explain the absence of true spiritual power in the lives of individuals. The annihilation of all morals through the "Death of God" ensures a world divided between a few moral champions (the master morality of high-caliber individuals) and herds of moral cowards (the slave morality of low-caliber individuals). The master morality (*Das Ubermensch*) is guided by reason, creativity, courage, authentic selfhood, and compassion (Apollo).

In the twentieth century, Nietzsche's views were used eisegetically to serve the political ambitions of Nazism; similar misuses were made of Plato and the Gospel of John, but Nietzsche gets the lion's share of blame for fueling fascism. Truthfully, Nietzsche preferred to categorize people according to a moral typology, often reserving some of his severest criticism for the Germans: "How much dreary heaviness, lameness, dampness, sloppiness, how much beer there is in the German intellect!" (*Twilight of the Idols*)

Nietzsche's work sets up many important observations for the development of modern existentialism, especially the theme that one must choose one's own way toward meaning and self-knowledge.

Principal works: *The Birth of Tragedy* (1872), *Human, All Too Human* (1878), *Beyond Good and Evil* (1886), *Thus Spoke Zarathustra* (1885), *The Genealogy of Morals* (1887), and *Twilight of the Idols* (1888)

"Creation—that is the greatest redemption from suffering, and life's easement. But that the creator may exist, that itself requires suffering and much transformation...For the creator himself to be the child new-born he must also be willing to be the mother and endure the mother's pain...All feeling 'suffers' in me and is in prison: but my willing always comes to me as my liberator and bringer of joy... Willing liberates: that is the true doctrine of will and freedom."

F .W. Nietzsche, *Thus Spoke Zarathustra*

References: *The New Nietzsche: Contemporary Styles of Interpretation*, ed. D. B. Allison; *Nietzsche*, Peter Bergman; *Nietzsche: Philosopher, Psychologist, Anti-Christ*, Walter Kaufmann

nihilism – n. in philosophy, the view that traditional values are without substance or foundation. It argues that life is senseless and useless. It also denies an objective ground for moral truths. Nihilism can be applied to politics, society, epistemology, religion, and theology, such that the perception of order and harmony as constituent qualities find no predictable history.

Nihilism finds expression in the views of Philipp Mainländer (1841–1876), author of *The Philosophy of Redemption* (1876). His arguments for theological nihilism, the death of God, run like this: 1) God is a unity but the world is a plurality, so God cannot be part of this scene, 2) God is joy but the world is dominated by suffering, so God is not part of this scene, 3) Nonexistence is better than existence, because unity and joy are not part of this world, 4) It is logical to admit that life is suffering and chaos, so death is redemption. From Mainländer, a student of Schopenhauer, the exposition of nihilism is taken up by Friedrich Nietzsche (1844–1900), who attempts to combat it with the theory of transvaluation and the introduction of "courage" as the cardinal virtue.

In Nietzsche, nihilism appears as a positive condition for the creation of new values, similar to positive arguments for anarchy. Catastrophe paves the way for the reconstruction of values.

References: *The Opening of Vision: Nihilism and the Postmodern Situation*, David M. Levin; *The Literature of Nihilism*, Charles I. Glicksberg; *The Dialectic of Nihilism*, Gillian Rose

nirvana – n. Sanskrit for "blown-out" or "extinguished." Buddhist philosophy uses this term to identify the elimination of worldly desires. In classic Buddhist fashion, whatever one says to describe nirvana will fail to describe nirvana. In the Hinayana school, nirvana means extinction. In the Mahayana school, nirvana means total bliss, although the Mahayana teachings of Nagarjuna (100–200 AD) argue that nirvana is itself merely another illusion among the countless illusions of this world. For Nagarjuna, author of *Treatise on the Middle Doctrine*, if nirvana exists then it is subject to nonexistence. Whatever is subject to nonexistence is an illusion.

"Nirvana, or self-extinction in Brahman, clearly implies extinction of the ego, the false self, in the Higher Self—the source of all knowledge, of all existence, and of all happiness."

Swami Prabhavananda, *The Spiritual Heritage of India*

nirvana principle – n. in psychology, a view ascribed to Barbara Low (1877–1955), a British psychoanalyst. She argues that the "nirvana principle" is the tendency to reduce internal pressures of excitement and desire. It is connected theoretically to masochism and the death instinct.

Reference: *The Language of Psychoanalysis*, Jean Laplanche and Jean-Bertrand Pontalis

niveous – adj. being snowlike, pure

nocent – adj. harmful or dangerous

nocturnal – adj. occurring at night or active at night

nocuous – adj. harmful

noegenesis – n. firsthand knowledge; knowledge acquired by intellect itself

noema – n. fr. the Greek *noema*, meaning thought, perception, or understanding. In the philosophy of Edmund Husserl (1859–1938), the term signifies the element of thought as material rather than as act. For Husserl, act is represented by "noesis."

noesis – n. thinking as act

noetic – adj. relating to the mind

nomology – n. the study of physical laws and/or the rules of reasoning

nosophobia – n. morbid fear of disease

nostomania – n. extreme homesickness

noxious – adj. distasteful; harmful to life in body or mind

nuance – n. a subtle distinction

nyctophobia – n. fear of darkness

obdurate – adj. hardened against tender feelings

obeisance – n. respect, submission, or homage

obfuscate – v. to confuse

objurgate – v. to scold or put down harshly

oblate – n. someone who is dedicated to monastic life

obliquity – n. deviation from normative values, as in moral philosophy; like its adjective *oblique*—meaning devious or not straightforward.

oblivescence – n. a state of forgetfulness

obscurantism – n. deliberate introduction of vagueness; concealment of understanding

obsequence – n. eagerness to please or satisfy

obsequious – adj. being servile or excessively submissive

obsolescence – n. the condition of being useless or technically out of date

obstreperous – adj. unruly, noisy; marked aggressiveness

obtest – v. to call forth as a witness

obtrusive – adj. annoyingly pretentious or showy; forward in manner

obtuse – adj. blunt; lacking sharpness of form; also, stupid

obumbrate – v. to cloud over

obversion – n. fr. Latin *obvertere*, meaning to turn toward. In logic, it refers to a form of immediate inference: the act of creating a logically equivalent statement. In obversion, a logical equivalent is created by changing the quality of a categorical statement and negating its predicate. For example: "All politicians are liars" is obverted to "No politicians are non-liars."

obviate – v. to make unnecessary

occidental – n. fr. Latin *occidere*, meaning to set or fall down. Thus, occidental refers to a member of peoples of the Western world.

occlusion – n. a complete obstruction; blockage of a passageway

ochlocracy – n. government by the masses

ochlophobia – n. fear of crowds

odalisque – n. a female slave in a harem; concubine

odium – n. fr. Latin *odi*, meaning hate. In Greek *odyssasthai*, meaning to be angry; marked by loathing and contempt.

odium theologicum – n. bitterness developed during a religious discussion; an unyielding refusal to philosophize about theological or religious differences

Oedipus complex – n. in psychology, the attachment of the child to a parent of the opposite sex, involving a hostility toward the rival, the parent of the same sex. Supposedly, it plays a role in the formation of the personality and the adjustment to sexuality. Freud argued it to be the result of maturing sexual and aggressive instincts.

In Greek mythology, Oedipus was the son of King Laius and Jacosta. Oedipus was abandoned on Mt. Cithaeron, because it was prophesized that he would kill his father and marry his mother. He was then found by a shepherd and raised by King Polybius of Corinth. Believing Polybius to be his father and fearing his own actions, Oedipus fled Corinth when he learned of the prophecy. On his journey, he killed a stranger. This stranger turned out to be his real father, Laius.

O

When Oedipus entered Thebes, he learned that the city was ruled by a sphinx who killed those unable to solve her riddle: "Who walks on four feet in the morning, two at noon, and three in the evening?" Oedipus became the hero of Thebes by replying, "Man, in the three ages of life." As a reward, he won the hand of the widowed queen, who turned out to be his mother, Jacosta.

Oedipus married Jacosta and they had two sons, Eteocles and Polynices, and two daughters, Ismene and Antigone. In time, Jacosta learned who her husband was and killed herself by hanging. Oedipus blinded himself as an act of atonement. Then Jacosta's brother, Creon, drove Oedipus away. His daughters, Antigone and Ismene, helped Oedipus to prepare for his own suicide at a sacred grove of trees.

Reference: *Oedipus: The Ancient Legend and Its Later Analogues*, Lowell Edmunds

oeillade – n. quick visual contact; affectionate glance

officious – adj. meddling interference

oligolalia – n. poverty of language; a mental condition complicated by a small vocabulary

oligophrenia – n. feeblemindedness; low mental inventory

oligopoly – n. a market in which there are many buyers and few sellers

oligopsony – n. a market in which there are many sellers and few buyers

omen – n. a phenomenon or event believed to predict the nature of a future event

omission – n. the act of leaving out

omnifarious – adj. of all sorts or all varieties

onanism – n. fr. *Onan*, son of Judah (Gen. 38:9); masturbation, self-gratification, or coitus interruptus

oneiric – adj. having to do with dreams

onerous – adj. being troublesome; involving an excessive burden

oniomania – n. in psychology, the neurotic need to shop or buy things; an irrepressible urge to spend money

ontogeny – n. the record of development of a particular organism or being

ontological force – n. in ethics, reference to the spiritual effects of an act on the life of the agent. The power of acts to shape the spiritual condition of the agent, positively or negatively. It is a measurement of the way life choices have an influence on the psychology of the person (think also of *karma*); related to the investigation of post-traumatic stress syndrome or suicide following a horrible experience of some kind. More positively, it is the observable therapeutic effect of things like friendship, peak experiences, love, and skill development.

ontology – n. in philosophy, the study of the origin, nature, and purpose of being; the study of existence, being vs. nonbeing. Ontology is a subbranch of metaphysics, stemming from the Greek *ontos*, meaning "existence" or "being," and *logos*, meaning purpose, reason, or study of. For ontology, Greek philosophy identifies Parmenides (being), Plato (forms), and Aristotle (causality, potentiality, and actuality). Martin Heidegger's work in ontology remains a benchmark for twentieth-century definitions of being, but he relies on Greek philosophy, as do most modern ontologists.

Ontological reflection on death is a universal theme, and this finds further contemporary expression through philosophers like Edmund Husserl, Jean-Paul Sartre, Paul Tillich, Karl Jaspers, Maurice Merleau-Ponty, Étienne Gilson, and Martin Heidegger.

On a practical level, thinking about death is thanatology (Kübler-Ross, Herman Feifel). Thanatology is not ontology, but it creates a more accessible discussion of being and nonbeing for most people. The way this can be connected to ontology is through the Socratic reflections on death in the *Phaedo*, where the attitude toward death and the nature of the soul are discussed at length.

> References: *The Basic Problems of Phenomenology*, Martin Heidegger; *The Courage to Be*, Paul Tillich; *Being and Nothingness*, Jean-Paul Sartre; *Way to Wisdom*, Karl Jaspers; *Being and Some Philosophers*, Étienne Gilson; *On Death and Dying*, Elisabeth Kübler-Ross

onus – n. a burden that is particularly disagreeable

opacify – v. to make impermeable to light

oppilate – v. to obstruct or block up

opprobrium – n. conduct that brings about disgrace, even contempt

oppugn – v. to fight against, especially with argumentation

orbicular – adj. circular

Ortega y Gasset, José (1883–1955) – an important Spanish philosopher of existentialism whose literary achievements helped to establish philosophical thought in Latin America.

Ortega begins with a biological emphasis on life. From there he builds reflection toward a metaphysical sense of reality. One finds an interesting bipolarity in his existentialism that helps to heighten enthusiasm for understanding life. He called this view "the metaphysics of vital reason." Things and persons are essential to each other, each complementing the other's existence. The ultimate setting of reality is always a setting of the self with things.

In his epistemology, he advocates a position called "perspectivism." All points of view are partial, limited, and specific. Each person is necessarily limited to his or her own experience of knowing reality. Ortega develops this into an awareness of what one's personal choices are to find a satisfying life. The specific nature of one's knowledge of the world leads him to argue that each person has one correct choice to make in forming a meaningful life: a vocation or mission.

Ortega's critique of society produced a reaction against the alienating effects of mass society. Only individuals can really plan in a specific direction. Masses of people aren't able to strive creatively or structure a truly meaningful existence. An awareness of this has, in Ortega's view, produced the weakened unity of community in societies throughout the world. The individual senses the compromised vitality of life in a mass society, thus moving away from its damaging effects is the existential answer.

Principal works: *Meditations on Quixote* (1914), *Invertebrate Spain* (1922), *Dehumanization of Art* (1925), *The Revolt of the Masses* (1929), *Toward a Philosophy of History* (1941), and *What Is Philosophy?* (1957)

"The most trivial and at the same time the most important note in human life is that man has no choice but to be always doing something to keep himself in existence. Life is given to us; we do not give it to ourselves, rather we find ourselves in it, suddenly and without knowing how. But the life which is given us is not given us ready-made; we must make it ourselves, each one his own. Life is a task…Each individual before doing anything must decide for himself and at his own risk what he is going to do. But this decision is impossible unless one possesses

certain convictions concerning the nature of things around one, the nature of other men, and the nature of oneself."

José Ortega y Gasset, *Toward a Philosophy of History*

Reference: *The Imperative of Modernity: An Intellectual Biography of José Ortega y Gasset*, R. Gray

Orwell, George (1903–1950) – a British social philosopher. Orwell's birth name was Eric Arthur Blair. He is remembered as the author of *Animal Farm* (1945) and *1984* (1949).

Orwell had a lifelong fear and loathing of totalitarian governments and the bureaucratic organization of life. In *1984*, Orwell predicts the future to be one governed by totalitarian control of thought and speech. The invention of "Newspeak" is a language devoid of philosophical vocabulary. In *1984*, everyone is kept under surveillance by "Big Brother," who maintains harmony by policing free thought.

Today, the prophetic nature of this book seems more relevant than ever before as mistrust generates a society under total surveillance. The unintended consequence of personal technology is the creation of surveillance source points for spy agencies, law enforcement, taxing authorities, etc., "Big Brother".

References: *George Orwell: A Reassessment*, P. Buitenhuis and I. B. Nadel; and *George Orwell: The Age's Adversary*, P. Reilly

osseous – adj. consisting of or being like bone; hardened. The verb: *ossify*, meaning to make rigid or inactive

ostiary – n. a gatekeeper or guardian

otic – adj. relating to the ear; also, showing an increase or a formation

otiose – adj. useless.

Otto, Rudolf (1869–1937) – a German philosopher of religion. Otto thought about the conceptual interpretation of religious phenomena, especially the spiritual attitude of the believer identifies as, 1) *numinous* – the feeling of awe that enters the believer in the presence of the holy place or sacred entity, and 2) *mysterium tremendum* – the apprehension of mystery that lies beyond all reasoning. This apprehension is a sense of the fathomless nature of reality. And finally, 3) *mysterium fascinosum* – the spiritual satisfaction of the believer in giving in to the enchantment of religious existence. These three elements together comprise Otto's theoretical basis for identifying "holiness," which has both rational and nonrational elements.

Otto's work incorporates a Kantian basis acquired from Jakob Fries (1773–1843) and the Neo-Kantian School of Göttingen.

Principal works: *The Philosophy of Religion of Kant-Fries and Its Application to Theology* (1909), *Darwinism and Religion* (1910), *The Idea of the Holy* (1917), and *Mysticism East and West* (1926)

"In every highly developed religion the appreciation of moral obligation and duty, ranking as a claim of the deity upon man, has been developed side by side with the religious feeling itself. None the less a profoundly humble and heartfelt recognition of 'the holy' may occur in particular experiences without being always or definitely charged or infused with the sense of moral demands."

Rudolf Otto, *The Idea of the Holy*

Reference: *Rudolf Otto: An Introduction to His Religious Philosophy*, Philip Almond

Overridingness, Principle of – n. in ethics, the view that certain situations of moral choice may present a dilemma of doing one good and ignoring another, because the greater good justifies the neglect of a lesser good (e.g., lying to protect a friend from serious harm).

Reference: *Ethics*, Louis Pojman and James Fieser

overweening – adj. being arrogant or presumptuous

P

pacifism – n. the belief that reconciliation of conflicts and differences should occur peacefully. Pacifists oppose war in all its forms, including the use of violence by revolutionaries, and coercive actions of government upon its people.

In the East, pacifism is emphasized in the Taoist ideal of *wu wei* (nonaction). In Jainism, it appears as the ideal of *ahimsa* (noninjury), later perfected politically and socially by Gandhi. In Greek philosophy, it appears in the doctrines of Stoicism. In Christianity, it appears in the teaching, "Love your enemies" and "Blessed are the peacemakers." In Judaism, it emerged in the philosophy of the Essenes as active withdrawal from war and politics.

Pacifism as a practice makes use of civil disobedience, and it has often been popularized by the horrors of war. Tactically, it stands at a disadvantage toward those who advocate war, as pacifists make easy military opponents. On war:

> *"What will it be like to see dead bodies? You may be struck by how similar the combatants are to you in age and appearance. You may be disgusted by the appearance and smell of the decaying flesh."*

> *"Does torture work? Most people break under torture, confessing or giving information. Torture also dehumanizes, humiliates, and irreparably damages victims both physically and mentally."*

Chris Hedges, *What Every Person Should Know about War*

References: *The Theological Basis of Christian Pacifism*, Charles Raven; *Getting to Yes*, Roger Fisher and William Ury; *Fighting Fair*, Mark Juergensmeyer; *Negotiation: Process, Tactics, Theory*, David Churchman; *What Every Person Should Know about War*, Chris Hedges

paction – n. contract

padrone – n. an employer who controls the lives of his employees

pagination – n. the act of assembling and numbering pages, as in a book

Paine, Thomas (1737–1809) – an American revolutionary leader. Paine argued for a democracy in which reason is more important than tradition. In society, individuals should have equal rights but leadership must reveal both talent and wisdom, implying that few are capable of effective leadership.

Paine was a deist. He professed a love of nature and held that it stands as proof of an order and design pointing to a Creator. Paine extended this belief in natural theology to learning, suggesting that human reason should imitate the work of God. With regard to the problem of evil, Paine argued that suffering is primarily rooted in social injustice.

Principal works: *Common Sense* (1776), *The Rights of Man* (1792), and *The Age of Reason* (1794)

"The true deist has but one Deity; and his religion consists in contemplating the power, wisdom, and benignity of the Deity in his works, and in endeavoring to imitate him in everything moral, scientific, and mechanical."

Thomas Paine, *The Age of Reason*

References: *Thomas Paine*, A. J. Ayer; *Citizen of the World*, ed. I. Dyck

paladin – n. an independent champion of a cause; a knight errant

palaver – n. a prolonged meeting between primitive people or traders; also, beguiling talk

paleontology – n. the study of life in past geological ages; fossil study

Paley, William (1743–1805) – an English philosopher who advanced the merit of natural theology. Paley recognized the historical decline of traditional religion and theology, since they had lost their power as theories of natural phenomena. Even though many tried to cling to religion's importance as a kind of logic of causality, the writing was on the wall and Paley and others knew it. Religion was being pushed into a smaller and smaller domain, the consequence of science's power to provide better explanations. For Paley, if the notion of God was to retain any place in human understanding, revelation would have to include scientific facts. He realized that nature could supply a proof for God's existence.

Paley argued that designs within nature implied a Designer. The possibility of complex designs emerging by mere chance was, in Paley's view, astronomically small and he believed it was sufficient proof of God's existence.

Paley used the example of the watchmaker: if one finds a watch on a desert island, one logically assumes that other humans have been there and that the watch is the product of a watchmaker. So, deism argues that even though God may no longer have a relation to this world, the world is still the result of God's design and creation.

Principal works: *The Principles of Moral and Political Philosophy* (1785), *The Evidences of Christianity* (1794), and *Natural Theology* (1802)

"*In what way can a revelation be made but by miracles? In none which we are able to conceive.*"

William Paley, *Evidences of Christianity*

Reference: *Natural Theology*, Frederick Ferre

palindrome – n. a word, phrase, or statement that reads the same way when read forward or backward; (e.g., 1991)

palingenesis – n. reincarnation; metempsychosis; renewal in Christian baptism

palliate – v. to moderate by the use of excuses

pallid – adj. without vitality

palmary – adj. worthy of praise; excellent

palpable – adj. evident by sensation; observable

panatrophy – n. the disintegration of a whole body structure

pandect – n. a comprehensive summary

pandemic – adj. found universally; occurring everywhere; affecting a very large portion of a population

pander – n. someone who profits from the weaknesses of others. Also: *pander* – v. to provide fulfillment for the vices of others

pandit – n. in India, a respected teacher or sage; fr. Sanskrit *pandita*, meaning a Brahman expert in the science, laws, and religion of Hinduism. (Often written as "pundit")

pandour – n. a soldier of fortune or a mercenary with a reputation for plundering

panegyric – n. formal praise; often a eulogy

panentheism – n. the view that God is in everything but not limited to it. Thus, it differs from pantheism in that God's existence is not limited to the material world. The being of all reality is part of the being of God, but the being of God is not limited to the being of all reality. The view attempts to preserve the theological properties of "transcendence" and "immanence" simultaneously. Gustav Fechner (1801–1887), German philosopher-psychologist, defended panpsychism and panentheism. A. N. Whitehead (1861–1947) and Charles Hartshorne (1897–2000) also defended connections between panpsychism and panentheism. For Hartshorne, God has an organic pole and a spiritual pole.

> References: *Philosophers Speak of God*, Hartshorne and Reese; *Omnipotence and Other Theological Mistakes*, Charles Hartshorne; *Divine Relativity*, Charles Hartshorne; *Process Theology*, ed. Ewert H. Cousins; *Panentheism: The Other God of the Philosophers*, John Cooper

panjandrum – n. an arrogant official; a pompous bureaucrat

panlogism – n. the view that "logos" is of ultimate importance as a key to structuring a coherent picture of reality. This belief defines the overall philosophy of Hegel, who sees the rational and the real as the same.

panpsychism – n. the view that all matter is ultimately "psychic" or "spiritual" in nature. Arthur Schopenhauer (1788–1860) presented a panpsychist philosophy by arguing that the world is infused with "will" that is more or less aware of its motion depending on the level of organized matter. One finds similar expressions in the ideas of A. N. Whitehead (1861–1947) and Charles Hartshorne (1897–2000).

References: *The World as Will and Idea*, Arthur Schopenhauer; *Nanna or Concerning the Soul-Life of Plants*, Gustav Fechner; *The Sensible and the Supersensible World*, Wilhelm Wundt

pansophism – n. the claim of having complete wisdom

pantheism – n. in philosophy and theology, the view that God and the world are one and the same. In the West, the term first appeared in the writings of John Toland about 1705. In the East, it appears in the Upanishads of Hinduism, where Brahman is described as the unifying Divine agency.

Benedict Spinoza (1632–1677) was a defender of pantheism in *Deus sive natura*. God is nature, and nature is God. Also, F. H. Bradley (1846–1924) promoted a view that included many pantheistic philosophical claims. The basic logic of pantheism derives its forcefulness from the observation that going from nothing to something is merely an addition to a preexisting nonmaterial Godness which is necessarily infused with Divine properties. If God created the world, how is it possible for reality to be separated from that source?

References: *Philosophers Speak of God*, Hartshorne and Reese; *The Philosophy of Spinoza*, Harry A.

Wolfson; *The Conception of God*, Josiah Royce; *Asvaghosha's Discourse on the Awakening of Faith in the Mahayana*, trans. Teitaro Suzuki

Paraclete – n. fr. Greek *Parakletos*, advocate or defender; interecessor as in Holy Spirit.

paradisiacal – adj. having the quality of paradise

paragon – n. an example of true superiority

paralogism – n. defective reasoning; a fallacious argument

paramimia – n. the use of gestures to express thought in an inappropriate way, producing an ambiguous effect

paramour – n. a mistress; an illicit lover

paranoia – n. fr. the Greek *paranoia*, meaning madness. In psychology, a state of mind marked by unproven beliefs that one is being hunted or persecuted by others. It is also called "delusional disorder," sometimes classified under schizophrenia. Mild paranoia can coexist with mental well-being, while strong paranoia leads to chronic misinterpretations of "signs" and unnatural concern about the behavior of others. In severe cases, there is social withdrawal, and it may be accompanied by auditory hallucinations.

One theory argues that paranoid persons project on to others the worst qualities they find in themselves. The "distrust" they experience is not based on objective fact but on the ego's need to defend against unconscious impulses. Some paranoid persons compensate through megalomania.

References: *Faces of the Enemy*, Sam Keen; *Paranoia: A Study in Diagnosis*, Joseph Agassi and Yehuda Fried

parapsychology – n. the investigation of clairvoyance, mental telepathy, psychokenesis, and other unusual events that cannot be accounted for by laws of nature. It tries to establish the missing scientific explanations through "psychical research." The problem it encounters in demonstrating psychic phenomena rests upon the need to repeat the results of experiments. Some experiments have employed hypnosis and the use of drugs, but overall, the conclusions of parapsychologists remain tentative, as in the case of ESP (extrasensory perception).

References: *Science: Good, Bad, and Bogus*, Martin Gardner; *Parapsychology: Frontier Science of the Mind*, J. G. Pratt and J. B. Rhine

parataxic – adj. characterized by conflict of an emotional nature; a mode of individual experience where there is a failure to see certain logical relationships between events

paregoric – n. a pain-relieving medical prescription; originally a reference to opium-based painkillers

pariah – n. a social outcast; someone who lives on the margins of society

parlance – n. the appropriate way of speaking of a particular subject; a manner of speaking

parlous – adj. dangerous; perilous

Parmenides (ca. 515–450 BC) – a pre-Socratic philosopher who founded a school of philosophy at Elea. His thinking produced important definitions of change. Parmenides held that existence or realness implies absoluteness. Being and nonbeing do not share any mutual contingence by their essence. Something is, or it "is not." For Parmenides, contingency is not a property of real being. If something were to arise from "nonbeing," then nonbeing as origination is something and not true "nonbeing."

The problem of making correct distinctions is compounded because humans have sense perceptions. Sense perception is a denial of the logic of "being" vs. "nonbeing," thus sense perception is an illusion.

The work of Parmenides was a challenge to the views of Heraclitus and a resource for the subsequent theories of Plato (see Plato's dialogues: *Parmenides*, *Theaetetus*, and *Sophist*).

Principal work: *On Nature*

"There is only one other description of the way remaining, (namely), that (What Is) Is. To this way there are very many sign-posts: that Being has no coming-into-being and no destruction, for it is whole of limb, without motion, and without end. And it never 'Was,' nor 'Will Be,' because it 'Is' now, a whole all together, One, continuous; for what creation of it will you look for? How, whence (could it have) sprung? Nor shall I allow you to speak or think of it as springing from Not-Being; for it is neither expressible nor thinkable that What-Is-Not Is."

Parmenides, *On Nature*, fragment #7

References: *Parmenides: Being, Bounds, and Logic*, Austin Scott; *The Route of Parmenides*, A. P. D. Mourelatos

Parousia – n. in theology, a belief in the future coming of Christ. Christ will judge both the living and the dead and finish up the present world order. Though early Christians believed the parousia to be imminent, the exact time and place are not truly specified. In fact, there is opposition to speculation about the exact details of the parousia.

Its original meaning is "presence" or "arrival." In Platonism the term "parousia" implies the presence of form in matter. In Teilhard de Chardin, "parousia" is the evolutionary and spiritual anticipation of Christ's return, as the culmination of human spiritual development.

References: *Jesus and His Coming: The Emergence of a Doctrine*, J. A. T. Robinson; *The Future of Man*, Pierre Teilhard de Chardin

parricide – n. the killing of a father, mother, or close relative.

parsimony – n. the exercise of caution in the use of money, to the point of being stingy.

In philosophy, the principle of parsimony refers to the simplification of theory and is also known as Ockham's Razor. If there are several logically equivalent ways of expressing an idea, then choose the simplest version.

parturient – adj. close to giving birth.

parvenu – n. an individual who suddenly becomes wealthy or acquires a position of importance but lacks refinement and social skills; an upstart.

Pascal, Blaise (1623-1662) – a French philosopher of mathematics, logic, and religion. Pascal accepted Descartes's mechanistic model of nature. He argued for certain fixed notions: number, matter, change, space, and time, but concluded that a knowledge of their origins and destiny were impossible.

Pascal doubted the possibility of proving God's existence but presented an interesting puzzle known as "Pascal's Wager": 1) God exists, or 2) God does not exist. If you wager that God exists, and it is true, then you win all. If God does not exist, you lose nothing. If you wager that God does not exist, and it is true, then you win nothing. If God does exist, you lose everything. So, the belief in God is a better wager than atheism.

Pascal regarded human existence as corrupt and that contemplative life is the only source of happiness. He emphasized that all reasoning concludes with uncertainty and fails to satisfy our deepest needs for love and spiritual unity.

Pascal died of cancer at age thirty-nine.

Principal works: *Essay on Conics* (1640), *New Experiments Concerning the Vacuum* (1647), *The Geometric Spirit* (1658), *Pensées* or *Reflections on Religion* (1669)

"Men never do evil so completely and cheerfully as when they do it from religious conviction."

Blaise Pascal, *Pensées*

References: *Pascal, the Life of Genius*, Morris Bishop; *Pascal*, Jean Mesnard, trans. by C. and M. Abraham

Passover – n. in Judaism, the seven-day celebration of the escape from captivity in Egypt. In killing the firstborn of Egypt, God would pass over the homes of the Jews. It is connected to an ancient spring festival (late March or early April) involving the eating of unleavened bread (*matzo*) and the sacrifice of a lamb.

The first two evenings are called Seder, where the story of the Exodus is retold. Unleavened bread and bitter herbs symbolize the occasion.

In Christianity, it is called Easter. The Passover lamb foreshadows the death of Jesus, who is seen as the Lamb of God.

> Reference: *The Origins of Seder*, B. M. Boksher

pathos – n. a quality or condition that arouses sympathy or concern (e.g., physical or emotional suffering)

patristics – n. the study of the philosophy, theology, and writings of the early church fathers. It stems from the word "*pater,*" meaning father. All important Christian writers up to the thirteenth century are referred to as "Fathers." In its strictest usage it ends with writers in the eighth century. Patristics examines the defense of traditional dogma and theology. Thus, it also studies the theological heresies that helped to forge the official theological doctrines of Christianity.

> References: *Patrology*, Berthold Altaner; *Handbook of Patrology*, Patrick J. Hamell; and *Patrology*, J. Quasten

peccable – adj. tendency to commit moral error

peculate – v. to steal or embezzle

Peirce, Charles Sanders (1839–1914) – an American philosopher of pragmatism, Peirce (pronounced "purse") developed important arguments for semiotics, the theory of signs.

Signs are basic to epistemology and involve four important features: 1) the sign or symbol (written or spoken), 2) an object corresponding to the sign, 3) a conceptual interpretation of the sign, and 4) a mind that is capable of using and interpreting signs.

Peirce was a realist and his theory of perception admits the facticity of the external world. The point of all thought, for Peirce, is to gain satisfactory results in life. The pursuit of truth is one of approximation. Truth is never finished (the principle of fallibilism). Though nothing is completely knowable, we accomplish ever-increasing certitude through aggressive and careful observation of the world.

Ontology and phenomenology aid us in the identification of reality. Matter, as it appears to us through the senses, is a collection of essences to be described.

Principal works: *Collected Papers* (1878–1914)

"Nothing is 'vital' for science; nothing can be. Its accepted propositions, therefore, are but opinions at most; and the list is provisional. The scientific man is not in the least wedded to his conclusions. He risks nothing upon them. He stands ready to abandon one or all as soon as experience opposes them."

C. S. Peirce, *Collected Papers*

"The person who confesses that there is such a thing as truth, which is distinguished from falsehood simply by this, that if acted upon it should, on full consideration, carry us to the point we aim at and not astray, and then, convinced of this, dares to know the truth and seeks to avoid it, is in a sorry state of mind indeed."

C. S. Peirce, *Fixation of Belief*

Reference: *Charles Sanders Peirce*, Karl-Otto Apel, trans. by J. M. Krois

pejorative – adj. having a bad effect, especially in terms of a thing's perceived quality or condition

pellucid – adj. transparent; easy to comprehend

Pentecost – n. in Christianity, celebration of the visitation of the Holy Spirit upon believers. Observed the seventh Sunday after Easter. In Judaism, the celebration of the harvest, occurring fifty days after Passover.

penultimate – adj. next to the last in a finite sequence

penurious – adj. influenced by greed to the impossibility of sharing; stinginess

peradventure – n. an unplanned event; chance; also, speculation

perambulate – v. to travel or journey on foot

perdition – n. an act capable of ruining the spirit or soul; eternal destruction

P

perdurable – adj. everlasting

peregrinate – v. to move across

peremptory – adj. in dictatorial fashion; without debate or notice

perfervid – adj. extremely intense, especially in regard to the emotions

perficient – adj. fr. Latin *perficere*, meaning to complete; thus, to have a decisive influence or authority over

perfidy – n. a violation of trust

perfunctory – adj. done with little interest

perfuse – v. to spread; to flow

pericope – n. a selection or extract from a book; especially a selection from the Bible for use in a sermon, reading, or exegetical study

permute – v. to alter; to change

pernicious – adj. harmful; dangerous

perspicacious – adj. having great insight

perspicuity – n. mental clarity

persiflage – n. useless talk

pettifogger – n. a lawyer whose practices are petty, underhanded, or disreputable; one given to quibbling over insignificant details

personalism – n. the view that the concept of "person" is the ultimate category of meaning. The person, self, or thinker stands in contrast to the impersonal nature of mechanistic materialism that makes up the bulk of modern life. Personalism emphasizes the importance of moral values, individual persons, and human freedom. This philosophy also poses the reality of God as personal and uncreated. Ethical principles gain their validity from God as Supreme Spirit or Personality. This in turn implies that God is present as a type of worker, attempting to impart moral and religious meaning to the world. E. S. Brightman (1884–1953) was a leading defender of this view. Walt Whitman (1819–1892) also promoted a personalist idealism in his writings, and some good arguments are also found in the writings of Emmanuel Mounier (1905–1950): *What Is Personalism?* (1947) and *Personalism* (1949).

Reference: *The Philosophy of Personalism*, A. C. Knudson

pertinacious – adj. stubborn; unwilling to concede

peruse – v. to examine carefully

petulant – adj. ill-tempered; hostile in attitude

peyotism – n. an intertribal Native American religious practice incorporating the sacramental use of peyote. It adapts Christian elements to traditional tribal beliefs and uses peyote as a spiritual technology in a controlled setting to achieve higher states of mind and soul

pharisee – n. (adj. "pharisaical") a sanctimonious hypocrite; a self-righteous person

phatic – adj. to be focused on feelings and emotional states rather than substantial ideas

phenomenology – n. in philosophy, study of human consciousness in relation to phenomena, especially its essence and use. Phenomenology is a preface to reasoning about reality. In the phenomenology of Edmund Husserl (1859–1938) consciousness is seen as the central fact to deciphering reality. The essence of consciousness is to indicate or point out an objective reality. Consciousness is always consciousness of something. The task of reason is to detail this consciousness, to describe its content and the very activity of structuring pictures of experience. It is along these lines that the work of phenomenology became important to the research of the existentialists (e.g., Jean-Paul Sartre, Martin Heidegger, and Maurice Merleau-Ponty). Phenomenology is almost a technical program for thought analysis, operating as the microscope to further elaborate insights and observation. It is particularly interesting in the way that it contributes to awareness.

References: *The Problems of Phenomenology*, Martin Heidegger; *The Phenomenological Movement*, Herbert Spiegelberg

philander – v. to make love without commitment

philistia – n. a reference to cultural barbarians

philistine – n. an individual who has no appreciation of aesthetic or philosophic values; one who has but the crudest understanding of life and reality

philippic – n. a verbal condemnation

philogyny – n. love for women. Also "philogynous" (adj.) – being fond of women

philology – n. the study of language, especially historical and comparative considerations

philoprogenetive – adj. having a love for children or offspring

philosopher's stone – n. fr. Latin *lapis philosophorum*; a legendary stone capable of turning ordinary metals into gold; also a reference to any principle or concept capable of renewing the soul.

philosophy – n. the love of wisdom. According to the ancient philosopher Pythagoras, the goal of wisdom was salvation and religious awareness. For Socrates, self-knowledge was the principle goal of philosophy, coupled with a commitment to clarity of ideas. During the Middle Ages, philosophy was regarded as an accessory to theology and the life of faith, or a threat to that faith, depending upon the degree of skepticism toward religious dogma. In the twentieth century philosophy has been concerned with expanding the influence of logic through positivism. It has also offered valuable insights into psychology through existentialism, and has witnessed the reemergence of spiritual philosophy through the influence of Eastern philosophy and Western process philosophy.

Philosophy divides itself into five primary branches of study:

1) *Logic* – the study of methods used to distinguish correct from incorrect reasoning.
2) *Epistemology* – the study of theories of knowledge; its sources, nature, and validity
3) *Metaphysics* – the study of the nature of reality, literally "beyond reality." It is subdivided into *ontology*, the study of being, and *cosmology*, the study of the origins, nature, and development of the universe.
4) *Aesthetics* – the study of beauty or value in things
5) *Ethics* – the study of human conduct in groups and individuals, with the aim of discerning "the good"

Reference: *A History of Philosophy*, Frederick C. Copleston; *The Encyclopedia of Philosophy*, ed. Paul Edwards

phlegmatic – adj. showing a temperament that is sluggish and not easily moved to emotion

phronesis – n. a special judgment or wisdom in deciding worthy goals and how to achieve them; practical wisdom

phylephebic – adj. relating to the phase of maximum vigor of a race

phylogeny – n. the historical study of the racial history of an organism; the study of the evolution of a group of organisms

piacular – adj. the quality of making up for some sin or wrong; expiation

Piaget, Jean (1896–1980) – a Swiss philosopher whose interest in logic, mathematics, and action became a lifelong study of knowledge in children, starting with his own. Piaget reexamined the whole issue of Kantian categories of thought and worked in the area of epistemology, as well as psychology.

Piaget studied the development of abstract concepts of classes and numbers and more physical concepts of speed, time, space, conservation, and chance, linking these to human action. With regard to language, math, and logic, Piaget believed the child comes to primitive acquaintance through play and only later takes up the conceptual arrangement of these notions. Play is simply a trial-and-error use of curiosity to understand one's surroundings. With the accumulation of experience, the child experiences a rational (ordered) awareness of its world. Mistakes occur primarily at the frontier of the child's experience, with past successes being the anchor for corrections. Piaget called this characteristic of thought "reversibility," and believed it to be the basis for deductive reasoning.

In reworking the Kantian notion of time, Piaget concluded that Kant was wrong in setting up time as an *a priori* intuition. Children often confuse time with notions of size, height, and other visible clues of age. It is similar to the child's early difficulty with shapes. Children first distinguish only open and closed configurations and lack an ordered system of perspectives.

> Principal works: *The Language and Thought of the Child* (1923), *The Child's Conception of the World* (1926), *The Child's Conception of Physical Reality* (1926), *The Mechanisms of Perception* (1961), and *Success and Understanding* (1974)

> *"All in all, it is thus clear that . . . the grasp of consciousness lags behind precocious successes in the field of action and that it progresses from the periphery to the central regions of that action, they (findings) also face us with the new*

situation of practical success attained by stages with gradual coordinations at distinct levels: in these cases, there is, first of all, a more or less long phase when the action and conceptualization are almost on the same level and when there are constant exchanges between them. Then (next stage) we find a complete reversal of the initial situation: conceptualization no longer provides action with limited and provisional plans that have to be revised and adjusted, but with an overall programme . . . when practice is guided by theory."

Jean Piaget, *Success and Understanding*

References: *Making Sense of Piaget: The Philosophical Roots*, C. Atkinson; *A Piaget Primer*, D. G. Singer and T. A. Revenson

pique – v. to cause resentment; to cause irritation

pistology – n. the study of faith

placate – v. to moderate feelings, especially by compromise; to appease

Planck, Max Karl Ernst Ludwig (1858–1947) – a German physicist, Planck developed the theory of quantum energy, essential to quantum mechanics. Having received his PhD at the age of twenty-one, Planck taught at the universities of Munich, Kiel, and Berlin.

Planck studied blackbody radiation in 1897. A blackbody is matter that absorbs the energy that falls upon it; lacking reflective properties, it appears black. Some surfaces absorb nearly 98 percent of energy. Absorption creates higher temperatures. Blackbodies are also perfect emitters of energy. Planck resolved problems related to the uniform expression of energy exchanges in blackbodies, meaning Planck used the concept of discrete *quanta* to reveal the nature of events in radiation and matter. This work was later useful to Albert Einstein and Niels Bohr in their own discoveries.

Principal works: *Scientific Autobiography and Other Papers* (1949), and *The Universe in the Light of Modern Physics* (1937)

"There have been times when science and philosophy were alien, if not actually antagonistic to each other. These times have passed. Philosophers have realized that they have no right to dictate to scientists their aims and the methods for attaining them; and scientists have learned that the starting-point of their investigations does not lie solely in the perceptions of the senses, and that science cannot exist without

some small portion of metaphysics. Modern Physics impresses us particularly with the truth of the old doctrine which teaches that there are realities existing apart from our sense perceptions, and that there are problems and conflicts where these realities are of greater value for us than the richest treasures of the world of experience."

Max Planck, *The Universe in the Light of Modern Physics*

References: *Thirty Years that Shook Physics*, George Gamow; *Scientific Autobiography and Other Papers*, Max Planck, trans. by Frank Gaynor

Plato (427–347 BC) – Greek philosopher; a student of Socrates and the teacher of Aristotle. The spirit of philosophical thought that makes up Plato's system is portrayed in his Allegory of the Cave (*Republic*, Book VII): In the Cave (ignorance), there are a number of prisoners who are fated by their chains (conformity) to play a game identifying shadows (appearances) on a wall. Prisoners receive awards for their ability to identify shadows and a kind hierarchy exists for these captives based on their little victories. One of the prisoners is freed and forcibly removed from the Cave, which he regards as his home. The initial encounter with the light of the outside world has a blinding effect (alienation), and it is difficult for the captive to resist running back to the cave. In time, the prisoner is liberated from ignorance (enlightenment), especially by the superior appearance (knowledge) of this outside world. In his excitement, he desires to liberate (education) his friends from their ignorance. When he returns to the cave, he experiences the reverse problem. He is blinded (alienated) by the darkness and stumbles in descent. The prisoners are sure their comrade is insane, for he can no longer identify shadows on the wall. He, in turn, insists that they are deceived by their ignorance of reality. Plato explains that the liberated prisoner (Socrates) will be killed by his fellows if he insists that they leave the cave.

Plato's thought is an example of classical idealism, since it maintains that ideas are the highest order of reality, while matter is subject to the formative effects of ideas. The physical world is an illusion due to its perishable nature. Ideas or forms are eternal archetypes that are imperfectly represented in the whole range of material objects we find around us.

Plato's cosmology includes the notion of a "World Soul," the original home of human souls. It also employs the notion of the Demiurge, a type of craftsman deity, that works with forms and matter to fashion the empirical world. Human souls inhabit bodies due to the loss of harmony, a "falling" from the World Soul.

Life is a kind of challenge to reestablish the harmony of the soul and return to the World Soul.

The soul is composed of three elements: reason, spirit, and desire. The confusion and conflict of life reflect the relative imbalance of the soul's elements. The imbalance is a consequence of ignorance, which is for Plato the source of all evil. Morality is a central issue in Plato's philosophy, conveying the importance of correct value formation in order that individuals and societies transmit such values to succeeding generations. Life is thus a *poiesis*, an art or creation.

Wisdom, courage, and temperance are central virtues of the soul, corresponding to the three elements— reason, spirit, and desire. By living according to these virtues, the soul experiences a fulfillment of function and design. Enlightenment ensues, shaping the daily life of the individual.

Socially and politically, the soul is manifested in class structures: "rulers," "warriors," and "artisan-merchants." Rulers represent wisdom; warriors represent courage; and merchants and artisans represent desire. Governments are defined by the rational constitution of the state and are ranked in a descending order by Plato: aristocracy—guided by reason; timocracy—guided by honor and glory in warfare; plutocracy—guided by the love of wealth; democracy—guided by the views of the masses; tyranny—guided by a despot or military council (oligarchy); kakistocracy—rule by criminals; and finally anarchy (chaos), or the absence of wisdom, courage, temperance, and justice.

The process of searching for true understanding takes the individual mind through four stages of development (Divided Line):

1) *Imagination* – the use of fantasy, as with poets and artists; the realm of subjective knowledge
2) *Belief* – the acceptance of the visible world as the source of truth
3) *Reason* – the mental movement to the principles of logic and mathematics
4) *Enlightenment* – the awareness of the unity of the world and its relation to forms

Principal works: *The Dialogues—Apology, Crito, Euthyphro, Ion, Protagoras, Gorgias, Meno, Cratylus, Phaedo, The Republic, Symposium, Parmenides, Sophist, Theaetetus, Phaedrus, Politicus, Philebus, Timaeus, Critias,* and *Laws*

"Surely the soul can reflect best when it is free of all distractions such as hearing or sight or pain or pleasure of any kind—that is, when it ignores the body and becomes as far as possible independent, avoiding all physical contacts and associations as much as it can, in its search for reality."

Plato, *Phaedo 65c*

References: *Preface to Plato*, Eric A. Havelock; *Plato's Progress*, Gilbert Ryle; *Plato: The Man and His Work*, 4th ed., A. E. Taylor

Platonic year – n. the time period in which a complete revolution of the equinoxes is achieved, about twenty-six thousand years; procession of the equinoxes

Platonism – n. the views and influence of Plato (427–347 BC). Plato's philosophy is recorded in the *Dialogues*, the most important of which are the *Phaedo* (a discussion of immortality; the relation of soul and body, and the role of eternal forms), *Symposium* (a discussion of eros, the meaning of beauty, and the value of contemplative life), *Protagoras* (a discussion of the notion of the good, the essence of knowledge, and the idea of goodness), and *The Republic* (a discussion of the ideal political state and the psychological nature of humanity).

Platonism influenced the theology of Christianity through the work of St. Augustine (Neoplatonism). Christianity can be seen as the survival of Platonism in a religious form. Jesus taught ethics but not systematic metaphysics, so Christianity's Hellenization is the result of a quest for metaphysics (theology).

pleasure principle – n. in Freudian psychology, the instinctual selection of actions by the agent to produce pleasure. The ego's assessment of obstacles to pleasure represents its desire to acquire satisfactions by the most direct route. It is complemented by the tendency to avoid pain. It predates Freud in the philosophy of Epicurus (hedonism), where the ethical discussion of self-mastery and pleasure is introduced to understand happiness.

References: *Beyond the Pleasure Principle*, Sigmund Freud; *Pleasure and Being*, M. Safouan

plebeian – adj. relating to the common person; crude, coarse, unremarkable

plenary – adj. complete; full

plenum – n. a general assembly of all the members of a legislative body

pleonasm – n. the use of words beyond what is necessary

Plotinus (204–270 AD) – an Egyptian philosopher and the founder of Neoplatonism. Plotinus invented the Metaphor of the Sun to describe God. God is like the sun, and, as "the One" or *nous* (mind), is the ultimate source of reality. From the One, there are rays of light representing emanations of reality, beginning with a World Soul, which has ascending and descending features (a motion for proximity or distance from God). The next emanation is the human soul, which possesses a "fallen" nature. Captive in bodily form, the soul is doomed to transmigrations until it can find complete salvation. The last emanation is the world of matter, which borders on darkness and nothingness. The soul's captivity in a material body forces it to struggle against the presence of formlessness. A disciplined life is necessary to create union with God, the One.

Principal works: *Enneads*, 6 vols.

> "If we do not possess good, we cannot bestow it; nor can we ever purvey any good thing to one that has no power of receiving good."

Plotinus, *Enneads*, vol. 4

References: *Plotinus: The Road to Reality*, John M. Rist; *The Philosophy of Plotinus*, William Inge, 2 vols.

pluralism – n. in philosophy, the view that the world is composed of multiple types of entities. It includes the view that ideological novelty and difference are proof of variety in reality. It stands in contrast to monism, which emphasizes the oneness of substance, and dualism, which offers a bipolar perception of reality.

poiesis – n. in philosophy, especially Aristotle, the term is a reference to productive science. It also refers to making, creating, playing, and producing. In *Finite and Infinite Games*, James Carse develops an understanding of life as *poiesis* or infinite play:

> "The finite play for life is serious; the infinite play for life is joyous." . . . "Surprise causes finite play to end; it is the reason for infinite play to continue." . . . "While finite games are externally defined, infinite games are internally defined."

James P. Carse, *Finite and Infinite Games*

pogrom – n. organized extermination or massacre

poignant – adj. deeply affecting; sharp

poltroon – n. a complete coward.

polyandry – n. the practice of having more than one husband simultaneously

portend – v. to warn

poseur – n. someone who works at styling life or his or her ideas in order to impress others

positivism – n. a philosophical movement emphasizing the scientific method as the only legitimate route to knowledge. Positivism is an open disagreement with the "truth" claims of religion and metaphysics. As part of the empirical tradition, it received its initial definition through the views of Auguste Comte and Ernst Mach. Later it developed into "logical positivism" and "analytic philosophy."

Reference: *Positivist Philosophy*, L. Kolakowski

postprandial – adj. after dinner

postrosse – adj. bent backward

potentiate – v. to give power; to make vital

pother – n. mental confusion; a burst of unorganized activity

pragmatism – n. the philosophical view that knowledge should be useful for the practice of living. It emphasizes the value of results, efficiency, and productive living. Truth is a product of correct applications of knowledge.

"Pragmatism" is derived from the Greek *pragmatikos*, meaning "deed" or "act." It was developed by three American philosophers: Charles Peirce, William James, and John Dewey. Pragmatism endorses the correspondence theory of truth and is closely aligned with realism as opposed to rational idealism.

> *"The pragmatist clings to facts and concreteness, observes truth at its work in particular cases, and generalizes. Truth, for him, becomes a class-name for all sorts of definite working-values in experience. For the rationalist it remains pure abstraction, to the bare name of which we must defer. When the pragmatist undertakes to show in detail just 'why' we must defer, the rationalist is unable to recognize the concrete from which his own abstraction is taken. He accuses us of "denying" truth; whereas we have only sought to trace exactly why people follow it always ought to follow it. Your typical ultra-abstractionist fairly shudders at*

concreteness: other things being equal, he positively prefers the pale and spectral. If the two universes were offered, he would always choose the skinny outline rather than the rich thicket of reality."

William James, *Pragmatism*

References: *Purpose and Thought*, John E. Smith; *The Origins of Pragmatism*, A. J. Ayer; *How We Think*, John Dewey; *Pragmatism*, William James

prandial – adj. relating to any meal

prattle – v. to engage in useless conversation; to chatter like a child

praxis – n. practice

prayer – n. fr. Latin *precaria*, meaning written petition; in theology, a thought or word directed toward God. Its efficacy rests on the transcendent and personal reality of God. It presupposes a relation that is disclosed through the atonement created by Jesus Christ. Moreover, it is the essence of the search for God, leading to union and spiritual likeness:

"You who are love itself, give me the grace of love. Give me Yourself, so that all my days may finally empty into the one day of your eternal life."

Karl Rahner (1904–1984), *Prayers for a Lifetime*

Reference: *The Theology of Prayer*, J. C. Fenton

preamble – n. an introductory set of remarks or statements

prebend – n. a financial compensation given to a clergyman, especially when working for a cathedral or college church

precatory – adj. relating to a request

precocious – adj. showing early independence or maturity of development

predaceous – adj. tending to live on others

presage – v. to warn; to indicate a foreshadowing of an event

preterhuman – adj. beyond what is human; Christ or Buddha

preternatural – adj. beyond what is natural or ordinary

prevaricate – v. to make misleading statements

prevenient – adj. occurring before

prig – n. a fussy, self-righteous person

prima donna – n. meaning "first lady"; a vain and undisciplined individual; one who finds it difficult to work as part of a team or under the direction of others

prima facie – adj. apparent

primal – adj. early; original; primitive

primogenitor – n. an ancestor

primogeniture – n. the right to property held by the eldest son; exclusive rights to inheritance

principle of participation – n. in philosophical anthropology, an idea from Lucien Lévy-Bruhl (1857–1939). Lévy-Bruhl's work on the thought of primitive people and prelogical consciousness. To describe this consciousness Lévy-Bruhl used the term *principle of participation*. It observes that contradiction in primitive societies is apparently acceptable in that any thing or person can be both itself and not itself. This is achieved through the emphasis on mystical factors in the thinking of primitive people. Life as "mystery" allows nonlogical judgment. Primitives are able to believe both sides of a problem that Westernized persons would regard as contradiction. Correspondence to reality or truth as we know it does not define or organize the thoughts of primitive societies.

> References: *The Mental Functions in Inferior Societies*, Lévy-Bruhl; *Primitive Mentality*, Lévy-Bruhl; *Mystical Experience and Symbols among the Primitives*, Lévy-Bruhl

pristine – adj. being of original form or purity

privy – adj. confidential

probity – n. integrity; honesty

procellous – adj. stormy, unstable, or chaotic

prochronism – n. the mistake of assigning an earlier date than the true one

proclivity – adj. a natural inclination

procumbent – adj. lying facedown

prodigal – adj. being extravagant; wasteful as in "the prodigal son"

prodigious – adj. being extraordinary

prodigy – n. a very talented child; an amazing event or deed

prodrome – n. a warning signal, especially of disease or decline

proem – n. introduction; preface

proffer – v. to present for consideration

profligate – n. a person completely given over to uncontrolled sensual hedonism; an immoral person

profluent – adj. to flow out smoothly

progeny – n. children; offspring; successors

projection – n. in psychology, the relocation of a psychological problem in some external object or person. It is a defense action associated with paranoia.

In Gestalt theory, projection is delivery of a biased interpretation on to external objects and persons. A carpenter views the world by the interests, habits, and experiences of making things. A businessperson sees the world as moments and units of profit and loss. A lawyer sees a legal dimension in many situations.

Projection is divided into three types: 1) *classical* – unconscious awareness of attributing one's own negative traits on to an other; 2) *attributive* – placing your own negative qualities on to someone you like; and 3) *complimentary* – blaming a negative feeling, such as fear, on another person.

Reference: *Ego Defenses and the Legitimation of Behavior*, Guy E. Swanson

prolepsis – n. in logic, the anticipation of a future conclusion as if already in existence

prolicide – n. killing one's children or offspring

prolix – adj. tediously wordy

prolocutor – n. one who presides; chairperson

prolusion – n. an introductory and sometimes experimental essay

promulgate – v. to make known publicly

pronto – adj. without hesitation

propaedeutic – adj. preparatory; introductory

propensity – n. a strong inclination or leaning

propinquity – n. nearness

propitious – adj. favorable

propter hoc – adj. fr. Latin meaning "because of this"

prorogue – v. to suspend or postpone

prosaic – adj. of the everyday world; dull

proscribe – v. to prohibit or forbid

Protagoras (490–410 BC) – a pre-Socratic philosopher and member of the Sophist school, Protagoras argued that all knowledge is subjective and a product of individual interpretation. He presupposed that our egocentric condition accounts for different philosophical attitudes toward moral issues. He held that everything is in a state of flux and that judgment could only be specific and never absolute. He devoted his philosophy to understanding rhetoric, skepticism, subjectivism, agnosticism, legal issues, and language.

Protagoras's fame rested on his reputation as a tutor for aspiring politicians, lawyers, and charlatans in the art of argument. He became wealthy by teaching students how to win any argument and professed that he knew how to attack an issue from all sides.

Principal works: *On Truth*, *On the Gods*, and *Antilogic*

"About the gods, I am not able to know whether they exist or do not exist, nor what they are like in form; for the factors preventing knowledge are many: the obscurity of the subject, and the shortness of human life."

P

Protagoras, *On the Gods*

Reference: *Sophists*, W. K. C. Guthrie.

protean – adj. versatile; after Proteus, a god of the sea and shape-shifter. Proteus was able to transform himself to handle situations of danger, perhaps a lion, a serpent, an eagle, a pig, or even water or trees. Robert Lifton refers to the "protean self," a person able to handle all life's challenges with skill and courage. (Check the ideas of Robert Lifton in *Trauma and Self*, eds. Strozier and Flynn. Lifton is a psychiatrist who studied Holocaust survivors, and he is the originator of the term "protean self".)

protract – v. to extend outward

protreptic – n. a statement used to persuade

provenance – n. origin

prurient – adj. causing or having restless sexual craving

pseudodementia – n. a temporary state of insanity due to emotional influences

pseudomania – n. pathological lying

pseudoscience – n. theories and systems of thought that are plausible but have no hard empirical basis for belief

psittacism – n. parrot-like talk; talk that is not comprehended by the speaker

psychagogy – n. the practice of leading souls, especially after death; also meaning a practice of influencing the conduct of others by the suggestion of exciting goals

psychasthenia – n. a neurotic disorder characterized by phobias and acute anxiety; it is manifested as perpetual doubt and a susceptibility to trivial fears

psychataxia – n. inability to concentrate

psychoanalysis – n. the methods and theories of Freud, with derivative effects in Carl Jung, Otto Rank, Alfred Adler, Erik Erikson, Melanie Klein, and others. Psychoanalysis is the picturing of the mental life of the individual with regard to specific theoretical concepts, including repression, the unconscious, regression, infant sexuality, defense, projection, the Oedipus complex, wish fulfillment, the damming of the libido, free association, and cathartic method.

Psychoanalytic treatment of neurosis requires several meetings per week for several years to outline the psychic arrangement of the patient's mind. While it is an important tool in the treatment of mental illness, the results are often questionable, and there is no clear consensus on the handling of symptoms and attitudes in the patient.

In some models, such as Erikson, there is an invariable theory of human development that does not admit the importance of human freedom or question the ethical assumptions in deciding what constitutes normal behavior. In fact, psychoanalysis often assigns "moral concerns" to religion, simultaneously discrediting it as a legitimate source of meaning and purpose.

References: *Psychotherapy and Morality*, Joseph Margolis; *The Myth of Mental Illness*, Thomas Szasz; *The Psychoanalysis of Children*, Melanie Klein; *Treating the Self*, Ernest Wolf; *The Scope of Psychoanalysis*, Franz Alexander

psychogenic – adj. originating in the mind

psycholagnia – n. intense imaginative preoccupation with erotic ideas

psycholepsy – n. a loss of drive; a sense of hopelessness

psychomachia – n. a conflict within the soul, especially with regard to good and evil

psychomancy – n. communication with spirits

psychomorphism – n. in primitive religion, the attribution of mental states to animals and nonliving things

psychopannychism – n. in theology, the view that the soul enters sleep at death and does not awaken until the resurrection of the body

psychostasia – n. in the ancient world, the belief in and the act of weighing souls or spirits

psychotechnics – n. the use of psychological theory for controlling human behavior, especially for practical purposes

psychotechnology – n. the study of psychic manipulation (e.g., in business, industry, and other institutional settings)

psychrophobia – n. morbid fear of anything cold. Compare to psychrophilia, the love of cold temperatures

pudency – n. modesty

puerile – adj. relating to childishness, immaturity

puerilism – n. childish behavior in an adult; a psychological disorder when chronic

pugnacious – adj. belligerent or troublesome

pullulate – v. to multiply or breed quickly; to swarm

punctilious – adj. showing great conformity to codes, rules, and conventions

pundit – n. expert or teacher; variation of *pandit*

purlieu – n. a favorite place; a haunt; an outlying area

purloin – v. to steal; to acquire wrongfully

purport – v. to imply or claim

pur sang – adj. genuine beyond question

pursuivant – n. a follower

purvey – v. to supply

purview – n. scope; a range of vision or understanding

putative – adj. generally regarded or supposed

putrefy – v. to make rotten

putrilage – n. rotten, putrid matter

pyknic – adj. short, muscular build (Socrates)

pyretic – adj. relating to fever

pyromancy – n. in religion, divination by the use of fire

pyromania – n. obsessive-compulsive incendiarism; irresistible need to set fires

pyrophobia – n. morbid fear of fire, especially its occurrence and immediacy

Pyrrho of Elis (ca. 365–275 BC) – in Greek philosophy, the founder of Skepticism. Pyrrho taught that absolute knowledge is unattainable. He believed that a person's happiness depended, in part, on the acceptance of knowledge as relative and an *agoge* (way of life). Be calm in the face of adversity. Learn from animals—concern about one's future is useless worry.

The legends about Pyrrho's life are based on fragments by Timon of Phlius, the writings of Diogenes Laertius, and stories attributed to Aenesidemus and Posidonius.

They leave us with two different impressions: 1) Pyrrho lacked common sense and often exposed himself to silly accidents due to his absent-mindedness, and 2) a more realistic Pyrrho living within the bounds of his own culture.

Reference: *Greek Skepticism*, Charlotte Stough

Pythagoreanism – n. in philosophy, a movement started by Pythagoras (570–500 BC). Famous for revering mathematics, Pythagoreans used numbers to outline a religious life, paying special attention to the number 10, believed to be a sacred number as the sum of 1,2,3, and 4. Pythagoreans believed astronomy revealed a mathematical harmony, and the analysis of harmony, and good health as a measure of harmony, provided a foundation for a philosophical mysticism.

Pythagoras's work with musical tones in the shortening and lengthening of a vibrating string deepened the belief that number is the secret to enlightenment. They believed that the universe is playing a song, and that we exist to hear that song.

Reference: *Pythagorean Precepts*, Thomas Taylor

pythonic – adj. being prophetic

"Q" – n. in theology, a reference to writings that may have contributed to the formation of the Gospels in the New Testament, especially Matthew and Luke. "Q" derives from the German *Quelle*, meaning "source." The "Q" theory was introduced by Adolf von Harnack and developed by B. H. Streeter.

Reference: *The Four Gospels*, B. H. Streeter

QED – abbr. (*quod erat demonstrandum*) fr. Latin meaning, "which was to be demonstrated"; often found in deductively reasoned work (Baruch de Espinoza)

quadrivium – n. in medieval schools, a curriculum composed of arithmetic, geometry, astronomy, and music

quaggy – adj. marshlike; compare "quagmire": a complex or precarious situation where disengagement is difficult

quandary – n. a practical dilemma; a mental state of doubt

quark – n. in physics, believed to be a constituent of matter more basic than protons and neutrons. Part of theories of matter that are interesting from the standpoint of Platonism and physics (Heisenberg). Since they have never been observed, they are a hypothetical reality. Some physicists believe they are unobservable. Their existence is based on indirect evidence. Quark theory was first put together by Murray Gell-Mann and George Zweig in 1963.

Reference: *Introduction to Quarks and Partons*, F. E. Close

quash – v. to suppress or nullify

quaternary – adj. having four parts

quercine – adj. relating to oak; hardness

querulous – adj. being of a complaining nature; whining

quiddity – n. essence

quidnunc – n. one who seeks to know all the latest gossip; a news monger who has an insatiable need for speculating and learning the foibles of others

quiescent – adj. quiet; silent

quietism – n. in theology, a seventeenth-century spiritual view that emphasizes the importance of withdrawing from the world and its affairs in order to discover God. It advocates an ethic of complete nonviolence and absence of effort. It recommends a life of prayer in which even the desire for virtue is an obstacle to entering a pure faith experience.

quietus – n. anything that ends a dispute

Quine, Willard Van Orman (1908–2000) – an American logician in the tradition of Whitehead and Russell. Quine specialized in the philosophical and metalinguistic problems of semantics, logic, and epistemology. Like most modern logicians, he rejects the value of traditional metaphysics, preferring to designate metaphysical issues as "ontic theory." As such, metaphysical reflection must conform to scientific observations of reality.

> Principal works: *Mathematical Logic* (1940), *Methods of Logic* (1950), *Word and Object* (1960), *Set Theory and Its Logic* (1963)

> Reference: *Words and Objections: Essays on the Work of W. V. O. Quine*, Donald Davidson and Jaakko Hintikka

quintessence – n. the purest example

quisling – n. a traitor who collaborates with the enemy

quittance – n. release from duty or obligation

Q

quondam – adj. previous; former

quorum – n. the minimum number necessary to transact a meeting

quotidian – adj. being ordinary

R

Radhakrishnan, Sarvepalli (1888–1975) – an Indian philosopher. His philosophy of spiritual simplicity and asceticism became part of his platform as a political leader (president of India, 1962–1967).

Radhakrishnan argued that *maya* (ordinary experience) is a middle zone between unreality and the Absolute, with its origins lying in the Absolute. God is also neither completely transcendent nor completely immanent. The true nature of God inspires a kind of ethical universalism and an attitude of religious tolerance. These things are learned through authentic meditation and the development of an ethical life.

> Principal works: *Indian Philosophy*, 2 vols. (1923), *The Philosophy of the Upanishads* (1924), *An Idealist View of Life* (1929), *Eastern Religion and Western Thought* (1939), and *Religion in a Changing World* (1967)

> *"The supreme reality is incomprehensible in the sense that it cannot be expressed in logical propositions but it is increasingly apprehensible to the purified mind."*

> S. Radhakrishnan, *Eastern Religion and Western Thought*

> *"Karma is not so much a principle of retribution as one of continuity. Good produces good, evil produces evil. Love increases our power of love, hatred our power of hatred. It emphasizes the great importance of right action."*

S. Radhakrishnan, *An Idealist View of Life*

Reference: *Radhakrishnan: A Religious Biography*, Robert N. Minor

raffish – adj. cheap; vulgar; crude

Rahner, Karl (1904–1984) – a German theologian and Jesuit priest. Rahner was regarded as a successor to Joseph Marechal, the "Father of Transcendental Thomism." His theology and philosophy reveal a phenomenology reminiscent of his teacher, Martin Heidegger.

Rahner's theology sees human existence as a becoming, drawn forward by the presence of God. It is God (being) alone who can provide people with the fulfillment they seek in every level of their existence. An awareness of spiritual being in one's self liberates the individual from the demands for success and material control of life. Rahner's thought introduces this awareness as a type of anthropology of transcendence. This anthropology is, in turn, shaped by a Christology in an evolutionary view of the world. There Rahner sees matter and spirit existing together and argues that *homo sapiens* is both observer and participant in the natural order. Christ is a subjective expression of God's willingness to self-communicate with mankind.

In his theology of death, Rahner argues that what human life becomes does not perish in death. A life inspired by faith is everlasting, finding its fulfillment in God (being). Our finitude, which is so real in death, is mitigated by the transcendent eternal properties of the soul.

Principal works: *Theological Investigations*, 22 vols. (1961–1989), *Foundations of Christian Faith* (1976), *On Prayer* (1969), *On the Theology of Death* (1969), *The Trinity* (1970), and *Theological Dictionary* (1965)

"If man is thus the self-transcendence of living matter, then the history of nature and of spirit from an intrinsic and stratified unity in which the history of nature develops toward man, continues on in him as his history, is preserved and surpassed in him, and therefore reaches its own goal with and in the history of man's spirit. Insofar as this history of nature is subsumed in man into freedom, the history of nature reaches its goal in the free history of spirit itself, and remains an intrinsic, constitutive element in it. Insofar as the history of man still encompasses within itself the history of nature as the history of living matter, in the midst of its freedom it is still based upon the structures and necessities of this material world. Because man is not only a spirit who observes nature, but is also a part of it, and because he is to

continue its history, his history is not only a history of a culture situated above the history of nature, but is also an active transformation of the material world itself. And it is only through action which is of the spirit and through the life of the spirit which is the action that man and nature reach their single and common goal."

Karl Rahner, *Foundations of Christian Faith*

Reference: *Karl Rahner: His Life, Thought, and Works*, Herbert Vorgrimier, trans. by Edward Quinn

raillery – n. good-natured criticism or ridicule

Ramadan – n. in Islam, a reference to the ninth month of the Islamic calendar. Because the Islamic calendar is based on lunar cycles, the month changes from year to year. Comprising one of the Five Pillars of Islam, Ramadan requires all those who are faithful to Allah to fast from dawn to dusk. It celebrates the month in which Mohammed received the teachings of the Koran. The word *Ramadan* (usually capitalized) translates as ninth month.

Ramakrishna (1836–1886) – an Indian religious leader whose real name was Gadadhar Chatterji. A pluralist, he taught that all religions point to the same reality. His student, Vivekananda, spread his principal ideas through the Ramakrishna Mission, founded in 1897.

Ramakrishna co-converted to the practice of Sufism and Christianity. He proclaimed the truth of both religions. He then taught a pluralistic monotheistic spirituality, particularly through his experiments with Tantra, Vedanta, Islam, Christianity, and Vaishnava.

Reference: *Ramakrishna and His Disciples*, Christopher Isherwood

ramification – n. outcome; a branching process

ramous – adj. having branches

rancor – n. deep-seated resentment

Rank, Otto (1884–1939) – an Austrian psychologist, whose work and emphasis on "birth trauma" marked his departure from the Freudian school of thought. Rank's interests focused on the hero, myth, the sexual self, feminine psychology, guilt, dreams, neurosis, and the techniques of psychoanalysis.

In his most famous book, *Beyond Psychology*, Rank provides insights into the fear of death, the nature of personality, the desire for immortality, the need for love, and the fear of destruction.

> *"Christianity as it emerged from the disintegration of the Old World of antiquity became a spiritual mass-movement of international scope inaugurating an entirely new philosophy of living and thereby precipitating a new psychological type of man. This we designated the 'inspirational' type because . . . it was built on a 'therapeutic' ideology that, by going beyond the mere preaching of an ideal for social conduct, inspired the common man . . . to live up to a spiritual plane much higher than he could possibly aspire to in reality."*

Otto Rank, *Beyond Psychology*

Reference: *Acts of Will: The Life and Work of Otto Rank*, E. James Lieberman

rankle – v. to continue to cause irritation, anger, and/or resentment.

rapprochement – n. the act of reconciliation; creation of a cordial relation

rarefy – v. to thin out or make less dense; to make spiritual.

Rastafarians – n. in religion, a reference to a Jamaican messianic movement that started in the 1930s (Marcus Garvey, 1887–1940). It defines itself as an Abrahamic faith, teaches that Ethiopia is Zion, and God was incarnated in Haile Selassie, the late Ethiopian ruler. Rastafarians also believe that Christian scholarship has been corrupted by white Christians who will not admit that Jesus was black. Rituals are punctuated by the use of marijuana and revivalist music, especially reggae. Their influence in Jamaica stresses the importance of black separatism…It was the religion of Bob Marley, whose reggae music criticized materialism, political corruption, oppression of the poor, and sensual hedonism.

Reference: *The Essence of Rastafari Nationalism and Black Economic Development*, T. C. Myers.

ratiocination – n. the process of reasoning; a logical train of thought

rationalism – n. in philosophy, a reference to the thought of René Descartes, Benedict Spinoza, and G. W. Leibniz.

According to rationalism, reason is the principle tool for gaining knowledge and explaining reality. The best ideas are "innate." This means that empiricism is a secondary instrument in the architecture of ideas. Sense data, due to the various limitations of perception, are not ultimately reliable in deciphering reality. Even empirical approaches aided by the technology of seeing (e.g., microscopes and telescopes) rely upon reason to order the world around us.

Rationalism emphasizes ideas themselves as the raw matter to be used in gaining a truthful definition of reality. It uses mathematics and logic as paradigms for the discovery of knowledge independent of sense data. Principles, laws, and concepts alone constitute knowledge. So, beliefs that cannot be logically justified should be rejected.

Reference: *A History of Western Philosophy*, vol. 4, Frederick Copleston, SJ; and *The Rise of Western Rationalism*, Paul K. Feyerabend

realism – n. in philosophy, the view that objects of knowledge exist independent of our thinking. John Locke was a predecessor for modern scientific views of realism. In his empiricism, he argues that our ideas are sense data based in nature, an external and independent reality.

Realism stands in contrast to idealism, which argues that the external world is secondary to the world of ideas, that the physical world is somewhat of an illusion, and that only ideas themselves can be handled as the truth (e.g., Plato). Realism works with the scientific method: the objects of sense provide us with a common world of thought that can be compared and tested for accuracy. Realists such as Friedrich Nietzsche (1844–1900), author of *Thus Spoke Zarathustra*, complain that afterworldliness or otherworldliness interfere with a grasp of reality here and now. In this sense, realists are referred to as "tough minded" and idealists referred to as "soft minded." Philosophies of realism include pragmatism and process philosophy.

References: *Rationalism and Progress of Science*, Peter Smith; and *Introduction to Realism*, John Wild

rebarbative – adj. being unattractive

reboant – adj. loudly echoing or reverberating

recalcitrant – adj. difficult to handle, treat, or operate

recension – n. revision of a text on the basis of reconsiderations in the resource materials

recherche – adj. rare, refined, exquisite

recidivism – n. the tendency to fall back into previous habits or conduct, especially with regard to criminal actions

reciprocate – v. to return in kind; to give and take equally, more or less

recognizance – n. responsibility for behavior

recondite – adj. esoteric; not easily or commonly understood

recreant – adj. cowardly (as a noun, also recreant: a coward)

recriminate – v. to make a retaliatory charge against an accuser

recumbent – adj. reclining or resting

recusant – adj. the quality or refusal to comply, especially to established authority

redaction criticism – n. a method of analyzing complex texts dealing with multiple authors and shared materials. In theology, the term "redaction criticism" was used by Willie Marxsen to examine the editorial work of New Testament authors, especially the Gospels of Matthew and Luke.

Reference: *What Is Redaction Criticism?*, Norman Perrin

redintegrate – v. to restore to a sound state

redivivus – adj. brought back to life

redoubtable – adj. producing fear; formidable

redshift – n. in cosmology, a shift in the spectrum of galaxies outside the local group that is interpreted as a Doppler shift. It increases in proportion to distance and constitutes evidence for the belief in an expanding universe (Big Bang Theory). It is a way of measuring and detecting whether stars are moving closer or farther from Earth.

Reference: *Astronomy*, 4th ed., Michael Zeilik

reflet – n. luster; brilliance at the surface

refluent – adj. flowing back; ebbing

refringent – adj. to throw back; refractory, as in light

refulgent – adj. shining; brilliant in appearance

regicide – n. killing of a monarch

regnant – adj. to exercise the main power; ruling over

regression – n. a movement backward, usually to a more diseased or inferior condition

Reich, Wilhelm (1897–1957) – an Austrian psychoanalyst and philosopher of human sexuality. He broke from the ranks of conventional psychology to explore the role of "psychological armor," also called "character armor." Reich argued that people who had been hurt by others developed attitudes against further injury. He believed this armor also functioned internally to protect the individual from repressed emotions, especially destructive ones. According to Reich, armor makes the individual less susceptible to bad experiences but also freezes the "libidinal and aggressive motility."

As an extension of this armor, patients also have a distrust of the psychologist who provides analysis. This is called "negative transference." According to Reich, this distrust is rooted in attachment to "neurotic equilibrium." To break down this distrust, the patient must feel free in attacking the analyst to discharge repressed rage and aggression.

> *"There are no symptoms without a disturbance of the total character. Neurotic symptoms are, as it were, nothing but peaks of a mountain chain representing the neurotic character."*

> Wilhelm Reich, *The Function of the Orgasm*

Considered a nihilist by his critics, Reich believed that an authoritarian society is a damaging influence on the development of children. He argued for "biologism" and "vegetotherapy", the latter being a form of meditation on the role of emotions in the cultivation of well-being. By giving greater freedom to sexual desire, the individual would exercise good judgment under more natural circumstances. His psychology was also critical of religion as repression.

As Reich became more radical in his approach to the psychology of sex, he aroused opposition wherever he went. Reich was eventually prosecuted for contempt of court regarding an injunction to stop the shipment of "orgone accumulators."

This was an outcome of his arguments for "orgone energy," a spiritual energy now equated with mindfulness (in Buddhism) or *prana* (in Hinduism). He was sentenced to two years in a US prison and died there of untreated heart complications.

Principal works: *The Mass Psychology of Fascism* (1933), *Character Analysis* (1933), and *The Function of the Orgasm* (1927)

Reference: *The Quest for Wilhelm Reich*, Colin Wilson

reify – v. to make that which is abstract take on physical characteristics

rejoinder – n. an answer to a reply

relativism – n. in philosophy, the view that no absolutes exist. This doctrine goes back to the thinking of Protagoras (490–410 BC), who argued that "man is the measure of all things." Relativism appears in epistemology as the effect of skepticism, and in ethical theory as the effect of cultural differences that cause different normative systems to collide.

Relativism has had particular impact on normative ethical values. This is traceable to a number of causes including:

1) The decline of religion
2) The mixing of cultures, which demands an acceptance of other values and brings about conflict
3) The decline of reason in modern society
4) The liberal intellectual climate of Western culture, which is reluctant to embrace objectivist thinking because of its commitment to subjectivism
5) The appeal of the word "freedom" over the word "authority"; including a fallacious dissociation of the notion of freedom from existential responsibility

References: *Patterns of Culture*, Ruth Benedict; *Ethical Relativity*, Edward Westermarck; and *Ethical Relativism*, John Ladd

religious cults – n. in religion, a reference to any sort of fanatical belief system that is devoted to the emotional needs of its practitioners. Cults usually derive their inspiration from a charismatic leader, whose spiritual credentials may be in doubt. Some cults survive the death of the leader to form churches.

Cults tend to be antirational and resistant to self-criticism. They often see themselves in conflict with the rest of society. They may endorse secret rituals for membership. They may also exploit vices that can act to attract disciples. They are a natural refuge for those without family or social support, and tend to endorse metaphysical views that rely on uncritical acceptance.

Reference: *Satan's Power: A Deviant Psychotherapy Cult*, William S. Bainbridge

remanent – adj. remaining or enduring

remigrant – n. one who returns

renascent – adj. showing new vitality

renifleur – n. a person who is sexually gratified by odors

renitent – adj. to be stubbornly opposed

renvoi – n. expulsion of an alien

replication – n. a reply; an answer; also, a copy

replete – adj. full

reposit – v. to replace

reprehend – v. to find fault

requital – n. a return or repayment; also, a reward

reseau – n. a network

res gestae – n. acts or deeds performed; facts surrounding a litigated issue

resupine – adj. prone or prostrate due to being bent back

reticent – adj. inclined to be silent

reticulation – n. a network; a formation of dots, lines, crosshairs, wires, etc.

retral – adj. at or near the back

retrocede – v. to recede; to move away

retrograde – adj. contrary to normal order or progress

revenant – n. one who returns, especially after a long absence

revile – v. to attack or abuse

rhathymia – n. a carefree disposition

rhexis – n. a break or rupture

riant – adj. cheerful, happy

ribald – adj. coarse, vulgar

rident – adj. a laughing attitude

risible – adj. able to laugh

risqué – adj. indecent; borderline actions or words

roborant – adj. tending to strengthen

rogatory – adj. concerning the process of questioning

Romero, Francisco (1891–1962) – an Argentine philosopher, Romero reflects the views of Wilhelm Dilthey, José Ortega y Gasset, and Nicolai Hartmann. He taught at the universities of Buenos Aires and La Plata.

Romero divided phenomena into four classes: *inorganic*—the physical world of atoms and space; *organic*—the vital world of flora and fauna; *psychic*—consciousness and intentional egoistic transcendence; and *spiritual*—complete non-egoistic transcendence. All four compose a whole in which transcendence is characteristic of development and higher forms of being.

> Principal works: *Logic* (1938), *Philosophy of the Person* (1944), *Man and Culture* (1950), *Theory of Man* (1952), and *What Is Philosophy?* (1953)

> *"The spiritual act is projected toward the object, and it remains there. In cognitive, emotional, and volitional activity, the self is concerned with the objectivities for what they are in themselves. In merely intentional activity the subject places the objects and then takes them to himself, whereas in the spiritual act he places the objects and then yields himself to them."*

Francisco Romero, *Theory of Man*

Rousseau, Jean-Jacques (1712–1778) – a French philosopher and romantic, Rousseau's philosophy helped ignite the French Revolution. He remained on the edge of society throughout his life, wandering from place to place, and in the end experienced a deep paranoia of the enemies he had created with his writing.

Rousseau believed that literature, science, and reasoning, as taught in the modern world, brought with it "garlands of flowers over the chains which weigh men down." He viewed art and literature as sources of conformity, making people think and act alike in dress, speech, and dispositions.

Rousseau criticized modern politicians for their failure to set good examples. He argued that ancient leaders lead their citizens toward virtue and morals, whereas modern politicians lead people toward an obsession with commerce and money. He contrasted this with the state of nature in which humans were essentially good and free of the corrupting influence of modern society (Rousseau's "noble savage").

The goal of Rousseau's thought was to outline a society committed to reestablishing values concerned with the moral development of all its citizens. Law should reflect the general well-being of citizens and avoid special interests and factions. Rousseau is "the father of liberalism."

Principal works: *Discourse on the Sciences and the Arts* (1750), *Discourse on the Origin of Inequality Among Men* (1755), *The Social Contract* (1762), *Emile* (1762), and *Confessions* (1782)

"Moral liberty . . . alone makes man truly master of himself; for the mere impulse of appetite is slavery, while obedience to a law which we prescribe to ourselves is liberty."

J. J. Rousseau, *The Social Contract*

"Where is there any respect for law? Under the name of law you have seen the rule of self-interest and human passion. But the eternal laws of nature and of order exists. For the wise man they take the place of positive law; they are written in the depths of his heart by conscience and reason; let him obey these laws and be free; for there is no slave but the evil-doer, for he always does evil against his

will. Liberty is not to be found in any form of government, she is in the heart of the free man."

J. J. Rousseau, *Emile*

Reference: *Rousseau: The Self-Made Saint*, J. H. Huizinga

ruction – n. a noisy, quarrelsome disturbance

rueful – adj. bringing about pity

Rūmī, Jalāl al-Dīn (1207–1273) – a Persian philosopher, jurist, poet, and advocate of Sufism. He used his poetry to define Islamic mysticism, especially in a work entitled *The Masnavi*. It portrays life as a mystical journey through love. Dance, music, and poetry are spiritual exercises to reach the Perfect One. According to Rūmī's exegetical rendering, Quranic revelations offer mystical opportunities for a perfection of love.

Reference: *Teachings of Rumi: The Masnavi*, by Rumi, trans. and ed. by E. H. Whinfield

ruminant – adj. inclined toward contemplation or meditation

Russell, Bertrand (1872–1970) – an English pluralist philosopher of logic, mathematics, and society. Russell liked to respond to critics by saying, "I always reserve the right to change my mind." He worked with Alfred N. Whitehead.

Russell's reputation as a philosopher was in the area of logic, mathematics, and language. His approach became known as "logical atomism." Russell believed that a perfect language would have logical properties that ensure correspondence between its component parts and facticity; the relation to reality. Use of language should concern itself with the simplest elements of language to identify their role in providing exact meaning. This concern led Russell to emphasize "atomic facts," facts of the simplest kind, and the expression of these atomic facts in "atomic propositions," the linguistic equivalent of physical atoms.

Truth and falsity depend upon a careful analysis of words and propositions corresponding to facts. Two or more atomic propositions constitute a "molecular proposition." The molecular propositions necessitate the use of "truth functions," symbols that guide us through a kind of arithmetic of truth calculations.

Problems in the application of Russell's theory led to a renewed interest in empiricism, especially the ideas of David Hume. This in turn weakened the metaphysical, or abstract, focus of Russell's logical atomism. To other logicians, like Ludwig Wittgenstein, the disparity between theory and practice forced a recognition of the propositions of science.

> Principal works: *Principia Mathematica*, 2 vols. (with A. N. Whitehead, 1910), *Our Knowledge of the External World* (1914), *Principles of Social Reconstruction* (1916), *Mysticism and Logic* (1918), *Education and the Social Order* (1932), *Unpopular Essays* (1950), *Logic and Knowledge* (1956), and *Essays in Skepticism* (1962)

> *"The fundamental argument for freedom of opinion is the doubtfulness of all our beliefs. If we certainly knew the truth, there would be something to be said for teaching it. But in that case it could be taught without invoking authority, by means of its inherent reasonableness. It is not necessary to make a law that no one shall be allowed to teach arithmetic if he holds heretical opinions on the multiplication table, because here the truth is clear, and does not require to be enforced by penalties. When the State intervenes to ensure the teaching of some doctrine, it does so 'because' there is no conclusive evidence in favor of that doctrine."*

> Bertrand Russell, *Skeptical Essays*

> Reference: *Bertrand Russell and the British Tradition in Philosophy*, D. F. Pears

rusticate – v. to live in the countryside (Cynics)

ruth – n. pity; compassion

Ruysbroeck, Jan van (1293–1381) – A Flemish philosopher of mysticism. At age sixty Ruysbroeck brought together his experience in religious reflection to form the monastic community of Groenendael in the forest of Soignes, (Belgium's largest urban forest). He taught that the soul finds God through a knowledge of itself, moving from the active life immersed in the world to the contemplative life that transcends the world.

> Principal works: *Adornment of the Spiritual Marriage*, *The Sparkling Stone*, *The Book of Supreme Truth*, and *The Espousals*

> *"The image of God is found essentially and personally in all mankind. Each possesses it whole, entire and undivided, and all together not more than one alone."*

Jan van Ruysbroeck, *Adornment of the Spiritual Marriage*

Reference: *The Land Within*, Paul Mommaers, trans. by N. D. Smith

S

Sabbath – n. fr. Hebrew *shabbath*, meaning "to rest." It commemorates the seventh day of Creation. In Exodus 20:8, it is an appointed day for prayer, worship, and meditation. It has historical roots as an act of resistance to cultural assimilation during the Egyptian captivity of the Israelites. By appointing one day each week to rest, the Jews built their devotion to Yahweh and resistance to Egyptian influence. It begins at sundown on Friday and ends at sundown on Saturday.

Saccus, Ammonius (175–242 AD) – the teacher of Plotinus, who founded the views of Neoplatonism. Saccus also taught Origen, who influenced the formation of Christian theology. Christian theologians borrowed ideas from Neoplatonism and Platonism. Saccus's work on Platonism seemed to be a reconciliation of the differences between Aristotle and Plato.

> Reference: *The Cambridge History of Later Greek and Early Medieval Philosophy*, A. H. Armstrong

sacerdotal – adj. priestly

sadism – n. in psychology, deriving sexual gratification from inflicting pain on another. It is derived from the name Marquis de Sade (1740–1814), who died in the lunatic asylum of Charenton. Sade wrote *Justine*, a novel depicting moral, sexual, and physical cruelty.

Sadism is the opposite of masochism, and reflects a need for sexual power over a sex partner. It is explained as a response to feelings of inferiority, which may include underlying hostility toward parental figures or others in authority. Some psychologists believe it can be culturally induced in value systems where the male dominates the female. It combines perfectly with masochism into "codependency" (Fromm).

Reference: *S and M: Studies in Sadomasochism*, eds. G. Levi Kamel and Thomas Weinberg

sagacity – adj. having acute mental apprehension, along with great practical wisdom

salacious – adj. given to sexual interests; lecherous

salubrious – adj. being conducive to good health

salutary – adj. bringing about improved health

samsara – n. fr. Sanskrit *samsara*, meaning passing through. In Hinduism, a reference to the cycle of existence or wheel of life—birth, growth, decay, and death. In this context death is merely a pause between lives. Life is repeated over and over until the effects of karma (the law of rewards) result in a final and eternal liberation of the soul.

sanative – adj. able to cure

sangfroid – n. deep-seated composure, especially in dangerous circumstances

sanguinary – adj. being bloodthirsty; combat ready

sanguine – adj. courageous disposition

Santayana, George (1863–1952) – a Spanish-American philosopher. Born in Madrid, Santayana remained emotionally attached to his Mediterranean roots. This was partly an apprehension about the structure of modern commercial-democratic society, which seemed to be an extension of the conflict between his Catholic spirituality and its Protestant counterpart.

Santayana's philosophy is a poetic reasoning with interests in social theory, morality, aesthetics, metaphysics, science, and religion. In his social theory, Santayana observed a hierarchy of organization: "natural society" cohering on basic human and biological needs; "free society," or institutions going beyond natural needs and addressing the individual needs of persons; and "ideal society"—a community built upon affection for science, art, and religion.

His moral theory identifies three stages of development: "pre-rational"—guidance provided by aphorisms and traditional sayings, being often inconsistent yet rich in meaning; "rational"—guidance from the advanced use of reasoning, given to a specific direction and goal; and "post-rational"—guidance by images of an afterlife, reflecting the growing pessimism characteristic of aging and decline of the body.

The best label for Santayana's philosophy may be philosophical naturalism, since he based so much of his reasoning on the ideal as found in nature. Even his religious sentiments are guided by this belief. He believed that without nature, religion itself would have no existence.

> Principal works: *Sense of Beauty* (1896), *Life of Reason*, 5 vols. (1906), *Scepticism and Animal Faith* (1923), *Realms of Being*, 4 vols. (1940), and *Dominations and Powers* (1949)

> *"Scepticism is the chastity of the intellect, and it is shameful to surrender it too soon or to the first comer; there is nobility in persevering coolly and proudly through a long youth, until at last, in the ripeness of instinct and discretion, it can be safely exchanged for fidelity and happiness."*

> George Santayana, *Scepticism and Animal Faith*

> References: *The Philosophy of George Santayana*, ed. Paul A. Schilpp; and *The Complete Poems of George Santayana: A Critical Edition*, William Holzberger

sapid – adj. tasty; palatable; also, agreeable to the mind

sapient – adj. revealing deep wisdom or discernment

Sappho (ca. 630 BC) – a Greek philosopher and poet of love. Born on the island of Lesbos (lesbianism), she became famous for her views on passion. Her poetry was usually addressed to women, and it is believed that she was a member of a literary circle of female correspondents. (See also "Lesbos, Sappho of")

> Reference: *Three Archaic Poets*, Anne P. Burnett

saprophagous – adj. feeding on decaying organic material

sarcasm – n. satirical comments designed to be painful

sardonic – adj. having a bitter character; derisive

Sartre, Jean-Paul (1905–1980) – a French philosopher of existentialism. Sartre popularized the phrase "existence precedes essence." The logical equivalent of this phrase is "being precedes meaning." One exists before one's life becomes something meaningful. Making it something is dependent upon personal choice. Failing to make it something is also a personal choice. For Sartre, the freedom of one's existence implies an openness that is unavoidable. There is no way to exchange this existential condition or contract for fatalism. Modern life is a complicated affair, and most people live in "bad faith" (*mauvaise foi*); they deny responsibility for who they are. They live "inauthentically," attempting to pass off an unsatisfactory existence on some external set of facts.

A life of action is the only reality. Besides the acts one chooses, one is nothing. Even God does not provide a solution, as Sartre argues for the truth of atheism. There is no God. The human situation is one of abandonment or forlornment. And, human anxiety is the product of an awareness of this abandonment, this finitude of existence. Those who cannot handle the reality of this awareness experience loneliness, despair, and perhaps guilt, because they adopt ready-made lives. They practice self-deception. They try to act as if it is not true that life bears no ready-made script. They get a job on compromised principles that do not really suit their authentic vision. They go to work, and it is perhaps a cheap substitute for choosing the life one really should live according to one's being.

A social consequence of our forlorn condition is that we may fail (narcissism) to see the "intersubjectivity" of persons. Our condition is universal. Everyone experiences what the other experiences, in terms of ontology. It is important to recognize this in order to prevent a sense of self-pity. Sartre also focuses on the Nietzschean use of courage. Sartre has been called a French version of Nietzsche.

Principal works: *Nausea* (1938), *The Transcendence of the Ego* (1936), *Being and Nothingness* (1943), *Existentialism Is a Humanism* (1946), and *Critique of Dialectical Reason* (1960)

"When, in all honesty, when I've recognized that man is a being in whom existence precedes essence, that he is a free being who, in various circumstances, can want only his freedom, I have at the same time recognized that I can want only the freedom of others.

"Therefore, in the name of this will for freedom, which freedom itself implies, I may pass judgment on those who seek to hide from themselves the complete arbitrariness *and the complete freedom of their existence. Those who hide their complete freedom from themselves out of a spirit of seriousness or by means of deterministic excuses, I shall call cowards.*"

Jean-Paul Sartre, *Existentialism Is a Humanism*

Reference: *Sartre: Romantic Rationalist*, I. Murdoch

saturnine – adj. having a cold, gloomy temperament

satyriasis – n. abnormal and uncontrollable sexual desire in the male; having Dionysian preferences

satyromaniac – n. a lustful male

scabrous – adj. difficult; rough; also, promoting scandalous themes

scatology – n. the study of obscene words and literature

schizoid – adj. disintegrating into mutually contradictory or antagonistic parts

Schleiermacher, Friedrich (1768–1834) – a German theologian. Schleiermacher thought of religion primarily as feeling or intuition rather than reason or ethics. True religion, in his view, stands independent of dogma and is primarily an experience of the infinite. He argued that religious feeling is an experience of complete dependence upon God.

Schleiermacher defended Christian monotheism, against other religious outlooks, as the highest form of religious experience. He acknowledges that a variety of religious forms exist in different individuals, but Christianity is among the truest.

Principal works: *Religion: Speeches to Its Cultured Despisers* (1799), and *The Christian Faith* (1822)

"*Second Theorem: In the uniting of the divine nature with the human, the divine alone was active or self-imparting, and the human alone passive or in process of being assumed; but during the state of union every activity was a common activity of both natures.*"

F. Schleiermacher, *The Christian Faith*

Reference: *The Philosophy of Schleiermacher*, Richard B. Brandt

Schopenhauer, Arthur (1788–1860) – a German philosopher. Schopenhauer divided reality into four kinds of objects: "physical objects" located in time and space (the content of scientific thought); "abstract objects"—the domain of logic and the principles of reason (e.g., rules of inference and the theories of metaphysics); "mathematical objects"—the geometrical analysis of space and the mathematical account of time; and "the self"—the will and its conscious exertion over life. Schopenhauer referred to these as objects or forms of the Principle of Sufficient Reason. The dynamics of interaction between these objects reveals a deterministic trend in the natural world.

Schopenhauer's account of change includes a highest metaphysical force that he calls "will." Will permeates everything, from the highest life form to the lowest objects. It acts in such a way as to be the "will to live." Everything seeks life over and against other life. Each member of a species is part of the drive for survival, expendable and replaceable. The world is basically a battlefield.

For humanity, Schopenhauer argued, the consequences of existence are bleak. Every move we make is directly or indirectly a calculated attempt to escape death. Life is evil. It is a steady annihilation of the race through disease, war, violence, and time. This prevents the attainment of true happiness. Life is fundamentally a struggle to survive, leading to aggressiveness, achievement, conflict, and self-centeredness.

Schopenhauer concludes that the only true source of peace comes from philosophical or artistic creativity. He advocates Buddhist principles with an ethic of sympathy to escape the destructive power of the universal will.

Principal works: *The Fourfold Root of the Principle of Sufficient Reason* (1813), *The World as Will and Idea* (1819), *On the Will in Nature* (1836), *The Two Basic Problems of Ethics* (1841), and *Essays of Schopenhauer* (T. Saunders, 1951)

"Great intellectual gifts mean an activity pre-eminently nervous in its character, and consequently a very high degree of susceptibility to pain in every form."

Arthur Schopenhauer, *Essay on Personality*

"Reading is merely a surrogate for thinking for yourself; it means letting someone else direct your thoughts. Many books, moreover, serve merely to show how many ways there are of being wrong, and how afar astray you yourself would go if you followed their guidance."

Arthur Schopenhauer, *Essays*

Reference: *Arthur Schopenhauer: Philosopher of Pessimism*, 2nd ed., Frederick C. Copleston

sciolism – n. superficial knowledge

scopophilia – n. the pleasure of looking at sensual and erotic images; literally "love of looking"

scrupulous – adj. having strong character; principled

scrutable – adj. able to be understood after detailed study

scurrilous – adj. given to gross descriptions; obscenely abusive

secern – v. to make careful distinctions

sedition – n. promotion of resistance or rebellion against lawful authority

sedulous – adj. working with careful persistence; diligent

self-abasement – n. attack on one's self based in feelings of guilt or inferiority

self-realization – n. developing one's talents and abilities as personal sources of meaning and purpose

semantics – n. the branch of linguistics concerned with meanings

sematic – adj. giving warning, especially to other animals by the use of special signals or markings (e.g., a rattlesnake's tail, a dog's growl, the red hourglass of a black widow)

semeiology – n. semantics; the study or art of signs; variation of semiology – n. the study of signs

semidiurnal – adj. relating to half a day

senescence – n. the process of aging; adj. senescent—the quality of aging

sententious – adj. aphoristic expression; compressed truths, often moralistic and often self-righteous

sequacious – adj. following intellectually, logically; also, being servile

sequent – adj. following

sequester – v. to put into solitude; to isolate

serendipity – n. accidental encounter with good fortune

seriocomic – adj. semi-serious and semi-comical

sesquipedalian – adj. given to the use of long words

Sextus Empiricus (ca. 225 AD) – a Greek philosopher and a key figure in the school of Skepticism. The goal of Skepticism wasn't truth or knowledge but inner peace. The endless conflicts between intellectuals taught Sextus the futility of gaining absolute knowledge of anything.

Ataraxia (peace of mind) was the final stage in the process of seeking knowledge. It followed *tropoi* (methods of argument) and *epoche* (the suspension of judgment). For Sextus, the mutilation of spiritual life through constant haggling over truth and knowledge simply proved the validity of moving beyond these toward an adjusted philosophy of *eudaimonism* (happiness). He realized he was still a practitioner of logic, because even to refute logic one must use logic.

> Principal works: *Pyrrhonic Sketches, Against the Dogmatists, Against the Intellectuals*, and *On the Soul* (no existing fragments)

> References: *The Modes of Scepticism*, Julia Annas and Jonathan Barnes; *The Skeptical Tradition*, ed. Myles Burnyeat

Shinto – n. the national religion of Japan, *Shinto* means "way of the spirits."

A phrase used conjunctively with Shinto is *kami-no-michi*, meaning "the path of the sacred." The *Kojiki* is the ancient manuscript of Shinto. It describes the creation of the world by two *kami* (sacred ones), *Izanagi* (male-who-invites) and *Izanami* (female-who-invites).

Shinto teaches that the emperor is the descendant of the sun goddess, *Ameterasu*. Japan itself is perceived as the center of the world, the land of the kami. Along with this belief is the "way of the warrior," *bushido*. Bushido is then the code of the *samurai*. Loyalty to Japan is at the center of Shinto's practices and teachings.

> References: *On Understanding Japanese Religion*, Joseph Kitagawa; and *A Study of Shinto*, Genchi Kato

Shiva – n. in Hinduism, the god which destroys. Hindus who worship Shiva are called *Shaivites*. Shiva is part of the Hindu trinity: Shiva, Brahman, and Vishnu.

sidereal – adj. relating to the stars or the heavens

Sidgwick, Henry (1838–1900) – an English philosopher noted mainly for his advocacy and defense of utilitarianism. Sidgwick connected ethics to common sense and three types of ethical reflection: "intuitionism"— advocating a pursuit of excellence from obvious principles like compassion, wisdom, and justice; egoism—advocating the pursuit of one's personal happiness over other considerations; and "utilitarianism"— advocating the greatest good for the greatest number. He used the principles of intuitionism to advance his brand of utilitarianism.

> Principal works: *The Methods of Ethics* (1874), *The Principles of Political Economy* (1883), and *Outlines of the History of Ethics* (1886)

> Reference: *Henry Sidgwick and Later Utilitarian Political Philosophy*, William Harvard

Sikhism – n. a religion that began as a protest to imperfections in Hinduism. Nanak (1469–1538), the founder of Sikhism, promoted a monotheistic doctrine with an ethical focus on philanthropy, loyalty, truth, honesty, justice, and nonpartisan life. Sikhism denounces wine, tobacco, idolatry, the caste system, slander, and hypocrisy. In time, Sikhism abandoned some of its pacifistic beliefs for its own survival in a hostile Muslim environment.

The Khalsa ("pure") Order of Singhs are guided by the phrase, "The Pure are of God, and the victory is to God." They wear the five Ks: (1) *kesh*—uncut hair, (2) *kachh*—military shorts, (3) *kangha*—comb, (4) *kara*—steel bracelet, and (5) *kirpan*—sword.

Sikhism combines elements of Islam with Hinduism to form a unique and durable syncretistic faith. It argues for the equality of men and women, and it reveals a "process" orientation in accepting the wisdom of gurus after Nanak. It seems to accept the possibility of a continuing revelation from God. It does not advocate asceticism, per se, since the support of family life requires a degree of wealth to ensure flourishing.

> *"There is pleasure in gold, pleasure in silver, and in women, pleasure in the perfume of sandal; there is pleasure in horses, pleasure in couches and in palaces, pleasure in sweets, and pleasure in meats. When such are the pleasures of the body, how shall God's name obtain a dwelling therein?"*

Guru Nanak, *The Sikh Religion* by M. A. Macauliffe

"Accursed the life of him in this world who breatheth without uttering the Name."

Guru Nanak, *The Sikh Religion* by M. A. Macauliffe

References: *The Sikh Religion: Its Gurus, Sacred Writings, and Authors*, M. A. Macauliffe; and *The Sikhs*, W. H. McLeod

silvicolous – adj. belonging to forest or woodland habitat; living in forests (e.g., monastic Buddhism as a "forest religion")

simony – n. the sale or trading of sacred things

simulant – adj. pretending

sinecure – n. an office or position yielding honor and profit with little or no work involved

sine qua non – Latin meaning "an indispensable thing"; a requirement

sinistrous – adj. unfavorable

sirenic – adj. dangerously attractive

sitomania – n. abnormal craving for food

skulk – v. to avoid observation, as with the habit of foxes

slake – v. to relieve by satisfying

slattern – n. a loose woman, especially a prostitute

Smith, Adam (1723–1790) – a Scottish philosopher of economics. Smith argued against the old view that wealth is the acquisition and retention of money. A nation is better off, reasoned Smith, if it can increase its productivity of goods. Thus, the successful capitalist is one who meets the need for desirable goods. The general welfare of society is improved even if the capitalist seeks only his own well-being, because his work satisfies the needs of others through productivity.

Smith's fame as an economist overshadows his refined personal views of ethics and its relation to a successful life. Building on a moral psychology of sympathy, he advocated moderation and self-control over a life of uncontrolled ambition and self-indulgence. Moral development is a key element in his view of success. Smith reasoned that there are three stages of moral development: pleasure—typical of youth and reflecting little restraint due to the absence of informed reasoning; emulation—the recognition of superior role models and the opportunity to model one's life accordingly, though often without any real appreciation for the last stage; and virtue—the authentic recognition of moral qualities which contribute to a happy life, individually and socially.

Principal works: *Theory of Moral Sentiments* (1759), and *An Inquiry into the Nature and Causes of the Wealth of Nations* (1776)

"In civilized society man stands at all times in need of the cooperation and assistance of great multitudes, while his whole life is scarce sufficient to gain the friendship of a few persons."

Adam Smith, *Theory of Moral Sentiments*

"Capitals are increased by parsimony, and diminished by prodigality and misconduct."

Adam Smith, *The Wealth of Nations*

Reference: *Adam Smith's Sociological Economics*, David A. Reisman

socialism – n. in philosophy, the political doctrine that group control of property is desirable, as is the production of goods and the possession of wealth. Some types of socialism are politically allied with communism, being differentiated only in degree. As a philosophy, and contrary to its claims, socialism stands counterposed to individualism and personal liberty. The values of equality and individual freedom make strange companions under the socialist canopy.

The first references to socialism are traced to France in the 1830s, also in Jean-Jacques Rousseau (the father of liberalism), but its basic beliefs can be traced back even further to Plato, the Hebrews, and the New Testament. It received greater definition in the work of Marx and Engels. Marxism then became the foundation for Russian and European socialism. John Stuart Mill counter-argued that socialism produces indolence.

References: *The General History of Socialism and Social Struggle*, Max Beer; *Essential Works of Socialism*, ed. Irving Howe

sociopath – n. a psychopath (1930). One who is a danger to society, possessing strong hostility toward others, but lacking the courage and intellectual honesty to examine the sources of this hostility. Characteristics include: superficial and glib communication with others, enlisting others to attack adversaries, vilifying those who are critical, perfectionistic dress, and mannerisms that mask inner hostility. The psychopath's lack of empathy for those who experience severe pain and suffering is contradicted by the psychopath's own outrage over trivial offenses.

According to Andrew Salter (1914-1996), the psychopath's goal is attainment of power at the expense of others. The psychopath needs to dominate and oppress others to avoid self-examination. With sardonic wit, Salter reminds his readers that in suicides by people who are dominated, many a suicide could have been prevented with a homicide.

> Reference: *Conditioned Reflex Therapy*, Andrew Salter, and *The Case Against Psychoanalysis*, Andrew Salter.

Socrates (470–399 BC) – a Greek philosopher. Socrates was a stonemason, a hoplite, and the teacher of Plato. Originally a philosopher of matter, he gradually abandoned his interest in physics and cosmology. Instead, Socrates became focused on ethical theory as it applied to individuals and society. He attended to the exploration of self-knowledge and its relation to human happiness (eudaemonism). The end of his life has become a model for facing death, living by one's principles, and doing what is best for society.

For Socrates, the secret to a successful life was *logos*, or reason. Reason was the key to psychological harmony. He stressed the relationship between reason and actions. This relationship was to be perfected by the use of *sophia*, wisdom. In turn, this provided the basis for the pursuit of *arete*, virtue: "Knowledge is virtue."

Socrates was known for a philosophical method, called "midwifery" or the "Socratic Method," employing the following elements: *conversation*—the use of a verbal exchange or dialogue, often in a question form; *definition*—the request for meanings in one's terminology; dialectic—the use of counterargument to deepen the theoretical understanding of some issue; *skepticism*—exercising doubt and a professed ignorance of the truth to find truth; induction—the use of empirical evidence, case examples; and *deduction*—conclusions derived from preexisting statements of supposed fact.

Principal works: None. The views of Socrates are recorded by Plato in the *Dialogues*.

"A man who is good for anything ought not to calculate the chance of living or dying; he ought only to consider whether in doing anything he is doing right or wrong."

Socrates in Plato's *Apology*

References: *The Socratic Enigma*, ed. H. Spiegelberg; and *The Trial and Death of Socrates*, G. M. A. Grube

sodality – n. comradeship

solecism – n. any mistake, but especially grammatical ones

solicitous – adj. filled with concern and anxiety

solifidian – n. one who believes in salvation by faith without works

solipsism – n. fr. Latin *solus*, meaning alone. It is extreme egoism, adopting the view that the self alone exists. The self is more real than other selves, who are merely sensory experiences. Solipsism is caused by radical skepticism of an external world. It is historically evident in the views of Gorgias, Descartes, and Berkeley. F. H. Bradley (1846–1924) explained solipsism as a failure to transcend the self, by communion with the Absolute. In logical terms, solipsism is a fallacy of subjectivity, meaning a failure to honor the objective facticity of an external world.

By definition, solipsism includes narcissistic concern with the self at the expense of social relationships.

Reference: *The Significance of Philosophical Scepticism*, Barry Stroud

somnifacient – adj. causing sleep

somniferous – adj. bringing about sleep

somnolence – n. sleepiness

sophism – n. an argument that appears to be correct but is actually invalid; an argument used to display intellectual brilliance or provide a deception

sophists – n. fr. Greek *sophist*, meaning craftsman, expert, or wise man. In philosophy, it is a reference to a group of thinkers known for their skepticism regarding knowledge. They taught politicians and lawyers how to argue any position. Active in the fifth and fourth centuries BC, they included: Protagoras, Gorgias, Hippias, and Thrasymachus. Their theoretical skepticism led directly to ethical skepticism, which translated into subjectivism and relativism. Sophists argued that knowledge is rhetoric, and the one who is more skilled at language shall appear to hold the correct view on any matter.

Reference: *The Sophists*, Mario Untersteiner, trans. by Kathleen Freeman

sophrosyne – n. moderation; self-control. In Plato's philosophy, this implies a balance between the needs of the body and those of the mind.

soporose – adj. abnormally sleepy

sordid – adj. dirty; squalid

sororicide – n. killing of a sister

sot – n. a chronic drunkard

soteriology – n. the theological study of salvation, especially as it relates to Christ

spavined – adj. in worn-out condition

specious – adj. superficially correct or good

spiel – n. an extravagant story

Spinoza, Benedict (1632–1677) – a Dutch philosopher and rationalist metaphysician. Spinoza was born and raised in Amsterdam. Moving to Voorburg (Netherlands) in 1660, he made a living by grinding and polishing lenses. During his life he rarely made contact with many other philosophers and lived in relative seclusion as he developed his theories. His theological opinions fostered contempt. Once, he was almost assassinated with a dagger (a button blocked the knife's penetration).

Spinoza presented a pantheistic version of reality: God and nature are one and the same (*Deus sive Natura*). He removed the idea of a "relation" with God, making the world and God a unity. This unity was argued as eternal, so God and matter have no prior cause. Matter, in turn, exhibits "attributes": essences perceived by the intellect.

God has an infinite number of attributes, but our human reasoning only recognizes two: thought and extension.

The universe is also characterized by necessity. The events of the universe are fixed from eternity. And, our knowledge of this universe is represented by stages of enlightenment: *imagination*—ideas derived from sense experience, the passive acceptance of sense data; *reason*—the use of mathematical and physical knowledge for the formation of abstract theories; and *intuition*—a transcendence of reason and imagination, a comprehensive intellectual grasp of how the whole universe hangs together.

Principal works: *Principles of Cartesian Philosophy* (1663), *Theological Political Treatise* (1670), and *Ethics* (published posthumously)

"Whatever is, is in God, and nothing can exist or be conceived without God . . . God is the indwelling and not the transient cause of all things."

Benedict Spinoza, *Ethics*

References: *The Philosophy of Baruch Spinoza*, ed. Richard Kennington; and *The Philosophy of Spinoza*, Harry A. Wolfson

sponsion – n. promise

sporadic – adj. occasionally

spurious – adj. of questionable origins; counterfeit

squalid – adj. extremely filthy, especially as a result of poverty or neglect

SS – n. fr. German *Schutzstaffel*, meaning defense echelon. Founded as a bodyguard for Hitler, it was expanded into an institution of Nazi terror. The SS used public executions to create compliance with fascist agendas. Under the direction of Heinrich Himmler, the SS controlled all elements of the German police system, including the Gestapo.

References: *A History of Nazi Germany*, Joseph W. Bendersky; and *The Ideological Origins of Nazi Imperialism*, W. D. Smith

staid – adj. steady in character; being serious or grave

stanchless – adj. incessant

stasis – n. a stoppage of the flow of body fluids; equilibrium

sthenic – adj. characterized by a strong build

stilted – adj. pompous; above it all; formal

stochastic – adj. involving chance or luck as a complication to prediction

stoicism – n. in philosophy, the view that indifference to pleasure and pain produces the best adjustment to human existence. It advocated a specific outlook with regard to logic and cosmology, and argues for resignation or acceptance of the circumstances one finds in the world. Stoics valued "apathy," since it protects one's happiness by being unmoved by the depravity of society. It emphasized a simple life, and taught that a world reason or "logos" is at the bottom of all events in this world. Representatives of the school include Zeno of Citium (335–263 BC), Seneca (3–65 AD), and Marcus Aurelius (121–180 AD).

> Reference: *Ethics and Human Action in Early Stoicism*, Brad Inwood

stolid – adj. unemotional; slow to reveal feeling

strappado – n. a special form of capital punishment in which the individual is hoisted to a height of about thirty feet, tied to a rope that is less than thirty feet long, and then dropped; also used as a type of torture, the degree of which was determined by the part of the body connected to the rope and the drop distance.

stricture – n. an abnormal narrowing; also, adversarial criticism

structuralism – n. in philosophy, the view that all cultures and societies possess a common structural foundation upon which secondary differences are built. The basic categorization of all cultures is possible in terms of psychology, anthropology, religion, economics, and philosophy, thus revealing a foundational order. Starting with the influence of Claude Levi-Strauss, ideological support expands with the works of Marx, Freud, Jung, Lacan, Foucault, and Merleau-Ponty. It minimizes differences and individuality by exposing the forms that exist in successive generations of culture everywhere.

> References: *The Language of the Self*, Jacques Lacan; *The Order of Things*, Michael Foucault; *The Words and the Things*, M. Foucault; and *The Archaeology of Knowledge*, M. Foucault

stupefacient – adj. causing unconsciousness or stupor

subjacent – adj. underlying

sublimate – v. to handle or express a primitive instinct in socially refined ways; to use the energy present in a primitive drive toward a creative act or project; to divert

subrogate – v. to substitute

sub rosa – adj. in secret (in ancient tradition a rose was placed over the meeting table to indicate an oath of secrecy on the part of all participants)

subterfuge – n. a deceptive maneuver; an evasion

succedaneum – n. a substitute, especially an inferior one

succubus – n. a female demon who has sex with men while they are asleep

succursal – adj. subsidiary, branch, or offshoot (as in a dependent monastery, or branch of a business)

suffuse – v. to spread over or through in the manner of light

Sufism – n. in Arabic philosophy, a contemplative form of Islamic mysticism that emphasizes a relationship with Allah through renunciation and love. Sufism has a pantheistic tone and is compatible with some types of Hinduism in northern India. The name *sufism* derives from the Middle Eastern word *suf*, meaning "wool." Wool was the favorite clothing of these ascetic philosophers.

Sufis gather in retreat houses called "khanqahs." These are often found near shrines of Sufi saints. There, "salat" or prayer takes on a special meditative dance form. Sufi masters are called "physicians of the heart." They are often persecuted by mainstream Muslims, who regard them as heretics. Sufis are apolitical and refuse to participate in violence, as the will of Allah is love. They make up less than 5 percent of Islam.

Reference: *What Is Sufism?*, Martin Lings

sultry – adj. with sweltering heat; strong passion, especially sexual

sumptuous – adj. luxuriously splendid

superable – adj. capable of being mastered

supercilious – adj. showing haughty contempt

superego – n. in Freud and psychoanalysis, that part of the self that acts as a control over the impulses of the id. The superego is the conscience. It is the result of education, training, and conditioning stemming from authority figures such as parents, teachers, and heroic personalities. It is the desire to comply with cultural rules. It is the source of feelings of guilt. It introduces resistance to impulsive behavior.

Reference: *Essays on Ego Psychology*, Heinz Hartmann

supererogatory – adj. in ethics, the quality of doing more than is required or needed; voluntary

supernal – adj. originating in heaven; of a spiritual character

supervenience – n. in logic, the condition of having something additional or unexpected occur, as in an unexpected logical derivation

supine – adj. inactive; indolent

supplicate – v. to pray or beg for humbly

supposititious – adj. not genuine; deceptively presented

surcease – v. to put an end to

surmise – v. to conclude on a little evidence

surrealism – n. the use of fantastic dreamlike effects in art, literature, or theater, especially unnatural combinations of elements in experienced reality

sybarite – n. a person who practices luxurious self-indulgence

sycophant – n. a flatterer; one who seeks benefits by providing excessive praise; a servile individual

sylph – n. a slender, graceful woman

sylvan – adj. of the woodland or forest; n. one who frequents the forest

syncretism – n. the blending of ideas from opposed systems of thought. It is an effort to create unity, usually at the expense of philosophical rigor

synderesis – n. an inborn sense of moral harmony. It derives from the Greek word *synteresis*, meaning spark of conscience

syndetic – adj. serving to link or join

synergetic – adj. a working together; being cooperative

syntality – n. the mental and behavioral conformity of a group to the personality of an individual

T

tabula rasa – n. fr. Latin, *tabula rasa* means blank slate. The term was made famous in the philosophy of John Locke (1632–1704), who used it to defend empiricism. Locke believed that the mind is blank until experience (sense data) writes upon it.

tacit – adj. implied but unspoken

taciturn – adj. disinclined to talk

Tagore, Rabindranath (1861–1941) – an Indian philosopher and recipient of the Nobel Prize for literature in 1913. Tagore had an important influence on the mixing of Western and Eastern philosophy. He was a leader of the Renaissance period of Hinduism. His philosophical position emphasized the need to reconcile opposites as part of a greater truth. The underlying harmony of the universe teaches us to subordinate our desires and avoid egoism. At times, he combined the insights of hedonists and ascetics, determinists and free-will advocates, idealists and realists.

Tagore's thought was expressed in philosophical poetry. His work characterized the role of emotion in thought. Tagore was interested to write poetry that addressed the value of action as well as contemplation. He believed that a philosophy that did not work out a doctrine of action was "escapist" and afraid of mastering real-life problems.

Principal works: *Sadhana* (1913), *Personality* (1914), *Creative Unity* (1922), *The Religion of Man* (1931), and *Towards Universal Man* (posthumously, 1961)

"Blessed am I, that I have searched for heaven's glorious light.
Blessed am I, that I have loved this lowly earth's delight."

Rabindranath Tagore, (poem) "Prabhat" in *Chaitali*

References: *An Introduction to Rabindranath Tagore*, Vishwanath S. Naravane; and *Rabindranath Tagore*, Mary M. Lago

talisman – n. a magical charm

Talmud – n. fr. Hebrew *talmudh*, meaning instruction. It is a collection of rabbinical sayings about the meaning of the Torah. It is the basis of Jewish law, ethics, customs, rituals, and philosophy. It includes the Mishnah and a commentary known as the Gemara. With these two, there is also material called the *haggadah*, which are authoritative statements on morals, faith, and narrative parables. Scholars have found the Talmud important to understand the background of Christianity.

Reference: *The Talmud: An Analytical Guide to Its History and Teachings*, Isaac Unterman

Tantrism – n. in Hinduism and Buddhism, a school of thought that arose around the sixth century. It is a formal part of Tibetan Buddhism in particular, but is also found in Bhutan, Nepal, and parts of India. It claims to unlock the psychophysical powers of the devotee through special practices and meditation. Through the use of special *mantras*, Tantric Buddhism seeks to bring about the purest balance of body and mind.

With the use of specific divine forms the practitioner strives to create a union of opposites within the body, especially the masculine (Shiva) and feminine (Shakti).

Reference: *The Tantric Tradition*, Agehananda Bharati

Taoism – n. a Chinese religion emphasizing a mystical treatment of life. The *Tao* or way is discovered in the unification of one's being. Life is mastered through silence, letting go, and living in harmony with the natural world. Life is made long by utilizing mind (meditation), matter (diet), and movement (tai chi). Remember that an ax falls first on the tallest tree. Learn to be like the bamboo shoot rather than the stone in the stream. The stone is worn into nothing. The bamboo shoot floats and drifts silently until it finds a place to flourish along the banks of the river. The secret lies in the recognition of opposites, *yin* and *yang*, which structure the flow of events in the universe. The Tao Te Ching is the scripture of the Taoists, supposedly written by Lao-tzu.

Chuang Tzu's (399–295 BC) Taoism claims that any skill can aid the practitioner in mastering the *Tao*. There are many ways to find the *Tao*. The key is to get past egotistical motives for excellence. For, the power of the *Tao* is a power of being.

> References: *What Is Taoism?*, H. G. Creel; *Taoism: The Parting of the Way*, Holmes H. Welch Jr.; and *The Tao is Silent*, Raymund Smullyan

tectonics – n. the science of building construction; *tekton*, a reference to the occupation of Jesus

Teilhard de Chardin, Pierre (1881–1955) – a French scientist, priest, and theologian. Teilhard argued that the universe is in physical and spiritual evolution, moving toward greater levels of complexity. The evolutionary process has moved through stages or critical boundaries, including the emergence of life, the appearance of higher animals (including man), and the emergence of rational consciousness. According to Teilhard, the last stage represents the creative and directed development of the earth, moving toward fulfillment in God.

Teilhard could see the coming dissolution of cultures and the emergence of a single technical culture. The rational consciousness of humanity imposes a *noosphere* over the biosphere, aided by technological evolution. This noosphere is directed toward completion of a cosmic or historical goal: the integration of all human consciousness in the *Omega* point (Christ/God) through love and global technological communication.

Exiled to China by Vatican authorities for heresy, Teilhard became involved in paleoanthropology. His exile freed him to pursue his scientific interests. This led to his discovery of the Peking Man.

> Principal works: *The Phenomenon of Man* (1955), *The Divine Milieu* (1956), *The Future of Man* (1964), *The Hymn of the Universe* (1965), and *Christianity and Evolution* (1969)

"The Primacy of Charity: Since the Christian universe consists structurally in the unification of elemental persons in a supreme personality (the personality of God), the dominating and ultimate energy of the whole system can only be a person-to-person attraction; in other words, a love attraction."

P. Teilhard de Chardin, *Christianity and Evolution*

References: *An Introduction to Teilhard de Chardin*, N. M. Wildiers; *Teilhard de Chardin: The Man and His Meaning*, Henri de Lubac

telegnosis – n. knowledge acquired supernaturally

telekinesis – n. moving objects without physical contact; part of parapsychology

teleology – n. fr. the Greek *teleos*; the study of purpose and cause as principles of explanation. Teleology is useful to theological speculations about the origins of the universe (e.g., the teleological argument for the existence of God: designs reveal a designer). "Teleology," as a term, was first used by Christian Wolff in 1728 to denote the science of final causes.

Reference: *Teleology*, Andrew Woodfield

telesthesia – n. sensation from a distance without the apparent use of the senses

telic – adj. tending toward a specific end

telluric – adj. of or relating to the terrestrial landscape; having to do with the earth

telos – n. an ultimate or highest end

temerity – n. recklessness; foolishness

tendentious – adj. being biased

tenebrific – adj. causing gloom

tenet – n. principle; a belief held to be true

tenuous – adj. flimsy; without strength

tepid – adj. lacking conviction or enthusiasm

teratology – n. in biology, the study of malformations and monstrosities

termagant – n. a woman who is overbearing, difficult, or stubborn

ternary – adj. involving three elements

terraqueous – adj. having to do with or constituted of land and water

terrene – adj. worldly; of the earth

terricolous – adj. having the quality of being on or in the earth

terrorism – n. the political use of violence. The goal of terrorism is to intimidate civilian populations in order to change government policies. Terrorists make use of murder, bombings, kidnapping, industrial sabotage, and other creative acts of mayhem.

Terrorism is distinguished from clandestine warfare used by resistance groups, because resistance fighters usually emphasize military targets.

According to terrorism expert Bernhardt Hurwood (1926-1987), the greatest threat to terrorism is the "moderate," one who works to reform a terrorist group from within and temper the use of violence. The "moderate" is most often the target of assassination.

References: *International Terrorism*, Yonah Alexander; *Understanding Terrorism: Challenges, Perspective, and Issues*, Gus Martin; and *Society and the Assassin: A Background Book on Political Murder*, Bernhardt J. Hurwood

terse – adj. concise; using as few words as possible

testy – adj. easily irritated

tetrad – n. a group of four

Thales (ca. 580 BC) – a pre-Socratic philosopher who argued that the universe is composed of a single substance (monism): water. He believed it was possible to account for all things with this substance, noting its self-motion, life-producing importance, abundance, and various forms (clouds, rain, lakes, seas, marshes, ice).

Thales predicted an eclipse during a battle between Lydeans and Persians, discovered proofs in geometry, devised systems of measurement for distant objects, and predicted an olive harvest, which made him a wealthy man.

References: *A History of Greek Philosophy*, vol.1, W. K. C. Guthrie; and *The Presocratic Philosophers*, G. S. Kirk and J. E. Raven

thanatology – n. the study of death; its nature, stages, and consequences. The name is taken from Greek *thanatos*, the god of death. Thanatos lived in the underworld with his brother Hypnos, the god of sleep. According to Greek mythology, Thanatos was the only god who did not accept offerings, although Thanatos was once fooled by Sisyphus. Socrates taught that philosophy is the practice of death.

Herman Feifel (1915-1987), a psychologist and leader in thanatology, introduced the systematic study of death in 1959 with the publication of *The Meaning of Death*. This book had a direct influence on Elisabeth Kübler-Ross and gave psychological and moral importance to understanding death and dying. Thanatology is now studied as an interdisciplinary subject of universal interest.

> References: *On Death and Dying*, Elisabeth Kübler-Ross; *The Meaning of Death*, Herman Feifel

thanatophobia – n. fear of death.

thanatopsis – n. contemplation of death.

thanatos instinct – n. in psychology, the instinctual tendency toward self-destruction; also called the "nirvana principle"; opposed to the eros instinct

thaumatology – n. the study of miracles; their nature, origin, and purpose

thaumaturge – n. a miracle worker

theanthropic – adj. being of man and god

theanthropism – n. the unification of human and divine

theism – n. maintains the view that God is both personal and transcendent. God is distinct from the world and its operations but is still the cause of all things. Theism is the main theological position of Islam, Christianity, and Judaism. It is distinguished from pantheism, deism, and panentheism.

> References: *The Degrees of Knowledge*, Jacques Maritain; *God and Philosophy*, Etienne Gilson; and *Thinking about God*, John MacQuarrie

theocentric – adj. putting God at the center of reality or one's philosophy

T

theogony – n. tracing the origins of the gods

theology – n. the study of God and God's relation to the universe. What distinguishes theology from philosophy is the addition of faith to reason. It is divided into dogmatic, philosophical, historical, scriptural, and practical theology, with each of these areas having further classifications.

> References: *Theological Dictionary*, Karl Rahner and H. Vorgrimler; *Naming the Whirlwind*, Langdon Gilkey; and *Principles of Christian Theology*, John MacQuarrie

theomachy – n. opposition to God or the divine will

theomania – a type of insanity in which one believes one's self to be God

therianthropic – adj. being part animal and part human

theriomorphic – adj. being of animal form, especially regarding gods

thersitical – adj. after Thersites, a Greek warrior known for his hypercritical attitude and who was killed by Achilles for insulting him; thus, meaning loud, abusive, and socially irritating

theurgy – n. the involvement of the gods in human affairs. It was practiced by the lesser Neoplatonists but regarded as a cult that used incantations and ritual to produce beneficent results

third sex – n. a homosexual

Thoreau, Henry David (1817–1862) – an American philosopher of nature, Thoreau became famous while living in a hut at Walden Pond near Concord (owned by Emerson). Thoreau wrote about life in the wilderness and its influence on his understanding of truth. His ideas have been interpreted as an endorsement of anarchism, since he argued that freedom was more attainable in the wilderness than in civil settings. He argued that the spontaneity and creativity found in nature are necessary for spiritual well-being. As little time as possible should be spent on commerce and political issues. In fact, Thoreau concluded that to do something for the sake of money is the worst use of time.

> Principal works: *Civil Disobedience* (1849), and *Walden, or Life in the Woods* (1854)

"All men recognize the right of revolution; that is, the right to refuse allegiance to, and to resist, the government, when its tyranny or its inefficiency are great and unendurable."

H. D. Thoreau, *Civil Disobedience*

Reference: *The New Thoreau Handbook*, Walter Harding

thrall – n. a slave; a state of complete absorption or servitude

thrasonical – adj. being a braggart

Thrasymachus (ca. 500 BC) – a Greek philosopher, Thrasymachus sided with the Sophists. He defended the view that justice is based on power: "Might makes right." Natural justice is the result of the strong overpowering the weak. He pointed out that political arrangements override the power of individuals, but politics too expresses the will to power, although in groups. Thrasymachus is mentioned in Plato's *Republic*, Book I.

Reference: *A History of Greek Philosophy*, vol. 3, W. K. C. Guthrie; and *Ancilla to the Pre-Socratic Philosophers*, Kathleen Freeman

threnody – n. a song, poem, or lamentation for the dead

throe – n. a painful struggle; punishment

Tillich, Paul (1886–1965) – a German philosopher and theologian who defined religious existentialism. Tillich moved to the US in 1933, because of Hitler's attack on academic freedom. He taught at Union Theological Seminary and the University of Chicago.

Tillich's thought is characterized by existential themes. His work on anxiety (*angst*) identified three primary sources: the awareness of death, the threat of a meaningless life, and the existence of guilt. Tillich poses God as a practical solution to human anxiety. God has the power of offering protection from these threats to being. Deep awareness of history is linked to the feeling of despair, the reaction to a world in perpetual conflict.

Tillich emphasizes ontology, and defines faith as "ultimate concern." This ultimate concern transcends art, science, the state, political movements, material goods, and social status. The problem of anxiety can only be resolved through an act of faith. Worldly values do not have the Ultimate as their ultimate concern. Since they do not determine the nature of reality, they cannot be Ultimate. Only God is the source of all meaning and being, and thus God or the religious life is the correct approach to being.

Principal works: *The Shaking of the Foundations* (1948), *Systematic Theology*, 3 vols. (1951–63), *The Courage to Be* (1952), *Dynamics of Faith* (1957), *Theology of Culture* (1959), and *Morality and Beyond* (1963)

"Anxiety and courage have a psychosomatic character. They are biological as well as psychological. From the biological point of view one would say that fear and anxiety are the guardians, indicating the threat of nonbeing to a living being and producing movements of protection and resistance to this threat... Courage is the readiness to take upon oneself negatives, anticipated by fear, for the sake of a fuller positivity. Biological self-affirmation implies the acceptance of want, toil, insecurity, pain, possible destruction. Without this self-affirmation life could not be preserved or increased. The more vital strength a being has the more it is able to affirm itself in spite of the dangers announced by fear and anxiety."

Paul Tillich, *The Courage to Be*

Reference: *Paul Tillich: His Life and Thought*, Marion and Wilhelm Pauck

timocracy – n. a government characterized by the love of honor or glory (e.g., Sparta)

timorous – adj. fearful

Tolstoy, Leo (1828–1910) – a Russian social philosopher. Tolstoy advocated religious anarchy. Influenced by J. J. Rousseau, he believed all governments to be corrupt and coercive toward citizens. Though our relationship toward one and other determines the possibility of a meaningful life, this is only possible when conditioned by a belief in God. He concluded from a study of the Bible, especially the Sermon on the Mount, that there should be five cardinal rules of action: suppression of all anger, the refusal to judge others, the avoidance of oaths, the avoidance of all sex outside of marriage, and an unconditional love of one's enemies. Tolstoy denied the divinity of Christ and the notion of the Trinity.

He viewed art as an emotional medium and a vehicle for morality, arguing that it conveyed the highest insights into human existence; human existence itself being influenced by various types of unseen fate.

Principal works: *War and Peace* (1873), *Anna Karenina* (1877), *What I Believe* (1882–84), and *The Christian Teaching* (1894–96)

"In quiet and untroubled times it seems to every administrator that it is only by his efforts that the whole population under his rule is kept going, and in this consciousness of being indispensable every administrator finds the chief reward of his labor and efforts. While the sea of history remains calm the ruler-administrator in his frail bark, holding on with a boat hook to the ship of the people and himself moving, naturally imagines that his efforts move the ship he is holding on to. But as soon as a storm arises and the sea begins to heave and the ship to move, such a delusion is no longer possible. The ship moves independently with its own enormous motion, the boat hook no longer reaches the moving vessel, and suddenly the administrator, instead of appearing a ruler and a source of power, becomes an insignificant, useless, feeble man."

Leo Tolstoy, *War and Peace*

References: *Tolstoy: A Biography*, A. N. Wilson; *Tolstoy the Rebel*, Leo Hecht; and *The Hedgehog and the Fox*, Isaiah Berlin

Torah – n. fr. Hebrew *Torah*, meaning instruction or precept. The Torah is composed of the first five books of the Old Testament: Genesis, Exodus, Leviticus, Numbers, and Deuteronomy. These five are also called the Pentateuch.

torpid – adj. being sluggish or dull

tour de force – n. French, an accomplishment that has no equal; a deed that reveals the highest level of skill, knowledge, or power

tractate – n. a lengthy essay or dissertation

traduce – v. to slander; to mistreat through false evidence

traducianism – n. in theology, the theory that souls are produced along with bodies; like biological regeneration, souls are also passed along from parent souls in a type of spiritual regeneration. Advocated by Tertullian (155–222 AD)

transect – v. to cut across

transempirical – adj. lying beyond or outside of sensory knowledge

transmogrify – v. to alter appearance, especially to that which is unsightly or grotesque

transpicuous – adj. easily seen through; easily known or understood

travail – n. adversity; suffering

travesty – n. a terrible and ludicrous alteration; a distortion

tremulant – adj. disordered; shaken

trenchant – adj. very effective

trepidation – n. anxiety; excessive worry

tribade – n. a lesbian

tribulation – n. trouble; suffering

trilemma – n. a situation in which there are three undesirable choices

triturate – v. to reduce to minute particles; to crush

trivium – n. in medieval schools, the university training in rhetoric, logic, and grammar

truckle – v. to be servile; to be submissive

truculent – adj. very hostile; capable of inflicting harm with little provocation

turgid – adj. excessively decorated; pompous

tutoyer – v. to address a person with familiarity, especially where no familiarity exists

tychism – n. in philosophy, the view that events can occur without apparent connection to outside causal forces; chance is active in the universe. Charles Peirce believed chance is an objective fact in the world. Tychism is taken from the Greek *tyche*, meaning chance; also the goddess of chance. *Tyche* fostered prosperity and fortune. She was the daughter of Zeus and Aphrodite.

tyro – n. a neophyte; a beginner in some art, craft, or discipline.

U

ubeity – n. the state of being in a specific location

ubiquitous – adj. being everywhere

ultraism – n. the advancement of extreme measures, views, or principles

umbrage – n. the feeling that one has been slighted, often accompanied by resentment

Unamuno, Miguel de (1864–1936) – a Spanish existentialist philosopher. Unamuno was influenced by Kierkegaard. His phrase *carne y hueso* (flesh and bone) defined the nature of humanity, noting the hunger for immortality within the human race.

Unamuno was sympathetic to the individual fate of human existence, which is a sense of uncertainty. Unamuno himself was torn between the offerings of faith and the demands of reason. As a Catholic, he loved the Church but couldn't abandon the power of rational criticism. Faith affirms immortality and reason denies it. Thus, Unamuno finds existence to be a dilemma of choices.

Conclusions found in Unamuno's arguments include: 1) human existence involves a painful awareness of transience and contingency, 2) to handle the anguish that is produced by this awareness, we explore the power of personal spiritual integrity, 3) life is essentially a mystery, 4) love is a property of life that can resolve the feeling of despair stemming from uncertainty, and 5) the goals we establish can only be self-created.

Principal works: *On Purism* (1895), *Love and Pedagogy* (1902), *Tragic Sense of Life* (1913), and *Saint Emmanuel the Good* (1933)

"All this talk of a man surviving in his children, or in his works, or in the universal consciousness, is but vague verbiage which satisfies only those who suffer from affective stupidity, and who, for the rest, may be persons of a certain cerebral distinction. For it is possible to possess great talent, and yet to be stupid as regards the feelings and even morally imbecile."

"Suffering is a spiritual thing. It is the most immediate revelation of consciousness, and it may be that our body was given us simply in order that suffering might be enabled to manifest itself. A man who had never known suffering, either in greater or less degree, would scarcely possess consciousness of himself."

Miguel de Unamuno, *Tragic Sense of Life*

References: *Miguel de Unamuno*, Martin Nozick; and *Unamuno: An Existential View of Self and Society*, Paul Ilie

unconscious, the – n. in philosophy, the view that a significant part of the mind's activity exists apart from conscious mental activity. The concept of the unconscious is used by many important thinkers (e.g., Plato, with his doctrine of anamnesis or recollection, or Arthur Schopenhauer with his the idea of a "blind will" as the force behind human effort). Also, Carl Jung expressed the idea of archetypes of the unconscious and their relation to dreams. Jung believed that depression during adolescence and midlife represented struggles with the unconscious needs of the soul.

References: *Memories, Dreams, Reflections*, Carl Jung; *The Discovery of the Unconscious*, Donald Meichenbaum and K. S. Bowers; and *The Essential Jung*, Anthony Storr

uncouth – adj. lacking in grace, style, or taste; also, awkward

unguinous – adj. being greasy; slippery; difficult to grasp

unitarianism – n. in theology, the view that God is one and that Jesus is not a supernatural being but merely a human being. Its anti-Trinitarian argument has its origins in Adoptionism, Monarchianism, and Arianism. It does not recognize the notion of eternal punishment and argues that goodness is part of human nature.

Reference: *The Philosophy of William Ellery Channing*, R. L. Patterson

U

usury – n. lending money at an excessively high interest rate

utilitarianism – n. in ethical theory, the view that "the greatest happiness for the greatest number" should guide ethical decisions. According to utilitarianism, the utility of values to produce the greatest degree of satisfaction for the greatest portion of society is the basis of "the good." Advocates include Jeremy Bentham, J. S. Mill, and Henry Sidgwick.

> References: *Utilitarianism*, John Stuart Mill; *Utilitarianism: For and Against*, J. J. C. Smart; *Studies in Utilitarianism*, ed. T. K. Hearn

utopia – n. fr. the Greek *outopos*, meaning no place. It refers to a state or place of ideal perfection. It also means an impractical ideal for social improvement; one that cannot be realized

uxorial – adj. of or benefiting a wife

uxoricide – n. the killing of one's wife

uxorious – adj. excessively submissive or affectionate toward one's wife

vagary – n. an unpredictable occurrence; chance

valetudinarian – n. a cripple; someone who is preoccupied or obsessed with his or her poor health

vapid – adj. lacking vitality; dull or lifeless

Value theory – n. in ethics, the study of moral worth, especially the worth of acts. It is also designated "axiology." Value theory seeks to clarify various methods for measuring the "rightness" or "wrongness" of acts. Oppositional thinking about values occurs in the following schools of thought: essentialism vs. existentialism, relativism vs. absolutism, objectivism vs. subjectivism, as well as cognitivism, naturalism, and determinism. Values are those things that are personally important to us individually and socially. As such, they represent our interests (Santayana). Interests, as values, lead to domains of action (chosen environments that present occasions for the exercise of reason).

Reference: *Ethics*, Louis Pojman and James Fieser

varlet – n. an unreliable person; a scoundrel

vastitude – n. the quality of immensity

vatic – adj. relating to the characteristics of a prophet

vaticide – n. the killing of a prophet

vaticinate – v. to foretell the future

Veblen, Thorstein Bunde (1857–1929) – an American philosopher of economics. Veblen was critical of religion, business, and political systems. Often at odds with college administrators, he taught at the University of Chicago, Stanford, and the University of Missouri.

Veblen argued that modern life is skewed by the philosophy of consumption presented by the business community. He argued that the "profit-making" values of business destroyed the creative values of workmanship, thus acting as a corruption of social psychology. He criticized the educational system for serving the needs and values of the business community, thus failing to educate. He believed the philosophy of "salesmanship" was apparent in religion and politics as well.

Veblen believed that the survival of society would, in the future, depend upon the smooth and efficient operation of its technological structure, but he hoped to preserve the creative values necessary for the structuring of an enlightened society.

Principal works: *Theory of the Leisure Class* (1899), *The Theory of Business Enterprise* (1904), *The Instinct of Workmanship* (1914), *Higher Learning in America: A Memorandum on the Conduct of Universities by Businessmen*, 1918 (originally subtitled "A Study in Depravity"), and *Absentee Ownership* (1923)

"Modern consumers in great part supply their wants with commodities that conform to certain staple specifications of size, weight, and grade. The consumer (that is to say the 'vulgar consumer') furnishes his house, his table, and his person with supplies of standard weight and measure, and he can to an appreciable degree specify his needs and his consumption in the notation of the standard gauge. As regards the mass of civilized mankind, the idiosyncrasies of the individual consumers are required to conform to the uniform gradations imposed upon consumable goods by the comprehensive mechanical processes of industry."

Thorstein Veblen, *The Theory of Business Enterprise*

References: *The Philosophy of Thorstein Veblen*, Stanley M. Daugert; and *Thorstein Veblen: A Critical Interpretation*, David Riesman

Vedas – n. in Hinduism, writings on religious practice and philosophical advice. "Veda" means knowledge. Vedas include *Samhitas* (hymns), *Brahmanas* (rules for sacrifices), *Aranyakas* (philosophical interpretations of the sacrifices), *Upanishads* (the main outline and details of Hindu philosophy), and *Sutras* (priestly matters, social duties, sexual conduct, the use of pleasure, etc.).

> References: *Hinduism: A Religion to Live By*, Nirad Chaudhuri; and *Vedic Literature*, Jan Gonda

velitation – n. a minor dispute

velleity – n. a weak will; a will that nets no result or action

venal – adj. open to influence, especially a corruption

venatic – adj. having connection to hunting

vendue – n. a public sale or auction.

venery – n. hunting, especially as an art or skill; also, the pursuit of satisfaction, especially sexual pleasure; sexual intercourse

ventose – adj. given to useless chatter; windy

venue – n. the location where an event takes place

verbiage – n. words that do not relate essentially to the respective topic; superfluousness

verbose – adj. being excessively wordy

verecund – adj. having no confidence to assert one's self; being embarrassed

veridical – adj. truthful

verism – n. in aesthetics, the view that reality is best represented in art through the inclusion of the ugly, the vulgar, and the ordinary as well as the grand and the beautiful

vernal – adj. having to do with spring

vertiginous – adj. inclined toward useless change; whirling

verve – n. enthusiasm, especially with regard to a talent or skill

vestal – adj. pure; unspoiled; chaste

viaticum – n. the resources for a journey; the essentials for travel

vicinage – n. closeness or nearness

viduity – n. widowhood

Vienna Circle – n. in philosophy, reference to a group of philosophers, mathematicians, and scientists (1920s) whose goal was to establish a modern and rigorous form of empiricism. The Circle's work was committed to clarifying the meaning of language. This group included Rudolf Carnap, Herbert Feigl, Phillip Frank, Victor Kraft, Kurt Gödel, Béla von Juhos, Felix Kaufmann, Moritz Schlick, Otto Neurath, and Friedrich Waismann.

The label "logical positivism" is used to describe the Vienna Circle. Their work involved the rejection of traditional metaphysics as meaningless, since metaphysics has no empirical foundation. The same concerns were extended toward the improvement of epistemology and ethics. The Vienna Circle was influenced by the philosophy of David Hume, because Hume demonstrated the importance of empirical reasoning.

References: *The Vienna Circle: The Origin of Neo-Positivism*, Victor Kraft; *Language, Truth and Logic*, A. J. Ayer

vilify – v. to put down; to defame

vilipend – v. to assign a low value or importance to something

virago – n. a woman with outstanding qualities of strength and courage

virgin birth – n. usually a reference to the birth of Jesus, especially the influence of the Holy Spirit on the life of Jesus. As a theological dispute, virgin birth resolves itself in two general ways: 1) the fundamentalist view that Mary was literally a biological virgin whose pregnancy was initiated by God, and 2) a more historical-cultural approach to the meaning of virgin birth, emphasizing other elements such as the historical existence of birth stories, noting the virginal birth of other great leaders.

The issue of virgin birth is important to the definition of who Jesus was.

V

Low Christologists discount the importance of the virgin birth, arguing its limited value in understanding the relationship between God and Jesus. High Christologists see the issue as one of sacred and holy intervention into the life of humanity.

References: *The Birth of the Messiah: A Commentary on the Infancy Narratives in Matthew and Luke*, Raymond E. Brown; *The Illegitimacy of Jesus*, Jane Schaberg; *Discovering the God Child Within*, Eugen Drewermann; *A Marginal Jew: Rethinking the Historical Jesus*, John P. Meier; and *Jesus: A Revolutionary Biography*, John Dominic Crossan

virulent – adj. powerfully poisonous; characterized by intense hostility

visage – n. appearance; face

vis-à-vis – prep. face to face; also n. counterpart

Vishnu – n. in Hindu philosophy, Vishnu is part of the "trimurti," or Hindu trinity. Vishnu is the preserver, Brahma is the creator, and Shiva is the destroyer. As a form of devotion it is called *Vaishnavism*. Incarnations of Vishnu are said to have occurred in Rama, of the epic *Ramayana*, and Krishna, indicated as a hero in the Bhagavad Gita.

Reference: *Vishnu and His Incarnations*, Shakti M. Gupta

vitalism – n. in philosophy, the view that a special essence distinguishes all living things from nonliving things. Its basic form produces a metaphysical dualism, meaning two realities are present simultaneously. There is also a presumption of teleological forces at work. Hans Driesch (1867–1941) based his arguments for vitalism in Aristotle's notion of entelechy. Driesch argued for a mind-like, non-spatial essence as an active agent in living things. Vitalism stands in opposition to Cartesian (Descartes's) notions of life as mechanisms.

Reference: *The Vitalism of Hans Driesch*, H. H. Freyhofer

vitiate – v. to impair or make defective, especially through the addition of some inferior quality or feature

vitreous – adj. transparent like glass; easily seen through

vocation – n. fr. the Latin *vocare*, meaning "to call." Traditionally, this term was used in Christianity to indicate the call to a religious life. In modern times, the term is regarded in a more personal way by philosophers like José Ortega y Gasset (1883–1955). For Ortega, vocation implies a radical call to pursue one's vitality through authentic selfhood.

vociferate – v. to shout

volant – adj. nimble or quick in movement

Voltaire, François-Marie Arouet de (1694–1788) – a French philosopher and social critic. Voltaire was the pen name of Francois-Marie Arouet. He adopted the name when he was imprisoned in the Bastille. He wrote against superstition and political corruption. Much of his thinking was influenced by the views of John Locke, and he criticized the work of Shakespeare as formless and crude.

Theologically, Voltaire was a deist who defended freedom of the will and doubted the immortality of the soul. He was a tireless critic of formal religion, regarding ecclesiastical domination as a sign of ignorance and prejudice.

Politically, Voltaire was a parliamentarian and a supporter of the upper classes. His liberalism did not include an admiration for the lower classes, because he considered them incapable of self-rule.

Principal works: *Essay on the Customs and Spirit of the Nations* (1756), *Candide* (1759), *Treatise on Toleration* (1763), and *Philosophical Dictionary* (1764)

"After our holy religion which would be the least bad? Wouldn't it be the simplest one? Wouldn't it be the one that taught a good deal of morality and very little dogma? The one that tended to make men just, without making them absurd? The one that wouldn't command belief in the impossible, contradictory things insulting to the Divinity and pernicious to mankind, and wouldn't dare threaten with eternal punishment anyone who has common sense? Wouldn't it be the religion that didn't uphold its beliefs with executioners, didn't inundate the world with blood for the sake of unintelligible sophisms? The one in which an ambiguity, a play on words, or two or three forged charters wouldn't make a sovereign and a god of a priest who is often a man who has committed incest, a murderer, and a poisoner? The one that wouldn't make kings subject to this priest? The one that taught nothing but the worship of a God, justice, tolerance, and humanity?"

Voltaire, *Philosophical Dictionary*

V

Reference: *The Intellectual Development of Voltaire*, Ira O. Wade; and *Voltaire and the Century of Light*, A. Owen Aldridge

voluble – adj. talkative; also, fluent.

voyeur – n. one who seeks sexual satisfaction and pleasure through seeing; also, one who hunts down that which is scandalous; a prying eye

Vulgate – n. the name given to Latin translations of the Bible, starting with the work of St. Jerome (342–420 AD), who made the first translation at the request of Pope Damascus (382). The Vulgate became the basis for the Wycliffe translation into English.

Reference: *Jerome: His Life, Writings, and Controversies*, J. N. D. Kelly

vulpine – adj. having the qualities of a fox; being clever or crafty

Warsaw Circle – n. a group of language philosophers whose aims mirrored the Vienna Circle. In fact, the two circles taught each other. The Warsaw group included Jan Łukasiewicz (1878–1956), Stanisław Leśniewski (1884–1939), and Alfred Tarski (1901–1984). Łukasiewicz was the first to develop a three-valued logic: "true," "false," and "possible." He also developed the Polish notation, which has become a standard in logic expressions. The teacher of Tarski, Leśniewski worked on problems presented by Russell with regard to the foundations of mathematics. Tarski was responsible for contributions to the development of metalogic, which included his adaptation of the Correspondence Theory of Truth to metalanguages.

weal – n. a healthy, stable society; well-being

Weber, Max (1864–1920) – a German philosopher of sociology. Weber was from the Neo-Kantian school. He was the older brother of another social philosopher, Alfred Weber (1868–1958), whose work distinguished "culture processes" from "civilization processes" (see *Principles of Culture-Sociology*, 1921, and *The Tragic and History*, 1943).

Max Weber developed a theory of "ideal types": rational individuals who are representative of a certain historical period; individuals whose manner of being is shaped by the specific social organization of an age.

Weber's interest in religion led him to examine the connections between religion, economics, and society. He described the influence of Lutheranism and Calvinism on the development of capitalist society. He determined that the true meaning of capitalism was the "rational organization of free labor" rather than the class struggle of Marxism. It is rational organization that produces the bureaucratic structure of modern capitalism. The structure of corporations, in turn, leads to bureaucratization.

The use of *Verband* (authority) is a trait of bureaucracies, going back even to Roman, Egyptian, and Chinese bureaucratic structures. Following this are the attendant "roles" that members of bureaucracies play. The social dynamic of *Verband* includes an acceptance of authority on the part of members.

Verband assumes three basic types that are recognized in a social order: "rational-legal"—the existence of laws and rules establishing authority on a "rational" model; "traditional"—referring to past institutions; and "charismatic"—where authority is created by an inspirational personality figure. Significant change is often accomplished by charismatic personalities, since their authority often extends beyond traditional and rational-legal types.

> Principal works: *Capitalism and the Protestant Ethic* (1905), *The Economic Ethic of the World Religions* (1915), *Economy and Society* (1922), *From Max Weber: Essays in Sociology* (1946), and *On the Methodology of the Social Sciences* (1949)

> *"Devotion to the charisma of the prophet, or the leader in war, or to the great demagogue in the 'ecclesia' or in parliament, means that the leader is personally recognized as the innerly 'called' leader of men. Men do not obey him by virtue of tradition or statute, but because they believe in him. If he is more than a narrow and vain upstart of the moment, the leader lives for his cause and 'strives for his work.' The devotion of his disciples, his followers, his personal party friends is oriented to his person and its qualities."*

> Max Weber, from *Max Weber: Essays in Sociology*

> References: *The Iron Cage: An Historical Interpretation of Max Weber*, Arthur Mitzman; *Max Weber: An Intellectual Portrait*, Reinhard Bendix

weltanschauung – n. a comprehensive view of the world or reality, especially from a specified logical and metaphysical viewpoint; fr. German *Weltanschauung*, meaning philosophy of life or worldview.

W

weltschmerz – n. a sadness or melancholy, caused by unrealistic expectations for a perfect or ideal life; also, apathy; fr. German *Weltschmerz*, meaning literally, world pain

Wertheimer, Max (1880–1943) – one of the principal founders of the Gestalt school of psychology. He authored *Productive Thinking* (1923), and taught the Gestalt approach to life as a quest for critical thinking, problem solving, and social effectiveness.

Reference: *The Task of Gestalt Psychology*, Wolfgang Köhler

whet – v. to sharpen or stimulate

Whitehead, Alfred North (1861–1947) – an English philosopher, Whitehead is the central figure of process philosophy. His original interest was mathematics, which included work with one of his best students, Bertrand Russell, on *Principia Mathematica*. Therein, Russell and Whitehead worked on a demonstration of mathematics' debt to logic.

Gradually, Whitehead lost interest in the abstract considerations of mathematics and language, moving toward questions of metaphysics that he felt were important to the further progress of science. Influenced by the work of Charles Darwin, Max Planck, Niels Bohr, and other scientists, Whitehead wanted a deeper framework for reality, which started with a substitution of traditional atomic notions of matter. In Whiteheadian terms, atoms are called "actual entities" or "actual occasions." Whitehead thought that these new names addressed the life-like nature of all reality, even its most primitive basis. It was his intention to emphasize the "organic" nature of reality over the mechanistic models of the past. He wanted to show the vitality of relationships in nature.

Whitehead uses the notion of actual occasions to argue for feeling and purpose in the universe. This universe is marked by "creativity," "novelty," and "becoming." The things we see are collections of actual occasions that Whitehead identifies as "societies." Whitehead uses the word "prehension" to identify a cohesiveness among actual occasions collected together into a "society" or "nexus." His theory of metaphysical unity also employs the term "concrescence."

Borrowing from Plato, Whitehead introduces "eternal objects" that act as a kind of polarity for actual entities. Actual entities align metaphysically with eternal objects through a process Whitehead calls "ingression." Actual entities derive their specific identity from simple eternal objects; in the case of complex objects (societies) there are complex eternal objects.

In his cosmology, Whitehead designates God as the timeless coagent of creation. The future represents God's "primordial nature," whereas the past represents God's "consequent nature." Guiding values for this coagency are the good, the beautiful, and the truth.

> Principal works: *Principia Mathematica* (1910), *The Concept of Nature* (1920), *Science and the Modern World* (1926), *Religion in the Making* (1926), *Process and Reality* (1929), *The Aims of Education* (1929), *Adventures of Ideas* (1933), and *Modes of Thought* (1936)

> *"A race preserves its vigor so long as it harbours a real contrast between what has been and what may be; and so long as it is nerved by the vigour to adventure beyond the safeties of the past. Without adventure civilization is in full decay.*

> *"It is for this reason that the definition of culture as the knowledge of the best that has been said and done, is so dangerous by reason of its omission. It omits the great fact that in their day the great achievements of the past were adventures of the past. Only the adventurous can understand the greatness of the past."*

> A. N. Whitehead, *Adventures of Ideas*

> References: *Whiteheadian Thought as a Basis for a Philosophy of Religion*, Forrest Wood Jr.; and *Alfred North Whitehead: The Man and His Work*, Victor Lowe

white supremacy – n. a political doctrine that claims whites are inherently superior to blacks. Moreover, within the doctrine's aims is the requirement that blacks be subordinate to whites in all areas of life. (Compare with black nationalism.)

William of Ockham (1290–1349 AD) – an English philosopher, Ockham is mainly remembered for his *Principle of Parsimony*, often called "Ockham's Razor": what can be said in few words should not be said or expressed in many words. Basically, do not extend things unnecessarily.

Ockham's position on nominalism was that there is no "beyond" with regard to things and universal terms used. The mind of man is the limited domain within which universals exist. Human reflection is limited to the objects of experience and does not imply some extra context outside the sensory world.

Principal works: *Summa Logicae* (1323), and *Treatise on Predestination and God's Foreknowledge of the Contingent Future* (1324)

"That no universal is a substance outside the mind can be evidently proved."

William of Ockham, *Summa Logicae*

References: *William of Ockham: The Metamorphosis of Scholastic Discourse*, Gordon Leff; and *The Theory of Demonstration According to William of Ockham*, Damascene Webering

wisdom – n. in philosophy, the Anglo-Saxon term for *sophia*. Wisdom is the possession of excellent judgment in the affairs of day-to-day existence. It is the maximization of opportunities to construct a satisfying life. In Plato, wisdom is a cardinal virtue, one from which other virtues flow. It is characterized by a degree of humility toward reality, a pronounced curiosity regarding the workings of the world, an interest in ethics, and a deep respect for the objective forcefulness that exists within things.

Wittgenstein, Ludwig (1889–1951) – an Austrian logician, Wittgenstein made important contributions to the understanding of language and logic. In the *Tractatus Logico-Philosophicus* he works to identify the basis of empirical science. Wittgenstein noted the role of language in the statement of facts. Language provides pictures of reality. It approximates facts. Facts in turn are the basic parts of the world we experience. Language that does not provide facts is just nonsense, including the statements of religion, metaphysical thought, and probably most of ethics. Wittgenstein concludes in a kind of mystical fashion that even the work of the *Tractatus* is nonsense, since it is metaphysical in nature, attempting to grasp at foundations of reality.

The later Wittgenstein adopts a more liberal view of language, assigning it multiple purposes. Thus, language patterns reveal ceremonial language, instructional language, emotional language, and investigative language.

Wittgenstein defined the idea of philosophy as a "sense of puzzlement" about reality. The role of logic and language is to reduce this sense of puzzlement by rendering a clear picture of reality.

Principal works: *Tractatus Logico-Philosophicus* (1921), *The Blue and Brown Books* (1933–35), *Philosophical Investigations* (1953), *Philosophical Remarks* on the *Foundations of Mathematics* (1956), and *Lectures and Conversations on Aesthetics, Psychology, and Religious Belief* (1966)

"4.05 Die Wirklichkeit wird mit dem Satz verglichen."

(4.05 Reality is compared with propositions.)

"4.06 Nur dadurch kann der Satz wahr oder falsch sein, in dem er ein Bild der Wirklichkeit ist."

(4.06 A proposition can be true or false only in virtue of being a picture of reality.)

Ludwig Wittgenstein, *Tractatus Logico-Philosophicus*

References: *The Claim of Reason: Wittgenstein, Skepticism, Morality, and Tragedy*, Stanley Cavell; and *Wittgenstein's Vienna*, A. Janik and S. E. Toulmin

wittol – n. a married man who knows of his wife's infidelity and does nothing about it

wroth – adj. extremely angry, to the point of destruction and violence

Wundt, Wilhelm (1832–1920) – a German doctor and the founder of experimental psychology. Wundt moved psychology away from metaphysics and rationalism, and into systematic laboratory studies.

Reference: *Basic Principles of Experimental Psychology*, O. Zinser

wu wei – n. in Chinese philosophy, the idea of emptiness or inaction. It is a central notion in the philosophy of Taoism and also in Zen Buddhism, especially in conjunction with understanding the essence of meditation and enlightenment.

> *"Without going out the door, one can know the whole world. Without looking out the window, one can see the Tao of heaven. The further one travels, the less one knows. So, the sage knows everything without traveling. He names everything without seeing it. He accomplishes everything without doing it."*

Ch'u Ta-kao, *The Tao Te Ching*

Xanthippe – n. fr. *Xanthippe*, the wife of Socrates; an ill-tempered woman

xenocentric – adj. oriented toward or preferring a culture other than one's own

Xenophanes (575–478 BC) – a pre-Socratic philosopher, aligned with thinkers in the Milesian school. Xenophanes argued for two primary elements, fire and air. He also taught that there are an unlimited number of suns in the universe.

xenophilia – n. love of things that are different, especially foreign cultures and ideas

xenophobia – n. a fear of things that are different, especially foreign cultures and ideas

Xenophon (ca. 430–354 BC) – a follower of Socrates in his youth, who later recorded details of Socrates's life in a work entitled *Memorabilia*

xeric – adj. ascetic; needing only very small amounts of moisture; being accustomed to dryness

xerophilous – adj. living in a very hot and dry environment; loving a desert life; desert monasticism

xylomancy – n. divination rituals that focus on the interpretation of dry twigs and pieces of wood found on the forest floor

Yahweh – n. a name for God used by the early Jews; the meaning of the tetragram YHWH. This indirect reference to God is important for the practice of reverence.

yin and yang – n. in Eastern philosophy, the reference to complementary principles or forces of the universe. "Yin" represents the feminine principle: negative, passive, destructive, weak. "Yang" represents the masculine principle: positive, active, creative. All change is the result of interaction between opposed principles or forces.

yoga – n. in Indian philosophy, a practical discipline of union between self and the universal soul. Deriving guidance from the Vedic scriptures, yoga is theistic and is expressed in different schools (e.g., *karma yoga* – the emphasis on duty; *raja yoga* – the emphasis on mental concentration; *jnana yoga* – the emphasis on knowledge; and *hatha yoga* – the emphasis on posture and physical conditioning of the body).

Reference: *Yoga: Immortality and Freedom*, Mircea Eliade, 2nd ed., trans. by Willard Trask

Yogacara – n. Buddhism that emphasizes yoga and *acara*, ethical conduct

Yogananda (1893–1952) – an Indian mystic. Yogananda studied as a monk in the Shankara order. He eventually moved to the United States and founded the Self-Realization Fellowship in Los Angeles in 1935.

Reference: *Autobiography of a Yogi*, Yogananda.

yogi – n. a practitioner of yoga; a contemplative person

Yom Kippur – n. in Judaism, the Day of Atonement. It is celebrated ten days after the Jewish New Year, Rosh Hashanah. In ancient times, a scapegoat symbolically carried the sins of the Jews into the desert.

Z

zeal – n. a striving interest to complete something

zealot – n. a partisan with a fanatical consciousness, including a commitment to militant opposition

zeitgeist – n. fr. German *Zeitgeist*, meaning time spirit. It refers to the intellectual or philosophical character of a time and culture.

Zen – n. a type of Mahayana Buddhism that emphasizes the importance of purity and sudden enlightenment, especially by intuitive and meditative processes of mind. The historical origins of Zen are obscure. A search for the beginning of this religious-philosophic discipline leads to several possibilities, all of them proven only by the existence of tradition as explanation. One story is that Zen was the creation of an Indian philosopher by the name of Bodhidharma (460–534). Other stories attribute Zen to the Buddha himself. Still other accounts point to Lao-tzu (ca. 500 BC) due to the striking similarities between Zen and Taoism. The strongest modern advocate of Zen is D. T. Suzuki (1870–1966), author of *Manual of Zen Buddhism*. It is perhaps best and in the spirit of Zen that its exact history is nameless, for Zen is the study of the nameless reality that surrounds us.

Zen is divided into two general schools or sects, Rinzai and Soto. Rinzai emphasizes sudden enlightenment and is less intellectually oriented, claiming that all perceptual and rational discriminations are illusions. All striving is useless, including the striving not to strive. Theoretical paradoxes are somewhat of a commodity in Rinzai Zen, aiding in the encouragement to "transcend" reality. Paradox is refined in the Zen use of *koans* (statements designed to frustrate rational analysis of reality). The Soto sect is a moderate representation of the principles of Zen. It is more popular and less rigorous than the Rinzai sect.

Zen actualizes its discipline and teachings through various arts, including archery, swordsmanship, the tea ceremony, and landscape gardening. This aspect of Zen extends the fruits of Mahayana Buddhism beyond the monastery, giving the hope of liberation to ordinary followers. The contemplative techniques embodied in the arts of Zen are usually administered by a master teacher or "*Roshi*." Vows of absolute obedience are used to preserve the spiritual discipline that Zen aims toward. Vows of obedience also serve to preserve the institutional authenticity of Zen, since Zen is considered a practice that can only be mastered with the guidance of a roshi.

> *"In the case of archery, the archer and the target are no longer two opposing objects, but are one reality. The archer ceases to be conscious of himself . . . completely empty and rid of the self, he becomes one with the perfecting of his technical skill."*

> Daisetz T. Suzuki, in the introduction to *Zen in the Art of Archery* by Eugen Herrigel

The pragmatic focus that is found in Zen arts has held a great fascination with Westerners, many of whom are disenchanted with the approaches of Western religion. Yet, the attraction to Zen arts is sometimes wrong, because the esoteric nature of Zen is not simply mastered by physical conformation. Zen masters are often reluctant to accommodate large numbers of students, because such accommodation may become a type of striving.

References: *Zen and Western Thought*, Masao Abe; *Zen and Japanese Culture*, D. T. Suzuki; *Zen: A Way of Life*, Christmas Humphreys; *The Spirit of Zen*, Alan Watts; *The Empty Mirror: Experiences in a Japanese Zen Monastery*, Janwillem van de Wetering

zenana – n. in Hinduism, a den of licentious pleasure; female sequestration

Zeno of Elea (490–430 BC) – a student of Parmenides, Zeno worked out refutations of plurality and especially motion. He developed a number of paradoxes to illustrate the weakness of common sense:

Z

1) *The Arrow:* for an arrow to exist it must occupy a space. To occupy a space means to be motionless. If an arrow moves, it is not occupying a space. If it is not occupying a space it does not exist. Thus, if it does not exist, it cannot move.

2) *Achilles and the Tortoise:* Achilles, running after a tortoise, cannot catch the tortoise because each time Achilles reaches the point where the tortoise last was, the tortoise has moved on. No matter how fast Achilles runs, each time he reaches the point at which the tortoise last was, the tortoise has moved on. The distance may appear to decrease, but no matter how many times Achilles reaches the point at which the tortoise last was, the tortoise will have moved on, however minutely. Theoretically Achilles cannot catch the tortoise.

3) *The Racecourse:* To travel from start to finish on a racecourse, the runner must travel from A to B. But, first the runner must travel halfway. And before reaching halfway, he must reach halfway to halfway between A and B. This requirement of running halfway to each halfway can be extended infinitely, since there are an infinite series of points between any two points, thus an infinite series of halfway points. The runner cannot move from A to B.

References: *A History of Greek Philosophy*, vol. 2, W. K. C. Guthrie; and *Modern Science and Zeno's Paradoxes*, Adolf Grunbaum

zephyr – n. a soft, gentle breeze usually coming out of the west; important to philosophers who sail

Zoroastrianism – n. though originally the faith of "*Parsis*" ("Persians" in Hindu) at about 500 BC (some sources go back to 1500 BC), this religion survives primarily in India where some 200,000–300,000 practitioners live. Its migration to India took place about 800 AD.

Zoroaster (also called "Zarathustra") became the namesake of this faith by healing an Aryan ruler's horse, declaring allegiance to *Ahura Mazda* (Wise Lord or Supreme Being) and making spiritual declarations based on visions and communion with the divine *Ahura Mazda*.

The Avesta is the sacred text of Zoroastrians, being a collection of hymns and instructions on worship and daily life. Within the text are the *Gathas*, or teachings of Zoroaster:

1) The universe is composed of opposing forces put in place by *Ahura Mazda*. These forces exist as a balance of good and evil.

2) The conflict between good and evil is visible in human life. Individuals have one lifetime to exercise their freedom, choosing either *asha* (truth) or *druj* (falsehood).

3) Reality, as we experience it, is a test of our spiritual powers. It is not a by-product of the senses. It exists and needs to be taken seriously.

4) Eshatologically, time ends and souls continue their existence in paradise or hell. Although hell exists to purify the damned, through punishment they are cleansed and return in a new age of innocence.

5) Believers must not spoil the earth with their actions and must enact the virtues of truthfulness, compassion, charity, and justice.

References: *A History of Zoroastrianism*, 2 vols., Mary Boyce; *The Dawn and Twilight of Zoroastrianism* and *The Teachings of the Magi: A Compendium of Zoroastrian Beliefs*, R. C. Zaehner; and *Textual Sources for the Study of Zoroastrianism*, Mary Boyce

A Concluding Mantra for Sati (Mindfulness)

My world religions students are sometimes required to begin sessions with this mantra, as they stand together in community. For some, it is their first encounter with prayer and meditation. This mantra has an interfaith orientation that all people can implement to generate mindfulness. When you are alone and looking for a simple solution to a stressful situation, try to recalibrate your mind.

Will you try it? Stop now. Sit quietly for 3-5 minutes and allow these words to produce a simple shift in awareness.

"Right focus - Right form - Right attitude - Right goals"

CHRONOLOGY OF PHILOSOPHY*

*Some dates are approximate as scholarship is inconclusive.

Thales 640?–546 BC
Anaximander 611–547 BC
Pythagoras c. 600 BC
Anaximenes 550–500 BC
Heraclitus c. 500 BC
Parmenides c. 500–450 BC
Anaxagoras c. 500–428 BC
Zeno of Elea (Paradoxes) c. 475 BC
Leucippus 500–450 BC
Empedocles 490–435 BC
Protagoras (Sophist) 481–411 BC
Gorgias (Sophist) 483–375 BC
Socrates 469–399 BC
Democritus (Atomist) b. 460 BC
Antisthenes (Cynic) 444–365 BC
Aristippus (Cyrenaic) 435–356 BC
Plato 427–347 BC
Aristotle 384–322 BC
Pyrrho (Skeptic) 360–270 BC
Zeno (Stoic) 350–258 BC
Epicurus (Epicureanism) 342–270 BC
Chrysippus (Stoic) 282–209 BC
Carneades (Skeptic) 214–129 BC
Panaetius (Stoic) 180–111 BC
Posidonius (Stoic) 130–150 BC

Cicero (Eclectic) 106–43 BC

Lucretius (Epicurean) 95–52 BC

Philo (Plato's Jew) b. 20 BC

Jesus 3 BC–30 AD

Seneca (Stoic) 4 BC–65 AD

Aenesidemus (Skeptic)/known – 50 BC–100 AD

Plutarch (Neo–Pythagorean) 46–120 AD

Epictetus (Stoic) 55–135

Marcus Aurelius (Stoic) 121–180

Clement of Alexandria (Christian) 150–215

Tertullian (Christian) c. 155–222

Origen (Christian) c. 185–254

Plotinus (Neoplatonist) 204–269

Irenaeus (Christian) "known" 130–202

Sextus Empiricus (Skeptic) c. 300

Iamblichus (Syrian Neoplatonist) 245–325

Julian the Apostate (Neoplatonist) 331–363

Augustine (Christian) 354–430

Proclus (Neoplatonist) c. 410–485

Boethius (Platonic–Christian?) 480–524

Closing of the Schools at Athens in 529. The end of ancient philosophy. Beginning of the Middle Ages.

Mohammed 569–632

John Scotus Eriugena c. 800–877

Avicenna 980–1036

Anselm 1033–1109

Avicebron c. 1050

Roscellinus c. 1050–1122

Peter Abelard 1079–1142

Averroes 1126–1198

Moses Maimonides 1135–1204

Albertus Magnus b.?1200–1280

Roger Bacon 1214–1294

Bonaventure 1231–1274

Thomas Aquinas 1225–1274

Meister Eckhart 1250–1329

Duns Scotus c. 1274–1308

William of Ockham c.1287–1347

CHRONOLOGY OF PHILOSOPHY*

John Buridan c. 1297–1358
The end of the Middle Ages. The fall of Constantinople. Beginning of the Italian Renaissance in 1453. Prelude to the Modern Period.
Leonardo da Vinci 1452–1519
Girolamo Savanarola 1452–1498
Niccolò Machiavelli 1469–1527
Nicolaus Copernicus 1472–1543
Erasmus 1466–1636
Martin Luther 1483–1546
Michel de Montaigne 1533–1592
Giordano Bruno 1548–1600
Francis Bacon 1561–1626
Johannes Kepler 1571–1630
Galileo Galilei (known mononymously as "Galileo") 1564–1641
Tommaso Campanella 1568–1639
Thomas Hobbes 1588–1679
Pierre Gassendi 1592–1655
René Descartes 1569–1650
Blaise Pascal 1623–1662
Arnold Geulincx 1624–1699
Benedict Spinoza 1632–1677
John Locke 1632–1704
Nicolas Malebranche 1638–1715
Isaac Newton 1642–1727
Gottfried W. Leibniz 1646–1716
Giambattista Vico 1668–1744
Christian Wolff 1679–1754
George Berkeley 1684–1753
François-Marie Arouet de Voltaire 1709–1751
Jonathan Edwards 1703–1788
Julian Offroy de La Mettrie 1709–1751
Thomas Reid 1710–1796
David Hume 1711–1776
Jean-Jacques Rousseau 1712–1778
Claude Adrien Helvétius 1715–1771
Condillac 1715–1780
Holbach 1723–1789
Immanuel Kant 1724–1804

Jeremy Bentham 1747–1832

Johann Fichte 1762–1814

Marie-François-Pierre Maine de Biran 1766–1824

G. W. F. Hegel 1770–1831

F. W. Joseph von Schelling 1775–1854

Arthur Schopenhauer 1788–1860

Antonio Rosmini-Serbati 1797–1855

Auguste Comte 1797–1855

John Stuart Mill 1806–1873

Charles Darwin 1809–1882

Søren Kierkegaard 1813–1855

Rudolf Hermann Lotze 1817–1881

Karl Marx 1818–1883

Herbert Spencer 1820–1903

Fyodor Dostoevsky 1821–1881

C. S. Peirce 1839–1914

William James 1842–1910

Friedrich Nietzsche 1844–1900

F. H. Bradley 1846–1924

Hans Vaihinger 1852–1923

Alexius Meinong 1853–1920

Josiah Royce 1855–1916

Henri Bergson 1859–1941

Samuel Alexander 1859–1938

John Dewey 1859–1952

Edmund Husserl 1859–1938

A. N. Whitehead 1861–1947

George Santayana 1863–1952

Max Schiller 1864–1937

Bertrand Russell 1872–1970

G. E. Moore 1873–1958

William E. Hocking 1873–1966

Giovanni Gentile 1875–1944

Ralph Barton Perry 1876–1957

Martin Buber 1878–1965

Moritz Schlick 1882–1936

Karl Jaspers 1883–1969

E. S. Brightman 1884–1953

CHRONOLOGY OF PHILOSOPHY*

Paul Tillich 1886–1965
C. D. Broad 1887–1971
Martin Heidegger 1889–1976
Gabriel Marcel 1889–1973
Ludwig Wittgenstein 1889–1951
Rudolf Carnap 1891–1970
Gilbert Ryle 1900–1976
Jacques Lacan 1901–1981
Jean-Paul Sartre 1905–1980
Maurice Merleau Ponty 1908–1961
A. J. Ayer 1910–1989
Michel Foucault 1926-1984
Jacques Derrida 1938–2004

A Philosopher's Library

F acts in this handbook have been cross-referenced as much as possible. The important books listed here are part of my personal library. Philosophy is a very stable field in general, and while new scholarship is always emerging, it is still very connected to the history of philosophy. Having a personal library is important for our education and intellectual growth. Having physical books on shelves allows us to sit quietly and privately among inspirational authors at any time.

Adams, R. M., *Leibniz: Determinist, Theist, Idealist.* (Oxford: Oxford University Press, 1994).

Adams, R. M. and M. McCord Adams, eds. *The Problem of Evil.* (Oxford: Oxford University Press, 1991).

Adelman, P. *Miriam's Well: Rituals for Jewish Women Throughout the Year.* (New York: Biblis Press, 1986).

Alcoff, L. and E. Potter, eds. *Feminist Epistemologies.* (New York: Routledge, 1993).

Alston, W. P. *Perceiving God: The Epistemology of Religious Experience.* (Ithaca, NY: Cornell University Press, 1991).

Annas, J. *The Morality of Happiness.* (Oxford: Oxford University Press, 1993).

Armstrong, D. M. *A Materialist Theory of the Mind.* (London: Routledge, 1968).

Arnold, E. V. *Stoicism.* (Cambridge: Cambridge University Press, 1911).

Ash, M. G. *Gestalt Psychology in German Culture, 1890–1967: Holism and the Quest for Objectivity.* (Cambridge: Cambridge University Press, 1995).

Atherton, M. *Berkeley's Revolution in Vision.* (Ithaca, NY: Cornell University Press, 1990).

Austin, S. *Parmenides: Being, Bounds, and Logic.* (New Haven, CT: Yale University Press, 1986).

Ayer, A. J. *Language, Truth, and Logic.* (New York: Dover, 1946).

Ayer, A. J. *Thomas Paine.* (Chicago: University of Chicago Press, 1988).

Barbour, Ian. *Religion in an Age of Science: The Gifford Lectures, 1989–91.* (New York: HarperCollins, 1990).

Barnes, J. *Aristotle.* (Oxford: Oxford University Press, 1982).

Barnes, J. *The Pre-Socratic Philosophers.* (London: Routledge & Kegan Paul, 1979).

Becker, Ernest. *The Denial of Death.* (Free Press, 1997).

Becker, Lawrence and Charlotte Becker. *Encyclopedia of Ethics*, vols. 1–2. (Garland Publishing, 1992). A very nice collection of short articles on ethics.

Bertocci, P. *The Person God Is.* (London: Allen & Unwin, 1970).

Biermann, Derek. *Samadhi.* (Shambala Publications, 2000).

Black, M. *Problems of Analysis.* (Ithaca, NY: Cornell University Press, 1954).

Blackmore, Susan. *The Meme Machine.* (Oxford: Oxford University Press, 1999).

Bloch, Ernst. *The Principle of Hope.* (Oxford: Blackwell, 1986).

Bok, Sissela. *Secrets: On the Ethics of Concealment and Revelation.* (New York: Oxford University Press, 1984).

Borg, Marcus. *Jesus and the Buddha: Parallel Sayings.* (Ulysses Press, 1999).

Bouveresse, J. and Carol Cosman, trans. *Wittgenstein Reads Freud: The Myth of the Unconscious.* (Princeton: Princeton University Press, 1995).

Boyce, Mary. *Textual Sources for the Study of Zoroastrianism.* (Manchester: Manchester University Press, 1984).

Bradley, F. H. *Essays on Truth and Reality.* (Oxford: Oxford University Press, 1914).

Brandt, R. *A Theory of the Good and the Right.* (Oxford: Clarendon Press, 1979).

Branham, R. B. and M. O. Goulet-Caze, eds. *The Cynics: The Cynic Movement in Antiquity and Its Legacy.* (Berkeley: University of California–Berkeley Press, 1996).

Bruns, G. L. *Hermeneutics: Ancient and Modern.* (New Haven, CT: Yale University Press, 1992).

Cassell, E. *The Nature of Suffering and the Goals of Medicine.* (Oxford: Oxford University Press, 1991).

Campbell, J. *Understanding John Dewey.* (Open Court Press, 1995).

Capaldi, Nicholas. *The Art of Deception.* (Prometheus Books, 1987).

Carr, K. *The Banalization of Nihilism: Twentieth-Century Responses to Meaninglessness.* (State University of New York Press, 1992).

Carruthers, P. *The Metaphysics of the Tractatus.* (Cambridge: Cambridge University Press, 1990).

Carver, T. *Friedrich Engels.* (New York: Macmillan, 1989).

Carver, T. *Marx and Engels: The Intellectual Relationship.* (Brighton: Harvester Wheatsheaf, 1983).

Cave, J. D. *Mircea Eliade's Vision for a New Humanism.* (Oxford: Oxford University Press, 1992).

Caws, P. *Structuralism.* (Humanities Press, 1988).

Chadwick, H. *Augustine.* (Oxford: Oxford University Press, 1986).

Chappell, V., ed. *The Cambridge Companion to Locke.* (Cambridge: Cambridge University Press, 1994).

Chatterjee, M. *Gandhi's Religious Thought.* (New York: Macmillan, 1983).

Chomsky, Noam. *Syntactic Structures,* Janua Liguarum no. 4. (The Hague: Monton, 1957).

Clark, J. M. *Meister Eckhart.* (London: Nelson, 1957).

Clark, J. P. *The Philosophical Anarchism of William Godwin.* (Princeton: Princeton University Press, 1977).

Clark, M. *Paley.* (Toronto: University of Toronto Press, 1974).

Clarkson, G. E. *The Mysticism of William Law.* (New York: Lang, 1992).

Coffa, J. A. *The Semantic Tradition from Kant to Carnap: To the Vienna Station.* (Cambridge: Cambridge University Press, 1991).

Cole, G. D. H. *A History of Socialist Thought,* 5 vols. (London: Macmillan, 1960).

Collingridge, D. *The Social Control of Technology.* (New York: St. Martin's Press, 1980).

Copleston, F. C. *Aquinas.* (Baltimore: Penguin, 1955).

Corbin, H. and L. Sherrard, trans. *History of Islamic Philosophy.* (Kegan Paul International, 1993).

Coyne, Richard. *Technoromanticism.* (Cambridge, MA: MIT Press, 1999).

Crosby, D. A. *The Specter of the Absurd: Sources and Criticisms of Modern Nihilism.* (State University of New York Press, 1988).

Cross, Frank L., ed. *The Oxford Dictionary of the Christian Church.* (Oxford: Oxford University Press, 1961). Highly recommended.

Daly, M. *Pure Lust.* (Boston: Beacon Press, 1987).

Dancy, J. *Moral Reasons.* (Oxford: Blackwell, 1993).

Davis, M. *Smut: Erotic Reality/Obscene Ideology.* (Chicago: University of Chicago Press, 1983).

Dawson, J. *Logical Dilemmas: The Life and Work of Kurt Godel.* (Wellesley, MA: Peters, 1997).

de Grazia, S. *Machiavelli in Hell.* (Princeton: Princeton University Press, 1989).

Dillon, J. *The Middle Platonists.* (London: Duckworth, 1977).

Donagan, A. *Spinoza.* (Chicago: University of Chicago Press, 1989).

Donagan, A. *The Theory of Morality.* (Chicago: University of Chicago Press, 1977).

Duden, B. *The Woman Beneath the Skin.* (Cambridge, MA: Harvard University Press, 1991).

Dummett, M. *The Origins of Analytic Philosophy.* (London: Duckworth, 1993).

Dundas, P. *The Jains.* (London: Routledge).

Durkheim, Emile and Joseph W. Swain, trans. *The Elementary Forms of Religious Life*, 2nd ed. (London: Allen & Unwin, 1912).

Edwards, Paul, ed. *Encyclopedia of Philosophy*, vols. 1–8. (New York: Macmillan Publishing, 1967). Still a very important resource.

Eliade, M., ed. *The Encyclopedia of Religion*. (New York: Macmillan, 1987).

Elon, M. and B. Auerbach and M. J. Sykes, trans. *Jewish Law: History, Sources, Principles*. (Philadelphia: Jewish Publications Society, 1994).

Engels, F., and E. Leacock, ed. *The Origin of the Family, Private Property, and the State*. (New York: International Publishers, 1972).

Esposito, John L., ed. *The Oxford History of Islam*. (Oxford: Oxford University Press, 1999).

Fackenheim, Emile. *To Mend the World*. (Bloomington, IN: University of Indiana Press, 1994).

Fakhry, M. *Ethical Theories in Islam*, 2nd ed. (Leiden: Brill, 1993).

Farrington, B. *The Philosophy of Francis Bacon*. (Liverpool: Liverpool University Press, 1964).

Farthing, G. W. *The Psychology of Consciousness*. (Prentice Hall Inc., 1992).

Feifel, Herman. *The Meaning of Death*. (New York: McGraw-Hill, 1959).

Fingarette, H. *Confucius: The Secular as Sacred*. (New York: Harper & Row, 1972).

Fischer, J. M. *The Metaphysics of Death*. (Stanford: Stanford University Press, 1993).

Fitzpatrick, M., M. Philp, and W. St. Clair, eds. *Political and Philosophical Writings of William Godwin*. (London: Pickering & Chatto, 1993).

Flavell, J. *The Developmental Psychology of Jean Piaget*. (Van Nostrand, 1968).

Flew, A. *The Presumption of Atheism*. (London: Pemberton Press, 1976).

Fodor, J. A. *Psychosemantics: The Problem of Meaning in the Philosophy of Mind*. (Cambridge, MA: MIT Press, 1987).

Foucault, M. *Discipline and Punish*. (London: Allan Lane, 1977).

Frank, J. *Dostoevsky: The Miraculous Years, 1865–71*. (Princeton: Princeton University Press, 1995).

Frei, H. and G. Hunsinger and W. Placker, eds. *Types of Christian Theology*. (New Haven, CT: Yale University Press, 1992).

Freud, S. *A General Introduction to Psychoanalysis*. (New York: Liveright, 1920).

Freud, S. *Jokes and Their Relation to the Unconscious*. (New York: Penguin, 1956).

Furley, D. *The Greek Cosmologists*. (Cambridge: Cambridge University Press, 1987).

Ganguli, K. M., trans. *Mahabharata*. (Calcutta: Oriental Publications, 1962). (also trans. by J. A .B. van Buitenen, University of Chicago Press, 1978.)

Gay, P. *Freud: A Life for Our Time*. (London: J. M. Dent, 1988).

Gaynor, Frank, ed. *Dictionary of Mysticism*. (Philosophical Library, 1953).

Gilligan, C. *In a Different Voice: Psychological Theory and Women's Development.* (Cambridge, MA: Harvard University Press, 1982).

Gilson, Etienne. *Being and Some Philosophers.* (Pontifical Institute of Medieval Studies, 1952).

Gilson, Etienne and L. K. Shook, trans. *The Christian Philosophy of St. Thomas Aquinas.* (New York: Random House, 1957).

Griffin, J. *Well-Being.* (Oxford: Clarendon Press, 1986).

Griffin, R. *Fascism: A Reader.* (Oxford: Oxford University Press, 1995).

Gove, Philip B., ed. *Webster's Third New International Dictionary of the English Language: Unabridged.* (G & C Merriam Co., 1976).

Guthrie, W. K. C. *A History of Greek Philosophy,* 6 vols. (Cambridge: Cambridge University Press, 1962–1978).

Guttenplan, S., ed. *A Companion to the Philosophy of Mind.* (Oxford: Blackwell, 1994).

Guttierrez, G. *A Theology of Liberation.* (Orbis Books, 1988).

Gutting, G., ed. *The Companion to Foucault.* (Cambridge: Cambridge University Press, 1994).

Guttman, J. *Philosophies of Judaism.* (Anchor Books, 1966).

Guyer, P., ed. *The Cambridge Companion to Kant.* (Cambridge: Cambridge University Press, 1992).

Hardman, O. *The Ideals of Asceticism: An Essay in the Comparative Study of Religion.* (New York: Macmillan, 1987).

Hare, R. M. *Moral Thinking.* (Oxford: Clarendon Press, 1981).

Harris, I. *The Mind of John Locke.* (Cambridge: Cambridge University Press, 1994).

Harrison, R. *Bentham.* (London: Routledge, 1983).

Hartshorne, C. *Man's Vision of God.* (New York: Harper & Row, 1941).

Hartshorne, C. *Omnipotence and Other Theological Mistakes.* (State University of New York Press, 1984).

Hartshorne, C. and W. Reese. *Philosophers Speak of God.* (Chicago: University of Chicago Press, 1953).

Harvey, P. *The Selfless Mind: Personality, Consciousness, and Nirvana in Early Buddhism.* (Curzon Press, 1995).

Hassan, R. *An Iqbal Primer.* (Lahore: Aziz Press, 1979).

Hausman, C. *Charles S. Peirce's Evolutionary Philosophy.* (Cambridge: Cambridge University Press, 1993).

Hempel, C. G. *Aspects of Scientific Explanation.* (Free Press, 1965).

Hetherington, Norris. *Encyclopedia of Cosmology: Historical, Philosophical, and Scientific Foundations of Modern Cosmology.* (Garland Publishing, 1993). A valuable survey of the key concepts in cosmology.

Hine, E. M. *A Critical Study of Condillac's Traite de Systemes*. (The Hague: Nijhoff, 1979).

Howells, C. ed. *The Cambridge Companion to Sartre*. (Cambridge: Cambridge University Press, 1992).

Hull, David. *Metaphysics of Evolution*. (State University of New York Press, 1989).

Hurley, S. *Natural Reasons*. (Oxford: Oxford University Press, 1989).

Ihde, Don. *Technics and Praxis*. (Dordrecht: Reidel, 1979).

Inwood, B. *Ethics and Human Action in Early Stoicism*. (Oxford: Oxford University Press, 1985).

Isaac, J. C. *Arendt, Camus, and Modern Rebellion*. (New Haven, CT: Yale University Press, 1992).

Jaeger, Werner and R. Robinson, trans. *Aristotle*. (Oxford: Oxford University Press, 1948).

Jaini, P. S. *The Jaina Path of Purification*. (Delhi: Motital Banarsidass, 1979).

Janaway, Christopher. *Schopenhauer*. (Oxford: Oxford University Press, 1994).

Janaway, Christopher. *The Cambridge Companion to Schopenhauer*. (Cambridge: Cambridge University Press, 1999).

Jonas, H. *The Gnostic Religion*. (Beacon Press, 1958).

Juergensmeyer, M. *Fighting with Gandhi*. (Harper & Row, 1984).

Kahn, C. H. *Anaximander and the Origins of Greek Philosophy*. (Indiana: Hackett, 1994).

Kahn, C. H. *Plato and the Socratic Dialogue*. (Cambridge: Cambridge University Press, 1996).

Kahn, C. H. *The Art and Thought of Heraclitus*. (Cambridge: Cambridge University Press, 1979).

Kegley, C. W., ed. *The Theology of Rudolf Bultmann*. (New York: Harper & Row, 1967).

Kelly, A. *Mikhail Bakunin: A Study in the Psychology and Politics of Utopianism*. (Oxford: Clarendon Press, 1982).

Kelly, J. N. D. *Early Christian Doctrines*, 2nd ed. (London: A & C Black, 1960).

Kenney, A. *What Is Faith?* (Oxford: Oxford University Press, 1992).

Keown, J., ed. *Euthanasia Examined*. (Cambridge: Cambridge University Press, 1995).

Kim, J. and E. Sosa, eds. *A Companion to Metaphysics*. (Oxford: Blackwell, 1995).

Kirkham, R. *Theories of Truth*. (Cambridge, MA: MIT Press, 1992).

Kitcher, P. *Freud's Dream: A Complete Interdisciplinary Theory of Mind*. (Cambridge, MA: MIT Press, 1992).

Koffka, K. *Principles of Gestalt Psychology*. (Harcourt Brace, 1935).

Kogan, B. *Averroes and the Metaphysics of Creation*. (State University of New York Press, 1985).

Kohlberg, L. *Essays on Moral Development*. (New York: Harper & Row, 1984).

Kolakowski, L. *Bergson*. (Oxford: Oxford University Press, 1985).

Korsgaard, C. *The Sources of Normativity.* (Cambridge: Cambridge University Press, 1996).

Kuhn, T. *The Structure of Scientific Revolutions,* 2nd ed. (Chicago: University of Chicago Press, 1970).

Kurtz, P. *A Skeptic's Handbook of Parapsychology.* (Prometheus Books, 1985).

La Fargue, M. *The Tao of the Tao Te Ching.* (State University of New York Press, 1992).

Larson, R. and G. Segal. *Knowledge of Meaning: An Introduction to Semantic Theory.* (Cambridge, MA: MIT Press, 1995).

Law, D. R. *Kierkegaard as Negative Theologian.* (Oxford: Clarendon Press, 1993).

Leary, J. E. *Francis Bacon and the Politics of Science.* (Iowa State University Press, 1994).

Leftow, B. *Time and Eternity.* (Ithaca, NY: Cornell University Press, 1991).

Lehrer, K. *Metamind.* (Oxford: Oxford University Press, 1991).

Levinson, H. *Santayana, Pragmatism, and the Spiritual Life.* (University of North Carolina Press, 1992).

Lucey, K. *On Knowing and the Known.* (New York: Prometheus Books, 1996).

MacKinnon, C. A. *Sexual Harassment of Working Women.* (New Haven, CT: Yale University Press, 1979).

Madison, G. *The Phenomenology of Merleau-Ponty.* (Ohio University Press, 1981).

Marciszewski, Witold and Martinus Nijhoff, eds. *Dictionary of Logic, as Applied in the Study of Language: Concepts, Methods, Theories.* (The Hague: Martinus Nijhoff, 1981). Especially useful for those interested in metalogic.

Marechal, J. and A. Thorold, trans. *Studies in the Psychology of the Mystics.* (New York: Magi Books, 1964).

Maritain, Jacques. *The Degrees of Knowledge.* (Charles Scribner Publications, 1959).

Marsh, C. *Reclaiming Bonhoeffer: The Promise of His Theology.* (Oxford: Oxford University Press, 1994).

Martin, M. *Atheism: A Philosophical Justification.* (Temple University Press, 1990).

McCool, G. *The Neo-Thomists.* (Marquette University Press, 1994).

McConica, J. K. *Erasmus.* (Oxford: Oxford University Press, 1991).

McIntyre, J. *St. Anselm and His Critics.* (London: Oliver & Boyd, 1954).

Mele, A. R. *Irrationality: An Essay in Akrasia, Self-Deception, and Self-Control.* (Oxford: Oxford University Press, 1987).

Minor, R. N. *Radhakrishnan.* (State University of New York Press, 1987).

Mitsis, P. *Epicurus' Ethical Theory.* (Ithaca, NY: Cornell University Press, 1988).

Moggridge, D. E. *Maynard Keynes: An Economist's Biography.* (London: Routledge, 1992).

Mohanty, A., A. Russo, and L. Torres. *Third World Women and the Politics of Feminism.* (Bloomington, IN: Indiana University Press, 1991).

Mohanty, J. N. *Reason and Tradition in Indian Thought.* (Oxford: Clarendon Press, 1992).

Moi, T. *Simone de Beauvoir: The Making of an Intellectual Woman.* (Oxford: Blackwell, 1994).

Moore, G. E. *Principia Ethica.* (Cambridge: Cambridge University Press, 1903).

Monk, R. *Bertrand Russell.* (London: Jonathan Cape, 1996).

Morais, H. M. *Deism in Eighteenth-Century America.* (New York: Russell and Russell, 1960).

Moser, P. *Knowledge and Evidence.* (Cambridge: Cambridge University Press, 1989).

Muller, Max. *Ramakrishna.* (Advaita Ashrama, 1899).

Murphy, N. *Theology in the Age of Scientific Reasoning.* (Ithaca, NY: Cornell University Press, 1990).

Nadler, S. *Malebranche and Ideas.* (Oxford: Oxford University Press, 1992).

Nagel, T. *The Possibility of Altruism.* (Oxford: Clarendon Press, 1970).

Nasr, S. H. *The Need for a Sacred Science.* (Richmond: Curzon Press, 1993).

Nead, L. *The Female Nude: Art, Obscenity, and Sexuality.* (London: Routledge, 1992).

Nehamas, A. *Nietzsche: Life as Literature.* (Cambridge, MA: Harvard University Press, 1985).

Neusner, J. *What Is Midrash?* (Fortress Press, 1987).

Neusner, J., ed. *Ethics of Family Life.* (Belmont, CA: Wadsworth, 2001).

Neusner, J., ed. *The Life of Virtue.* (Belmont, CA: Wadsworth, 2001).

Nozick, M. *Miguel de Unamuno.* (New York: Twayne, 1971).

Nozick, R. *Anarchy, State, and Utopia.* (Oxford: Blackwell, 1974).

Nozick, R. *Philosophical Explanations.* (Cambridge, MA: Harvard University Press, 1981).

Oates, W. J., ed. *The Stoic and Epicurean Philosophers: The Complete Extant Writings of Epicurus, Epictetus, Lucretius, Marcus Aurelius.* (New York: Random House, 1940).

O'Flaherty, W. D. *Karma and Rebirth in Classical Indian Traditions.* (Berkeley: University of California–Berkeley Press, 1985).

Olivelle, Patrick, trans. *Upanishads (800–300 BC).* (Oxford: Oxford University Press, 1996).

Oman, J. *Grace and Personality.* (Cambridge: Cambridge University Press, 1917).

Otto, R. *The Idea of the Holy.* (Oxford: Oxford University Press, 1958).

Papineau, D. *The Philosophy of Science.* (Oxford: Oxford University Press, 1996).

Parkin, F. *Durkheim.* (Oxford: Oxford University Press, 1992).

Pasnan, R. *Theories of Cognition in the Later Middle Ages.* (Cambridge: Cambridge University Press, 1997).

Paz, O and L. Kemp, trans. *The Labyrinth of Solitude: Life and Thought in Mexico.* (New York: Grove Press, 1961).

Pelikan, J. *Christianity and Classical Culture.* (New Haven, CT: Yale University Press, 1993).

Penelhum, T. H. *David Hume: An Introduction to His Philosophical System.* (Purdue University Press, 1992).

Phillips, D. Z. *Faith and Philosophical Inquiry.* (Schocken Books, 1971).

Phillips, S. H. *Aurobindo's Philosophy of Brahman.* (Leiden: Brill, 1986).

Piaget, J. *The Moral Judgment of the Child.* (New York: Free Press, 1932).

Pickering, M. *Auguste Comte: An Intellectual Biography.* (Cambridge: Cambridge University Press, 1993).

Plantinga, Alvin. "Is Belief in God Properly Basic?," *Nous* 15 (1): 41–51, 1981.

Polanyi, Michael. *Knowing and Being.* (Chicago: University of Chicago Press, 1969).

Popper, Karl. *The Logic of Scientific Discovery.* (London: Hutchinson, 1959).

Potter, K. H., ed. *Encyclopedia of Indian Philosophies.* (Princeton: Princeton University Press, 1981).

Poulain, A., and L. Y. Smith and J. N. Bainvel, trans. *The Graces of Interior Prayer.* (London: Routledge & Kegan Paul, 1950).

Prior, W. J. *Virtue and Knowledge: An Introduction to Early Greek Ethics.* (London: Routledge, 1991).

Purlin, S., ed. *A Handbook for the Study of Suicide.* (Oxford: Oxford University Press, 1975).

Putnam, R. A., ed. *The Cambridge Companion to William James.* (Cambridge: Cambridge University Press, 1997).

Quimette, V. *José Ortega y Gasset.* (Boston: Twayne, 1982).

Quinn, P. and Taliaferro, C. *A Companion to Philosophy of Religion.* (Oxford: Blackwell, 1997).

Rahner, K. *The Practice of Faith: A Handbook of Contemporary Spirituality.* (Crossroad Press, 1983).

Raskin, V. *Semantic Mechanisms of Humor.* (Dordrecht: Reidel, 1985).

Rasmussen, L., ed. *Reinhold Niebuhr: Theologian of Public Life.* (London: Collins, 1989).

Reber, Arthur. *The Penguin Dictionary of Psychology.* (New York: Penguin Books, 1985). One of the best reference manuals for psychology.

Reese, William L. *Dictionary of Philosophy and Religion.* (Humanities Press, 1989). Highly recommended.

Reich, W., ed. *Encyclopedia of Bioethics.* (New York: Macmillan, 1994).

Reichenbach, B. *The Law of Karma.* (University Press of America, 1983).

Reps, Paul, comp. *Zen Flesh, Zen Bones: A Collection of Zen and Pre-Zen Writings.* (Anchor Books, 1989).

Rescher, Nicholas. *The Coherence Theory of Truth.* (Oxford: Oxford University Press, 1973).

Richards, R. *Darwin and the Emergence of Evolutionary Theories of Mind and Behavior.* (Chicago: University of Chicago Press, 1987).

Robinson, J. M. *The Nag Hammadi Library.* (Leiden: Brill, 1988).

Ruland, Vernon. *Imagining the Sacred.* (Orbis Press, 1999).

Ruland, Vernon. *Sacred Lies and Silences: A Psychology of Religious Disguise.* (Michael Glazier Books, 1994).

Ruse, Michael. *Sociobiology: Sense or Nonsense?* (Dordrecht: Reidel, 1979).

Salmon, W. C. *Zeno's Paradoxes.* (Bobbs-Merrill, 1970).

Sanchez Reulet, A., ed.; and W. R. Trask, trans. *Contemporary Latin-American Philosophy.* (University of New Mexico Press, 1954).

Sayre, F. *The Greek Cynics.* (Baltimore: Furst, 1948).

Sayre, K. M. *Cybernetics and the Philosophy of Mind.* (London: Routledge, 1976).

Scarre, G. *Logic and Reality in the Philosophy of John Stuart Mill.* (Dordrecht: Kluwer, 1989).

Schiappa, E. *Protagoras and Logos: A Study in Greek Philosophy and Rhetoric.* (University of South Carolina Press, 1991).

Schilpp, P. A., ed. *The Philosophy of Sarvepali Radhakrishnan.* (New York: Tudor, 1952).

Schleiermacher, Friedrich, trans. by E. Lawler and T. N. Tice. *On What Gives Value to Life.* (Edwin Mellen Press, 1995.)

Schmithausen, L. *The Problem of Sentience of Plants in Earliest Buddhism.* (Tokyo: Institute for Buddhist Studies, 1991).

Schofield, M. *The Stoic Ideal of the City.* (Cambridge: Cambridge University Press, 1991).

Schutte, O. *Cultural Identity and Social Liberation in Latin American Thought.* (State University of New York Press, 1993).

Service, R. *Lenin: A Political Life.* (Indiana Univ. Press, 1995).

Sheehan, T. *Karl Rahner.* (Ohio University Press, 1987).

Sider, D. *The Fragments of Anaxagoras.* (Meisenheim am Glan: Verlag Anton Hain, 1981).

Singer, P., ed. *A Companion to Ethics.* (Oxford: Blackwell, 1991).

Smart, N. *Doctrine and Argument in Indian Philosophy.* (London: Allen & Unwin, 1964).

Solomon, R. C. *From Rationalism to Existentialism.* (New York: Harper & Row, 1972).

Sorell, T., ed. *The Cambridge Companion to Hobbes.* (Cambridge, MA: Cambridge University Press, 1995).

Spiegelberg, H. *The Phenomenological Movement.* (The Hague: Nijhoff, 1960).

Sprigge, T. L. S. *Santayana.* (New York: Routledge, 1995).

Stadler, F., ed. *Scientific Philosophy: Origins and Development.* (Dordrecht: Kluwer, 1993).

Stadler, F. and E. Nemeth, eds. *Otto Neurath.* (Dordrecht: Kluwer, 1996).

Stirner, M. and J. Carroll, trans. *The Ego and His Own.* (Harper & Row, 1971).

Streng, F. *Emptiness: A Study in Religious Meaning.* (Abingdon Press, 1967).

Stroud, B. A. *The Significance of Philosophical Scepticism.* (Oxford: Clarendon Press, 1984).

Sumner, L. W. *Welfare, Happiness, and Ethics.* (Oxford Univ. Press, 1996).

Suzuki, D. T. *An Introduction to Zen Buddhism.* (New York: Grove Press, 1964).

Swinburne, R. *The Coherence of Theism.* (Oxford: Oxford University Press, 1993).

Swinburne, R. *The Concept of Miracle.* (New York: Macmillan, 1970).

Swinburne, R. *The Existence of God.* (Oxford: Oxford University Press, 1979).

Szasz, Thomas. *The Myth of Mental Illness.* (New York: Hoeber-Harper, 1961).

Thrower, J. *A Short History of Western Atheism.* (London: Pemberton Press, 1971).

Tillich, P. *Biblical Religion and the Search for Ultimate Reality.* (Chicago: University of Chicago Press, 1955).

Torrance, J. *Karl Marx's Theory of Ideas.* (Cambridge: Cambridge University Press, 1995).

Tucci, G. *The Religions of Tibet.* (London: Routledge, 1980).

Urmson, J. O. and J. Ree, eds. *The Concise Encyclopedia of Philosophy and Philosophers.* (Allen & Unwin, 1991).

van Parijs, P. *Real Freedom for All.* (Oxford: Oxford University Press, 1995).

Varley, P. *Warriors of Japan, as Portrayed in War Tales.* (University of Hawaii Press, 1994).

Verbeek, T. *Descartes and the Dutch: Early Reactions to Cartesianism (1637–1650).* (Carbondale: Southern Illinois University Press, 1992).

Vermes, P. *Buber on God and the Perfect Man.* (London: Littman Library of Jewish Civilization, 1994).

Vorgrimler, H. *Understanding Karl Rahner.* (Crossroad, 1986).

Walker, Ralph C. S. *The Coherence Theory of Truth.* (London: Routledge, 1989).

Ward, James. *The Will to Believe and Other Essays.* (New York: Dover, 1956).

Warren, H. C. *Buddhism in Translation.* (Atheneum Publications, 1962).

Weiss, P. *Sport: A Philosophical Inquiry.* (Carbondale, IL: Southern Illinois University Press, 1969).

Weizenbaum, J. *Computer Power and Human Reason.* (W. H. Freeman & Co., 1976).

Wildiers, N. M. *Teilhard de Chardin.* (Harper & Row, 1963).

Williams, B. & J. J. C. Smart. *Utilitarianism: For and Against.* (Cambridge: Cambridge University Press, 1973).

Williams, B. *Moral Luck.* (Cambridge: Cambridge University Press, 1981).

Wojtyla, K. and H. T. Willits, trans. *Love and Responsibility.* (New York: Farrar, Strauss, & Giroux, 1981).

Wolenski, J. *Logic and Philosophy in the Lvov-Warsaw School.* (Dordrecht: Kluwer, 1989).

Wollheim, R. *Art and Its Objects.* (Cambridge: Cambridge University Press, 1980).

Wood, T. *Nagarjunian Disputations.* (University of Hawaii Press, 1994).

Worster, D. *Nature's Economy: A History of Ecological Ideas.* (Cambridge: Cambridge University Press, 1994).

Zaehner, R. *Mysticism.* (Oxford: Oxford University Press, 1961).

Ziarek, Ewa P. *An Ethics of Dissensus: Postmodernity, Feminism, and the Politics of Radical Democracy.* (Stanford: Stanford University Press, 2001).

Zimmerman, M. *Heidegger's Confrontation with Modernity: Technology, Politics, Art.* (Indiana University Press, 1990).

Zimmerman, M. J. *The Concept of Moral Obligation.* (Cambridge: Cambridge University Press, 1996).

Zolo, D. *Reflexive Epistemology: The Philosophical Legacy of Otto Neurath.* (Dordrecht: Kluwer, 1989).

ABOUT THE AUTHOR

Joseph van de Mortel is Professor of Philosophy and Religion at Cerritos College and a recipient of the Templeton Award in Science and Religion. He is also active in the American Philosophical Association, the American Academy of Religion, and Greenpeace.

He has organized many workshops on philosophy of religion and meditation throughout Southern California, including Rinzai-ji Temple in Los Angeles and Ramakrishna Monastery in Trabuco Canyon. In his spare time he enjoys ocean sailing in and around Channel Islands National Park.

NOTE ON COPYRIGHTS

Care has been taken not to infringe on copyrights. Quotes have been provided under the guidelines of the 1976 US Copyright Act in conjunction with the definition of "fair use" as very small extractions. In every case, the respective author has been noted. If there are exceptions and a copyright has been mistakenly infringed upon, proper acknowledgement shall be included in future editions upon satisfactory notice of an error.

CPSIA information can be obtained
at www.ICGtesting.com
Printed in the USA
FSHW022035231219
65422FS

9 781635 053623